SAMS Teach Yourself
Cisco Routers
in 21 Days

SECOND EDITION

SAMS
201 West 103rd St., Indianapolis, Indiana, 46290 USA

Sams Teach Yourself Cisco Routers in 21 Days

Copyright ©2002 by Sams Publishing

All rights reserved. No part of this book shall be reproduced, stored in a retrieval system, or transmitted by any means, electronic, mechanical, photocopying, recording, or otherwise, without written permission from the publisher. No patent liability is assumed with respect to the use of the information contained herein. Although every precaution has been taken in the preparation of this book, the publisher and author assume no responsibility for errors or omissions. Nor is any liability assumed for damages resulting from the use of the information contained herein.

International Standard Book Number: 0-672-32296-X

Library of Congress Catalog Card Number: 2001093562

Printed in the United States of America

First Printing: December 2001

04 03 02 01   4 3 2 1

Trademarks

All terms mentioned in this book that are known to be trademarks or service marks have been appropriately capitalized. Sams Publishing cannot attest to the accuracy of this information. Use of a term in this book should not be regarded as affecting the validity of any trademark or service mark.

Warning and Disclaimer

Every effort has been made to make this book as complete and as accurate as possible, but no warranty or fitness is implied. The information provided is on an "as is" basis. The author and the publisher shall have neither liability nor responsibility to any person or entity with respect to any loss or damages arising from the information contained in this book.

ASSOCIATE PUBLISHER
Jeff Koch

ACQUISITIONS EDITOR
William E. Brown

DEVELOPMENT EDITOR
Mark Renfrow

MANAGING EDITOR
Matt Purcell

COPY EDITOR
Jerome Colburn,
Publication Services, Inc.

PRODUCTION EDITOR
Theodore Young, Jr.,
Publication Services, Inc.

INDEXER
Richard Bronson,
Publication Services, Inc.

PROOFREADER
Publication Services, Inc.

TECHNICAL EDITOR
Andre Paree-huff

TEAM COORDINATOR
Denni Bannister

INTERIOR DESIGNER
Gary Adair

COVER DESIGNER
Aren Howell

PAGE LAYOUT
Michael Tarleton,
Jim Torbit,
Publication Services, Inc.

Contents at a Glance

	Introduction	1
Week 1 At a Glance		**5**
Day 1	Introduction to Routing	5
Day 2	Understanding Cisco Hardware	25
Day 3	Understanding the Cisco IOS	39
Day 4	Learning the Cisco Interface	59
Day 5	Understanding How Routers Move Data	85
Day 6	Getting the Router Up and Running	103
Day 7	Backing Up Router Configurations	137
	Week 1 In Review	???
Week 2 At a Glance		**155**
Day 8	Understanding Routed Protocols	155
Day 9	Learning IP Basics	175
Day 10	Learning How to Configure IP on Cisco Routers	187
Day 11	Understanding Segmented Networks	213
Day 12	Learning How to Configure IPX	233
Day 13	Understanding WAN Protocols	253
Day 14	Understanding Routing Protocols	273
	Week 2 In Review	
Week 3 At a Glance		**283**
Day 15	Learning How to Configure RIP	283
Day 16	Using IGRP and EIGRP	309
Day 17	Configuring OSPF	327
Day 18	Understanding BGP	347
Day 19	Learning IS-IS	379
Day 20	An Introduction to Basic Cisco Security	417
Day 21	Understanding Cisco Catalyst Switch Routing and PNNI	472
	Week 3 In Review	

Appendix A Cisco Command Reference   457
Index   491

Contents

Introduction	**1**
Week I Cisco Routing Basic Elements	**3**
1 Introduction to Cisco Routing: The Technology and the Company	**5**
The History of Cisco Routers	10
The Advent of the PC	12
The Birth of Cisco	15
Routing and the Internet	16
Routing in Everyday Life	19
Summary	24
Q & A	24
Quiz	24
Questions	24
Answers	24
2 Understanding Cisco Hardware	**25**
General Cisco Router Hardware Components	26
External Hardware	27
Internal Hardware	32
Series-Specific Router Hardware	33
Routers for Small to Midsize Businesses	33
Enterprise Series Routers	36
Summary	37
Q&A	38
Quiz	38
Questions	38
Answers	38
3 Understanding the Cisco IOS	**39**
Behind the Cisco IOS	40
Obtaining IOS Updates	41
Router Memory Architecture	44
Upgrading Run-from-Flash IOS Images	48
Upgrading Run-from-RAM IOS Images	51
The Cisco IOS Command Interpreter	56
Summary	57
Q&A	57
Quiz	58

Questions	58
Answers	58
Exercises	58

4 Learning the Cisco IOS User Interface — 59

Navigating the IOS	60
The IOS User Interface Basic Elements	66
IOS Messages at Startup	71
Accessing Cisco's IOS Help	73
Full Help	74
Context-Sensitive Help	76
Basic IOS Commands	76
`ping`	77
`show`	78
Summary	82
Q&A	82
Quiz	82
Questions	82
Answers	83
Exercises	83

5 Understanding How Routers Move Data — 85

Cisco Routers and the Network Layer	86
Protocol Routing	88
Protocol Headers	91
Data Packeting	93
The Mechanics of Routing	93
Simple Network Routing	94
Complex Network Routing	97
Routing Tables	98
Achieving Convergence	100
Routed Protocols vs. Routing Protocols	101
Summary	101
Q&A	102
Quiz	102
Questions	102
Answers	102

6 Getting the Router Up and Running — 103

Configuring a Clean Router	104
Connecting to the Router	105
Using the Setup Dialogs	107
The Basic Management Setup	109

Extended Setup Dialog 115
The Configuration Files 117
    The `startup-config` File 117
    The `running-config` File 118
    Viewing and Editing the Configuration Files 118
Reconfiguring an Existing Router 121
Changing Individual Configuration Items 122
    Setting the Hostname..123
    Router Passwords 123
    The Secret Password 124
Viewing and Configuring Interfaces..129
Creating a Banner 132
Summary 133
Q&A 133
Quiz 133
    Questions 133
    Answers 133
Exercises 134

7 Backing Up Cisco Routers   137

Physical Backups 138
    Cisco Multiple Power Units 141
    Backup Routers 141
Cisco IOS Configuration File Backups 147
    The What and Why of Router Configuration Backups.................148
    `running-config` and `startup-config`..148
Summary 152
Q&A 152
Quiz 152
    Questions 152
    Answers 152
Exercises 153

Week 2   Week Title   155

8 Understanding Routed Protocols   157

Protocol Categorization 158
The OSI Model 159
    The Application Layer...160
    The Presentation Layer 161
    The Session Layer 161
    The Transport Layer 161
    The Network Layer 163
    The Data Link Layer 164
    The Physical Layer 165

Protocol Divisions and Classifications	166
Connection-Oriented Versus Connectionless Protocols	167
Classful Versus Classless Protocols	169
Protocol Encapsulation	171
Summary	172
Q&A	173
Quiz	173
Questions	173
Answers	173

9 Learning IP Basics   175

IP	176
Class A Addresses	177
Class B Addresses	178
Class C Addresses	178
Network Subnetting	180
Supernetting an IP Network	183
IP and Cisco Routers	184
Summary	184
Q&A	185
Quiz	185
Questions	185
Answers	185

10 Learning How to Configure IP on Cisco Routers   187

IP and Cisco Interfaces	188
ICMP	193
Using ICMP Tools	193
Ping	194
`ping` (User Mode)	195
`ping` (Privilege Mode)	198
`traceroute`	202
`traceroute` (Privilege-Mode)	202
Telnet	204
Remote Administration Using Telnet	204
`rlogin`	209
Summary	209
Q&A	210
Quiz	210
Questions	210
Answers	210
Exercises	210

11 Understanding Segmented Networks   213

- Identifying the Need for Subnetting 214
- Subnetting an IP Network 215
  - Placing Cisco Routers within Segmented Environments 224
- Configuring Static Routes Between Subnets 228
- Summary 231
- Q&A 231
- Quiz 231
  - Questions 231
  - Answers 232
- Exercises 232

12 Learning How to Configure IPX (Internetwork Packet Exchange)   233

- Introduction to IPX 234
- IPX Addressing 235
  - Configuring IPX on Cisco Routers 237
  - IPX Encapsulation 240
  - Ethernet Encapsulation Fields 241
- IPX Routing 244
- Summary 250
- Q&A 250
- Quiz 250
  - Questions 250
  - Answers 250
- Exercise 251

13 Understanding WAN Protocols   253

- ISDN 255
  - ISDN Technology 256
  - ISDN Terminology 257
  - ISDN Functionality 259
  - Configuring ISDN 261
- X.25 265
  - Permanent Virtual Circuits 265
  - Switched Virtual Circuits 266
- Frame Relay 267
  - Frame Relay Technology 267
  - Configuring Frame Relay 269
- Summary 271
- Q&A 271
- Quiz 271
  - Questions 271
  - Answers 272
- Exercises 272

14 Understanding Routing Protocols	**273**
Routing Algorithms	274
Distance Vector	276
Link State	277
Dynamic Updates	277
Convergence	281
Summary	281
Q&A	281
Quiz	282
Questions	282
Answers	282

Week 3   283

15 Learning How to Configure RIP	**285**
An Overview of the Routing Information Protocol (RIP)	286
The Technology That Built RIP	287
The RIP Routing Table	288
RIP Routing Algorithm	294
How RIP Works	295
Routing Updates within RIP	298
Configuring RIP	299
Maintaining RIP	301
Setting RIP Timers	301
Manually Configuring RIP Neighbors	302
Working with Multiple Versions of RIP	304
Viewing RIP Stats	305
Summary	306
Q&A	306
Quiz	307
Questions	307
Answers	307
Exercise	307
16 Using IGRP and EIGRP	**309**
IGRP and EIGRP Versus RIP	310
IGRP Technology	313
IGRP Metrics	313
Increased Hop Count	314
Load Balancing	315
IGRP Updates	316
Configuring IGRP	317
Establishing Unequal-Cost Load Balancing	318

    Modifying Update Timers 319
        Enabling/Disabling Split Horizon and Hold-Down Timers 320
    EIGRP Technology 321
    Configuring EIGRP 322
    Summary 323
    Q&A 324
    Quiz 324
        Questions 324
        Answers 324
    Exercise 324

17 Configuring OSPF   327

    Introduction to OSPF 328
    OSPF Technology 328
        Link State Algorithms 332
        OSPF Updates 335
        OSPF Areas 337
        Stub Areas 338
        NSSA 338
        Route Distribution 340
    Configuring OSPF 340
    Summary 344
    Q&A 344
    Quiz 344
        Questions 344
        Answers 344
    Exercise 345

18 Understanding Border Gateway Protocol (BGP)   347

    Autonomous Systems 349
        Obtaining an Autonomous System Number 351
        ASNs and IP Addresses 355
    Configuring the Exterior Border Gateway Routing Protocol 360
        BGP Route Maps 363
        BGP Route Flapping and Flap Dampening 366
    Configuring Interior Border Gateway Routing 372
        BGP Confederations 372
        BGP Synchronization 375
        BGP Route Reflection 377
    Exercises 378

19 Learning IS-IS   379

    IS-IS and DECnet 380
        DECnet Areas and Nodes 382
        DECnet Nodes 384

DECnet Routing Basics	386
DECnet Phase V	389
How IS-IS Relates to CLNP	389
IS-IS Link State Routing	391
Controlling Link State Floods	393
IS-IS Metrics and Algorithms	396
IS-IS Addressing, Areas, and Domains	398
IS-IS Areas	399
IS-IS Addresses	401
IS-IS Packets	403
Hello Messages	405
Link State Packets	406
Sequence Number Packets	407
IS-IS Routing	408
Designated IS	409
Pseudonodes	410
IS-IS Routing	411
Configuring IS-IS	414
Summary	416
Q&A	416
Quiz	416
Questions	416
Answers	416
Exercise	416

20 Introduction to Basic Cisco Security — 417

IP Access Lists	418
NAT	423
Summary	425
Q&A	425
Quiz	426
Questions	426
Answers	426
Exercises	426

21 Understanding Cisco Catalyst Switch Routing and PNNI — 427

The ATM Architecture	429
ATM Network Layout	432
The UNI Signaling Protocol	434
The ATM Cell Structure and Signaling Protocol	436
PNNI Hierarchy	438
PNNI Peer Groups	439
PNNI Routing Protocol	444

PNNI and QOS 447
PNNI Signaling Protocol 449
PNNI Crankback 452
Configuring PNNI 454

Appendix Cisco Command Reference   **457**

User Mode Examples 458
   access-enable 458
   access-profile 458
   connect 459
   disable 459
   disconnect 459
   enable 460
   exit 460
   help 460
   lock 460
   login 461
   logout 461
   name-connection 461
   pad 461
   ping 462
   ppp 462
   resume 462
   rlogin 463
   show 464
   slip 467
   systat 467
   telnet 467
   terminal 468
   traceroute 471
   tunnel 472
   where 472
   x28 472
   x3 473
Privilege Mode Commands 473
   access-template 474
   cd 475
   clear 475
   clock 480
   copy 480
   debug 481
   delete 481

`dir`	484
`erase`	484
`more`	484
`pwd`	485
`reload`	485
`rsh`	486
`setup`	486
`test`	487
`verify`	488
`write`	488

Index 491

About the Author

JEROME F. DIMARZIO is a network engineer with 10 years of experience in system design and administration. He has worked as a consultant since 1991 for companies such as the Walt Disney Company and the United States Department of Defense.

Currently Jerome F. DiMarzio is a technical consultant for a large financial institution in central Massachusetts. He has achieved the certifications of MCP, MCP+I, MCSE, and CCNA. He is also a GOLD (Graduate Of the Last Decade) member of the Institute of Electrical and Electronics Engineers (IEEE), serving on the IEE Computer Society Task Force on Virtual Intelligence and the Task Force on Information Technology for Business Applications.

About the Reviewers

MICHELLE TRUMAN, CCIE # 8098, has a degree in Telecommunications Technology as well as a BA from the College of St. Catherine in St. Paul, MN. Michelle has spent 8 years working as a Lead Engineer and Project Manager in the banking and Food/Beverage industries for several large corporations including AgriBank, Pillsbury, Burger King, Guinness Brewing, and Häagen Dazs. She has taught courses in LAN and WAN technologies and routing protocols such as BGP and OSPF. She is currently a Principal Consultant for AT&T Business Internet Services.

About the Tech Editor

ANDRÉ PAREE-HUFF (CCNP, CCDA, MCSE+I, ASE, A+, Network+, I-Network+, Server+) has been working in the computer field for over 10 years. He is currently working for Compaq Computer Corporation as a Network Support Engineer level III for the North America Customer Support Center in Colorado Springs, Colorado. André handles troubleshooting of network hardware, specializing in layers 2 and 3 of the OSI model. He has co-authored five network-related books and has been a technical editor on more then two dozen others. He is currently working toward his CCDE and CCIE.

Dedication

To my amazing family: Suzannah, Christian, and Sophia

Acknowledgments

I would first like to thank William E. Brown, Mark Renfrow, Matt Purcell, and the team at SAMS Publishing, and Molly Redenbaugh, Jerome Colburn, Dave Mason, and the rest of the team at Publication Services.

I would also like to thank, in no particular order, Walt Adams of Double Eagle Services in Central Florida; Lou Vella, and the team at Allmerica Financial; Heather Osterloh; and everyone who made this book possible.

My sincere thanks also go to my wife, Suzannah, and my two beautiful children, Christian and Sophia, for making the drudgery of countless hours of work and research worth every minute. I would also like to thank Diana Mitchell. Finally, I would probably end up grounded for life if I didn't thank my parents Jerome and Agnes (and my brother Matt too).

I thank everyone who helped to make this book happen, and my sincere apologies go to anybody I forgot or left out.

Tell Us What You Think!

As the reader of this book, *you* are our most important critic and commentator. We value your opinion and want to know what we're doing right, what we could do better, what areas you'd like to see us publish in, and any other words of wisdom you're willing to pass our way.

As an Associate Publisher for Sams Publishing, I welcome your comments. You can fax, e-mail, or write me directly to let me know what you did or didn't like about this book—as well as what we can do to make our books stronger.

Please note that I cannot help you with technical problems related to the topic of this book, and that due to the high volume of mail I receive, I might not be able to reply to every message.

When you write, please be sure to include this book's title and author name as well as your name and phone or fax number. I will carefully review your comments and share them with the author and editors who worked on the book.

Fax: 317-581-4770

E-mail: feedback@samspublishing.com

Mail: Jeff Koch
Sams Publishing
201 West 103rd Street
Indianapolis, IN 46290 USA

Introduction

SAMS Teach Yourself Cisco Routers in 21 Days is focused on providing readers with the basic building blocks of knowledge needed to learn Cisco routing successfully. The topics within this book offer a certification-independent look at the more important concepts any novice Cisco user should know.

The examples and subject matter contained in this book are derived from the author's over 10 years of experience in the fields of networking and routing technologies. Jerome F. DiMarzio has structured this book to be a concise primer for those who desire a base on which to build their future routing experience.

How This Book Is Organized

SAMS Teach Yourself Cisco Routers in 21 Days covers all of the information needed to learn Cisco routers. The lessons contained within this text are divided into three weeks, each week covering a more advanced subject matter.

The first week introduces you to the basic Cisco elements:

Day 1 "Introduction to Cisco Routing: The Technology and the Company"—This lesson introduces basic concepts, briefly discusses the history of Cisco and the problems its products have been designed to solve, and sets the tone for the remaining lessons.

Day 2 "Understanding Cisco Hardware"—This lesson helps the reader recognize the differences in routing hardware and aids in identifying the parts of the routers used within the book.

Day 3 "Understanding the Cisco IOS"—This lesson explains and examines the Cisco router operating system and how to get it and upgrade it.

Day 4 "Learning the Cisco IOS User Interface"—This lesson explains how to navigate and use the Cisco IOS user interface, from which all router configuration tasks are performed.

Day 5 "Understanding How Routers Move Data"—Taking a small break from the Cisco-specific topics, this lesson covers the technical aspect of how data is moved from place to place.

Day 6 "Getting the Router Up and Running"—This lesson explains, step by step, how to configure a Cisco router "out of the box" for basic operation.

Day 7 "Backing Up Cisco Routers"—The last lesson this week covers the procedures needed to back up and retain the configurations made during the previous lesson.

The second week focuses on teaching the basic protocols used in router operations:

Day 8 "Understanding Routed Protocols"—This lesson will explain, in terms not specific to any particular vendor, how routed protocols function.

Day 9 "Learning IP Basics"—This lesson introduces the reader to the most popular routed protocol today: the Internet Protocol (IP).

Day 10 "Learning How to Configure IP on Cisco Routers"—In this lesson the reader learns how to configure a Cisco router to run IP and IP-related tools.

Day 11 "Understanding Segmented Networks"—This lesson, also IP related, focuses on subnetting and routing within subnetted and segmented networks.

Day 12 "Learning How to Configure IPX (Internetwork Packet Exchange)"—This lesson examines the processes for configuring a Cisco router to route the Internetwork Packet Exchange (IPX) protocol.

Day 13 "Understanding WAN Protocols"—Lesson 13 explains the functionality of wide area network (WAN) protocols such as Frame Relay.

Day 14 "Understanding Routing Protocols"—This last lesson of week 2 introduces the reader to routing protocols, the major subject of the following week.

The final week discusses and examines more advanced topics, such as security and routing protocols:

Day 15 "Learning How to Configure RIP"—This lesson focuses on learning the commands needed to configure the Routing Information Protocol (RIP) on a Cisco router.

Day 16 "Using IGRP and EIGRP"—Using the same format as the previous lesson, this lesson explains how to configure the Interior Gateway Routing Protocol (IGRP) and the Enhanced Interior Gateway Routing Protocol (EIGRP) on a Cisco router.

Day 17 "Configuring OSPF"—Another popular protocol, Open Shortest Path First (OSPF), is examined in this lesson.

Day 18 "Understanding Border Gateway Protocol (BGP)"—The commands needed for configuring Border Gateway Protocol (BGP) are discussed in this lesson.

Day 19 "Learning IS-IS"—This lesson focuses on a seldom covered protocol often considered an advanced topic. The commands used in configuring the Intermediate System to Intermediate System (IS-IS) protocol are the focus here.

Day 20 "Introduction to Basic Cisco Security"—This lesson introduces the reader to Network Address Translation (NAT) and IP Access Lists.

Day 21 "Understanding Cisco Catalyst Switch Routing and PNNI"—The final lesson of the book deals with another advanced topic: configuring a Cisco Catalyst switch for routing PNNI (Private Network-to-Network Interface).

Who Should Read This Book

This text does not cover every subject and every concept needed to master the myriad Cisco commands and functions available. However, anyone interested in learning Cisco routers should start with this book. This text covers all of the basic information needed by IT professionals and other readers who do not have any practical experience with routers in general. Anyone who is looking to begin building a path toward routing, networking, or both will profit greatly from the experience and subject matter covered in this book.

Conventions Used in This Book

Features in this book include the following:

Notes provide you with comments and asides about the topic at hand.

Cautions explain roadblocks you might encounter when you work with Cisco and tell you how to avoid them.

Tips offer shortcuts and hints on getting the task done.

At the end of each chapter, you'll find handy Summary and Q&A sections. Many times, you'll also find a New Terms section.

In addition, you'll find various typographic conventions throughout this book:

- Commands, variables, directories, and files appear in text in a special `monospaced font`.
- Commands and such that you type appear in **boldface type**.
- Placeholders in syntax descriptions appear in a `monospaced italic` typeface. This indicates that you will replace the placeholder with the actual filename, parameter, or other element that it represents.

WEEK 1

Cisco Routing Basic Elements

1 Introduction to Cisco Routing: The Technology and the Company

2 Understanding Cisco Hardware

3 Understanding the Cisco IOS

4 Learning the Cisco IOS User Interface

5 Understanding How Routers Move Data

6 Getting the Router Up and Running

7 Backing Up Cisco Routers

WEEK 1

DAY 1

Introduction to Cisco Routing: The Technology and the Company

Welcome to *Sams Teach Yourself Cisco Routing in 21 Days*. This book will cover the lessons needed to understand the routing process as it applies to Cisco routers. Technically able people are in very high demand today, and nowhere are they more desired than in the field of routing. Information routing is what "makes the world go 'round" in our ever-evolving society as it becomes more and more dependent on data and the movement of data from place to place.

Imagine all of the technological advances of the last decade. Many of them have revolved around the Internet (or some other form of anytime, anywhere technology). Now imagine these same advances without the ability to route information. Many services we take for granted, such as e-mail, e-shopping, and the latest in computer telephony, become nearly impossible. Many people do not realize just how important routing is to a technological society. The global economy is dependent on the ability to route information from system to system.

Cisco has long been the leader in routing technology, so Cisco-experienced engineers are highly valued in the corporate market. However, there has always been a conundrum in the routing world. Routing equipment is fairly expensive, and the data flowing across it can be very critical to a company's existence, so many companies will hire only experienced engineers, so as to minimize the newly hired techs' ramp-up time as well as the risk of them breaking a $50,000 router. Many people trying to start a career in routing therefore face the question: How do you get experience without a job, and how do you get a job without experience?

In the past the answer was expensive routing certification classes. Why would you want to attend a routing certification class if all you wanted was to learn the basics of the technology? The simple answer is that certification classes were the only choice. No formal introductory classes in Cisco routing existed at the time. Therefore, if you wanted to know the basics, you had to participate in Cisco Certified Network Associate (CCNA) training classes.

> **Note** Cisco Career Certifications are a valuable asset to any routing engineer. However, the classes and course material can be expensive, and, by Cisco's own guidelines, you should have at least two years of routing experience (preferably with Cisco equipment) before attempting the certifications. Once again, how do you get the experience you need to move your career on the right path?

Now, many people seem to be choosing forms of self-study material. However, there is a noticeable lack of training materials (books or CD-ROMs) that are not geared to obtaining certification. There is a very reasonable explanation for this as well. Because employers want engineers with experience, what better way is there to prove the breadth of your knowledge than with a Cisco Career Certification? Therefore, the bulk of the demand for training materials, and therefore the bulk of the money to be made, is in certification, so that is where most of the books will lean. What is wrong with that? Many certification training books have two major flaws.

The first flaw is that these books assume that the reader has a certain level of Cisco experience already. (Again, Cisco's guidelines say that an engineer should have two years of experience before getting certified. These materials are marketed to people who are trying to advance their current careers in routing, not to start new ones.) This means that any reader who has little or no routing experience is behind from the beginning. Many basic concepts, such as the hardware configuration of the router and interfacing with it, are not covered.

> **Note:** Many Cisco Certified Exam books are so well written that they need to give you only the information needed to pass the exam. If you don't have previous routing knowledge, or even access to a Cisco router, you may feel very lost.

The second flaw of many certification training books is that (by definition) they teach you only what is needed to pass the particular test the book was written for. This leaves a lot of basic and more advanced topics out of the scope of discussion. Because Cisco certifications are hierarchical, the specific knowledge points needed to pass the first test (CCNA) will not be revisited in the more advanced Cisco Certified Network Professional (CCNP) and Cisco Certified Internetwork Engineer (CCIE) certifications. Conversely, a book gearing someone to pass the CCNA would not tackle the topics needed to pass the CCIE. Therefore, books designed for certification may not cover the breadth of knowledge required to give a beginning engineer a good grasp of Cisco's routing concepts.

SAMS Teach Yourself Cisco Routing in 21 Days covers all of the topics an engineer should learn to know basic Cisco routing. By the end of this book you should be able to configure a Cisco router from scratch and adapt it to function in almost any local area network (LAN) or wide area network (WAN) scenario. Concepts that are usually not covered, such as interfacing to routers, upgrading the IOS, and working with different hardware configurations, will be discussed in detail.

> **Note:** Although this book will not explicitly present the material needed to pass a Cisco Career Certification (such as the CCNA), you will learn much of what is needed to pass the exam. However, if you are looking to pass a CCNA exam, do not rely solely on this book. This book is geared toward learning the technology—not passing a test.

The lessons are divided into three weeks' worth of material (seven days per week). Every day is a new lesson, many of which build on previous days. Therefore the knowledge required to learn Cisco routing successfully can be learned in a gradual and logical manner.

The format of this book lends itself to teaching you the concepts of Cisco routing the way you would learn them on the job, from the more basic topics to the more advanced. Even if you have minimal routing experience, the lessons are laid out in a way that makes them easy to follow. Routing novices will learn the basics, starting with "Introduction to Cisco Routing: The Technology and the Company" and "Understanding Cisco Hardware" (Days 1 and 2) through the most advanced topics "Understanding Cisco Catalyst Switch Routing and PNNI" (Day 21).

Note: Scenarios and troubleshooting tips will be provided through the book to give it a more "hands-on" feel. Many of the examples and issues used throughout the book are taken from real-life situations and experiences.

Skipping chapters is not recommended, but engineers with some Cisco experience can easily move on to the more advanced chapters. Regardless of whether you follow the book from beginning to end, or skip from day to day, each lesson will stand on its own to provide the most information about the subject.

The first lesson in this book introduces you to Cisco the company, the history behind its product, and the concepts of routing.

The History of Cisco Routers

Prior to 1984, there was no proven way to route digital information intelligently from location to location. Even though packet switching has existed since the mid-1960s, the demands of the new computer networks and communication protocols (such as TCP/IP) were pushing for a change in the technology. Computer networking itself was barely a decade old at this point and was just beginning to catch on in the public sector.

Through the 1960s and 1970s the lack of proven routing tools was not a major problem (for those who needed network interconnection, packet switching was a workable solution). Many computer networks at the time consisted of five or six larger mainframes with possibly 10 terminals attached to each. The mainframes were all (usually) centrally located, minimizing the need for long runs of network cabling. The close proximity of the mainframes made networking the large device fairly easy. A network of 60 users might have only six network connections, all in the same area, to connect the mainframes; the terminals attached to each mainframe do not need a network connection. Figure 1.1 illustrates the mainframe-based networks.

Note: Although many people will consider the attachment of serial terminals to a mainframe "networking," for the purposes of this discussion, it is not. We are dealing with the network used *and shared* by the mainframes—in other words, shared network connections, whereas serial connections are not shared.

FIGURE 1.1

Mainframe-based network.

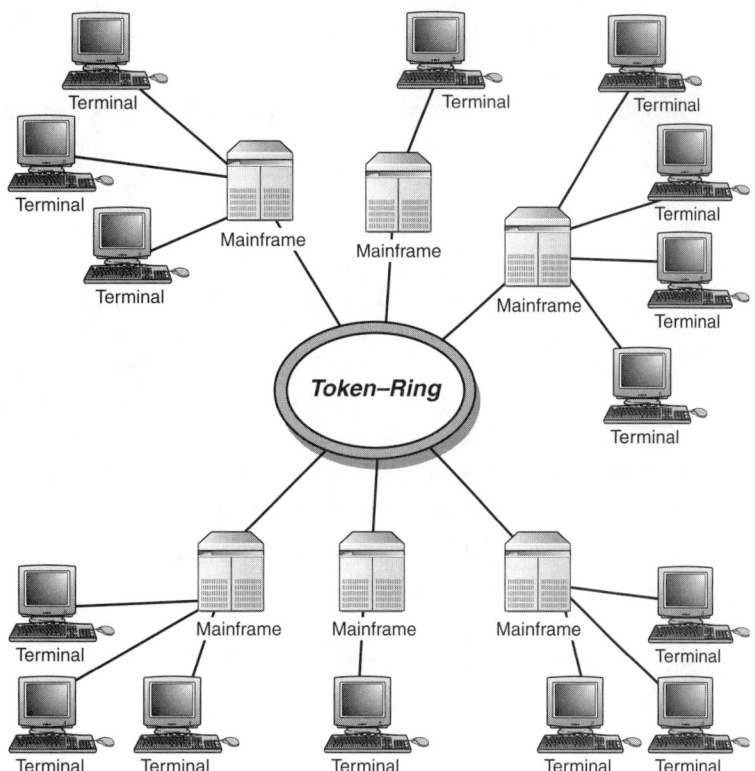

The larger switched networks in the 1960s and 1970s were confined to institutions that could afford the hardware; as with most advances in technology, the earlier you invest in a product, the more expensive it is. For example, the U.S. government operated one of the largest networks in the world, and one of the first: ARPAnet (later to become DARPAnet). The hardware needed to provide a sound large-scale environment using the impressive packet-switching technology that made ARPAnet a reality was so expensive that it remained out of the reach of many U.S. companies.

By the early 1980s, the personal computer (PC) revolution had begun. The computer was becoming smaller and more self contained. Hard drive, processing, and networking abilities that were once the sole domain of the mainframes could now fit on a user's desktop and be dedicated to the needs of that one user. This made the PC very attractive to the business community.

The Advent of the PC

As the personal computer gained acceptance in the workplace (as well as the home), administrators were faced with a new set of problems. The same 60-user network that once required only six network connections in a relatively confined space could now need as many as 66 connections (60 PC users plus 6 mainframes) spread over a large area.

To use the PC's capabilities effectively, it could not be simply serially connected to the mainframe like a terminal. Instead, each PC would require the same form of network connection that the mainframes needed; for example, if the mainframes were connected with Token Ring, each of the PCs would also require a Token Ring connection. As a result, not only would the physical limits of the technology, such as Media Access Units (MAUs) and cabling, be tested, but so would the transmission and bandwidth limits. A network that once handled the traffic of six devices now saw a more than tenfold jump in bandwidth usage. This jump was especially noticeable in Token Ring environments, which at the time only produced about 4Mbits of bandwidth.

PCs would also require the same protocol and addressing considerations as their larger mainframe counterparts. That is, every PC on a network would require its own address space (related to the protocol being used) to participate in the environment. However, this was the least of the administrator's problems.

The second problem that businesses and network administrators faced, which led more directly to the advent of the router, was the cost of PCs. The new, networkable PCs were many times more cost efficient than their mainframe counterparts. As a result, businesses began adding more and more PCs to their networking environments. Administrators were faced with the possibility of unlimited numbers of devices occupying a network environment.

The most popular network topologies at the time, Token Ring and Ethernet, were developed before PCs were in the picture. The added network burden that PCs had begun to create cast light on what could and could not be done with the existing network designs. Figure 1.2 illustrates a single networking environment that is at its limits.

FIGURE 1.2

A large networking environment.

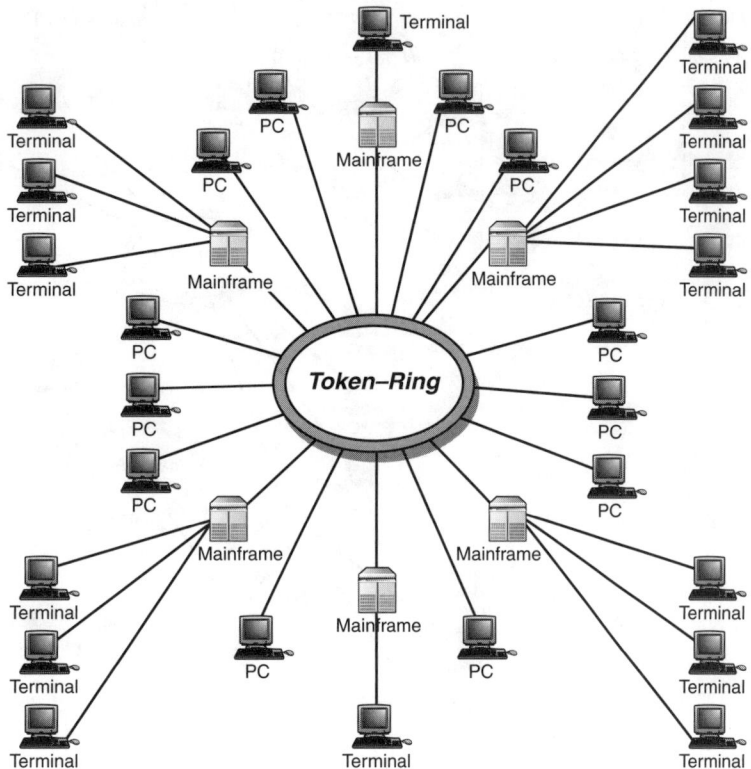

Under the pressures of the new network load, something had to break at last. The blueprints for network design were thrown out the window. Large, open-environment networks were abandoned for smaller, departmentalized ones. A single, larger networking environment would be broken up (on logical lines) into smaller, easier-to-handle pieces. Figure 1.3 illustrates the segmented network structure.

If you are familiar with network design, you already know that breaking larger networks into smaller subnetworks has clear advantages over keeping larger environments. Smaller networks can usually clear issues caused by traffic congestion and make the process of managing the network easier. However, these smaller, easier-to-manage networks posed a larger issue. How could users on one network segment access resources on another? The answer was routing.

FIGURE 1.3

A segmented network.

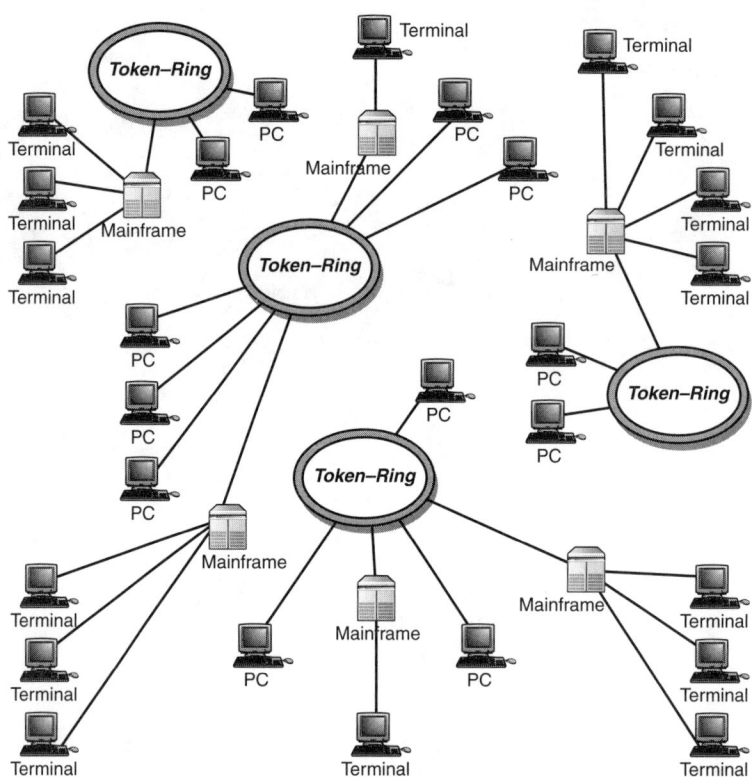

Without receiving much outside funding, Lerner and Bosack self-funded the research and development of a possible routing solution. The design process proved to be harder than expected. However, within two years they had developed their first router and begun to wire the Stanford campus.

 Note — Two Stanford University staff members, Sandy Lerner (Director of Computer Facilities for the Department of Computer Science) and Leonard Bosack (Director of Computer Facilities for the Graduate School of Business), began working on a solution for the university's growing networking problem. In the process, Lerner and Bosack also began working on a much larger issue: the problem of intersystem protocol routing.

Eventually their hard work and innovation paid off. They successfully connected the Stanford University environment using their new routers, creating one of the largest educational computing environments to date.

Seeing the overall technological (and marketable) potential of their routers, Lerner and Bosack next turned to Stanford University for the possible commercialization of their product. (At the time Stanford was also looking for a way to commercialize its network and technology.) The two parties seemed a perfect solution for each other's problems. Lerner and Bosack could get the help they needed producing their routers for a larger market, and the university could get the commercialization it was looking for.

However, Stanford did not elect to promote the new routing technology, so Lerner and Bosack were forced to market the product themselves. They continued to produce their routers and formed the company Cisco.

The Birth of Cisco

Cisco released its first router to the general public in October of 1984. At that time, Lerner and Bosack were continuing to fund the company from private sources and revenue returns. However, the quickly growing demand was outweighing the supply for the product. The tide of network computing was turning. Companies that either had no use for, or could not afford, a packet-switching solution began to look at Cisco's routing products. Networks of any size could be interconnected (relatively) easily. The foundation of the Internet (as we know it today) was being laid.

To keep up with the growing demand for routers, Lerner and Bosack turned to a venture capitalist group to fund the resources they needed to keep up with demand and grow Cisco in the direction where it needed to go. However, many (if not all) venture capitalists want to sit on the board of the company they invest in so that they can be satisfied with, and retain some control over, the way their money is being used. In the case of Cisco the venture capitalists eventually gained control over the company, and Lerner and Bosack moved on from the company they had formed.

In 1991, John Chambers joined Cisco from Wang as a senior vice president, and in 1995 he was named President and CEO of Cisco. Cisco has grown to over 20 billion dollars per year of revenue under Chambers's leadership. Although the internal culture has changed since Sandy Lerner and Leonard Bosack started Cisco Systems at Stanford University, the goal remains the same: to provide the best routing equipment in the world.

Cisco routers are widely recognized as the best in the industry. They provide a strength, reliability, and scalability that are unmatched in the world today. Nowhere are these characteristics better shown than in the varied environments of the Internet.

Routing and the Internet

One of the most important technological innovations of modern times has been the Internet. What started as a form of communication between U.S. military installations has become a multibillion-dollar-per-year industry. The Internet is now used to provide everything from news and information, shopping, and gaming to television and telephone service. Without a doubt, the Internet is an integral part of today's society.

The first incarnation of the Internet was not comparable to the cyberworld of today. That is, the Internet was a completely different place in its infancy. Through the early 1980's, as the first personal computers began flooding the stores, small networks of bulletin board servers (BBSs) began cropping up around the country. The servers were generally on the campuses of larger universities (the entities who could afford the technology), but the users could dial into them from the comfort of their own homes.

These conglomerations of BBS users could dial into specific hosts and access information, news, chat, and messaging services (early e-mail). These small (by today's standards) clusters of users, all connected via modem to large dial-in BBSs, formed the first loose meshes of what would become the Internet. However, the e-mail wonders that were the beginnings of mass computer communication were by no means perfect (yet).

The major flaw of the BBS systems was the lack of interconnectivity between them. For more than five years (a virtual lifetime in the world of technology), users around the world knew nothing but the joys of dialing into their local University's BBS and "talking" to a stranger (in the next county). People were communicating with each other, but unless you know what number to call and how to log in, you could only stay within your specific community.

Eventually, as Cisco's routing products began showing up in businesses and universities everywhere, the individual BBS systems began to communicate with each other. Now, not only could a user who dialed into the MIT BBS find out the temperature of a soda in the science building; they could finger the University of Washington for the latest geoseismic readings.

Cisco spent the 1980s strategically laying the groundwork for the Internet. It was Cisco's routers that would enable the easy and seamless integration of hundreds of different systems, starting with the early BBSs. What the early BBS users did not see were the hundreds of Cisco routers that were carrying their signals from MIT to the University of Washington. The dawn of the Internet was close at hand.

By the late 1980s the University of Minnesota had begun work on Gopher. Expanding on technologies such as Lynx and Trumpet, Gopher would allow BBS users to view graphics on the once text-dominated computers. For all intents and purposes the Internet was born. People signed up by the thousands for a chance to surf the web with online services like Genie, Prodigy, and CompuServe. However, no one saw (or cared) how the information of the Internet was delivered to their screens. The power of routing made all of this possible.

In the early days of the Internet, the function of a router was clear and well defined. Routers needed to move data from system to system in an efficient manner. Early routers functioned in much the same way as routers do today. Technically, they examine packets, calculate paths, and make intelligent routing decisions. These processes enable a router to determine where data originated from, where it is going, and how to get it there. It is fair to say that without routers and their capabilities, the Internet as we know it today would not exist.

What sets Cisco routers that are on the market today apart from their predecessors is the wealth of functions they have accumulated over the years. As the technology has changed, so have routers. Many of the advancements and achievements in routing technology that we see today have come from Cisco. Other manufacturers quickly copy many of the items and functions that are built into Cisco routing environments, proving that Cisco is an industry leader in information technologies.

Modern Cisco routers can translate public IP addresses, act as firewalls, provide remote access to an environment, filter out unwanted traffic, and much more. However, the main duty of a router has remained the same over the years: to move data efficiently between systems.

Let's examine how a Cisco router works in relationship to the Internet. Figure 1.4 illustrates a user viewing a web site on the Internet.

FIGURE 1.4

The routing process on the Internet.

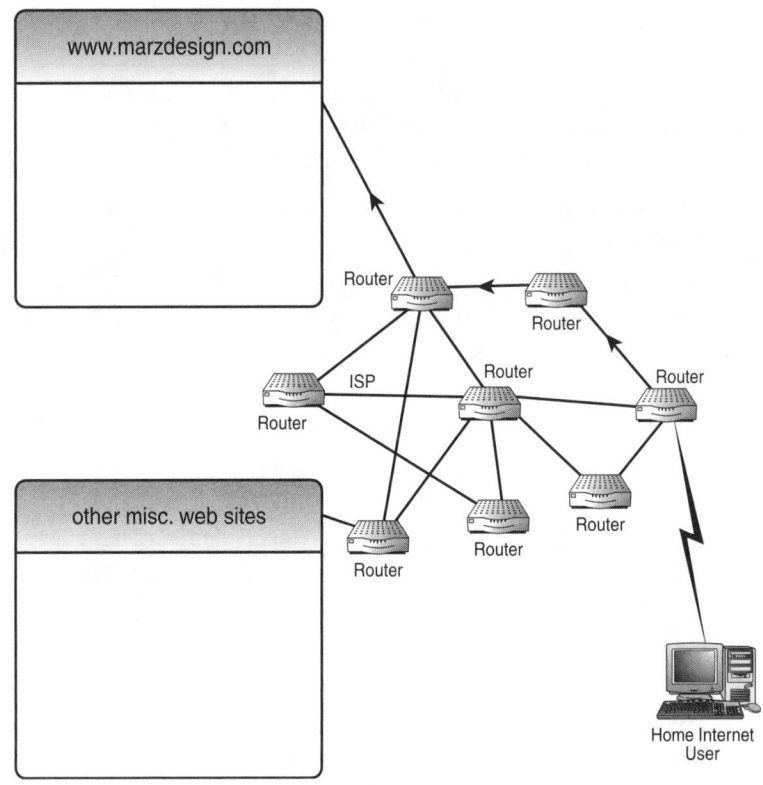

The first place a user might encounter a Cisco router is during login, especially if the user is connecting to the Internet through a broadband connection.

> Cisco routers can handle multiple types of interfaces. From WAN interfaces such as ISDN (Integrated Services Data Network), DSL (Digital Subscriber Lines), and T-lines to LAN links like Ethernet, a single Cisco router can handle multiple connections on multiple media. Therefore, it is not unlikely to have the first point of contact on an Internet service provider's (ISP's) network be a Cisco router with firewall enabled.
>
> Depending on the setup of the ISP's environment, the firewall can be before the Network Authentication Device, after the Network Authentication Device, or both.

For most ISPs, a Cisco router can be placed on the outermost border of the network. This router acts as a first line of defense in their security scheme. Any router placed on the border of a network like this (where users can connect through it) will most likely run anything from a firewall to NAT (natural address translation).

> **Note** Usually someone who refers to a "border router" is talking about a router that is running BGP (Border Gateway Protocol). However, in this scenario, a user of an ISP would not be able to connect to the network through a BGP border router.

In our example the router on the border of the ISP's network runs a firewall to protect the Network Authentication Device. Once authenticated by the ISP's network, the user can begin "surfing" the web.

> **Caution** The following explanation of how routers work on the Internet has been simplified. By the end of the book you will understand the whole picture.

Suppose the user wants to visit the site www.marzdesign.com. The user's browser alerts the ISP to retrieve information from IP address 207.217.96.36, corresponding to the domain name www.marzdesign.com. The request travels through the ISP's routers. Each router examines the request, determines which IP address is being requested and which is the requester, and matches that information against its own *routing table*. The routing table tells it where to find the IP address being requested, or (if the routing table does not know where to find the address) it will know the address of another router that might know (kind of a "friend-of-a-friend" arrangement). This process continues until the request finally reaches www.marzdesign.com. At this point the routing tables (because they have been keeping track of who made the request) send the requested information back to the user. This scenario is repeated millions of times a day, most of the time without the users knowing.

Routing in Everyday Life

By the mid-1990s the hardware forming the technological base for the Internet was well in place. The majority of the routing hardware used to power the Internet comes from Cisco. Its routers, switches, and other connectivity products make the Internet more reliable, more scalable, and faster then ever before.

So how does Cisco's ability to power the Internet translate to everyday life? Not long after Cisco began finding new ways to connect businesses, businesses began looking for new ways to branch out. Many companies started to experiment with allowing workers to perform their daily job duties from home.

Cisco, working to accommodate the current technological business needs, released its line of small office/home office (SOHO) hardware in the mid-1990s. Cisco's SOHO line of routers provides all of the functionality of the enterprise on a much smaller scale. Features such as access lists, WAN links, and firewalls, normally found on higher-end equipment, could now be purchased by the home user. Whether you run a home network with Internet access to multiple machines or use your home as a satellite office, a Cisco router can handle the routing requirements.

Many businesses have employees who spend some time working from home-based offices. There are several ways to accomplish this, and Cisco routers can be used in every one. One way is to connect the remote office to the main office with a WAN link. Figure 1.5 illustrates a typical home office.

FIGURE 1.5

A typical home office.

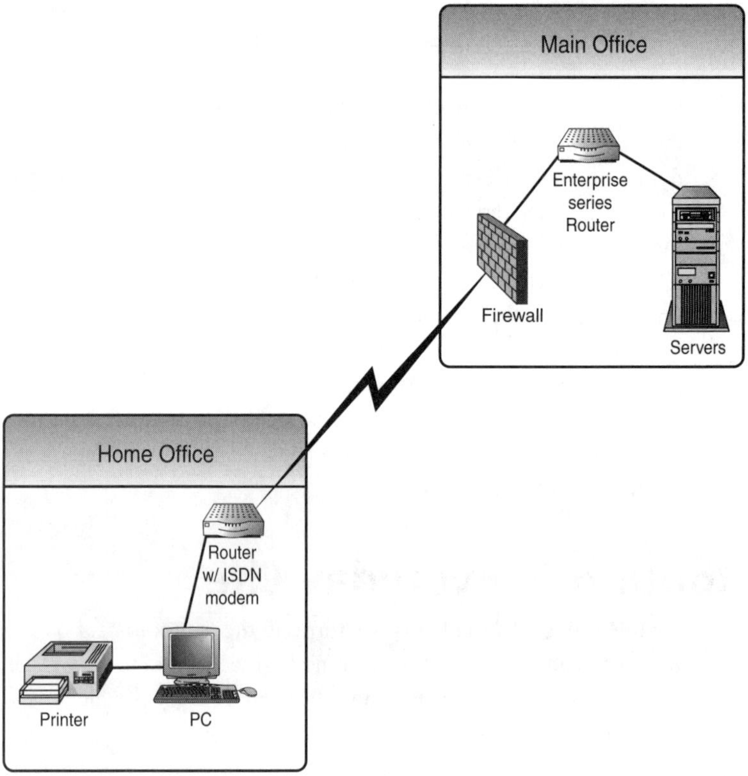

The home office in Figure 1.5 is connected to the main office by ISDN. A larger Cisco router (like the 7500 Series) is placed at the main office. An ISDN modem is installed as a board peripheral on the larger router, and a smaller SOHO router (say, Cisco 1600 Series) is placed in the user's home and equipped with another ISDN board peripheral to accept the other end of the ISDN connection. The two remotely connected offices can now communicate as if they were in the same building.

> **Note** Cisco has done an exceptional job of ensuring that its home products are every bit as compatible with existing technologies as the enterprise products are. Not only do most accept the same software (Cisco IOS), but most can also use the same hardware, such as volatile and nonvolatile memory and expansion cards.

Although WAN technologies such as ISDN and frame relay are common forms of remote (home) networking technology, there is a more popular choice. WAN technologies can be very costly for businesses with great numbers of employees working from home. Therefore more companies are choosing to implement VPN (virtual private network) technologies.

Figure 1.6 illustrates a home-to-business network that implements a VPN. If you look closely, you will notice that there is only a small difference between this network and the one pictured in Figure 1.5. The network in Figure 1.6 lacks a home routing device. A device such as a Cisco 1600 Series is not needed in the user's home to implement a VPN, as long as the user has a sustained Internet connection.

However, an even more interesting feature of this particular network can be seen on the company's side. The same Cisco 7500 series that was used to create the WAN link can be used to implement the VPN. In fact, the same router can run the two scenarios simultaneously. Therefore a single Cisco router can handle the remote networking needs of almost any business.It is nearly impossible to design, work on, or otherwise come into contact with a network and not encounter a Cisco router. They have a strong market base and an even stronger reputation for producing a superior routing product.

Now that you have made the decision to learn Cisco routing and you know the history behind the product, let's explore the hardware that makes it all possible. The next day's lesson discusses the hardware involved in Cisco routing.

FIGURE 1.6

A home-to-business VPN.

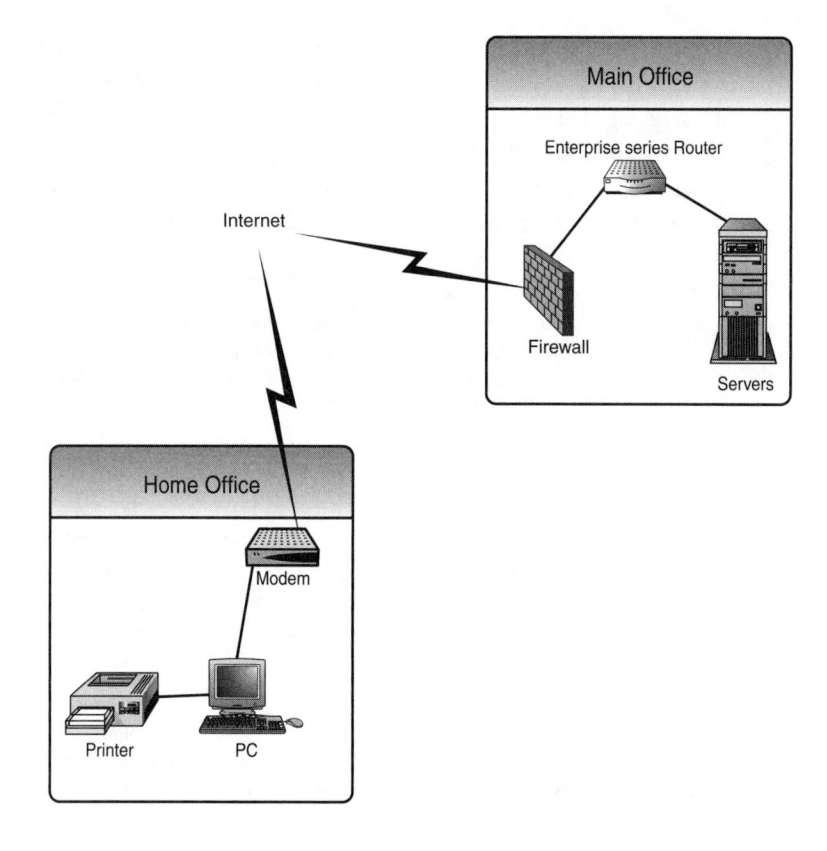

Summary

Today's lesson has focused on providing the base of knowledge needed to understand the origins of inter-computer routing fully. The concepts introduced in this lesson, such as the use of protocols and the differences between PCs and specialized routing hardware, will become more apparent as we progress through the book.

- For many years the only way to learn Cisco routing was to endure classes geared toward Cisco Career Certification. However, by Cisco's own standards, you shouldn't attempt certification without at least two years of routing experience.
- The remainder of this book will give you the skills needed to break into the wonderful world of routing.
- Cisco began as a technological "experiment" at Stanford University.

- After University officials chose not to market the new routing technology, Cisco began selling its routers to private companies.
- Cisco leads the world in routing technology, and its routers carry the majority of the traffic on the Internet today.

Q&A

Q **If networks existed before routers, how was information moved from network to network?**

A The main form of interconnecting networks was through the use of switches. Switching technology had already been in place on the public telephone network. Also, routing protocols were implemented on computers, allowing these devices to act as routers.

Quiz

Questions

1. What is the purpose of a router?
2. Where did Cisco routers originate?

Answers

1. To move data from one network to another
2. Stanford University

WEEK 1

DAY 2

Understanding Cisco Hardware

In this lesson, we will be discussing the hardware behind Cisco's routing products. Before you can truly begin working on and learning Cisco routers, you need to familiarize yourself with the router's hardware. Routing hardware, such as memory, expansions, and port configurations, can change from manufacturer to manufacturer and even vary within one manufacturer's line of products. Therefore, we need to cover the variety of hardware that can be found with Cisco's product lines before we discuss anything else.

> **Note** Keep in mind that the software that runs the Cisco routers—the Cisco IOS—is the same for all Cisco routers. There are added features for some router series, but the base IOS is the same. Therefore, the major differences between Cisco routers will be in the hardware. The Cisco 700 series, however, is a notable exception to this rule. These routers run a modified version of the Cisco IOS, known as the Cisco IOS-700. These routers have a fixed configuration and are the only ones to support a different operating system.

Cisco's routers are classified by series. Just as two trucks in different series from one maker differ from each other, such as a Ford Explorer and a Ford Expedition, Cisco routing hardware varies from series to series. The hardware differences can be slight (maybe an extra Ethernet port), or they can be great (the ability to add dozens of ports via expansion slots). Either way, you should be familiar with these differences to recognize what type of router you are dealing with. For example, you wouldn't want to waste your time trying to configure a router for ISDN support if it doesn't have a physical ISDN port.

> **Note** This lesson serves to provide an overview of the hardware that you will encounter when dealing with Cisco routers. We will not be looking at any one router or hardware component in depth. Rather, you should be familiarizing yourself with the broad scope of hardware that can be found in routers.

When dealing with Cisco routers, we can divide the routing hardware into two categories: general routing hardware and series-specific routing hardware. General hardware includes items that all Cisco routers have, such as random access memory (RAM), ports, and flash memory. Series-specific hardware includes the overall look of the router, port configurations and locations, and expansions.

Choosing the specific model of Cisco router for a network can be one of the most important decisions a designer can make (or at least the one with the most repercussions). Knowing the hardware characteristic of the specific Cisco series and models will help an administrator choose the correct router for any environment.

To aid in the decision-making process, this lesson will cover the following topics.

- General Cisco router hardware components
- Series-specific router hardware

While reviewing the following hardware specifications, be mindful of the limitations and capabilities of each router model. These specifications should then be applied against the needs of working environments to identify the correct routing device.

General Cisco Router Hardware Components

Every Cisco router has components that are common across all series. That is, certain pieces of hardware will be found in all Cisco routers regardless of the series that the routers belong to.

Certain components, such as flash memory and ports, are common among all Cisco routers. These pieces of hardware should be fairly recognizable to anyone with hardware experience (PC or otherwise). To examine these components in a logical manner, we will discuss them in categories. The common hardware for Cisco routers can be divided into two categories: external hardware and internal hardware.

Internal common hardware includes RAM and other components that are generally accessible only from within the router's chassis. External hardware, on the other hand, can include ports, power, and expansion cards. Let's take a look at the external features common to Cisco routers.

External Hardware

Discussing the external features of a Cisco router may seem rudimentary; however, a lot of design work has been put into making Cisco routers as user-friendly as possible. These features include placing the ports in an area that is easily accessible and putting the series designator of the router where it can easily be read. The features of the external hardware components are key in determining what kind of Cisco router you are working with. Therefore we will begin by discussing the features found on the case of the router.

The Case

When discussing external features of Cisco routers, the first thing that we should identify is the case. The case is one of the most distinctive parts of a Cisco router. The blue or gray coloring (and the Cisco logo) should indicate to you that the router is from Cisco. However, the case has other features that help you identify the series, model, and other information that is critical to the performance of the router.

The Cisco logo and the series number should be prominently displayed on the front of the router. For most Cisco routers, like the 2500 Series, the logo and series designation are located at the left and right sides of the front panel, respectively.

Note Keep in mind that there can be several models within a certain series of router. For example, the Cisco 2500 Series of routers includes the 2501, 2502, 2503, 2504, 2505, 2507, 2509, and 18 other models. The series designator on the front panel will tell you only which series the router belongs to, not the model, because one case design can be shared by all of the routers in a series.

Routers on which the logo is placed on the front of the case are often intended to be mounted in a rack, particularly for the higher series. Rack-mount routers are usually viewed and accessed from the front only, and in most situations you will find that all of the available ports are also located on the front panel.

For some of Cisco's small-business routers, such as the 1600 Series, the Cisco logo and series marker can be found on the top of the case. The small-business series routers are generally meant for desktop placement or side mounting.

> **Note** When a Cisco router is side mounted, the unit is usually hung like a picture; that is, the bottom (or foot) of the router is attached to the side of a rack or other suitable space.

On most Cisco routers that are not rack mounted, the logo and series designator are the only items you will find on the front of the case. However, some routers, such as the 1600 Series have a status panel. These status panels are generally located on the front or top of the unit. The status panel contains a set of LED lights corresponding to different activities, such as power, system integrity, and port status. You can use the status lights to determine the functionality of a port or an abnormal collision rate.

The lights for port status will differ depending on the router you have. On the 1605, there are two pairs of lights for Ethernet (ETH0 and ETH1) and one pair for a WAN interface card (WIC). On the other hand, the 1603 has one light for ISDN (BRI0) and one for a WAN interface card (WIC).

For routers with no forward-facing status panel, such as the 2500 Series, there are status lights on the rear access panel. These lights are located adjacent to each port and, like those on the 1600 Series status panel, indicate the port's status. Normally the port's status is marked by a connectivity light and either a collision light or an error light.

The connectivity light for a port indicates whether the cable connected to the port has through communication. The collision or error light of a port shows the current error rate of a link (on an Ethernet network this indicates the overall collision of packets on a line).

Although the status indicators are not in the same location on all routers—on the front of some routers, on the top or rear of others—there are some hardware items that can always be found in the same place. Let's take a look at what common external hardware components can be found to the rear of a router.

Items Located on the Rear of the Case

The most common (and most recognizable) items located to the rear of the router's case are the power plug and the power switch.

In contrast, the higher-end Cisco routers can accept power from DC power sources. These routers require a little more setup then simply plugging in a power cable. Many larger companies utilize the DC capabilities of the high-end Cisco routers to provide battery backup power to their environments. The power supply itself is modular. That is, the standard AC power supply can be removed and replaced by the DC (in models that accept both).

Like the power supply, one feature that all Cisco routers will have (but the type will change) is a console port.

The Console Port

Another feature that you will always find to the rear of a router is the console port. The console port is your initial link to the router's interface. The console port will look like a standard RJ-45 port. However, if you try to use a standard RJ-45 cable, you will find that it will not work.

> **Note** Once you start looking at the higher-end routers (some enterprise and ISP series routers) the console will be a serial port rather than a RJ-45. Routers with a serial port for the console will accept a standard terminal rather than needing to be connected to a PC. However, not all of these console ports support a modem connection as their RJ-45 counterparts do. These routers will generally have a separate serial port for direct modem access.

> **Note** We will cover using the console port on Day 3, "Understanding the Cisco IOS." Now you should be aware that, even though the console port looks innocent enough, it has been the grief of many an engineer. Every Cisco router will come bundled with a special *console cable* (usually colored blue); this cable is the only one that should be used in conjunction with the console port.

Cisco routers can be accessed and administered through multiple interfaces. It is possible (on a fully configured Cisco router) to interface with the router over the console port, the Ethernet ports, or by Telnet over an IP port. However, the only interface that is initialized by default is the console interface. Therefore it is important to be able to recognize the console port and know how to connect with it.

Though we will not get into the details now, you should realize that connecting to the console port via a PC requires an RJ-45 rollover cable (which are slightly different from both standard Ethernet cables and Ethernet crossover cables). Because rollover cables are hard to find (and even harder to make successfully) you should always have a standard issue Cisco console cable on hand. Every router is packaged with at least one.

The anatomy of Cisco rollover cables will be covered on Day 6, "Getting the Router Up and Running."

> I can't emphasize enough the importance of having a Cisco console cable available at all times. Trust me—there is never one around when you need it. If anything goes wrong with the router, the console port is the only guaranteed way to access the router.

Two more features can be located on the rear of the case on a Cisco router. Not every router will have both of these components, but most will. They are a WAN expansion port and a removable flash RAM card.

WAN Expansion Ports

A blank plate should protect the WAN expansion port, located on the rear of most Cisco routers. The blank plate can be easily removed to reveal a very versatile feature of most Cisco routers. To remove the blank plate and access the WAN expansion port, simply remove the screws holding the plate in place.

Note Some Cisco routers can be purchased with a "WAN enabled" option and have a WIC already installed in the WAN expansion port. Even if your router has a WIC installed, it can be removed and replaced with others for added capabilities.

The technology behind many of the WAN cards, including ISDN and T1, will be discussed on later days.

The particular WICs that can be installed in a router depend on the series and model of the router; a list for each model is provided in the section "Series Specific Router Hardware" later in this lesson). Some WAN abilities that can be added to routers through the WAN expansion port are ISDN ports and T1 interfaces.

> You should always check with your router model's specific documentation to ensure that you are adding a WIC that is compatible with your series. You should also verify that you have the proper IOS release to provide the functionality needed to operate the WIC installed.

Expanding a router's capabilities through the use of WICs is a good way to use your equipment to its fullest potential. Although many people underestimate the abilities of smaller devices, even a small router like the Cisco 1605 can simultaneously handle WAN routing (through the WIC) and multiple LAN routing (through the two Ethernet ports). The simple addition of a WIC can double a router's productivity. By recognizing a router's potential, you will be a better engineer.

Another upgrade that can save the life (and increase the productivity) of a Cisco router is the flash memory.

Flash Memory

Most Cisco routers are equipped with a removable (thus upgradeable) flash memory card. The capacity of the card varies depending on the router (anywhere from 4MB to 24MB), but they can be swapped out and replaced.

The router uses the flash memory to store configuration files and IOS images. Therefore it is very important to verify that all files have been copied off the flash card before replacing it. Otherwise you may boot your router only to find your configurations missing (not good). We will discuss moving files from (and the general use of) the flash memory on Day 3, when we discuss the Cisco IOS.

> **Note** Some models of Cisco routers actually run directly from the flash memory, whereas others run from internal RAM and only store their data in the flash memory. In most cases the designation between the two can be found in the model name. Routers with R after the model name (such as the Cisco 1605 R) run from RAM.
> Both types still use the flash memory to store files.

By this point you should be fairly well acquainted with the common external hardware of the Cisco routers. Before we look at the series-specific hardware components, let's discuss the internal router hardware.

Internal Hardware

If you are familiar with PC hardware, the view inside a Cisco router will not be much different. All of the familiar device components—a processor, RAM, and other internal circuits—exist in all routers.

Most Cisco routers use a processor from the Motorola 68000 family (usually a 68360 or a 68030 running around 28MHz). These processors are very good at handling the complex calculations required for making routing decisions. Another advantage of modern 68000 processors is their ability to operate efficiently while using minimal power. Because the processor does not use as much power, it does not generate as much heat. This characteristic is important because it means that some Cisco routers (primarily those in the small business line) will not require a cooling fan. The absence of a fan makes these routers very quiet and energy efficient.

The RAM used by most Cisco routers is dynamic RAM (DRAM) on single inline memory modules (SIMMs), installed in expandable slots as in many computers. This makes the RAM just as upgradeable as in its PC counterparts. (You may find yourself upgrading both the flash and the DRAM at least once over the life of a router.)

> **Note**
>
> Dynamic memory needs to be *refreshed*—that is, "reminded" of its contents by reading, writing, or a special refresh signal—on a regular basis. If the memory is not refreshed fairly regularly, the contents can be corrupted. However, the chips themselves are very fast and can hold large amounts of information. In contrast, static RAM (SRAM) does not have to be refreshed, but it has much less capacity per chip or per dollar.
>
> DRAM works well in a routing environment, because the information in a router's memory changes so often that refreshing it is not an issue. Also, the speed of DRAM gives it a definite advantage.

We have now covered all of the hardware components that are common to many Cisco routers. Let's take a look at some series-specific hardware.

Series-Specific Router Hardware

Each router series has hardware that is specific to that series. (Otherwise there would be no need for the different series.) The series are designated by their hardware-specific capacities. In other words, the hardware in the enterprise series routers has a greater capacity for handling traffic and route calculations then the small-business routers.

> **Note** A third group of routers, the Service Provider Series, are geared specifically to the needs of ISPs. Because these routers are of such a high level, they are outside the scope of a book like this.

This section describes the series-specific hardware (such as available ports, their capacities, and upgrades) for the more popular small-business and enterprise routers. These are the routers that you are most likely to see in a production environment. This section will provide a good reference for future projects (both in conjunction with the lessons in the book and after you finish).

Routers for Small to Midsize Businesses

Cisco's small-business routers are great for businesses that do not need the multiport connectivity of the Enterprise level routers. However, just because these routers are not built to handle the overwhelming loads of Enterprise routers, do not write them off as lightweight.

The small-business routers are every bit as robust as their larger counterparts. In fact, because of their greater cost efficiency, many engineers choose to purchase small-business series routers for personal use and practice. They have most (if not all) of the functionality of many enterprise-level routers at a fraction of the cost. Let's take a look at the more popular small-business routers.

The 800 Series

The 800 Series router is the most popular for home and small network use. Its simple design allows it to route effectively between smaller LAN and WAN links. Home users will like the simplified nature of the router's interface, whereas small businesses will gain from its versatility.

The Cisco 805 is the router of choice in the 800 series. The 805 comes with everything needed to provide a WAN or PPP connection to a (small) LAN networking environment. This is important for users who want a device that requires as little (postsales) modification and maintenance as possible.

The Cisco 805 is equipped with one Ethernet port and one serial port (along with the standard console port).

The Ethernet port on the Cisco 805 has a feature, not found on many routers, that makes it a great router for home use. A well-marked "HUB/NO HUB" switch beside the Ethernet port allows the user to forgo the use of a crossover cable when connecting the router directly into a home PC. If the router will reside on a small network (in other words, be attached to a hub), the "HUB/NO HUB" switch just needs to be set accordingly.

The Cisco 805 serial port is used for WAN (or modem) connections. The serial port can be set for asynchronous connection to a modem for PPP (Point-to-Point Protocol) communication or for synchronous connection to a CSU/DSU (channel service unit/data service unit) for Frame Relay communication, to handle almost any need. The settings for the serial port are made within the IOS.

Table 2.1 summarizes the features of the 805 router.

TABLE 2.1 Cisco 805 Hardware

Component	Standard	Upgrade
RAM	8MB	16MB
Flash	4MB	12MB
Processor	Motorola 68000	N/A
Ports		
Ethernet	1 (10BaseT)	N/A
Serial	1 (Sync/Async)	N/A
WAN	N/A	N/A

The 1600 Series

The Cisco 1600 Series routers are perfect entry-level routers for midsize companies, because they are the most cost-effective Cisco routers that offer both upgradeable flash cards and WIC expansion ports. There are five routers in the Cisco 1600 line. Each router provides a different support function. The table below illustrates the hardware available on the different 1600 series models.

TABLE 2.2 The Cisco 1600 Series Models

Router	Ethernet Ports	Serial Ports	WAN Ports
1601	1	1	1 (open interface slot)
1602	1	1 serial with integrated 56-kbps DSU/CSU	1 (open interface slot)
1603	1	0	1 ISDN and 1 open interface slot
1604	1	0	1 ISDN, 1 s-bus for ISDN phones, and 1 open interface slot
1605	2	0	1 (open interface slot)

The 1603 is popular among small business users that may have an ISDN connection to a remote office. However, the most popular router in the 1600 series is the 1605, in part because of its dual Ethernet ports, which enable it to route effectively between two LANs and a WAN. The following table shows the standard and upgradeable hardware for the Cisco 1605. (The WICs listed can be installed in any 1600 Series router with a WIC interface.)

TABLE 2.3 Cisco 1605 Hardware

Component	Standard	Upgrade
RAM	8MB	24MB
Flash	4MB (removable card)	16MB
Processor	Motorola 68360 33MHz	N/A
Ports		
Ethernet	2 (10BaseT)	N/A
Serial	0	N/A
WAN	WIC interface	Serial (Sync/Async)
		56k CSU/DSU
		Fractional T1 CSU/DSU
		ISDN BRI with S/T interface
		ISDN BRI with integrated NT1, U interface

The 2500 Series

Also meant for medium-sized businesses, the Cisco 2500 Series rack-mount routers can adapt to any LAN setting. Many large enterprises also use the 2500 Series routers to segment larger networks.

There are over 20 models in the Cisco 2500 series of routers, and there is not enough room in this section to supply a profile of all of them. The more popular ones are used to connect remote offices. The versatility of the 2500 series literally allows it to conform to almost any environment.

One of these more popular 2500 series routers is the Cisco 2520, which is equipped with multiple serial ports and Ethernet ports. The serial ports can be used for modems, CSD/DSUs, and other WAN serial interfaces. However, it should be stated that the 2525 and 2524 are the only two routers in the 2500 series to have WIC interfaces. The other models in the 2500 series have built-in WAN components. Table 2.4 shows the hardware components for the Cisco 2520.

TABLE 2.4 Hardware Components for the Cisco 2520

Component	Standard	Upgrade
RAM	8MB	24MB
Flash	4MB EPROM	12MB
Processor	20-MHz Motorola 68EC030	N/A
Ports		
Ethernet	1 Ethernet (AUI or 10BaseT)	N/A
Serial	2 (Sync/Async), 2 sync	N/A
WAN	Built-in	1 ISDN BRI port

Enterprise Series Routers

The enterprise series routers are the workhorses of the Cisco routing line, and they begin to incorporate many high-end features that are really outside of the scope of this book; for example, the 7000 series and the 12000 series include technologies such as VOIP (voice over IP) and complex PPP routing.

One series of routers at the enterprise level that is worth noting here is the Cisco 4000 Series. Though still a high-end router, the 4000 Series is common enough that you may find it in many different settings. The reason for its popularity is that is has support for fiber and FDDI.

Understanding Cisco Hardware

> **Note:** FDDI (Fiber Distributed Data Interface) has a high-bandwidth ring topology. By running the fiber in double rings, the topology has a built-in redundancy that makes it very attractive to companies that need high bandwidth and high visibility.

The Cisco 4000 Series routers are modular. That is, they can use hardware routing modules. One of the most popular modules is the FDDI card, which provides built-in support for FDDI rings. Table 2.5 illustrates the hardware in the Cisco 4000.

TABLE 2.5 Hardware in the Cisco 4000

Component	Standard	Upgrade
RAM	4MB	16MB
Flash	4MB EPROM	8MB
Processor	40MHz Motorola 68EC030	
	N/A	
Ports		
Ethernet	0	Module
Serial	1	Module
WAN	Network Modules	Ethernet
		Serial
		Token Ring
		FDDI

Summary

This lesson should provide you a good overview of the hardware the makes the Cisco routers work. Understanding the hardware behind the technology will better prepare you for the lessons that constitute the remainder of the book. The next lesson deals with the operating system that runs Cisco routers. Knowing something of the hardware structure of routers now gives you a better perspective of why the Cisco IOS works the way it does.

The Cisco IOS is the operating system that drives all Cisco routers. The next lesson will take you through navigating the Cisco IOS and performing some simple configurations. We will discuss the user interface of the IOS along with its command structure and help systems.

Q&A

Q Does the selection of a particular Cisco router make a difference in the overall performance of the network?

A Absolutely. Each router is placed into a specific series based on its features and functionality. Choosing a router that is too powerful for your network may be cost ineffective, whereas an underpowered router will not adequately handle the daily load on the environment.

Quiz

Questions

1. What type of RAM is normally installed in Cisco routers?
2. What is the name of the port used to add WAN capabilities to a router?

Answers

1. DRAM
2. WIC (WAN Interface Card)

WEEK 1

DAY 3

Understanding the Cisco IOS

In this lesson (Day 3) we will discuss the Cisco IOS (Internetwork Operating System), the operating system that drives most Cisco routers (except the 700 Series). Before we examine any other features of Cisco's routers (such as configurations and operations), we need to understand the basic IOS elements. Therefore, this lesson will focus primarily on providing you that key knowledge base that is essential to understanding the rest of this book and successfully mastering Cisco routers.

The IOS features a complete set of tools to help administrators monitor and configure Cisco routers. One of these tools is the Exec, or command interpreter. The Exec is the engine that drives the Cisco IOS.

The command interpreter is the core of the Cisco IOS. Any command entered into the Cisco IOS needs a master process to act upon it and supply an appropriate response. This is the basic job description of the Exec.

The Cisco command interpreter is divided into two modes, or levels. The lower level, offering the most basic interpretation of commands, is the *user mode* command interpreter. The highest level is known as the *privilege mode* command interpreter. We will cover the procedures required to use both modes of the Exec.

> **Note**
>
> If you have a Cisco router that you will be using to follow the lessons in this book, do not use it here. This lesson serves as an introduction to the Cisco IOS. Therefore it would be better just to read along and absorb the information rather than trying to reproduce the examples on your own. (Beginning with the next lesson, sample exercises will appear at the end of each day. These exercises will allow you to practice what you have learned in the day's lesson.)
>
> If you do have a Cisco router, and have yet to turn it on for the first time (or you have turned it on and were confused by what you saw), don't use it until Day 6, "Getting the Router Up and Running." All Cisco routers enter what is known as *setup mode* the first time they are powered up. Setup mode allows the administrator to provide the initial configuration to the router. Therefore, if you do not already have a basic understanding of the Cisco IOS, you may feel lost during the process. That is why we will be covering the concepts behind the Cisco IOS here, on Day 3.

This lesson, covering the basic elements of the Cisco IOS, will tie directly into Day 4, "Learning the Cisco User Interface." Together, these two lessons will completely introduce you to the operating system of Cisco routers: the Cisco IOS.

Two major topics are covered in this lesson:

- What the Cisco IOS is and how to upgrade it
- The Cisco IOS command interpreter

Behind the Cisco IOS

Like any computer (and most other electronic devices), Cisco routers require an operating system to perform their primary functions. The heart of every Cisco router is the Cisco IOS. The Cisco IOS contains the instruction sets needed to configure, maintain, and run a Cisco router successfully in any environment.

Routers, like PCs, are complex devices capable of incredible calculations. Cisco routers apply complicated formulas to sets of criteria (representing routing paths and options), ultimately producing a desired result of the "best path" for information to traverse. Calculations such as these require an operating system that is both robust and user friendly. However, this operating system needs to be lightweight and fast to handle the load of today's routing environments.

The Cisco IOS is a robust operating system that is fully featured but at the same time very streamlined. The operating system that runs all Cisco routers is packed with features that allow for the most complex configurations (meaning the routers can be adapted to work in almost any situation). However, there are no superfluous or "seldom used" functions. The Cisco IOS is a very efficiently assembled package of commands and functions for managing routers.

As you will discover, the Cisco IOS is more than just a set of commands for running routers. The IOS provides tools for file storage, memory management, and other services that an administrator would use to operate within a given environment.

You might think, however, that with such a powerful command structure (and given the complexity of router operations), the Cisco IOS would be complicated or hard to use. In fact, the Cisco IOS is extremely user friendly and easy to learn. Anyone familiar with basic PC functions and terminology can easily learn the Cisco IOS.

However, before we explore the structure of the Cisco IOS, let's examine it as an operating system—in other words, the important stuff, such as where you buy it and how you install it.

After we examine these topics, we will look into the technology that drives the Cisco IOS. By the conclusion of this lesson, you will be familiar with the overall architecture of the Cisco IOS.

Obtaining IOS Updates

Operating systems, regardless of platform, need to be flexible to be successful. That is, the more control you as an administrator have over the operating system, the more satisfied you will be with its results. Part of being flexible is the ability to be replaced or modified.

Almost every operating system on the market today can be considered flexible. For example, if you own a PC, you can install Microsoft Windows 2000, upgrade it to Microsoft Windows XP, or keep it and modify it through the use of service packs.

The Cisco IOS is just as flexible. You can install IOS version 12.0(3) on your router, upgrade it to 12.2, or keep it and modify it through the use of feature packs.

> **Note** A Cisco IOS feature pack is a version of the IOS software that contains added functionality not available in the basic IOS, such as the ability to run a firewall or utilize virtual private networks (VPNs).

Every router is packaged (unless otherwise stated) with the Basic Cisco IOS. The Basic IOS usually supports routing one routed protocol, such as IP or IPX. To give a router with the Basic IP Cisco IOS the ability to router both IP and IPX, you would need to install the IP/IPX feature pack.

In contrast to most PC operating systems, a Cisco IOS feature pack actually contains the entire operating system within it—not just the parts needed to add the new features. Therefore, when you add a feature pack to your router, you should be sure that the feature pack includes all of the functionality you currently have.

For example, suppose an administrator has a router running the Basic Cisco IOS that routes IP, decides that the particular router also needs to route IPX, and therefore installs the Cisco IPX IOS feature pack. The error in the administrator's logic is that installing a feature pack is not a cumulative process. What the administrator has actually done is overwrite the current IP IOS with IOS that routes IPX (and only IPX), thus losing the ability to route IP. To be able to route both the IP and IPX protocols, the administrator should have installed the Cisco IP/IPX IOS feature pack. Therefore it is important to be aware of your needs when you look to upgrade a router with an IOS feature pack.

After the decision to upgrade the Cisco IOS has been made, you need to acquire the desired software.

The Cisco IOS, unlike many operating systems, can be obtained only through Cisco, simply because you can run it only on Cisco products. When you purchase a Cisco router, it should come with a preloaded version of the latest IOS. This is all that you need to get your router operational. However, given the reliability of Cisco's equipment and the loyalty of its customers, many people may want to upgrade their IOS when a new version is released. Moreover, the needs of a network may change over time, and a new feature pack may need to be installed. Where do you find these updates?

Understanding the Cisco IOS

There are two ways to obtain the "latest and greatest" that Cisco has to offer. The first (and recommended) way is to register your router and purchase a service agreement. This book does not cover all the details of the various service agreements that Cisco has to offer, but most of the agreements include access to Cisco's secure Web site, shown in Figure 3.1.

FIGURE 3.1

The Cisco secure download page for IOS upgrades.

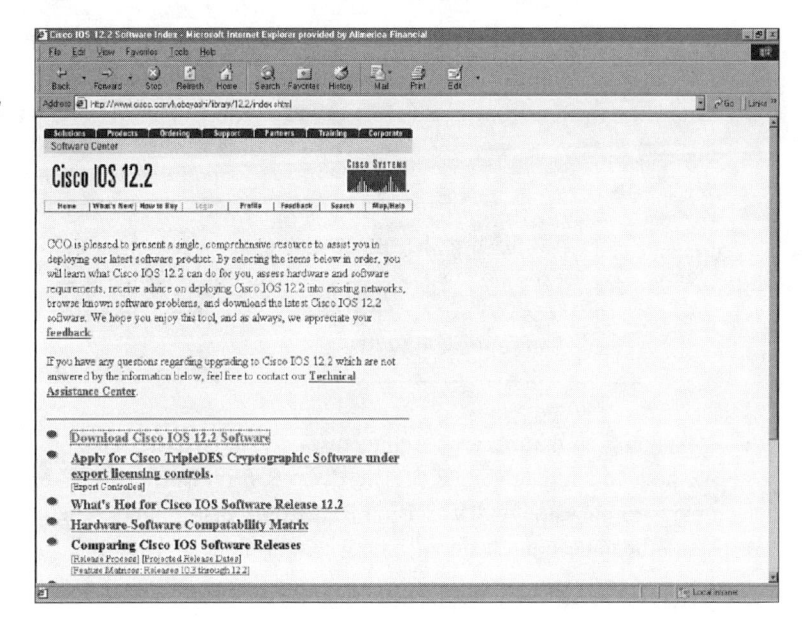

From Cisco's secure site you can freely download (as covered by your particular service plan) the latest Cisco IOS updates and feature packs. IOS images (the files that contain the installable Cisco operating system) are available for the current release and most past releases as well. Therefore, administrators with older equipment can still find the IOS they need to keep their network running.

The Cisco CCO (Cisco Connection Online) secure site is a great tool not only for obtaining the IOS releases but for accessing many of Cisco's technical documents and specifications as well.

Obtaining the Cisco IOS is only the first step. Next you need to upgrade the IOS (or apply the specific feature pack, as the situation may be).

Router Memory Architecture

Before attempting to upgrade your router's IOS, you need to understand the memory architecture of your router. Different models of Cisco routers run the Cisco IOS from different locations. Knowing where the IOS is running on your particular router can be the difference between a successful upgrade and a corrupt IOS image.

Cisco routers fall into two categories, depending on the way in which they run the Cisco IOS. Run-from-RAM (RFR) routers are Cisco routers that load the IOS into RAM to be run, whereas Run-from-Flash (RFF) routers will run the IOS directly from the flash memory.

> **Note**
> The letter R after the model number identifies a Run-from-RAM router. For example, the Cisco 1605R is a Run-from-RAM router.
>
> It can be assumed that any router without an R after the model name is a Run-from-Flash router.

Depending on the memory architecture of your specific router, you may use different methods to upgrade your IOS. The Cisco IOS on Run-from-RAM routers cannot be upgraded the same way as it is on Run-from-Flash routers. Therefore, we must understand the underlying difference between the two architectures.

Run-from-Flash Routers

The nature of flash memory is to retain information regardless of whether the device it is installed in is powered on or off. This nonvolatility—the ability to retain information when the power is off—is the reason that Cisco uses flash memory as its primary means of storage in most of its routers.

All files, configurations, and IOS images are stored in the router's flash memory, regardless of the router's memory architecture. On both Run-from-RAM and Run-from-Flash routers, an IOS image is stored in the Flash memory. It is where the IOS image goes after the router boots that creates the difference between the two architectures.

Run-from-Flash routers boot up like all other Cisco routers. During the boot process, the loader calls and executes the images in the Flash memory directly. Figure 3.2 illustrates the boot process in a Run-from-Flash router.

FIGURE 3.2

Loading an RFF IOS image.

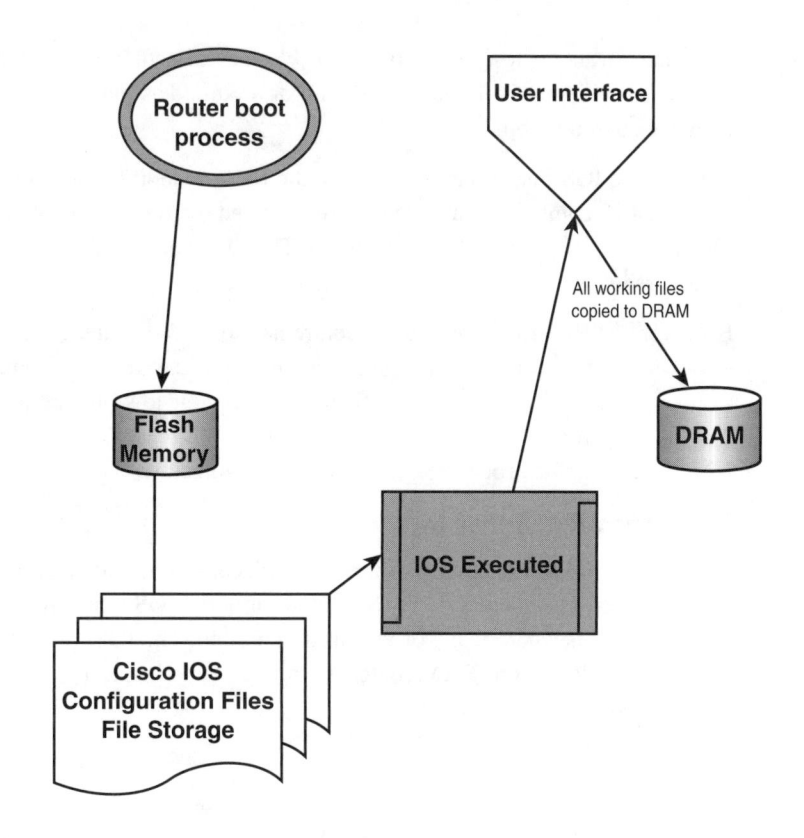

The boot process executes the uncompressed IOS image directly from flash. The IOS runs from the flash memory, while all working files are copied to the RAM.

This process has some advantages over other memory architectures. The first advantage is boot speed. Because the IOS image does not need to be decompressed to run, the router can boot quicker. This can be important in environments where every minute counts. (Where a Run-From-RAM router will generally take 2 to 3 minutes to boot, a Run-From-Flash router can boot in less than a minute.)

Running directly from flash memory also frees up RAM. Because the working IOS files (the running-config, routing tables, and other files required for immediate operation) are the only IOS components occupying the RAM space, the IOS can access them more quickly. This adds another advantage over other router architectures.

The final advantage to using a Run-from-Flash architecture is a reduced risk of corruption. The IOS image is not tampered with or modified as much as it would be in other memory configurations.

Because the IOS image that is stored on the flash memory is not modified at a binary level (that is, compressed and decompressed) and the image is relatively stationary, the router can run in a more stable condition. The likelihood of a file-level corruption is then greatly reduced.

However, the Run-from-Flash architecture has some disadvantages as well. The major disadvantage is that the IOS image is actually being run from the router's sole source of storage. As a result, the router's IOS cannot be upgraded while the IOS is in use. While this may sound operationally counterintuitive, it will make sense. However, before we look at the upgrade process, let's discuss the architecture of Run-from-RAM routers.

Run-from-RAM Routers

Run-from-RAM routers take a different approach to router loading. Like their Run-from-Flash counterparts, Run-from-RAM routers store the IOS image in the flash memory. However, this is where many of the similarities end. The IOS image that is stored in flash memory on a Run-from-RAM router is compressed, whereas on a Run-from-Flash router it is not compressed.

> **Note** Regardless of their architecture, all Cisco routers utilize the provided flash memory as storage. All IOS images, compressed or uncompressed, are stored on the flash.

During the boot process, the compressed IOS image is extracted from the flash memory and decompressed. During the decompression process the image is restored to a working executable operating system. Figure 3.3 illustrates the boot process for Run-from-RAM routers.

The decompressed IOS image is then copied to the router's RAM. Because the image is copied to the router's RAM, it must share the available RAM space with the router's working files. As a result, routers with a Run-from-RAM architecture are usually equipped with more base RAM than Run-from-Flash routers.

Understanding the Cisco IOS

FIGURE 3.3

Loading an RFR IOS image

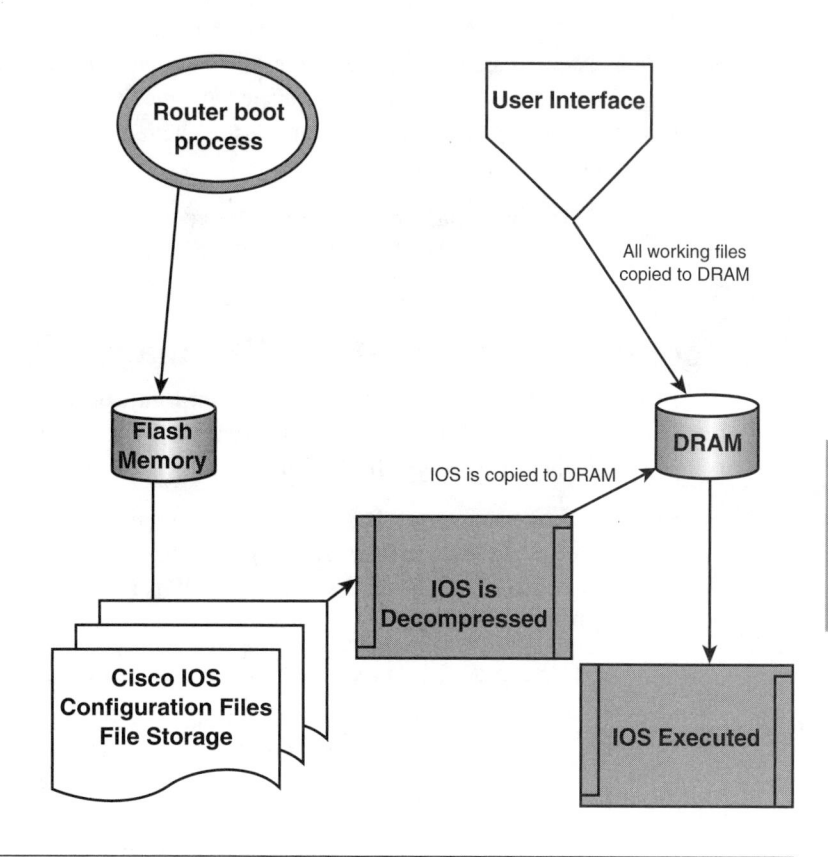

[Diagram: Router boot process → Flash Memory (containing Cisco IOS Configuration Files File Storage) → IOS is Decompressed → IOS is copied to DRAM → DRAM ← All working files copied to DRAM ← User Interface; DRAM → IOS Executed]

> **Note:** Recall from Day 2 that the RAM in most Cisco routers is DRAM.

After the IOS image is decompressed and copied to the RAM, the router executes it. This starts the router's operational systems. The router will continue all standard operations from the system RAM, leaving the flash open for router storage.

Run-from-RAM architecture has its advantages, as Run-from-Flash does. The foremost advantage is the freeing of the Flash memory. Because the IOS is run from RAM, the flash memory is free to accept a replacement for the IOS image without disturbing the running software. As a result, upgrading the IOS is much easier on a Run-from-RAM system than on a Run-from-Flash router.

However, a disadvantage to using Run-from-RAM routers is the increased risk of IOS corruption. Because the IOS is manipulated and modified much more in a Run-from-RAM router than in a Run-from-Flash system, the chances of a binary-level corruption of the operating system are increased.

Therefore, it is very important in Run-from-RAM router maintenance to keep backups of your router's configuration and IOS files. (Router backup methods and procedures will be covered on Day 7, "Backing Up Router Configurations.")

Upgrading Run-from-Flash IOS Images

There are generally two ways to upgrade the IOS of Run-from-Flash routers. The most common way is by using the Flash Load Helper (FLH), a separate command space that can be used to gain access to the flash memory independent of the IOS.

The other way is by using a dual flash bank. This method utilizes one larger flash SIMM that has been partitioned into two areas, thus giving the administrator the ability to access the unused flash regardless of whether the IOS is running. Let's examine the procedures for using both methods.

> **Note** Feel free to read through these procedures. However, do not be discouraged if you cannot follow the IOS functions being used. The Cisco IOS user interface concepts and functions involved here will be explained in more depth on Day 4.

Using Dual Flash Banks

Although using dual flash banks to upgrade an IOS image is fairly simple and relatively straightforward, there is considerable preparation time needed. In most cases, however, this is a procedure that needs to be performed only once.

Keep in mind that not every Cisco router has the capability to run a dual flash bank. To tell whether your router can be set up for dual flash banks, check the router's specific documentation, or open the case and check the flash SIMM. If the router's flash SIMM contains more than one set of four memory chips, the router can be set up to use dual flash banks.

> **Note** The minimum number of memory chips that can be used as a flash partition is 4.

By partitioning the flash memory you are creating two logical areas in which data can be stored and accessed by the router. This allows the administrator to write an IOS image to one partition of the flash while a separate image is running in the other partition.

One advantage to this method is that no router downtime is required to upload a new IOS image, whereas using the Flash Load Helper requires a minor amount of router downtime.

After determining whether the router is capable of being partitioned for dual flash banks, use the following steps to set up the flash banks.

First, enter the privilege mode command interpreter.

```
Router>enable
Router#
```

In privilege mode, enter the global configuration program.

```
Router#configure
Configuring from terminal, memory, or network [terminal]? terminal
```

Enter configuration commands, one per line. End with Ctrl-Z.

```
Router(config)#
```

Within the global configuration program, you can issue the commands needed to partition the flash memory.

```
Router(config)# partition flash
```

This command will accept parameters relating to the number of partitions you want and the desired size of each.

```
Router(config)#partition flash ?
  <1-8> Number of partitions in device

Router(config)#partition flash 2 ?
  <1-64> Size of partition 1
```

After partitioning the flash memory, upgrading the IOS becomes rather easy. Using the copy command, copy a suitable IOS image to the unused Flash partition.

> **Note** For now, do not be overly concerned with the underlying operation of the commands listed during this process. As we progress through the lessons, the purpose and function of all the commands will become much clearer.

The copy command is used to move files from one location to another, regardless of memory architecture or method of upgrade. Therefore, you will be using the copy command quite often during normal router operation.

`Router#copy tftp flash`

This command structure copies an unspecified file from a TFTP (Trivial File Transfer Protocol) server to the flash memory. Entering this command will cause the IOS to prompt you for several pieces of information before the actual copy can continue. The parameters you will be prompted for are:

- TFTP server name
- IOS image file name
- Destination flash partition
- Destination file name

> **Note** TFTP server programs can be downloaded (usually for free) for almost any operating system. However, be advised that FTP software is generally not the same as TFTP. Most FTP clients cannot handle TFTP transactions.

Once the desired IOS image is copied to the desired partition, you need to specify to the router what image to use. That is, you now have a router with two flash memory areas, each with a working operating system. Therefore, the router needs to know which IOS to use for daily operation.

To indicate to the router which flash partition to boot, use the boot command from within global configuration mode.

`Router(config)#boot system flash 2`

This command specifies that the router is to boot the system from the second flash partition.

The router should now be fully configured to run the new IOS. However, if your Run-from-Flash router cannot utilize multiple flash partitions, you must use the Flash Load Helper.

Using the Flash Load Helper

Using Flash Load Helper is a far easier method to upgrade Run-from-Flash routers. The FLH is a small preinstalled utility that automates the upgrade system. However, not every Run-from-Flash router can run Flash Load Helper.

To run the Flash Load Helper, simply use the same commands that you would use to initiate a file copy. If your router is configured to run Flash Load Helper, the FLH notification message will appear after you enter the copy command.

```
Router# copy tftp flash
**************** NOTICE ***************************
Flash load helper v1.0
This process will accept the TFTP copy options and then terminate the current
system image to use the ROM based image for the copy. Router functionality will
not be available during that time. If you are logged in via telnet, this
connection will terminate. Users with console access can see the results of
the copy operation.
********************************************************
```

This message indicates that the router is ready to run Flash Load Helper and you can proceed with the IOS upgrade.

After the FLH notification message is displayed, you will be prompted for several pieces of information. The FLH will ask you for the address of the TFTP server from which to obtain the desired IOS image, the file name of the image, and the destination file name. The FLH will then ask you to confirm your actions, and the upgrade will begin.

The only major disadvantage to using the FLH is that, when the process is complete, FLH reboots. The router needs to be rebooted to load the new image (because the old one no longer exists). Therefore, a small amount of system downtime is required to complete an upgrade using Flash Load Helper.

Upgrading Run-from-RAM IOS Images

There are two different ways to upgrade the Cisco IOS on a Run-from-RAM router. The first is by using a Cisco-supplied program known as the RSL (Router Software Loader). The RSL will connect to your router, determine its current IOS version, and allow you to upgrade it. However, to upgrade the IOS you do need to supply a new IOS image, as described in the previous section. Figure 3.4 illustrates the RSL.

FIGURE 3.4

The Cisco Router Software Loader.

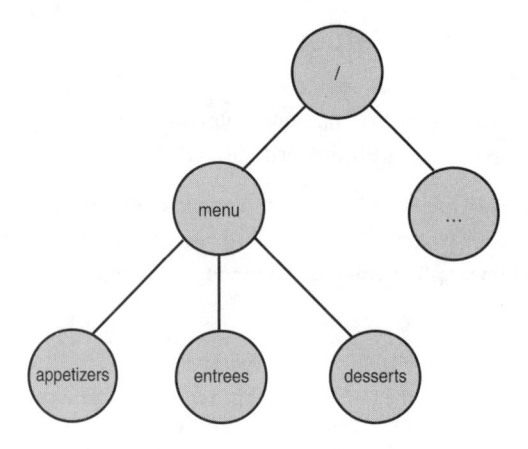

After successfully connecting to your router and examining its flash memory, the RSL will allow you to either back up or overwrite the existing IOS and install the new one. However, one problem you will inevitably encounter is a warning about the IOS you are installing not being an official release. This error is illustrated in Figure 3.5.

FIGURE 3.5

An RSL error.

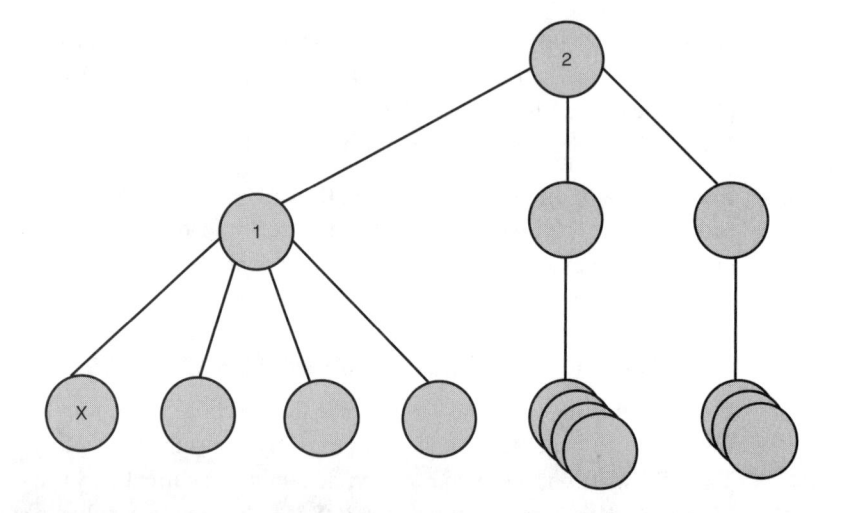

This error is generated by the RSL because the file you are trying to install to the router is not named correctly even though it is a valid IOS image. For example, the Basic IP release of IOS 12.0(3) for a Cisco 1600 Series router is downloadable as a file named c1600-y-mz.120-3.bin. However, the RSL wants the file to be named aaa0269.bin. Why the discrepancy? I really can't say. Either way most engineers find it much easier to upgrade the IOS manually.

Understanding the Cisco IOS

The following instructions will walk you through upgrading the Cisco IOS. Even though you will not understand most of the commands now, it will give you a good look at router maintenance. You can also refer back to this section later, when you know more of the router functions. (As with any configuration-altering process, it is recommended that you make a backup copy of your existing flash memory before you begin. You can back up your flash memory to the TFTP server by executing the command copy flash TFTP.)

To upgrade the IOS, you need to enter (or enable) privilege mode.

Router>**enable**

Within privilege mode, use the copy command to start the dialog. The copy command simply states that you want to copy something from a TFTP server to the flash memory.

Router#**copy tftp flash**

The router will prompt you for three pieces of information: the TFTP server's IP address (or DNS name), the IOS image file name, and the destination file name.

```
Address or name of remote host []? 10.16.4.152
Source filename []? c1600-y-mz.120-3.bin
Destination filename [c1600-y-mz.120-3.bin]?
```

You will notice that the destination file name (which is the name you want applied to the image file after it is copied to the flash memory) will default to the name of the source file. After starting the download, the router will ask you if you want to erase the current IOS image file. Answer yes and continue:

```
%Warning: Run from flash images are recommended for this platform.
Erase flash: before copying? [confirm]
Erasing the flash filesystem will remove all files! Continue? [confirm]
Erasing device... eeeeeeeeeeeeeeeeeeeeeeeeeeeeeee ...erased
Erase of flash: complete
Loading c1600-y-mz.121-8a.bin from 10.16.4.152 (via Ethernet0):
!!!!!!!!!!!!!!!!!!!!!!!!!!!!!!!!!!!!!!!!!!!!!!!!!!!!!!!!!!!!!!!!!!!!!!!!
!!!!!!!!!!!!!!!!!!!!!!!!!!!!!!!!!!!!!!!!!!!!!!!!!!!!!!!!!!!!!!!!!!!!!!!!
!!!!!!!!!!!!!!!!!!!!!!!!!!!!!!!!!!!!!!!!!!!!!!!!!!!!!!!!!!!!!!!!!!!!!!!!
!!!!!!!!!!!!!!!!!!!!!!!!!!!!!!!!!!!!!!!!!!!!!!!!!!!!!!!!!!!!!!!!!!!!!!!!
!!!!!!!!!!!!!!!!!!!!!!!!!!!!!!!!!!!!!!!!!!!!!!!!!!!!!!!!!!!!!!!!!!!!!!!!
!!!!!!!!!!!!!!!!!!!!!!!!!!!!!!!!!!!!!!!!!!!!!!!!!!!!!!!!!!!!!!!!!!!!!!!!
!!!!!!!!!!!!!!!!!!!!!!!!!!!!!!!!!!!!!!!!!!!!!!!!!!!!!!!!!!!!!!!!!!!!!!!!
!
[OK - 2868332/5736448 bytes]

Verifying checksum... OK (0xD6C8)
2868332 bytes copied in 106.936 secs (27059 bytes/sec)
```

Finally, after the new IOS image has been copied to the router, run the reload command to restart your device.

Router#**reload**

When your device restarts, you will have a shiny new IOS to "play with." You might not get away that easily, though. One common problem with installing an IOS via TFTP occurs after the router is restarted. The router may display an error on startup explaining that the device cannot load the IOS image. Don't worry; not only will the router continue to load, but the error is easy to clear up.

One common result of loading an IOS image from a TFTP server is that, after the image is loaded, the Cisco IOS Boot Loader wants to continue looking for the file on the TFTP location. After the router realizes that the file is no longer on the TFTP site, it will look to the flash memory and load the image from there. To keep this from happening, you need to edit the `startup-config` file, which can be done from within privilege mode.

```
Router#configure terminal
Router (config)# no boot tftp 1: <image file name>
Router (config)#z
Router#reload
```

> **Note:** In the previous sample, replace `<image file name>` by the name of the IOS image file that the boot loader is trying to load.

These steps should fix any error from trying to boot the IOS from TFTP. However, there is one more issue that you should be aware of when upgrading a Cisco IOS.

Pay very close attention to the DRAM requirements of the particular IOS version you are downloading. It is very possible to copy an IOS image to your router and not have the memory to run it. Keep in mind that the `copy` command does not monitor what is being copied; it simply moves binary data from location to location.

You may have more than enough physical space to store a particular IOS image in flash memory. However, if you do not have the minimum required DRAM to run it, your boot loader will become stuck in a loading loop. The boot loader will load the image, try to run it, realize it can't, and try to load it again, resulting in an infinite loop.

Even though it is a bit more complicated, there is a way to remedy this problem as well. You will need the following items:

- A PC running terminal software that is capable of sending a "break" key sequence and performing Xmodem file transfers
- A backup copy of your original IOS image (or other comparable IOS image). This image should be on the terminal PC.
- Lots of patience

> **Note**
>
> The key to being able to perform this fix successfully is using a terminal program that is capable of sending a break key sequence. Many people use HyperTerminal, supplied with most Microsoft operating systems. However, HyperTerminal on Windows NT4 is not able to utilize a break sequence. Therefore, you may want to look into the various other terminal emulators that can be downloaded for the platform.

The first step in curing the loading loop problem is to restart the router. Right when the router powers up, send a break to it. This will put the router into monitor mode. You can tell the router is in monitor mode by the following prompt:

```
rommon 1 >
```

From this monitor prompt, start the XModem protocol on the router:

```
rmonitor 1 >xmodem -r -s9600 aaa0269.bin
```

This command states that you want to start an XModem download to the router (`xmodem`), copy an image file directly to the DRAM and execute it (`-r`), copy the file at 9600 bps (`-s9600`), and name the file aaa0269.bin (`aaa0269.bin`). (Replace this name with the name of the file you want to send to your router.)

There are two reasons for copying the image directly to DRAM and not to flash. First, you cannot delete the image that is currently on the flash, so you most likely will not have room for the new one. Second, if you could fit the image on the flash, your router would still want to boot the old one. Therefore, you want to copy the good image directly to the DRAM.

When the router alerts you that it is ready to receive the file, start the XModem protocol on your terminal emulator. You want to send your router the backup file of the original IOS image for your router. After the XModem transfer has finished (which could take a little while over serial lines), the router will restart with the version of the IOS you sent it. You are not finished yet, though.

The remainder of today's lesson will introduce you to the IOS and its commands and functions—skills that you will need for successfully retaining and understanding the information provided in the remaining lessons). Before we examine the command set of the Cisco IOS, let's look at how the user interface (UI) is organized.

The Cisco IOS Command Interpreter

Now that we have installed (or upgraded) the router's IOS, it is time to look inside and see what makes the IOS work. The core component of the Cisco IOS is the Cisco command interpreter, also known as the Exec. This section will introduce you to the command interpreter and its different modes.

As was mentioned in the "Introduction" at the beginning of today's lesson, the Cisco IOS provides two levels of access to the IOS command structure. These levels are known as Exec modes or command interpreter modes. If you look back at the procedures for upgrading the IOS in the preceding section, you will notice that there are two different prompts at which commands can be entered within the Cisco IOS. These prompts represent the mode under which the user is accessing the command interpreter.

The first (most basic) mode is known as user mode. User mode is signified by a > sign as a command prompt.

```
Router>
```

From user mode the router engineer can execute the more basic commands, such as those used to view router properties or make temporary changes to the terminal settings. No password access is required to access the user mode of the Exec.

The following are some of the more common user mode commands:

- `ping`
- `rlogin`
- `telnet`
- `show`

Although these commands are not capable of setting global configurations or permanently changing the router's functionality, they offer enough power to gather information and track a router's general health.

The second (more advanced) level of the Exec is privilege mode. The privilege mode command prompt is indicated by a # character.

```
Router#
```

To access the privilege mode of the command interpreter, use the `enable` command from the user mode command prompt.

```
Router>enable
Password:
Router#
```

For security reasons, access to the privilege mode command interpreter can be blocked by a password. (We will discuss setting these passwords in Day 6, "Getting the Router Up and Running.")

Within privilege mode, the router engineer can access all of the functionality of the router. Tools for configuring the router's interfaces, connecting to external sources, loading protocols, and moving and deleting files are all available through the privilege mode of the command interpreter.

Some commonly used privilege level commands are

- `configure`
- `erase`
- `setup`

The next lesson, "Learning the Cisco User Interface," will dive deeper into the commands and tools that can be accessed from the two modes of the command interpreter. While you are learning the Cisco user interface, you will use and become acquainted with the various commands used to maintain the router. Before going on to the next lesson, try some of these questions based on today's lesson.

Summary

The brains (or thoughts) behind any Cisco router reside in the Cisco operating system. The IOS enables the router to perform all of the tasks needed to route data successfully between networks.

To enable functionality on a Cisco router that may not have been installed by default, IOS feature packs need to be installed. Feature packs can add the ability to run firewalls, protocols, and VPNs.

Cisco routers are produced in two memory configurations: Run-from-RAM and Run-from-Flash. The type of memory configuration for a router will determine the location for running the IOS.

Q&A

Q Why do the Cisco 700 series routers use a different IOS?

A The 700 series router is a specialized router produced by Cisco. This router is meant to have (more or less) a fixed configuration. The operating system that is default on the 700 series router lends itself to this functionality.

Quiz

Questions

1. What are the two memory configurations Cisco routers can be produced in?
2. What is the default feature pack installed on most Cisco routers?
3. What are the two basic modes of the Cisco command interpreter?
4. What transfer protocol is used to move IOS images to and from Cisco routers?

Answers

1. Run-from-RAM and Run-from-Flash
2. IP Basic
3. User and Privilege
4. TFTP

Exercises

1. Name the two different memory architectures for Cisco routers.
2. What are the two methods for upgrading the IOS in Run-from-Flash routers?
3. What is the major difference between how the IOS image is stored on a Run-from-Flash router and how it is stored on a Run-from-RAM router?
4. What are the two modes of the Cisco Exec?
5. What is the purpose of user mode?

WEEK 1

DAY 4

Learning the Cisco IOS User Interface

Today's lesson is going to focus on familiarizing you with the user interface (UI) of the Cisco IOS. From Day 3, you should now have some acquaintance with the IOS and its command interpreter modes. The UI and the commands can now be discussed in greater detail.

The following topics will be discussed in examining the Cisco UI.

- Navigating the IOS
- The IOS user interface basic elements
- Accessing Cisco's IOS help
- Basic IOS commands

The Cisco IOS user interface is the only direct window into the router. That is, the UI is the means through which an administrator accesses the command interpreter. If you are unfamiliar with routers and router interfaces in general, the first thing you will notice about the Cisco IOS is its apparent lack of a GUI (graphical user interface). In fact, the Cisco IOS is a command line operating system. For those of you who have worked on command line systems in the past, the Cisco UI will not appear very different from those of many Unix or DOS systems. However, if you have worked only with GUIs such as Windows or MacOS, you may have some adjusting to do.

Therefore, let's waste no time and plunge right into the specifics of the UI. At the heart of the Cisco IOS user interface are the command sets, which directly relate to the two modes of the command interpreter.

Navigating the IOS

The command sets for Cisco routers are divided into two categories: the user mode commands and the privilege mode commands. The user mode commands, the more basic of the two command sets, provide such functionality as viewing IOS versions and running Internet Control Message Protocol (ICMP) tools. When a user logs in to a Cisco router, it defaults to user mode. Table 4.1 illustrates some of the various commands available to users in both user and privilege modes.

TABLE 4.1 Sampling of User and Privilege Mode Commands

Mode	Command
User	`ping`
	`traceroute`
	`help`
	`terminal`
Privilege	`ping`
	`traceroute`
	`help`
	`configure`
	`erase`

Notice that many of the commands available in user mode are also available in privilege mode. The command modes of the Cisco IOS are hierarchical. That is, the higher you are in the command structure, the more commands you have access to (while retaining access to many of the lower commands).

Although there are two modes of the Cisco IOS (user and privilege), there are 17 access levels within these modes (16 definable and 1 fixed). User mode is the lowest level of the command hierarchy. The most basic commands are available in user mode. The more advanced commands are available in privilege mode.

Privilege mode is actually a conglomeration of 16 customizable command levels (0 through 15). An administrator can define certain privilege level commands to be available only within a specific level. This allows for greater control of router access.

> **Note** If no privilege mode levels have been defined, the IOS will default to level 15 (showing access to all privilege mode commands).

Configuring privilege mode levels will be discussed on Day 6, "Getting the Router Up and Running." There, all of the processes needed to set all 16 levels of access will be examined.

> **Note** In the examples throughout this book, when a privilege mode example is given, it can be assumed that the IOS is not configured for access levels and that the router is in the default mode level 15.

As was mentioned on Day 3, the privilege mode of the IOS command interpreter is separated from the user mode and protected by password. To access the privilege mode command set, the user must enter the correct password to change to privilege mode. The privilege mode commands enable an administrator to change configurations and system variables and to administer ports. All file management takes place from within the privilege mode command set. Router administrators will usually spend most of their time in privilege mode. Therefore, you should pay particular attention to the commands of the privilege mode.

The Cisco IOS also includes a very thorough help program for the IOS command set to aid the administrator in the configuration process, but those unfamiliar with the interface may find it a bit daunting. Mastering Cisco's IOS context-sensitive help system is key to navigating the router's functions and properties.

> **Note:** Most Cisco switches (and higher-end routers with switching capabilities) offer an HTML-based GUI to interface with the Cisco IOS. However, the core operating system is still command line based. This book will examine only the command line Cisco IOS interface.

The reason for using a command line operating system on a router is simple. The absence of a GUI allows the IOS to be relatively small in size and not very processor intensive (leaving the majority of processing time available for the routing functions). The average Cisco IOS release is 16MB (most are smaller depending on the feature set), and in most Cisco router models the processor runs at less than 100MHz. A small operating system lets the router do what it was meant to do—routing data, not worrying about drawing windows on a monitor and keeping track of mouse locations.

> **Note:** Given that the Cisco IOS has a command line interface, navigating through a series of commands should not be very difficult. Even so, there are also some built-in function keys that make using the IOS even easier to use.

Cisco routers help users navigate the IOS through the use of function keys. These function keys are shortcuts for commands or navigation tools. For example, function keys can represent the keystrokes needed to scroll through an entire line of text or recall previous commands.

> **Note:** Cisco IOS advanced command editing system keys are not customizable. These functions have been predefined in the IOS.

If you notice that the function keys, also known as the advanced command editing system, are not working on your router, they may have been turned off. The function keys can be disabled from the command prompt by typing

```
Router>terminal no editing
```

Luckily, using the following command can easily enable the editing features.

```
Router>terminal editing
```

Learning the Cisco IOS User Interface

> **Note** You will see this type of command structure fairly often in the Cisco IOS. That is, to turn off a function, use the command `no` before the same command that is used to turn an option on. By this logic, `no editing` turns off editing, and `editing` turns it on.

The two function keys you will use the most are the Enter key and the spacebar. Aside from their obvious functions of ending a line of input and character spacing, these keys also provide scroll control. When the output from the IOS is too long to fit on the terminal screen, the following prompt appears, letting the administrator know that more information is available:

```
--More--
```

Pressing the Enter key after the scroll prompt appears will display the next line of information, whereas pressing the spacebar will show the next full screenful of data. For example, viewing the router's current configuration may yield the following output. (For now, don't worry about what these outputs actually mean.)

```
Current configuration:
!
version 12.0
service timestamps debug uptime
service timestamps log uptime
no service password-encryption
!
hostname Router
!
boot system flash
no logging console
!
ip subnet-zero
!
!
!
interface Ethernet0
 ip address 10.16.4.153 255.240.0.0
 no ip directed-broadcast
!
interface Ethernet1
 no ip address
 --More--
```

Because there is more information in the output than can fit on the terminal screen, the IOS displays the scroll prompt. Pressing the Enter key at this point will produce the following result.

```
!
version 12.0
service timestamps debug uptime
service timestamps log uptime
no service password-encryption
!
hostname Router
!
boot system flash
no logging console
!
ip subnet-zero
!
!
!
interface Ethernet0
 ip address 10.16.4.153 255.240.0.0
 no ip directed-broadcast
!
interface Ethernet1
 no ip address
 no ip directed-broadcast
 --More--
```

The result of pressing the Enter key was the addition of the following line to the output display:

```
no ip directed-broadcast
```

This function is very useful when you are looking for a particular line of data in a list. Because routers operate in real time, output results change often; therefore you may want to scroll one line at time to catch the particular results you are looking for. This will ensure that you do not miss any list details. However, if you want to view the next full page of results, use the spacebar.

Using the spacebar in our previous example will yield the following output.

```
 --More--
 no ip directed-broadcast
 shutdown
!
ip classless
!
!
line con 0
 exec-timeout 0 0
 transport input none
line vty 0 4
 login
!
end
```

The full-page scroll is useful when you need to scroll quickly through pages of data. Both commands allow you to move through lists with ease.

- The Ctrl+B and Ctrl+F functions will operate just like the back arrow and forward arrow keys on the keyboard, respectively. They will navigate either forward or back through a line of text one character at a time. This can be convenient if you need to correct one character in a long command string. However, if you are dealing with a really long command string, and moving one character at a time is not fast enough, you can use the Esc+B and Esc+F functions, described next.
- The Esc+B and Esc+F functions move backward and forward, respectively, one full word. Therefore, if you have just finished a long command string (Cisco commands can tend to be quite lengthy) and need to edit it somewhere, you can use these functions to skip through the command word by word.
- To jump right to the beginning or the end of an entire string, use the Ctrl+A and Ctrl+E functions. Ctrl+A will carry you to the first character on the current line, whereas Ctrl+E will bring you to the last. I find myself using these functions to add options to the end of a long command string.
- The last two (and in my opinion, most useful) IOS function key combinations are Ctrl+P and Ctrl+N. These two function keys are also known as the command history keys. By using these functions an administrator can recall commands from the list of previously entered commands.

> **Note** The up-arrow and down-arrow keys can replace the Ctrl+P and Ctrl+N keys, respectively.

The Ctrl+P function is used to recall the last command executed. Suppose you wanted to run a directory list on the Cisco flash memory. You would use the following command structure:

```
Router#dir
Directory of flash:/

  1  -rw-    2202092       <no date> aaa0269.bin

4194304 bytes total (1992148 bytes free)
Router#
```

When the `dir` command is completed, the IOS returns to a blank prompt. If you wanted to run this command again, you could use the Ctrl+P keystroke combination (or the up arrow). Shortcuts like this can be big timesavers when you are using commands that require multiple parameters.

The Ctrl+P function is also used to recall multiple previous commands. For example, let's say you executed the following string of commands.

```
Router#
Router#dir
Directory of flash:/

  1  -rw-    2202092        <no date> aaa0269.bin

4194304 bytes total (1992148 bytes free)
Router#ping 10.16.4.152

Type escape sequence to abort.
Sending 5, 100-byte ICMP Echos to 10.16.4.152, timeout is 2 seconds:
.....
Success rate is 0 percent (0/5)
Router#sho flash

PCMCIA flash directory:
File Length  Name/status
  1  2202092 aaa0269.bin
[2202156 bytes used, 1992148 available, 4194304 total]
4096K bytes of processor board PCMCIA flash (Read/Write)

Router#
```

To re-execute the first command, simply use the Ctrl+P keystroke combination three times. This will bring the `dir` command back to the command prompt.

While using the Ctrl+P key, you may accidentally move past the command that you intend to recall. If this happens, simply use the Ctrl+N command to scroll forward through the recalled commands.

All of the advanced command editing functions can be valuable assets. Take the time to learn them, and try using them as you configure and maintain routers. Now, let's take a look at the basic elements of the Cisco IOS user interface.

The IOS User Interface Basic Elements

The Cisco IOS comprises four main components: status messages, input requests, IOS prompt, and the cursor. Figure 4.1 illustrates the main components of the Cisco IOS.

FIGURE 4.1

The Cisco IOS user interface.

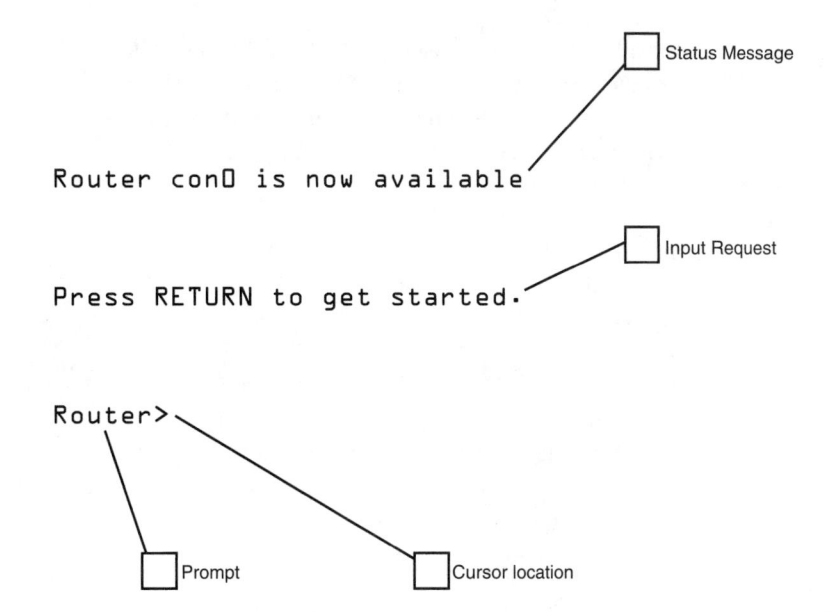

```
                                                    □ Status Message
                                                   /
        Router con0 is now available
                                              □ Input Request
                                             /
        Press RETURN to get started.


        Router>
              \
               \
         □ Prompt        □ Cursor location
```

Of the four basic elements pictured in Figure 4.1, the one you will deal with the most, obviously, is the command prompt. Notice that the command prompt is indicated (in Figure 4.1) by the word Router followed by the > character. Each of these two components has its own significance within the IOS.

> **Note** A fifth UI element, the banner message, is a configurable message that you can have the router display on login. However, because the banner is more of a configuration setting than a basic element, we will cover it on Day 6, "Getting the Router Up and Running."

The Cisco IOS command line prompt is divided into two logical parts: the hostname and the mode indicator. The first part of the prompt, the hostname, is always the first word in the display (excluding any words in parentheses). For example, within the following prompt, the router's hostname is "Frank".

Frank(config)#

The hostname is the name assigned to the router by the administrator. This name is completely arbitrary and can be changed at any time. The command prompt will always display the router's hostname. (In all of the examples throughout this book, the hostname Router is used.)

The second part of the command prompt is the mode indicator. The symbol > indicates that the administrator is logged in under user mode. The other symbol used to indicate the mode is #, which indicates that the administrator is logged in under privilege mode. Therefore, the command prompt

`Router>`

indicates that the IOS Exec on router `Router` is running under user mode and can execute only user mode commands, whereas the prompt

`Router#`

indicates that the IOS Exec on the router named `Router` is running under privilege mode and can execute privilege mode commands. By simply looking at the command prompt, you can easily determine what router you are working on and what mode you are currently accessing on it. This is especially useful in larger environments, where the chance of accessing multiple routers from one interface is greater.

When we first defined a hostname, we said it was the first word appearing in the command prompt *excluding any words in parentheses*. If a command prompt contains words in parentheses, these words indicate submodes. For example, the following command prompt indicates the router `Router` is in the "global configuration mode" of the privilege mode exec.

`Router(config)#`

Table 4.2 illustrates the different submodes of the privilege mode exec and their indicators.

TABLE 4.2 Submode Indicators

Submode	Indicator
Global configuration mode	`(config)`
Router configuration mode	`(config-router)`
Interface configuration mode	`(config-if)`

The least commonly used portion of the UI is the startup status message (simply because it is seen only at startup). The status messages of the Cisco IOS UI simply indicate the current condition of the port (terminal) the IOS is using. The example shown in Figure 4.1 illustrates that con0 (console port 0) is in an available condition. If there were any current messages about the condition of the port, they would be displayed here.

Other, more common status messages can be seen directly under the command prompt. The Cisco IOS will relay any status messages to you directly under the command that produced them.

Learning the Cisco IOS User Interface

> **Note:** Any status message that appears below the command prompt originates from the Cisco command interpreter.

An example of this can be seen when an incorrect command is entered at a prompt. Figure 4.2 illustrates a status message resulting from an incorrect input.

FIGURE 4.2
A status message resulting from an incorrect command.

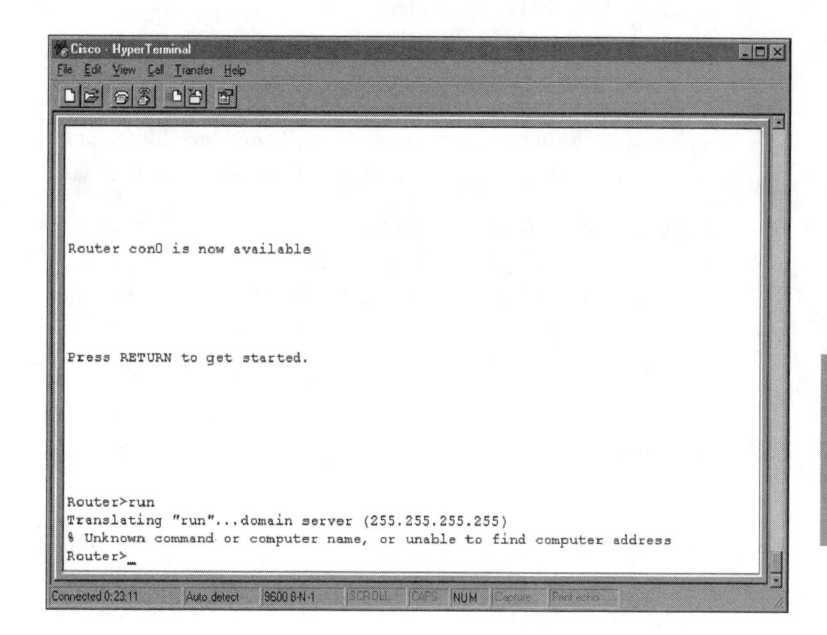

```
Router con0 is now available



Press RETURN to get started.




Router>run
Translating "run"...domain server (255.255.255.255)
% Unknown command or computer name, or unable to find computer address
Router>
```

In Figure 4.2 the word run was entered at the command prompt. run is not a command recognized by the Cisco IOS; therefore, the IOS generated a status message to alert the user that the router was trying to decipher what was input.

The first of the two lines illustrated in Figure 4.2 immediately following the command prompt is the status message, which reads

`Translating "run"...domain server (255.255.255.255)`

Without going into too much detail about the meaning of the message (we will do that later in this lesson), we can see that the IOS was (at the time) trying to translate the command given. Therefore the status of the router was translating.

In Figure 4.2 the second line of the status message, `% Unknown command or computer name, or unable to find computer address`, is an *alert* message that illustrates the result of the status. In other words, after the router attempted to translate the command run, the result was that it found that run was an unknown command.

A status alert will always start with the % character. However, alerts will not necessarily occur only after status messages. While a status alert message will follow status messages, you will also see alerts when you are using the Cisco IOS help system.

The final element of the Cisco IOS user interface is the input request. The input request portion of the Cisco IOS UI is the IOS's way of indicating when specific input is required. In most cases the desired or default response will be displayed immediately following the request. For example:

```
Would you like to enter the initial configuration dialog? [yes/no]:
```

The first portion of this statement is the message itself. That is, the question that the router is asking. In this case, would the administrator like to start the initial configuration process? However, it is the second part of the statement that we are concerned with.

The portion of the statement marked by the [ ] (square bracket) characters is the input request. The Cisco ISO will (in most cases) supply to you a list of possible answers to the question it is asking. The answers will always be within a pair of square brackets and separated by a / (forward slash). In the previous example, the IOS is looking for either a yes or no response. The user must enter one of these responses for the IOS to continue.

If only one choice appears between the brackets, then that answer is the default answer. For example,

```
Enter host name [Router]:
```

The Cisco IOS is asking for a new hostname for the router. It has supplied a default host name of Router. Pressing the Enter key at this prompt will accept the default answer, or the administrator can overwrite the default answer by typing a new hostname.

Often, if the administrator wants to change a configuration setting on the router that has previously been set (such as the IP address of a particular port), the IOS will supply the configured setting as the default response. For example, let's say that a router has an Ethernet port with the address 10.19.25.1. If an administrator wanted to change this address, the following message would appear:

```
Enter IP address for Eth0 [10.19.25.1]:
```

This indicates that the first Ethernet port (Eth0) is already configured with the address 10.19.25.1. To keep the address, simply press Enter, and the default value will be retained. However, if the administrator does want to change the address of the port, a new address can be typed in at the prompt.

Now that you are familiar with the four basic elements of the user interface of the Cisco IOS, let's take a look at the IOS message that can appear at system startup.

IOS Messages at Startup

There are several IOS messages that you will notice when you boot a Cisco router. Although most will either seem like gibberish or simply go by too fast to be comprehensible, they all have some significance. Let's take a quick look at the startup messages from the Cisco IOS.

The first group of messages you will notice is from the Cisco Boot Loader. These are general messages pertaining to the system image used to load the router. In most cases these messages will go by pretty quickly; however, if you can read them, you will see the following information.

1. Cisco System Bootstrap version
2. Physical router model
3. Router memory configuration
4. Startup image entry point memory address

Figure 4.3 illustrates a Cisco router at startup. Notice the information that is provided.

FIGURE 4.3
Cisco IOS startup messages.

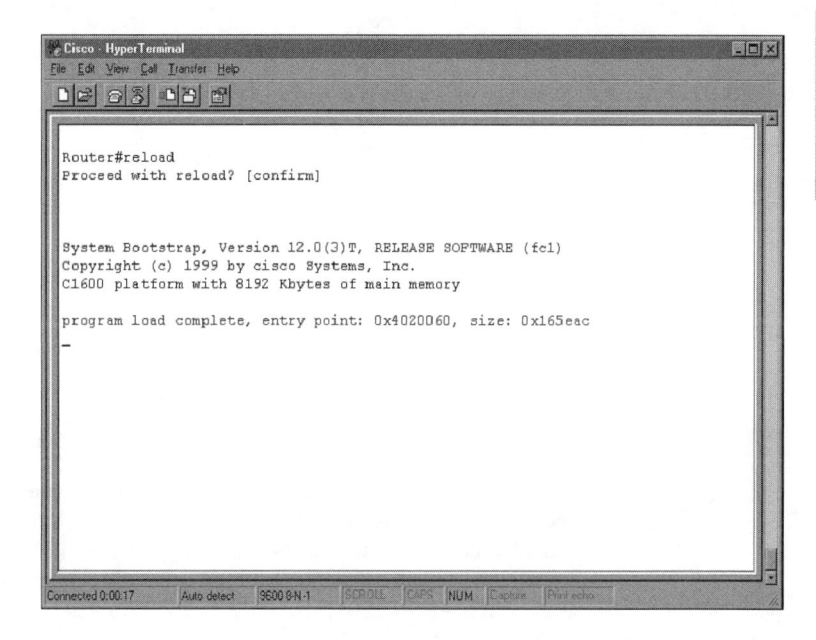

```
Router#reload
Proceed with reload? [confirm]


System Bootstrap, Version 12.0(3)T, RELEASE SOFTWARE (fc1)
Copyright (c) 1999 by cisco Systems, Inc.
C1600 platform with 8192 Kbytes of main memory

program load complete, entry point: 0x4020060, size: 0x165eac
```

The message shown in Figure 4.3 all appear before the startup image is even loaded. The purpose for this is to diagnose any potential problems with either the router or the startup image before any data is loaded to the router's memory. As with most digital systems, such a system check reduces the potential for corrupting any configuration files.

The decompression progress is marked by a series of # symbols. When the entire image has decompressed into memory, the IOS will return a status of [OK]. This indicates that the image has successfully decompressed and the router is ready to continue loading the configuration parameters.

After the image is decompressed into memory, the standard "Restrictive Rights Legend" will be displayed. Finally the IOS will display its version information. Both the Restrictive Rights Legend and the IOS version information are illustrated in Figure 4.4.

FIGURE 4.4

IOS version information after router power-up.

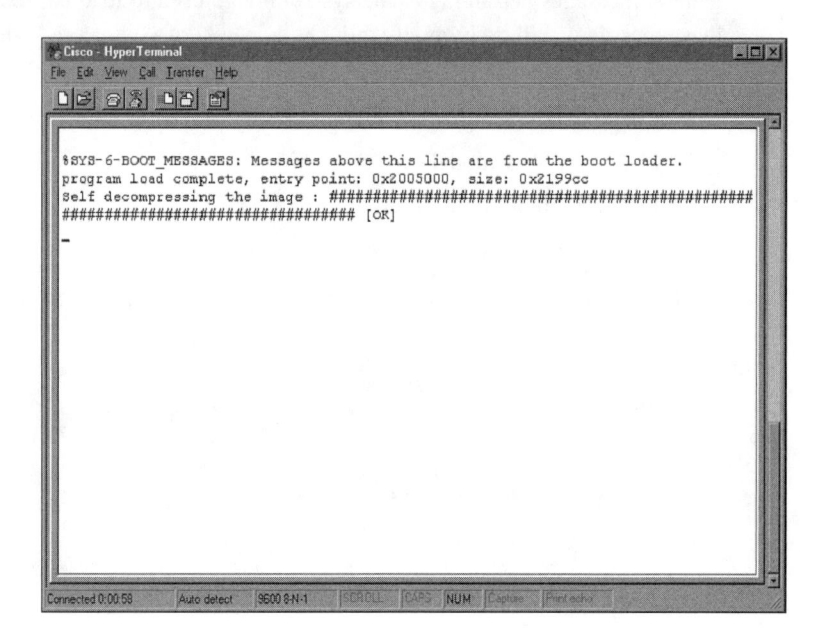

The last IOS status messages to be displayed at startup indicate the amount of memory available on the router. The router then enters user mode.

> **Note**
>
> If the router is started for the first time, it will not enter user mode at this point. Rather, the routers will enter setup mode. This mode comprises a series of prompts that help the administrator configure the router. Setup mode is discussed in Day 6, "Getting the Router Up and Running."

The Cisco IOS is packaged with a very comprehensive help system. This help system can be an invaluable tool for an administrator working on Cisco routers, but even the best help system in the world will be useless if you do not know how to use it. Even now I find myself looking through reference books for definitions of vague functions, or explanations of keywords and command structures.

In the final parts of this lesson we will discuss the concepts behind the Cisco IOS help system and examine the basic commands needed to navigate through a router's internal structure. Mastering these basic commands, and being able to use the Cisco help system, will well prepare you for the remainder of this book. Therefore let's discuss the Cisco IOS help system.

Accessing Cisco's IOS Help

The basic help functionality of the Cisco IOS provides the user with low-level assistance with the operation of the router. The basic help functions can be accessed by typing `help` from the user mode command prompt:

`Router>help`

The message that is returned from the `help` command shows that two levels of help are available. The first level of help is referred to as full help. Full help is used to determine what commands can be run from the command prompt. Full help can also be used to determine what commands can be run in conjunction with other commands.

Help may be requested at any point in a command by entering a question mark ?. If nothing matches, the help list will be empty, and you must back up until entering a ? shows the available options.

Two styles of help are provided:

- Full help is available when you are ready to enter a command argument (for example, `show ?`) and describes each possible argument.
- Partial help is provided when an abbreviated argument is entered and you want to know what arguments match the input (for example `show pr?`).

Full Help

Using Cisco full help to determine what commands can be executed at a particular time is as easy as entering a ? at the command prompt. This ? command, typed by itself, will list all the commands that can be run from your specific prompt. For example, entering a ? at the user mode command prompt will yield the following list of commands:

```
Router>?
Exec commands:
  access-enable    Create a temporary Access-List entry
  access-profile   Apply user-profile to interface
  clear            Reset functions
  connect          Open a terminal connection
  disable          Turn off privileged commands
  disconnect       Disconnect an existing network connection
  enable           Turn on privileged commands
  exit             Exit from the EXEC
  help             Description of the interactive help system
  lock             Lock the terminal
  login            Log in as a particular user
  logout           Exit from the EXEC
  name-connection  Name an existing network connection
  pad              Open a X.29 PAD connection
  ping             Send echo messages
  ppp              Start IETF Point-to-Point Protocol (PPP)
  resume           Resume an active network connection
  rlogin           Open an rlogin connection
  set              Set system parameter (not config)
  show             Show running system information
  slip             Start Serial-line IP (SLIP)
  systat           Display information about terminal lines
 --More--
```

This output from the full help function consists of a list of the commands that can currently be run from within user mode. If you are looking for a command to perform a particular function, that command will appear on this list if it exists.

The full help capabilities of the Cisco IOS can also tell you what commands can be used with a particular command. For example, if you typed `terminal` at the privilege mode command prompt, you would get the response

```
Router#terminal
% Incomplete command.
```

However, using the ? character after the `terminal` command will list the commands that can follow the `terminal` keyword.

Learning the Cisco IOS User Interface

```
Router#terminal ?
  autohangup              Automatically hangup when last connection closes
  data-character-bits     Size of characters being handled
  databits                Set number of data bits per character
  default                 Set a command to its defaults
  dispatch-character      Define the dispatch character
  dispatch-timeout        Set the dispatch timer
  domain-lookup           Enable domain lookups in show commands
  download                Put line into 'download' mode
  editing                 Enable command line editing
  escape-character        Change the current line's escape character
  exec-character-bits     Size of characters to the command exec
  flowcontrol             Set the flow control
  full-help               Provide help to unprivileged user
  help                    Description of the interactive help system
  history                 Enable and control the command history function
  hold-character          Define the hold character
  international           Enable international 8-bit character support
  ip                      IP options
  length                  Set number of lines on a screen
  monitor                 Copy debug output to the current terminal line
  no                      Negate a command or set its defaults
  notify                  Inform users of output from concurrent sessions
  padding                 Set padding for a specified output character
  parity                  Set terminal parity
  rxspeed                 Set the receive speed
  special-character-bits  Size of the escape (and other special) characters
  speed                   Set the transmit and receive speeds
  start-character         Define the start character
  stop-character          Define the stop character
  stopbits                Set async line stop bits
  telnet                  Telnet protocol-specific configuration
  terminal-type           Set the terminal type
  transport               Define transport protocols for line
  txspeed                 Set the transmit speeds
  width                   Set width of the display terminal
```

> **Note**
>
> Notice the spacing between the command `terminal` and the help character `?`. This spacing is very important. For example,
>
>   Router>**terminal** ?
>
> will yield very different results than
>
>   Router>**terminal**?.
>
> Where the first example will list all of the keywords and parameters associated with the `terminal` command, the second will list all of the commands that begin with the word `terminal`.
>
> This character spacing is the difference between full help and partial help (also known as context-sensitive help), which is covered in the next section.

Another function of the full-featured help system is to point out to you when you enter a command that does not exist. If you try to enter a nonexistent command at the command prompt, the IOS will display the following message.

```
Router>run
Translating "run"...domain server (255.255.255.255)
```

Context-Sensitive Help

Cisco's partial help system, or context-sensitive help, allows users to search for results on incomplete commands. For example if you knew that the command to name a physical port begins with name-, but you just couldn't remember the rest, you could use the context-sensitive help to find it.

The IOS help system treats the ? character as a wildcard, using it to obtain any results that match the character patterns that appear before it. In other words, entering name-? at the command prompt will yield the following results. (Notice the lack of spacing between the command and the question mark.)

```
Router>name-?
name-connection
```

The only user mode command beginning with name- is **name-connection**. This is the command to name a physical port on the router.

Context-sensitive help can also be used to do searches with as little as one letter of the command you need to know. For example, look at the following search using context-sensitive help.

```
Router>t?
telnet terminal traceroute tunnel
```

```
Router>t
```

Notice the state of the command prompt after a context-sensitive search is completed. The Cisco IOS will always return the characters you search on to the command prompt. In the previous example, our search t? returns the character t to the command prompt. Anything that you now type at this prompt will follow the letter t.

Basic IOS Commands

Now that you have a good idea of how the Cisco IOS works and can easily navigate through the user interface and help systems, it is time to explore some basic IOS commands. The remainder of today's lesson will introduce you to some of these commands. Learning them will give you more confidence on the router and prepare you for the more complex functions you will encounter in the rest of this book.

> **Note**
>
> One great feature of the Cisco IOS is its ability to recognize partial commands. That is, if you enter tr at the command prompt, the IOS will recognize that as the command traceroute, because, as it happens, no other user mode commands in the IOS start with the characters tr.
>
> On the other hand, there are four commands other than traceroute that begin with the letter t. So, if you typed just t at the command prompt and pressed Enter, you would receive the following message:
>
>   % Ambiguous command: "t"
>
> Most of the examples in this book will use the abbreviated commands when possible. Therefore, try to familiarize yourself with the command abbreviations; they tend to make router administration easier.

The fist command you need to learn is the enable command. Enable is a user mode command that switches the Cisco command interpreter from user to privilege mode.

```
Router>en
Router#
```

You, as a routing administrator, will find that most (if not all) of the commands that you work with throughout the course of your daily duties will reside in privilege mode. Therefore you will need to know how to access this mode of the command interpreter. However, getting into privilege mode is only half the battle. You need to know how to return to user mode as well.

```
Router#disa
Router>
```

The disable command will switch the command interpreter from privilege to user mode.

The exit command will leave the user interface entirely. Now, using enable and disable, you have mastered switching between command interpreter modes.

ping

You may already be familiar with the command ping. "Ping" is a common, cross-platform, networking term for using ICMP packet echoes to test for the existence of certain addresses. The Cisco IOS is capable of running the ping command from the user mode command prompt.

```
Router>ping 10.16.4.152
Type escape sequence to abort.
Sending 5, 100-byte ICMP Echos to 10.16.4.152, timeout is 2 seconds:
.....
Success rate is 0 percent (0/5)
```

Examining this output, we can see that the `ping` command tried sending five 100-byte packets to the specified address. The series of dots below the message are *status icons* that indicate that the packets did not reach the intended recipient, which is reinforced by the following message "`Success rate is 0 percent (0/5)`". The following table shows the different status icons for ping. Table 4.3 illustrates the ping/traceroute status icons.

TABLE 4.3 ping Status Icons

Icon	Meaning
!	Receipt of a reply
.	Failure of a reply
U	Destination unreachable
C	Congestion
I	Test interrupted by user
?	Unknown packet type
&	Time to live expired

Let's take a look at some more basic commands.

show

The `show` command is a privilege mode command that is used to view router configurations. A full help search on `show` displays the various commands that it can utilize to provide detailed router information. Table 4.4 represents the possible command arguments for the `show` command

TABLE 4.4 Possible Arguments for show Command

Command	Purpose
`access-expression`	List access expression
`access-lists`	List access lists
`accounting`	Show accounting data for active sessions
`aliases`	Display alias commands
`arp`	Display Address Resolution Protocol (ARP) table
`async`	Display information on terminal lines used as router interfaces
`bridge`	Display Bridge Forwarding/Filtering Database (may or may not be `verbose`)
`buffers`	Display buffer pool statistics

continues

TABLE 4.4 Continued

Command	Purpose
cdp	Display Cisco Discovery Protocol (CDP) information
clock	Display the system clock
compress	Show compression statistics
configuration	List contents of nonvolatile (flash) memory
controllers	Display interface controller status
debugging	Display the state of each debugging option
dhcp	Display Dynamic Host Configuration Protocol (DHCP) status
diag	Display WAN daughter card diagnostic information
dialer	Display dialer parameters and statistics
dnsix	Show Department of Defense Intelligence Information System Network Security for Information Exchange (DNSIX) Message Delivery Protocol (DMDP) information
dxi	Show Asynchronous Transfer Mode (ATM) Data Exchange Interface (DXI) information
entry	Show queued terminal entries
file	Show file system information
flash:	Display information about `flash:` file system
flh-log	Show Flash Load Helper log buffer
frame-relay	Show Frame Relay information
history	Display the session command history
hosts	List Internet Protocol (IP) domain name, lookup style, nameservers, and host table
interfaces	Interface status and configuration
ip	Display IP information
key	Display key information
line	Display TTY line information
llc2	Display IBM LLC2 circuit information
location	Display the system location
logging	Show the contents of logging buffers
memory	Display memory statistics
modemcap	Show Modem Capabilities database
ppp	Display Point-to-Point Protocol (PPP) parameters and statistics
privilege	Show current privilege level

continues

TABLE 4.4 Continued

Command	Purpose
`processes`	Show statistics on active processes
`protocols`	List active network routing protocols
`queue`	Show queue contents
`queueing`	Show queueing configuration
`registry`	Show function registry information
`reload`	Display scheduled reload information
`rhosts`	List remote host/user equivalences
`rmon`	Display `rmon` statistics
`route-map`	Display route-map information
`rtr`	Show Response Time Reporter (RTR) data
`running-config`	List current operating configuration
`sessions`	Show information about Telnet connections
`smf`	Show Software MAC filter information
`snapshot`	Show snapshot parameters and statistics
`snmp`	Display Simple Network Management Protocol (SNMP) statistics
`sntp`	Show Simple Network Time Protocol (SNTP) information
`spanning-tree`	Show spanning tree topology
`stacks`	Display process stack utilization data
`standby`	Display hot standby protocol information
`startup-config`	List contents of startup configuration
`subscriber-policy`	Display subscriber policy
`subsys`	Show subsystem information
`tacacs`	Show Terminal Access Controller Access Control System (TACACS+) server statistics
`tcp`	Status of Transmission Control Protocol (TCP) connections
`tech-support`	Show system information for tech support
`terminal`	Display terminal configuration parameters
`traffic-shape`	Show traffic rate shaping configuration
`users`	Display information about terminal lines
`version`	Display system hardware and software status
`whoami`	Display info on current TTY line
`x25`	Display X.25 information
`x29`	Display X.29 information

The three most popular items you will view using show are interfaces, running-config, and startup-config.

The show interfaces command will display the port status information for your physical router ports. Viewing interface status information is usually the first step in determining whether there is a problem with one of your router's ports (such as a physical port problem or a network problem). Executing the show interfaces command will produce results similar to what is depicted in the following sample. (Don't concern yourself with the meaning of the output right now; we will discuss that later. For now, just familiarize yourself with how commands and their output are structured.)

```
Router#sh int e0
Ethernet0 is up, line protocol is down
 Hardware is QUICC Ethernet, address is 00d0.58a8.e150 (bia 00d0.58a8.e150)
 Internet address is 10.16.4.153/12
 MTU 1500 bytes, BW 10000 Kbit, DLY 1000 usec, rely 128/255, load 1/255
 Encapsulation ARPA, loopback not set, keepalive set (10 sec)
 ARP type: ARPA, ARP Timeout 04:00:00
 Last input never, output 00:00:00, output hang never
 Last clearing of "show interface" counters never
 Queueing strategy: fifo
 Output queue 0/40, 0 drops; input queue 0/75, 0 drops
 5 minute input rate 0 bits/sec, 0 packets/sec
 5 minute output rate 0 bits/sec, 0 packets/sec
  0 packets input, 0 bytes, 0 no buffer
  Received 0 broadcasts, 0 runts, 0 giants, 0 throttles
  0 input errors, 0 CRC, 0 frame, 0 overrun, 0 ignored, 0 abort
  0 input packets with dribble condition detected
  6496 packets output, 389772 bytes, 0 underruns
  6496 output errors, 0 collisions, 1 interface resets
  0 babbles, 0 late collision, 0 deferred
  6496 lost carrier, 0 no carrier
  0 output buffer failures, 0 output buffers swapped out
```

Notice that the actual command executed was sh int e0. The e0 argument tells the show command that I wanted to view the status information for only the port Ethernet 0. Had I entered the command without the e0 option, the IOS would have displayed to me the status of all ports on the router.

The commands show running-config and show startup-config are used to view the configuration files that drive the router. We will discuss setting a router's configuration in the next lesson; the files can be viewed through the show command.

We will obviously be discussing many more IOS commands throughout the course of this book. However, if you want to practice some basic commands, look at the exercises at the end of this lesson.

Mastering the Cisco IOS user interface is a very big step in learning Cisco routing. Now that we have passed this hurdle, we will discuss "How Routers Move Information" in the next day's lesson.

Summary

The user interface of the Cisco IOS is not unlike that of other command-line operating systems (such as Linux or MSDOS).

Cisco provides multiple function keys (also know as the advanced command editing system) to simplify commonly executed tasks.

The Cisco command prompt is split into two main modes, the user mode and the privilege mode. The privilege mode of the IOS exec can be divided into 16 different access levels.

The Cisco IOS help system is divided into two distinct functional commands. The full help system provides command parameter assistance, while the context-sensitive help system provides syntax help.

Q&A

Q Why is there no GUI (graphical user interface) provided with Cisco routers?

A GUIs occupy a lot of system resources. The main function of routers is to move data from place to place, not to display it on a screen. By eliminating the GUI, Cisco kept the functionality of the router as streamlined as possible.

Quiz

Questions

1. What are the two modes of the Cisco IOS exec?
2. The placement of the "?" in the following example demonstrates the use of which help system? `Router>sho?`
3. What command is used to enter the privilege mode of the Cisco command interpreter?
4. When is the "Restrictive Rights Legend" displayed?

Answers

1. User and Privilege
2. Context-sensitive
3. Enable
4. During startup

Exercises

1. Setting the system clock:

   Try setting the system clock using the `clock` command. An output of the answer appears in the following note.

   > **Note**
   > ```
   > Router#clo ?
   >   set  Set the time and date
   >
   > Router#clo set ?
   >   hh:mm:ss  Current Time
   >
   > Router#clo set 09:32:00 ?
   >   <1-31>  Day of the month
   >   MONTH   Month of the year
   >
   > Router#clo set 09:32:00 07 July ?
   >   <1993-2035>  Year
   >
   > Router#clo set 09:32:00 07 July 2001
   > Router#
   > ```

2. Viewing the system memory:

   Now try viewing the system memory.

> **Note**
>
> ```
> Router#sh flash
>
> PCMCIA flash directory:
> File Length   Name/status
>  1   2202092  aaa0269.bin
> [2202156 bytes used, 1992148 available, 4194304 total]
> 4096K bytes of processor board PCMCIA flash
> (Read/Write)
> ```

Week 1

Day 5

Understanding How Routers Move Data

The purpose of this lesson is to introduce you to the processes involved in moving data from system to system. We will discuss the roles protocols take in the routing process and how routers use them to pass data over a network.

The topics covered in this lesson include:

- Cisco routers and the network layer
- Protocol routing
- Mechanics of routing
- Routed protocols versus routing protocols

These topics comprise a broad range of concepts that, together, form the theories and processes behind the movement of data through a networked environment. Understanding these processes will help solidify the later lessons of this book (those dealing specifically with routing and routed protocols).

By the end of today's lesson you will have a complete picture of the routing process on many levels. We will examine routing from the point of view of the Open Systems Interconnect (OSI) model and consider protocols, packets, and hardware. The information you will learn in this lesson will help strengthen the base of knowledge on which basic Cisco engineering experience should be built.

This lesson will serve as a gateway to the lessons that lie ahead. Once you have learned how routers move data, you can easily handle configuring the Cisco IOS to run different protocols and route between different environments.

Let us now take a closer look at how Cisco routers work (on a binary level) and what role the OSI model plays in their operation.

Cisco Routers and the Network Layer

All protocols in use today for moving data on a network conform to one common specification. These protocols have been designed to work within the specifications set forth in the OSI model. The OSI model is a common framework by which developers model their protocols to work with other developers' products. This common set of rules ensures that computers and other devices can all communicate with each other seamlessly, regardless of manufacturer, developer, or platform.

> **Note** The concept of interoperability is paramount when discussing router technologies. With the amount of different systems, protocols, and data types that make up the Internet, a router manufacturer could never predict what their products will be used for.

There are two fundamental reasons to base all protocols on a common framework. First, following a preset guideline for how a protocol should be written protects the developer against leaving out any critical functionality. For example, if a protocol development team begins working on a new transport layer protocol, it needs to follow the rules of the transport layer of the OSI. It follows automatically that the new protocol must be connection oriented and handle flow control (among other things). Keeping all of these requirements intact, the development team can be assured that their new transport layer protocol will work with every other device that is compatible with the transport layer of the OSI. This creates a very harmonious environment within which to build a network.

Routers use this common framework to their advantage. The process of moving data from one location to another is strictly based on the principles of the OSI model and protocol encapsulation. Cisco routers function on the network layer of the OSI model. This allows them to work with any protocol created to work within that specification.

> **Note** Being *able* to route any protocol written for the network layer and actually *routing* every protocol are two different things. In other words, even though Cisco routers can, in theory, route any protocol written for the network layer of the OSI, that does not mean that a particular router's IOS can hold the configurations to allow such operation. A Cisco router may not be able to route a specific protocol, simply because the IOS is not configured to handle it.

All routers operate on the network layer, for one simple reason. The network layer is the layer responsible for protocol addressing. Therefore, any protocol written on the network layer must be able to address each system within an environment. These addresses are the key to routing.

To help understand the concepts of routing, addressing, and protocols, let's look at an analogy from daily life. For example, a protocol address is comparable to an address of a house. This address specifies street number, street, town, and state where the house is located.

```
123 Maple Street
Anytown, Massachusetts
```

Given the address of a house, there is no confusion about its location. Protocols address computers in the same way.

The protocol address of a computer acts like the street address of a house. The address indicates the network and number of the specific computer. Any information bound for that one computer needs to know only the computer's address.

Let's look at a scenario that corresponds to routing information from one computer to another. If a person wants to send a letter to a friend's house in another state, several processes must take place. The person sending the letter puts it into an envelope. The address of the intended recipient is placed on the front of the envelope. The letter is then carried to the sender's local post office.

After receiving the letter, the post office reads the address to determine where the letter should go. The post office sends the letter to the local post office of the recipient. A letter carrier then delivers the letter to the recipient's house.

> **Note**
>
> Do not confuse protocol addressing with system addressing. The data link layer of the OSI model is responsible for system addressing. System addresses, such as the media access control (MAC) address of the data link layer, are normally hard-coded identifiers that are unique to the systems. Protocol addresses, on the other hand, are assigned by a protocol and can be duplicated among devices (hopefully not within the same network).
>
> Although the system address will not change, the protocol address can differ depending on the protocol being used. Some protocols, such as IPX, use the system address as a part of the protocol address. However, do not confuse the two.

In our scenario the post office corresponds to the router. The router reads the destination address from every packet to determine where the information should go. However, the router (like the post office) can understand the destination address only if it is written in a specific format. The format of the address is the responsibility of the protocol.

In short, whereas the router is concerned with moving information from place to place, it is the protocol that ensures that the router can understand that information.

This is a rough summary of the routing process. It is not very complicated. The main process does not change from this description. However, if it were always that easy, there would not be a need for a book such as this.

The complicated processes that people usually associate with routing come into play when we start to add metrics and other policies on top of the basic routing process. The added rules are what give routing its bad rap for being hard to understand. Let's pass over those complications for the moment, and focus on basic routing. The more complicated concepts will be covered later in the book.

The next section of this lesson examines the purpose of protocols in the routing equation. One of the functions protocols play to aid the routing process is to encapsulate the data being transported. This helps the routing process in many ways.

Protocol Routing

Before we look too deep into the actual act of routing (through the eyes of a router), we need to discuss exactly what role protocols play in the routing process. More precisely, what does it mean to say that protocols encapsulate data, and why does that help the routing process? To answer these questions, we need to discuss what happens to the data before the router gets involved.

When a device such as a PC wants to send data to another device, the data is subjected to the protocol residing on the PC. This protocol performs the task of encapsulating the data and preparing it for delivery.

This process of data encapsulation is the one key factor that makes information routing possible. Routers cannot move raw data. The data needs to be structured in a way that the router can easily determine what the data is, and where it needs to go. The purpose of encapsulation is to provide these two pieces of information.

By encapsulating the data, the protocol adds to it the destination address for the router to send the data to.

> **Note** Before the data is encapsulated (and the destination address is added), the router has no way to know where the data is to be sent.

Even though the protocol can address the data to a specific location, the router still needs to know what the data is. For example when a person receives a letter in the mail, they know that envelope (containing the address) is not part of the information being sent to them. It is merely the container to carry the letter. Encapsulation provides the same kind of envelope for routers to use when delivering data.

The protocol formats the data to fit within a certain size limit (much like an envelope). The router then knows that the information being sent (to the provided address) is x bits long. All of this information is provided through pieces of data known as protocol headers.

Protocol Headers

When a stream of data is passed to a protocol to prepare it for transmission, one of the protocol's duties is to encapsulate the data. By encapsulating the data stream, the protocol can format the data in a way that it can be easily understood by any other systems that may encounter it. However, the protocol does not want every other device to have to read the entire data stream. Rather, the information is formatted in such a way that the other devices need to read only very little of the data to understand whom the packets are meant for.

To do this the protocol adds protocol headers to the data stream. These headers contain information that every device using the same protocol can understand about the encapsulated data.

> **Note** When encapsulating data from a device, the protocol does not alter its content. Headers are prepended to the data without changing it in any way.
>
> Do not confuse encapsulation with encryption. Encryption alters the data in such a way that no other systems (with the exception of the deciphering device) can discern the contents of the packets.

To illustrate the purpose of protocol headers, let's take a look at the header fields for IP. When a data stream is passed to IP to be transmitted over a network, one of the functions IP performs is to add the following header data to the information. This header gives any device that comes into contact with the data stream (such as a router) several key pieces of information about the encapsulated data. Figure 5.1 shows the fields of the IP header.

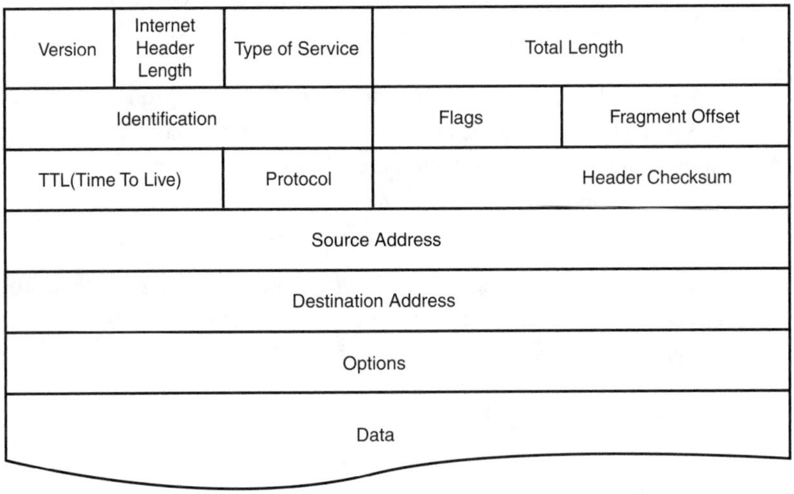

FIGURE 5.1

IP header fields.

Version	Internet Header Length	Type of Service	Total Length	
Identification			Flags	Fragment Offset
TTL(Time To Live)		Protocol	Header Checksum	
Source Address				
Destination Address				
Options				
Data				

The first field, "version," tells the router what version of IP was used to encapsulate the package. IP-4 is the current version of IP in use today, but IP-6 is quickly becoming a reality (and several firms have already begun testing IP-8). Therefore, routers need a standard way of knowing what version of a protocol they are dealing with.

The next field in the IP header is the header length. As it states, this field indicates to the router the size of the protocol header. By determining the size of the header, the router knows where the header ends and the encapsulated data begins.

The "type of service" (TOS) field assigns a priority to the encapsulated packet. Although this is an advanced routing topic, many Cisco routers can utilize or participate in what is known as TOS routing, which routing moves data based on this field. Therefore, while you may not have any need for the field now, the TOS field does have an impact on the way information is moved from one place to another.

The "total length" field is the length of the entire encapsulated packet. From this the router can derive the length of the data that follows the header (that is, total length – header length = data length).

The identifier field contains a unique number assigned to each packet. These numbers help the target device reassemble the packets after they are received.

The next field, the flag field, is used to indicate whether the packet can be fragmented. If the packet can be fragmented, the flag field will also indicate whether the current packet is the last in the fragment array. Cisco routers can fragment packets further for delivery.

Cisco routers can be configured not to route packets over a certain size. For example, if a particular link has low bandwidth, the router can be adjusted to pass packets over that link only if the packets are within a specified size range. The Cisco routers can then be configured to take any packets that are too large to meet the new requirements and break them into smaller pieces. The flag field aids in that process. However, it needs the help of the next field, the fragment offset field, to complete the process.

The "fragment offset" field is closely related to the "flag" field. The "fragment offset" field indicates the byte at which the fragmented packet ends. This allows the destination device to reassemble the fragmented packets correctly into full packets (for reassembly later into a full data stream).

Routers will generally carry a packet only for a specific amount of time. That is, if a router cannot locate a packet's intended destination within a given amount of time, it stops looking. The "Time to Live" (TTL) is used to specify the packet's expiration date. This field specifies a maximum amount of time that a router can continue trying to deliver a packet before discarding it as undeliverable. When a router attempts to deliver a packet and the target system is not available, the router notes the time indicated by the TTL field and begins counting down from there. If the packet cannot be delivered to the target system before the TTL expires, it is discarded.

> **Note** A low TTL can cause problems on larger networks. For example, if a packet needs to pass through multiple router hops (spanning multiple networks) and it has a low TTL, the TTL may expire before the packet even reaches the destination. Therefore, target systems that otherwise appear functional may not be receiving information, because of low TTL settings.

The "protocol" field is used by the target device (rather than a router). The protocol field tells the target device which protocol to pass the information to after it has been delivered and reassembled.

The "header checksum" is calculated from the contents of the header and safeguards against packet corruption. By checking this sum, the router can ensure that no corrupted packets get forwarded along.

The next field is one of the two most important pieces of information for the routing process. The "source address" tells the router who sent the packet. This address can be used to apply filters and determine path integrity. For example, a router may be configured to forward packets from one location to a specific network. The router would use this source address field to determine whether the packet meets those criteria. The "destination address" field appears directly after the source address and is arguably the most important field in the routing process. The destination address field will show the address of the target device. Obviously, without the benefit of a destination address, routing would be impossible.

The "options" field is for IP-specific options, and, finally, the "data" field is the actual information being sent between the systems.

The protocol provides most of the information needed for routing in the protocol headers. These headers pass all of the necessary data for moving a packet from one location to another. Routers read through these protocol headers to determine the critical material needed to route information successfully.

Another important function of data encapsulation is to break a data stream into small, manageable pieces. These small pieces are easily read and processed by routers.

Data Packeting

Protocols also break data streams into manageably sized packets during the encapsulation process. This breakup spares the routing hardware the work of trying to route large bursts of data. Even in today's age of seemingly endless bandwidth, bursting data without the advantage of segmentation would cause far too many clog-ups.

However, traffic is not the only problem solved by protocol encapsulation. When data is sent in short (mostly uniform) packets, there is a better chance that the target device will remain online during the entire transmission, thus increasing the chances that the information will be routed successfully.

During the encapsulation process the data marked for transmission is cut into variable-length pieces by the protocol. Then each piece or packet is identified, and a header is attached. Because the header is attached to each individual packet, the packets can be released at different times.

> **Note** Every protocol has different specifications for the size of individual frames or packets. In the event of network problems, examining the sizes of the packets through a packet viewer can identify certain protocols.

When the packets reach their destination, the target system can read each header to determine the sequence of packets (this will tell the target system what order to reassemble the packets in). The device can then strip the header off each packet and reassemble them into one continuous data stream.

This section of the lesson should have provided you with enough information to understand how protocols aid in the routing process. However, these functions, provided by routed protocols, are only one-third of the entire picture. The router hardware still has a lot of work to do before the data can reach its target.

The Mechanics of Routing

Contrary to popular belief, routing itself is fairly simple to understand. All routing is based on logical rules and policies. Routing becomes complicated when layers of security, secondary and tertiary protocols, and complex network divisions are added.

The remainder of this lesson is geared to presenting you with the information required to understand how routing works and how Cisco routers in general move data from system to system.

Simple network routing consists of moving data from one network to another, whereas complex routing can entail moving data across several routers or through a router that spans more than two networks. There is a high chance of encountering complications such as multiple metrics in complex routing environments.

Therefore, let's examine the physical routing process separately as it applies to each kind of routing environment—simple and complex.

Simple Network Routing

Simple routing (for this scenario) takes place when information needs to be moved between only two networks. Figure 5.2 illustrates a simple two-network environment.

Notice that the environment is divided into two separate networks (labeled A and B), each with its own IP address. Because these networks are separated physically, and they are using different IP addressing schemes, data cannot freely flow between them. The solution here is to create a very simple routing environment.

Figure 5.2

A simple networking environment.

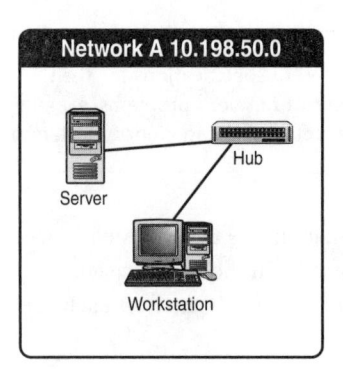

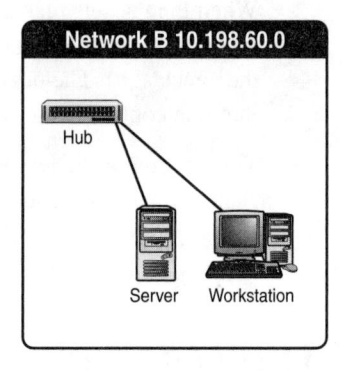

> **Note**
>
> The scenario and solution provided here is extremely simplistic. However, all routing environments (no matter how simple or complex) are all based on the same mechanics.

Let's examine how a router will function if placed between the two networks.

The PCs and other addressed systems (servers and such) should be configured with the address of the new router. Usually labeled as "default gateway", the parameter for the location of the router can vary dependent on the operating system in use. However, no matter the label, each system needs to know the address of the router. Figure 5.3 illustrates these same two networks with a router between them.

Notice that the router is actually linked to a hub on each network. Routers cannot route to individual systems; rather, the job of routers is to move information between networks. Therefore, another connectivity device must be employed to connect the devices of the two networks with the router.

> **Note**
>
> Although this example uses hubs, it is more desirable to use a switch, especially in high-traffic areas. Switches are capable of moving data to specific devices, rather than broadcasting every piece of data to every device on a network as a hub does.

Understanding How Routers Move Data

FIGURE 5.3

Two networks joined by a router.

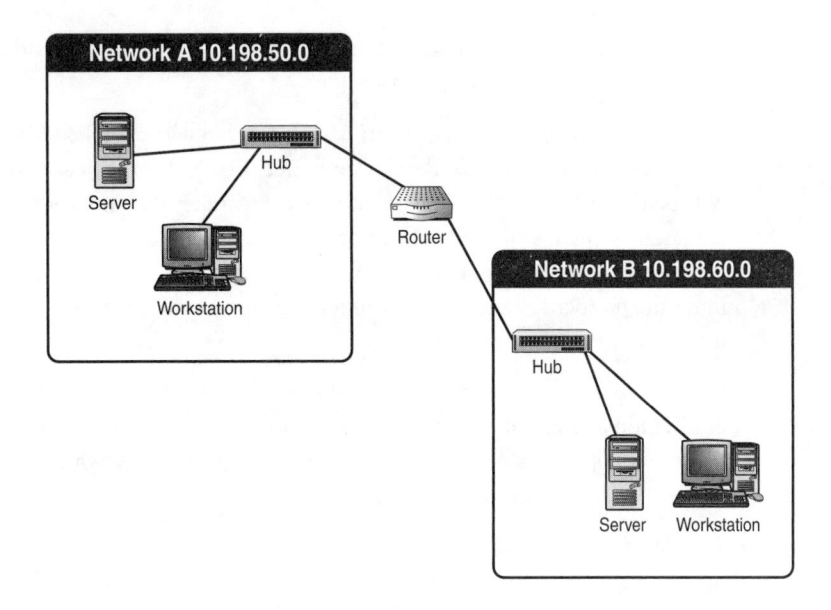

Placing the router correctly between the two networks may be the hardest part of the process, for one reason. You must assign a valid address on each router interface for the network to which it will be connected. In other words, the interface connected to network 10.198.50.0 needs an address in the 10.198.50.x range, whereas the interface connected to network 10.198.60.0 needs an address in the 10.198.60.x range.

> **Note**
> In most networking environments the first five to ten addresses in a network are reserved for routers. Although this is not a written rule by any means, it is a convention that most engineers seem to abide by.

Now that the router is in place and each PC has been configured with its address, we can see how data will move from network A through the router to network B.

PCs on network A (10.198.50.0) normally send messages to each other through the hub. That is, a packet from 10.198.50.5 meant for 10.198.50.8 is sent out of the PC. From the PC it has only one place to go: the hub. The hub (being an unintelligent device) simply relays that packet to every other device physically connected to it. The protocol header of the packet indicates the addresses of the device that sent the packet and the device to which it should be sent. Each device attached to the hub determines whether or not the packet is for it by reading the protocol header. One of those devices is 10.198.50.8. When this device receives the message, it processes it and sends the appropriate response.

The other devices read the header and determine that the packet is not meant for them, so they simply discard it and wait for more.

With the router in place, devices in network A can address packets to PCs in network B. When such a packet leaves the device in network A that created it and hits the hub, it will be discarded by every device in network A other than the router, because its recipient address is none of theirs. The packet also reaches the router. Rather than discarding the packet automatically like the other devices on network A, the router will begin examining the protocol header to determine whether it knows the location of the intended recipient.

First the router opens and reads the header. From the header, the router ascertains the destination address of the packet. Taking this destination address (10.198.60.17), the router applies the subnet mask for its interface with network A to determine the destination network (10.198.60.0).

The router then searches through its internal configuration to determine whether any configured interfaces match this network address. The router should find that the interface 10.198.60.1 is on the 10.198.60.0 network. The 10.198.50.1 interface now passes the packet to the 10.198.60.1 interface, which in turn forwards the packet to the hub on network B.

This rather simplistic view of how routers move protocols, and how protocols help to carry data, from network to network is actually very accurate. However, the chances of finding a routing environment that is configured like this are pretty slim. Rather, most networks today fall under the category of complex routing environments.

Complex Network Routing

A complex routing environment consists of multiple routers and multiple networks (producing multiple paths between each two networks). Figure 5.4 illustrates a complex routing environment.

Let's suppose a device from Network A wants to send information to a device in Network D. In logical order, the steps taken by the routing equipment are as follows:

1. The packet routed protocol encapsulated packet reaches Router A.
2. Router A searches through its routing table for an entry indicating the location of Network D. With the routing table, Router A finds that there are two paths to reach Network D. The first path is through Router F to Router G, whereas the other is through Router H to Router G.
3. Router A runs its routing algorithm based on the routing protocol in use—in this case we are using Open Shortest Path First (OSPF)—against the stored metrics for both paths and finds that of the two, the route from Router F to Router G is the best.

FIGURE 5.4

A complex routing environment.

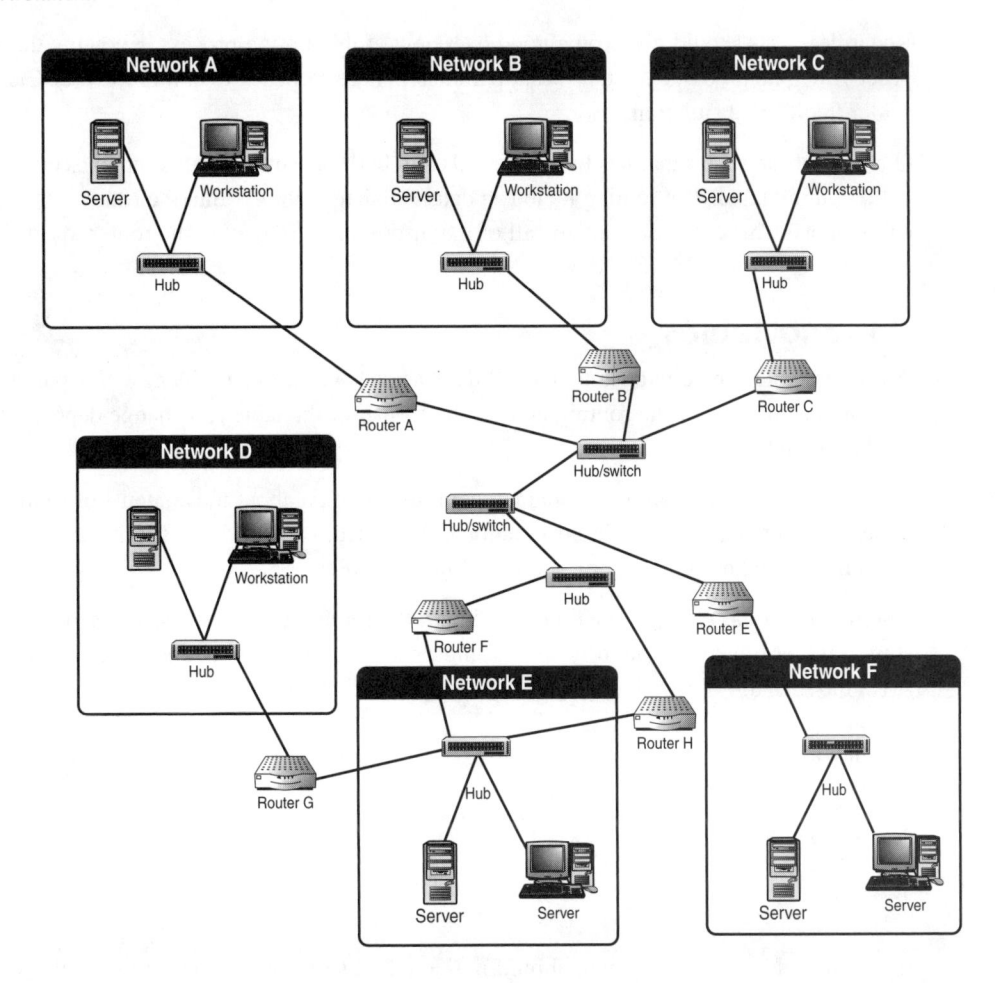

4. Router A encapsulates the packet (which was already encapsulated by IP) in OSPF. It then sets the destination field of the OSPF header to the address for Network D.
5. Router A now sends the OSPF-encapsulated packet to Router F.
6. Router F reads the OSPF headers and sees that the packet is targeted for Router G.
7. Router F searches its routing table to find that it has a physical link to Router G, and it forwards the packet over that link.
8. Router G receives the packet, strips off the OSPF header, and forwards the IP-encapsulated packet to Network D.

This scenario could be even more complex. In most environments there are access lists and multiple metrics to deal with (both of which will be covered later in this book).

Regardless, this should give you a good overview of the routing process. Knowing this process will help you understand what parameters need to be set to configure your Cisco router in different situations.

One part of the router that has been referred to in both the simple and complex scenarios is the routing table. The routing table is a database that resides within the router's physical memory. This database contains all of the information needed by the router to find the location of a destination network.

Routing Tables

A routing table can be likened to a small database. However, the problem with trying to explain the contents of the routing table is the format of the table can change depending on the routing protocol in use.

Therefore, this discussion will contain general information about the contents of routing tables. If there is more specific information to be added, we will discuss it in the lesson concerning the particular routing protocol (such as RIP).

One important piece of information stored with the routing table is a one-to-one relationship of router to network address. For example, an excerpt of the routing table for Router A (in the scenario illustrated in figure 5.4) may look like this.

```
Network A - ME
Network B - Router B
Network C - Router C
Network D - Router F
Network D - Router H
Network E - Router F
Network E - Router H
Network F - Router E
```

Examining this list closely, you should notice one discrepancy between the routing table and the environment in Figure 5.4. Router G is actually the gateway router for Network D, but Router A sees Routers F and H as the routers to Network D. The reason for this is that most routing protocols do not allow a router to see more than is currently physically connected to it. In other words, because Router G is not directly connected to Router A, Router A will recognize only Routers F and H as the path to network D.

Router A will know about the existence of Network D, but it will not care about how to get there. Rather, it will concern itself only with knowing whom it needs to send packets to when they are bound for Network D. In this case, Router A could send the packets to either Router F or Router H. Then, within the routing tables on both Router F and Router H is the entry:

```
Network D - Router G
```

By organizing routing tables in this way, specific routers do not need to be responsible for the entire environment. Rather, each router watches over is own little (physically connected) portion of the network. If every router had a full copy of the routing table for the entire environment, several problems would emerge. The first problem is the sheer size of the table itself. As a routing table becomes larger and larger, looking through it for entries takes longer and longer, thus increasing the amount of time needed to route data. Also, the larger a routing table gets, the more memory is required to store it, taking memory away from the routing algorithms and the configuration files.

The second problem that would surface as a result of owning a full copy of the database is knows as *convergence*. Convergence is the condition in which every router on the network has a routing table that agrees with the routing tables on all the other routers. A goal in routing is to reach convergence as quickly as possible when routing table information changes. If every router had a full table, a change made on one end of the network could take a long time to be reflected in the routing table of a router on the other end. Therefore, convergence would take a long time to achieve, creating routing holes and loops in which information would simply be lost.

Another important function of routing tables is to track and store *routing metrics*. Routing metrics are the deciding factor in one route being chosen over another. That is, the metrics within the routing table that are assigned to each route are used to calculate whether a packet will be forwarded over one router as opposed to another route to the same destination.

In the scenario shown in Figure 5.4, Router A had two routes to choose from when sending packets to Network D. The data could be forwarded to Router F or Router H, both of which eventually lead to Network D. Router A used the metrics assigned to each path to decide which router to use.

The specific metrics used by a router to determine what route to use vary from protocol to protocol. Whatever the protocol, one property of metrics remains the same: 99% of them are arbitrary numbers assigned by the network administrator or router engineer.

Metrics like "cost" are engineer-assigned numbers that indicate the relative value of using one path over another to a specific destination. There are any number of factors that would cause an administrator to assign a lower value to one link and a higher value to another. Factors such as traffic flow, equipment reliability, and line cost (in dollars) can all be influential in causing one value to be assigned over another. However, the metrics themselves are ultimately at the discretion of the engineer.

In our example, the route via Router H could have been assigned a metric of 200 while the route via Router F was assigned a metric of 100. When Router A's routing protocol is run against all of the metrics (some protocols can use up to ten metrics), a final figure is produced. The route with the lowest figure is chosen as the best path.

Earlier in this section, the topic of convergence was introduced. In fact, the concept of router convergence deserves more coverage than just an introduction. Therefore let's examine on a higher level the ever-important topic of convergence.

Achieving Convergence

Router convergence across a network is just as integral to router functionality as any of the other factors we have discussed thus far. Put simply, if each router is operating from a different routing table, then each router is going to move data differently. This will result in many problems, and most likely the network will cease to operate.

Therefore, a system needs to be implemented to ensure that every router within a given environment will be working from the same table. The result of this system is router convergence.

The responsibility of achieving router convergence belongs to the routing protocol. Therefore, there are just as many ways to achieve total convergence, as there are protocols. However, the basic concept behind the process remains the same.

To arrive at a state of router convergence, each router on the network passes a piece of its routing table to every other router within the same environment. After the target routers receive their updates, they apply the changes to their own tables and then send out more updates. This process continues until every router has the same view of the network as every other router.

> **Note** As we cover different routing protocols in this book, we will discuss their particular ways of achieving convergence.

Routed Protocols vs. Routing Protocols

Throughout this lesson we have used the terms "routed protocol" and "routing protocol." When more then one router is involved, both routing and routed protocols are needed for the routing process, and both are very important.

Most likely you are very familiar with routed protocols. These are the common LAN and WAN protocols such as TCP/IP and Frame Relay. Between routers, packets formed under these protocols are carried by packets formed by the routing protocols. Routing protocol packets are also used to carry routing updates and metric values. Without routing protocols, information sent under routed protocols could not move from router to router.

> **Note** A routing protocol is not needed in cases where only one router is used. That is, routing protocols carry data only between routers. Therefore, if you use only one router, you do not need a routing protocol.

Now that we have introduced and covered the concepts behind routing, both from a protocol and from a hardware point of view, in the next lesson we will be "getting our hands dirty." That is, the next lesson will discuss configuring your Cisco router from scratch.

Summary

Cisco routers (like all routers) need the assistance of protocols to facilitate the movement of data in the routing process. Protocols help routers move data through a process known as encapsulation.

Through encapsulation protocols format data according to a standard template. The protocols add necessary information to the data by routed in the form of protocol headers.

All of the routing information acquired by a particular router is stored in a simple database known as the routing table. The routing table holds information such as the destination addresses and locations of networks the router has delivered data to.

Routers share these routing tables with each other through routing updates. Routing updates ensure that every routing within an environment has the same view of the network. Network convergence is achieved when every router is sharing the same picture of the networking environment.

Q&A

Q Why can routers move data only on the network layer of the OSI model?

A The network layer of the OSI is responsible for the addressing for internetwork devices. With such addresses, routing to any specific destination is nearly impossible.

Q Are routing metrics necessary, and why?

A Routing metrics are used by routers to help determine the best path between two networks. While it is possible to code routes into a router statically, the use of metrics allows the routers to change their actions according to changes in the environment.

Quiz

Questions

1. What are the two main responsibilities of routed protocols?
2. Which field of the IP header acts as the packet's expiration date?
3. To achieve convergence, routers must share what information with each other?

Answers

1. Packet addressing and encapsulation
2. TTL (Time To Live)
3. The routing table

WEEK 1

DAY 6

Getting the Router Up and Running

In today's lesson we will examine one of the most important procedures in router setup and maintenance: supplying a configuration. The configuration is the heart (or brains) of the router's functionality. Your router's configuration is going to determine almost everything about the router, from the names and addresses of its ports to the protocols it can run and recognize.

To examine in full the process of configuring a Cisco router, we will look into the following topics.

- Configuring a clean router
- The configuration files
- Reconfiguring an existing router
- Changing individual configuration items
- Viewing and configuring interfaces
- Configuring banners

The process of configuring a router can be divided into two categories: a *clean configuration* and a *reconfiguration*. A clean configuration is supplied to a router that has no previous configuration installed. That is, either the router is new and has never been used, or the previous configuration has been completely wiped out. A reconfiguration occurs when the existing configuration of a router is altered. Although the same items of information may be supplied to the router during each process, they are accessed and executed differently.

For this chapter (and the majority of the remainder of the book) the configuration examples will be from a Cisco 1605R using IOS version 12.0(3). This particular router has two built-in Ethernet ports (Eth0 and Eth1), a WAN expansion slot, and a console port. This router is fairly cost effective; therefore, if you are considering purchasing a router for practice, I would suggest the 1605R. However, most of the examples given in this book will work on any Cisco router (especially if it is running IOS version 12.0(3)).

> **Note** If you do not have a router to practice on, try to complete the exercises at the end of each chapter on paper. The exercises are designed to help you retain the major points of each chapter. The answers for each exercise are supplied after the problem in a Note box similar to this one.

Let's look at our first configuration process: configuring a clean router.

Configuring a Clean Router

When you purchase a new Cisco router, it will arrive at your site with no routing configuration onboard. The reason is that Cisco has no idea what the specific layout and address scheme of your network are, so the company would find it a little difficult to supply a configuration with the router at the factory. Therefore, your first duty when hooking up your router will be to supply this initial configuration to the router.

The initial configuration process consists of answering a series of prompts. These answers will determine the configuration of the router. However, the IOS cannot anticipate and prompt you for every configuration possibility. Therefore, the configuration setup (known as the Basic Management Setup) is meant to supply only enough information to get the device operational. Once the router is up and running, you can fill in the details of the configuration as you see fit.

Before we can discuss configuring the router, however, we need to understand how to connect a terminal or PC in order to communicate with the router. If you have never worked on a Cisco router before, pay close attention to this section.

Connecting to the Router

If this is your first time around Cisco routers (or routers in general), you should notice one thing about the back of your router: the absence of a monitor or keyboard port. This is not a mistake. Most routers (and all Cisco routers) lack the capability to drive their own monitors and keyboards. Therefore, you must connect to the devices from an external source.

On further examination of the rear panel of the router, you will notice a console port—in most cases an RJ-45 jack, but on some high-end routers a DB9 serial port. As was discussed on Day 2, the console port is the direct access port, which you need to locate to access the router.

If you are working on a new router (one that has never been configured), the console port will be the only active port on which you can gain access to the router.

> **Note** You may be able to gain access to Cisco routers with existing configurations by Telneting to one of the Ethernet ports. However, even this capability must be enabled through the console port. Therefore, when in doubt, use the console port.

The console port, regardless of the physical port type (that is, RJ-45 or DB9), will always communicate serially. Therefore, if you are using your PC to communicate with the router, you must connect the console port of the router to the serial port of the PC. This connection can be made by using the supplied Cisco rollover cable and the RJ-45-to-DB9 adapter.

> **Note** The different types of cable that can connect to an RJ-45 connector—crossover, rollover, and standard Ethernet cables—differ from each other in several important ways.
>
> A standard Ethernet cable, used to connect an Ethernet port on a computer to an Ethernet hub, has eight multicolored wires leading to eight pins. If you hold the two ends of a standard Ethernet cable together, you will notice a one-to-one correlation between the eight colored wires of the cable at each end. Table 4.1 shows the relationship between the pins on an Ethernet cable.

TABLE 4.1 Standard Ethernet Pinouts

Ethernet Pins	Function
1 ‡ 1	Receive
2 ‡ 2	Receive
3 ‡ 3	Transmit
4 ‡ 4	Not used
5 ‡ 5	Not used
6 ‡ 6	Transmit
7 ‡ 7	Not used
8 ‡ 8	Not used

An Ethernet *crossover* cable is somewhat different. Normally used to connect Ethernet ports directly to each other rather than through a network, a crossover cable inverts wires 3 and 1 and wires 6 and 2. Table 4.2 shows the pinouts for an Ethernet crossover cable.

TABLE 4.2 Ethernet Crossover Pinouts

Ethernet Pins	Function
1 ‡ 3	Receive ‡ Transmit
2 ‡ 6	Receive ‡ Transmit
3 ‡ 1	Transmit ‡ Receive
4 ‡ 4	Not Used
5 ‡ 5	Not Used
6 ‡ 2	Transmit ‡ Receive
7 ‡ 7	Not Used
8 ‡ 8	Not Used

The Cisco-supplied *rollover* cable is a unique cable. All eight wires in the Ethernet cable are flipped to create a mirror image. Then the RJ-45-to-DB9 adapter is added. Table 4.3 illustrates the Ethernet rollover cable's pinouts and how they relate to the DB9 connector.

TABLE 4.3 Rollover Cable and DB9 Pinouts

Ethernet Pins	Ethernet to DB9 (pin 9 is not used)	Function
1 ⇄ 8	8 ⇄ 8	Receive ⇄ Transmit
2 ⇄ 7	7 ⇄ 6	Not Used
3 ⇄ 6	6 ⇄ 2	Transmit ⇄ Receive
4 ⇄ 5	5 ⇄ 5	GND
5 ⇄ 4	4 ⇄ 5	GND
6 ⇄ 3	3 ⇄ 3	Receive ⇄ Transmit
7 ⇄ 2	2 ⇄ 4	Not Used
8 ⇄ 1	1 ⇄ 7	Transmit ⇄ Receive

After connecting your PC to the console port of the router, you should be able to communicate using a standard terminal emulation program.

> **Note**
>
> If you are having problems connecting with your terminal emulation software, make sure that you are using the default port values for the console port:
>
>   Baud: 9600
>   DataBits: 8
>   Parity: None
>   StopBits: 1
>   Flow Control: Hardware

Once we have a working connection to the router's console port, we can discuss supplying a configuration to a clean router. The console connection will be our window to the configuration menus, so we need to get it working before we can begin configuring any options.

Using the Setup Dialogs

After unpacking (and registering) your new router, you should try to place it in the physical location where you expect it to reside when it is finally installed and running on the network. This will enable you to avoid having to move the router after the configuration is complete (possibly affecting a functional network). Another practical reason for putting the router in its final "production" location is that you will have access to the ports and cables that will ultimately connect to the router.

Using a terminal emulator, you should be able to watch the router's boot process. When the router has completely booted, it will realize that there is no existing configuration and will enter the setup dialog. The startup process (from boot to setup dialog) should look similar to this.

```
System Bootstrap, Version 12.0(3)T, RELEASE SOFTWARE (fc1)
Copyright (c) 1999 by cisco Systems, Inc.
C1600 platform with 8192 Kbytes of main memory

program load complete, entry point: 0x4020060, size: 0x165eac

%SYS-6-BOOT_MESSAGES: Messages above this line are from the boot loader.
program load complete, entry point: 0x2005000, size: 0x2199cc
Self decompressing the image : ##################################################
################################## [OK]
            Restricted Rights Legend

Use, duplication, or disclosure by the Government is
subject to restrictions as set forth in subparagraph
(c) of the Commercial Computer Software - Restricted
Rights clause at FAR sec. 52.227-19 and subparagraph
(c) (1) (ii) of the Rights in Technical Data and Computer
Software clause at DFARS sec. 252.227-7013.

           cisco Systems, Inc.
           170 West Tasman Drive
           San Jose, California 95134-1706


Cisco Internetwork Operating System Software
IOS (tm) 1600 Software (C1600-Y-M), Version 12.0(3), RELEASE SOFTWARE (fc1)
Copyright (c) 1986-1999 by cisco Systems, Inc.
Compiled Mon 08-Feb-99 20:15 by phanguye
Image text-base: 0x02005000, data-base: 0x02455958

cisco 1605 (68360) processor (revision C) with 7680K/512K bytes of memory.
Processor board ID 17531816, with hardware revision 00000002
Bridging software.
X.25 software, Version 3.0.0.
2 Ethernet/IEEE 802.3 interface(s)
System/IO memory with parity disabled
8192K bytes of DRAM onboard
System running from RAM
8K bytes of non-volatile configuration memory.
4096K bytes of processor board PCMCIA flash (Read/Write)
        --- System Configuration Dialog ---

Would you like to enter the initial configuration dialog? [yes/no]:
```

Getting the Router Up and Running

The last line of the setup process is the one that you need to pay attention to. A clean router will pause indefinitely waiting for your response to the question "Would you like to enter the initial configuration dialog?" If your router does not prompt you for the initial configuration dialog and wait for your answer at this point, then your router has an existing configuration. Configuring a router with an existing configuration is covered in the next section, "Reconfiguring an Existing Router."

> **Note**
>
> How does the Cisco IOS know whether this is the first time a router has been powered on? The short answer is that it doesn't. During the boot process the IOS tests for the existence of a file named `startup config`. This file holds all of the configuration information for the router.
>
> If the file exists, the router reads it and loads the configuration. If the file does not exist, the router realizes that there is no current configuration, so it enters setup mode.

To continue with the configuration process, answer yes to the prompt "Would you like to enter the initial configuration dialog?"

> **Note**
>
> If you respond with no, you will exit the System Configuration Dialog and go to the user mode command prompt. The router will not be configured.

Upon receiving a yes response from the user, the router begins the setup dialog: a series of menulike questions designed to gather enough information to make the device operational. Configuring the router through this dialog is known as Basic Management Setup.

Let's examine the Basic Management Setup and configure a Cisco router for operation.

The Basic Management Setup

After answering "yes" to enter the "initial configuration dialog" the Cisco IOS will display the following message.

```
At any point you may enter a question mark '?' for help.
Use ctrl-c to abort configuration dialog at any prompt.
Default settings are in square brackets '[]'.

Basic management setup configures only enough connectivity
for management of the system, extended setup will ask you
to configure each interface on the system
Would you like to enter basic management setup? [yes/no]:
```

Notice the last message before the prompt. The router software is reminding you that the basic management setup only gathers minimal information, and it mentions something called *extended setup* that is more detailed. You might guess that by entering no in response to the question "Would you like to enter basic management setup?" you would be able to enter extended setup instead. This is true, and we will cover the extended setup dialog later in this section. For now, let's focus on the basic management setup.

Respond yes to begin the basic management setup. At this point, the router will prompt you for the first piece of information that will be configured on the router.

```
Would you like to enter basic management setup? [yes/no]: y
Configuring global parameters:

  Enter host name [Router]:
```

The first piece of information the router asks for is the hostname that will be assigned to the router. The hostname is a way by which other devices, including other Cisco routers, can refer to the device you are configuring.

Theoretically you could refer to a router by its protocol address (for example, its IP address if the router is running IP). However, there are three reasons why you may not want to do so:

1. The router hasn't asked you for an address yet; therefore it doesn't know what its address is.
2. Routers tend to have more then one addressable port, so one would have to be chosen as the "hostname."
3. Names are just much easier to remember and identify than the long strings of numbers used to create addresses.

When choosing your router's hostname, try to use something descriptive enough that you can identify the router from a list. For example, MyCorp1 or Floor4A might be better hostnames than Router1. However, in today's security-conscious corporate landscape, a hostname like MainSecurityFirewallForTheOfficesFinancialCenter might just be a little too descriptive (moreover, you are limited to 30 characters for a hostname).

After you have chosen a hostname, type it at the prompt and press the Enter key. The setup dialog will move to the next question.

```
  Enter host name [Router]: STYSCisco

  The enable secret is a password used to protect access to
  privileged EXEC and configuration modes. This password,
  after entered, becomes encrypted in the configuration.
  Enter enable secret:
```

The router will now prompt you for the "enable secret" password. As the message states, the enable secret password is used to secure access to the privilege mode of the command interpreter.

> **Note**
>
> Once the secret password is configured, a user attempting to enter privilege mode will encounter the following prompt:
>
> ```
> Router>enable
> Password:
> ```
>
> Using the `enable` command will still put the router into privilege mode, but the router user will now have to enter the password to enter privilege mode.

Another interesting property of the enable secret password is that it is encrypted within the Cisco IOS, whereas the other passwords in the IOS are stored as plain text. (There are five Cisco IOS passwords all together, but you will be prompted for only two more during the Basic Management Setup dialog.) Anyone accessing your router for less than trustworthy purposes can theoretically find your other passwords spelled out within the IOS. However, they will have a much harder time deciphering the secret password.

Why protect the secret password and not the others? The reason is that the entire configuration of the router is done in privilege mode. Therefore, if you can block access to privilege mode, knowing the other passwords won't help any would-be intruders.

> **Note**
>
> Even though the password is encrypted in the IOS, it can be seen as plain text at the time you configure it. Therefore, you may want to clear your screen after configuring the router.

Choosing a secret password that is easy for you to remember will save you the added misery of performing a password recovery. After configuring the secret password, the dialog will prompt you for the `enable` password.

```
The enable password is used when you do not specify an
enable secret password, with some older software versions, and
some boot images.
Enter enable password: Enable
```

As the IOS illustrates, the `enable` password is used when there is no secret password. Keep in mind that you cannot enter a blank password during the setup dialog. However, you can go into the configuration at a later time and create a null password.

The last password that the setup dialog prompts you to configure is the virtual terminal password.

```
The virtual terminal password is used to protect
access to the router over a network interface.
Enter virtual terminal password: vterm
```

The virtual terminal password is used to secure access by Telnet to the ports of the Cisco router. Users can access networked Cisco routers by Telneting to a specific port of the router. For example, if a Cisco router was configured to span two networks, users on one of the networks could Telnet to the router through the port that corresponds to that particular network.

The virtual terminal password secures access to the router through this port. After configuring the password, users accessing the virtual terminal will need to supply the appropriate virtual terminal password to gain access.

> **Note** As you can see, Cisco routers have many different passwords (five in total; two are not configurable from within the setup dialog). Keeping them in order and being able to distinguish between them are very important.

Once the virtual terminal password is configured, the router will ask you whether you want to configure SNMP (Simple Network Management Protocol).

```
Enter virtual terminal password: vterm
  Configure SNMP Network Management? [yes]:
```

Notice that the default answer is yes. I tend to answer no here. Unless you have a compelling reason to answer yes, then just skip the question. Typically, you will see SNMP running only in areas with more than one router, by administrators with a need to monitor the status of various router statistics. (Even if you find that you do need SNMP configured on a port, you can add it after the setup dialog. SNMP tends to be a more advanced routing subject and will not be covered in great detail by this book.) Responding no will continue the setup dialog.

```
  Configure SNMP Network Management? [yes]: n

Current interface summary
Any interface listed with OK? value "NO" does not have a valid configuration
  Interface    IP-Address      OK? Method Status          Protocol

  Ethernet0    unassigned      NO  unset  up              down
  Ethernet1    unassigned      NO  unset  up              down

Enter interface name used to connect to the
management network from the above interface summary:
```

At this point, the router will display for you the current list of physical ports on your router and their statuses. Because this is the first time you have used this router, all of the ports should show "NO" under "OK?" and "down" under "Protocol." These two items tell you that the specified ports are not configured and they have no active protocol bound to them. Thus, in their current state, the interfaces are not functional.

For a router interface to be fully functional, two conditions need to be met. The first condition is that the interface needs to be turned on. By default, all of the interfaces on a Cisco router are turned off. (Continuing with the configuration dialog will turn the desired interface on.)

> **Note**: Turning a router's interface on refers to a software switch rather than a hardware switch. With the Cisco IOS you can indicate to the router whether a specific interface should be turned on or off.

The second condition for having a fully functional router interface is to configure a protocol to run on the desired interface. Because routing is fully dependent on the use of protocols, a Cisco interface will not be "up," or functional, without the presence of a configured protocol. Continuing with the setup dialog will supply the router with the required information to bring the interface up.

The setup dialog is now prompting you for them name of the one interface (physical port) you wish to configure. In our example we will be configuring the "Ethernet0" interface.

```
Enter interface name used to connect to the
management network from the above interface summary: Ethernet0

Configuring interface Ethernet0:
  Configure IP on this interface? [yes]:
```

The dialog now allows you to configure IP on the selected interface. Responding no to this question will conclude the setup dialog and leave your router's interfaces unconfigured. Therefore, because you most likely want at least one functioning interface, you should respond yes.

```
Configuring interface Ethernet0:
  Configure IP on this interface? [yes]: y
    IP address for this interface:
```

The dialog will prompt you for an IP address and subnet mask for the interface, as mentioned on Day 5.

```
IP address for this interface: 10.162.24.153
    Subnet mask for this interface [255.0.0.0] : 255.0.0.0
```

Finally, after you supply the IP information for the interface that you are configuring, the dialog will end and a summary of the configuration will be displayed.

```
Class A network is 10.0.0.0, 8 subnet bits; mask is /8

The following configuration command script was created:

hostname STYSCisco
enable secret 5 $1$ohv2$phQNY94qZoJAZ2h7XBigG0
enable password enable
line vty 0 4
password vterm
no snmp-server
!
no ip routing

!
interface Ethernet0
no shutdown
ip address 10.162.24.153 255.0.0.0
!
interface Ethernet1
shutdown
no ip address
!
end


[0] Go to the IOS command prompt without saving this config.
[1] Return back to the setup without saving this config.
[2] Save this configuration to nvram and exit.

Enter your selection [2]:
```

The Cisco IOS now asks you to either confirm your configuration, reconfigure, or simply abort and exit (selection 2 will save your configuration and reboot the router). Notice that if you think you might have made any errors configuring your router, you can rerun the setup by choosing 0. All of the configuration choices you made the first time will appear as the default responses the second time.

Note that the basic management setup dialog has allowed you to configure only one interface, even though there is more than one port on the router. This exit after you have configured one interface is one difference between the basic and extended setup dialogs. The extended dialog allows you to configure as many of your interfaces as you need.

Extended Setup Dialog

Let's take a look at the extended setup dialog. To enter the dialog, simply respond no when the IOS prompts you to enter the basic management setup.

```
Would you like to enter basic management setup? [yes/no]: no

First, would you like to see the current interface summary? [yes]:
```

The dialog immediately asks you whether you want to view the current interfaces. Answering yes will display the same interface summary seen in the basic setup after you respond no to setting up SNMP.

After the current interface summary is displayed, the dialog will prompt for the same information as the basic setup. You will be prompted for the hostname, secret password, enable password, and virtual terminal password.

Finally, you will be prompted to configure SNMP. After you respond no, the extended setup begins to differ from the basic setup.

```
Configure SNMP Network Management? [yes]: n
  Configure IP? [yes]:
```

The setup, rather than ask for an individual interface name to configure, asks if you want to configure protocols globally. The router will first determine what routing and routed protocols you want to configure on the router. After the dialog has determined exactly what protocols you want to use, it will then prompt you for the specific information needed to configure each protocol on each interface.

> **Note**
>
> As we discussed on Day 5, routed protocols are protocols that devices use to communicate with each other, such as IP or IPX; These protocols are deemed "routed" because routers route them. Routing protocols, on the other hand, are the protocols routers use to route routed protocols. (Try saying that five times quickly; read it slowly, it does make sense. To review these concepts, see the sections "Complex Network Routing" and "Routed Protocols versus Routing Protocols" from Day 5.)
>
> The routed protocols you will be allowed to configure are determined by the feature pack installed on your router. For example, if you have the IP feature pack installed (the most common), you will be able to route only IP, whereas if you have the IP/IPX feature pack, you can route both IP and IPX.

```
Configure IP? [yes]: y
    Configure IGRP routing? [yes]: n
    Configure RIP routing? [no]: n

Configuring interface parameters:
```

(Notice I responded no to configuring the two routing protocols IGRP and RIP. Because we have not discussed the purposes and functions of those protocols yet, we should just skip them and configure IP. You may be uncomfortable with configuring IP; just follow along. Be assured that we will discuss IP, IGRP, and RIP later in this book.)

The dialog now prompts you to configure all of the selected protocols on each of your interfaces.

```
Configuring interface parameters:

Do you want to configure Ethernet0  interface? [yes]:
```

The prompts encountered during the interface configuration are the same as those used during the basic management setup.

```
Do you want to configure Ethernet0  interface? [yes]: y
  Configure IP on this interface? [yes]: y
    IP address for this interface: 10.162.24.153
    Subnet mask for this interface [255.0.0.0] : 255.0.0.0
    Class A network is 10.0.0.0, 8 subnet bits; mask is /8

Do you want to configure Ethernet1  interface? [yes]:
```

However, rather then end after configuring the first interface, the extended setup dialog now prompts you to configure any other interfaces that are present on the router. After all of the interfaces are configured, the extended setup concludes, and you are prompted to save, discard, or reconfigure your settings.

> **Note**
>
> Unless you have your router connected to another device through the interface you just configured, you may see several errors after rebooting.
>
> ```
> 00:38:14: %QUICC_ETHER-1-LOSTCARR: Unit 0, lost carrier.
> Transceiver problem?
> 00:39:14: %QUICC_ETHER-1-LOSTCARR: Unit 0, lost carrier.
> Transceiver problem?
> 00:40:13: %LINK-5-CHANGED: Interface Ethernet1, changed state to
> administratively down
> 00:40:14: %QUICC_ETHER-1-LOSTCARR: Unit 0, lost carrier.
> Transceiver problem?
> ```
>
> These errors indicate that even though you just configured the particular interface, the router still cannot detect any other devices through it. Simply connecting an Ethernet hub to the interface should eliminate the errors.

Another option is to use the 'shutdown' command, thus disabling the interface.

```
Router#config t
Enter configuration commands, one per line.  End with CNTL/Z.
Router(config)#int e0
Router(config-if)#shutdown
```

(Replace the e0 in the example above with the type and number of the interface you wish to shut down, such as e1, bri0, or token1.)

By now you may be wondering where the IOS stored these configurations. The files the IOS uses to hold configuration information are discussed in the next section.

The Configuration Files

So where does the configuration you just created go after you are finished? The Cisco IOS actually stores the configuration in two different files. The first file is known as startup-config, and the second is running-config. Both files are stored on the router, but they serve very different purposes.

The startup-config File

When your router steps through its boot process, it needs the guidance of a configuration file to know what the specific parameters of the device are. This file is the startup-config file.

Note Those of you familiar with earlier Microsoft operating platforms can think of the startup-config file as the equivalent of autoexec.bat for a Cisco router.

If the router detects the presence of a file named startup-config within the router's flash memory, it will proceed to open and read the file. The file contains all of the information obtained during the setup dialog. When the router finishes stepping through the startup-config, the router should be fully operational (or at least as operational as you have configured it to be).

> **Note:** The next step in the startup process is extremely important. Understanding what happens to the `startup-config` file after the router boots will save you a lot of confusion and hassle down the road.

After the router has finished booting, it copies the information within the `startup-config` file to the `running-config` file. The router then uses the `running-config` file during all daily activities to obtain configuration information.

The `running-config` File

The `running-config` file is stored in a volatile part of the router's memory (known as the "system"). That is, every time the router is powered off, the `running-config` file is lost. After the router successfully boots up, the current `startup-config` is copied to the system and renamed `running-config`.)

The `running-config` file stores any configuration changes made to the router during the operation of the router. For example, if you were to change the IP address of port Eth0, the change would be reflected only in the `running-config`. If the router were rebooted, the changes would be lost.

There is a way to retain any configuration changes you make to the router. However, before we can discuss making your changes permanent, you need to understand how to view and edit the information within the different config files.

Viewing and Editing the Configuration Files

The contents of both the `startup-config` and `running-config` files can be viewed from privilege mode. The files are stored within the router's memory as text files (allowing the router to read through them like instruction sheets).

The location of the `running-config` and `startup-config` files can be viewed from privilege mode. To locate the `running-config` file, change directories to `system` and run the `dir` command.

```
STYSCisco#cd system:
STYSCisco#dir
Directory of system:/

    2  dr-x           0       <no date>  memory
    1  -rw-         541       <no date>  running-config
```

Getting the Router Up and Running

The `startup-config` file resides in the flash memory, referred to by the device name nvram (for "nonvolatile RAM"):

```
STYSCisco#cd nvram:
STYSCisco#dir
Directory of nvram:/

    1  -rw-         604               <no date>  startup-config
    2  ----           5               <no date>  private-config
```

(The file `private-config` is used for encryption information and cannot be accessed.)

To view the `startup-config`, use the `show` command. (Recall from Day 4 that the Cisco IOS understands partial commands.)

```
STYSCisco#show startup-config
Using 604 out of 7506 bytes
!
version 12.0
service config
service timestamps debug uptime
service timestamps log uptime
no service password-encryption
!
hostname STYSCisco
!
enable secret 5 $1$8HHJ$6dzol4.tGP2gUB6uFfwHS0
enable password enable
!
ip subnet-zero
!
!
!
interface Ethernet0
 ip address 10.16.4.153 255.240.0.0
 no ip directed-broadcast
 no cdp enable
!
interface Ethernet1
 no ip address
 no ip directed-broadcast
 shutdown
 no cdp enable
!
ip classless
!
dialer-list 1 protocol ip permit
dialer-list 1 protocol ipx permit
!
```

```
line con 0
 exec-timeout 0 0
 transport input none
line vty 0 4
 password vterm
 login
!
end
```

You should be able to match up the responses you gave during the setup process with the information contained within the `startup-config`. The router records all of the setup dialog information in this file.

The contents of the `running-config` can be viewed similarly by running the following command:

`Router#`**`show running-config`**

At this point we will assume that the contents of the two files are the same. Because you have just created your first `startup-config`, and because the `startup-config` becomes the `running-config` after bootup, the two files should be identical. However, that doesn't mean they have to stay that way.

The `startup-config` can be edited through the `setup` command. The `setup` command (which we will discuss in the next section, "Reconfiguring an Existing Router") tells the router to start the setup dialog, even if there is an existing `startup-config` file. The setup dialog initiated by the `setup` command is the same one used by both the basic and extended setup dialogs. These processes are the only way to edit the contents of the `startup-config` directly. After you have edited the `startup-config`, the router will always ask you to restart; this lets the router read the instructions you just entered. (Remember that the router loads the `startup-config` only during the boot process.)

> **Note** The `startup-config` can be totally replaced by copying the `running-config` over it. However, this is not considered editing the `startup-config` file itself; it is more of a replacement operation.

Most of the other operation-altering commands in the Cisco IOS affect only the `running-config`. This allows the users to make changes to the router's configuration without the risk of losing any previous settings. Commands such as those used to configure the IP address of an interface will write only to the `running-config`.

For example, suppose RouterA is configured to run IP on two Ethernet ports, and an administrator reconfigures the addresses on the ports to test a new IP scheme. After the testing is complete, the administrator wants to restore the router back to its previous operational state. The administrator simply needs either to reboot the router or to copy the startup-config over the running-config. This will reload the configuration within the router's running-config.

To copy the startup-config over the running-config, thus restoring the router back to its previous state without having to reboot, use the following steps.

1. First, confirm (using the show command) that the startup-config contains the configuration that you want.
2. Then, after switching to privilege mode, run the following command:
   ```
   STYSCisco#copy starting-config running-config
   Destination filename [running-config]?
   604 bytes copied in 2.136 secs (302 bytes/sec)
   ```

   This will copy the current startup-config to the running-config. Accepting the default filename, running-config, will ensure that the router correctly recognizes the configuration.

However, if the user wants to keep the new configuration and does not want it to be lost after the router is rebooted, follow the process in reverse. That is, copy the running-config over the startup-config. Doing so will take the current running configuration and ensure that the router uses it the next time it is rebooted.

```
STYSCisco#copy running-config startup-config
Destination filename [startup-config]?
Building configuration...
```

Now that we have successfully configured a router from scratch, let's discuss the step for reconfiguring a router that has already been set up.

Reconfiguring an Existing Router

When you boot your Cisco router, you may find that it goes directly to the user mode prompt instead of the setup dialog. If this happens, it means that the router has found an existing configuration in the flash memory. If you want to reconfigure the router, you have two options.

The first is to delete the current startup-config and reboot. This will erase the router's configuration and force it to enter the setup dialog.

```
STYSCisco#erase startup-config
Erasing the nvram filesystem will remove all files! Continue? [confirm]

Erase of nvram: complete
STYSCisco#
```

Either using the physical power switch or entering the reload command can restart the router.

```
STYSCisco#reload
Proceed with reload? [confirm]

02:33:39: %SYS-5-RELOAD: Reload requested
```

At this point the router will be void of any configuration and will begin the Initial Setup Dialog just as if it were brand-new.

The other process to reconfigure an existing router is to run the `setup` command within privilege mode. This command accesses the setup dialog of the router without (immediately) destroying the existing `startup-config`.

```
STYSCisco#setup


          --- System Configuration Dialog ---

Continue with configuration dialog? [yes/no]: y
At any point you may enter a question mark '?' for help.
Use ctrl-c to abort configuration dialog at any prompt.
Default settings are in square brackets '[]'.


Basic management setup configures only enough connectivity
for management of the system, extended setup will ask you
to configure each interface on the system

Would you like to enter basic management setup? [yes/no]:
```

From this point the setup is identical to the other setup dialogs. Simply follow the prompts, and your router should be operational in no time.

Changing Individual Configuration Items

The first half of today's lesson walked you through the various ways to configure a router. However, all of the processes covered had one thing in common: They gather a minimal amount of information for a broad range of subjects.

Most of the time you will want to configure one or two attributes on one or two interfaces and not have to change the virtual terminal password. Conversely, you may want to change the secret password without worrying about what protocols to configure on the Eth0 port.

The remainder of this lesson is going to show you how to configure all of the elements in the setup dialog individually. This will give you greater control over exactly what you want to configure.

Setting the Hostname

To set (or change) the hostname of your Cisco router, you must be in privilege mode. To execute the majority of the configuration commands, you will need to be in the configuration mode (accessible from within privilege mode).

As was mentioned, the hostname of the router is used to distinguish the router from other devices on the network. The `hostname` command allows you to edit and change the hostname freely. (Keep in mind that any configuration changes made outside of the setup dialog will affect only the `running-config`. Unless the `running-config` is then copied to the `startup-config`, these changes will not be retained.)

```
Router>enable
Password:
Router#configure
Configuring from terminal, memory, or network [terminal]? terminal
Enter configuration commands, one per line.  End with CNTL/Z.
Router(config)#
```

The `config` (`configure`) command opens the `running-config` file and prepares it for editing. As the preceding IOS message illustrates, there are three items that can be configured with the `config` command: terminal, memory, and network; right now we will be working with terminals. As far as the Cisco router is concerned, a "terminal" is any port or interface, physical or logical.

```
Router(config)#hostname STYSCisco
STYSCisco(config)#
```

The `hostname` command, followed by the router's new hostname, will set the value. You can see that the router immediately updates the privilege mode command prompt to reflect the new hostname.

Pressing Ctrl+Z will save the `running-config` and exit back to the privilege mode command prompt.

```
STYSCisco(config)#^Z
STYSCisco#
00:12:39: %SYS-5-CONFIG_I: Configured from console by console
```

Next we will configure the router's passwords.

Router Passwords

Both the basic and extended setup dialogs allow you to configure a total of three passwords: the `enable secret`, the `enable`, and the virtual terminal. However, there are a total of five configurable passwords within the Cisco IOS. The other two passwords—the auxiliary and console passwords—are configurable only from the command prompt. Let's discuss the configuration of all five IOS passwords.

The Secret Password

The secret password, which controls access to the privilege mode of the command interpreter, can be modified using the `configure` command.

```
STYSCisco#configure terminal
Enter configuration commands, one per line.  End with CNTL/Z.
STYSCisco(config)#enable secret 0 secretpassword
STYSCisco(config)#^Z
STYSCisco#
```

After entering the terminal configuration, use the `enable` command to indicate that you want to change one of the `enable` passwords. The command string `enable secret 0 secretpassword` is simple to follow. You are specifying that you want to change the secret enable password to `secretpassword`. The `0` preceding the new password indicates that the password you are entering is not encrypted.

> **Note**
>
> You could have used a 5 to indicate that you wanted to specify an encrypted password; that is, you could have entered the string `enable secret 5 secretpassword`. If you then used a `show` command to read the configuration file, you would see the password encrypted as 1SuLj$3frAA0Qrjkr3GyBT7371k1.

The `enable` Password

The `enable` password, which is used only when the secret password is not defined, is configured the same way as the secret password.

```
STYSCisco#configure terminal
Enter configuration commands, one per line.  End with CNTL/Z.

STYSCisco(config)#enable password newpassword
STYSCisco(config)#
```

Notice that one difference between the `enable` password and the secret password is that the `enable` password cannot be encrypted. Otherwise the processes for changing them are the same.

The Virtual Terminal Password

The virtual terminal password, which is used to protect access to the Telnet ports, is configurable through the `line` option of the `configure` command.

```
Router#configure terminal
Enter configuration commands, one per line.  End with CNTL/Z.
Router(config)#line vty 0 4
Router(config-line)#login
```

```
Router(config-line)#password 0 vterm
Router(config-line)#^Z
Router#
```

To configure the virtual terminal password, you must go beyond the general `configure terminal` and configure the line properties.

> **Note:** The `line` properties are any options that directly affect the operation of the physical and logical ports of the router.

Using the `line` command, we specify to the IOS that we want to change the virtual terminal characteristics for lines 0 through 4.

```
Router(config)#line vty 0 4
```

After executing this command the router will enter line configuration mode. At this point we can specify that we want to edit the login features and set the password for line 0 to vterm:

```
Router(config-line)#login
Router(config-line)#password 0 vterm
```

As always, we end the command with a Ctrl+Z to exit the configuration mode.

The Auxiliary Password

The auxiliary password protects access to the auxiliary port if your router has one. The auxiliary port is used for attaching an external modem (providing dial-in access to the router, not to the network the router is attached to). Not every Cisco router has an auxiliary port, so not every router will be capable of setting this password.

```
Router#configure terminal
Enter configuration commands, one per line.  End with CNTL/Z.
Router(config)#line aux 0
Router(config-line)#login
Router(config-line)#password 0 auxpassword
Router(config-line)#^Z
Router#
```

The last password you can configure on a Cisco router is the console password.

The Console Password

The console password controls access to the console port. Because passwords are easily lost or forgotten, I rarely set the console password; however, it is your decision to set or not set the password. The console password can be set as follows:

```
Router#configure terminal
Enter configuration commands, one per line.  End with CNTL/Z.
Router(config)#line con 0
Router(config-line)#login
Router(config-line)#password 0 conpassword
Router(config-line)#^Z
Router#
```

You have just successfully configured all of the passwords afforded to you by the Cisco IOS. However, you may have noticed that you cannot enter blank passwords. How, then, do you remove a password that you no longer want? Furthermore, how do you access your router when you have devised a password so secure that even you can't remember it?

Password Recovery and Removal

Removing unwanted passwords is a fairly easy procedure. Actually, it is the same process for removing almost any unwanted property on a Cisco router. In most cases, to remove an attribute or property, you run the same command that originally set the property but place a no in front of it.

For example, to remove the console password that was set earlier, we would run the following command:

```
Router#configure terminal
Enter configuration commands, one per line.  End with CNTL/Z.
Router(config)#line con 0
Router(config-line)#login
Router(config-line)# no password 0 conpassword
Router(config-line)#^Z
Router#
```

Notice the no preceding the word password. This tells the IOS that you no longer want to use the password for the console port. However, the IOS does not know what password you want to leave out unless you tell it. Therefore, you must include the password in the no statement.

> **Note**
>
> Leaving the password out of the no statement, as in the following example, will only tell the IOS to suppress a blank password.
>
> ```
> Router#configure terminal
> Enter configuration commands, one per line.  End with CNTL/Z.
> Router(config)#line con 0
> Router(config-line)#login
> Router(config-line)# no password 0
> Router(config-line)#^Z
> Router#
> ```
>
> Because the blank password does not exist, the command will not work.

Getting the Router Up and Running

> **Note**
>
> This same process works for many of the attributes that can be set within the Cisco IOS. For example to remove the IP address from an Ethernet port, run the following command.
>
> ```
> Router#configure terminal
> Enter configuration commands, one per line.  End with CNTL/Z.
> Router(config)#interface ethernet 0
> Router(config-if)#no ip address 10.52.189.122 255.255.0.0
> Router(config-if)#^Z
> Router#
> ```
>
> Again, the no is placed before the attribute you wish to remove.

Removing unwanted passwords is great if you can remember the passwords you want to remove. However, what can you do if you have forgotten the passwords? You need to follow the procedures for password recovery.

Most people overlook the obvious when it comes to password recovery. All of the system passwords (with the exception of the `enable secret`) are stored as plain text in both the `running-config` and `startup-config`. Therefore, before you try altering any memory registers, look at the `running-config` and the `startup-config`.

However, if the lost password is the `enable secret`, you must perform a password recovery.

> **Note**
>
> Although the following steps should work on most small and medium business-based routers (along with some enterprise series routers), you should check with the Cisco web site for the password recovery process for your particular router.

The first step you need to take is to run the `show version` command from the user prompt. This will display for you the memory register of the configuration.

```
Router>show version
Cisco Internetwork Operating System Software
IOS (tm) 1600 Software (C1600-Y-M), Version 12.0(3), RELEASE SOFTWARE (fc1)
Copyright (c) 1986-1999 by cisco Systems, Inc.
Compiled Mon 08-Feb-99 20:15 by phanguye
Image text-base: 0x02005000, data-base: 0x02455958

ROM: System Bootstrap, Version 12.0(3)T, RELEASE SOFTWARE (fc1)
ROM: 1600 Software (C1600-RBOOT-R), Version 12.0(3)T,  RELEASE SOFTWARE (fc1)
```

```
Router uptime is 1 hour, 8 minutes
System restarted by power-on
System image file is "flash:aaa0269.bin"

cisco 1605 (68360) processor (revision C) with 7680K/512K bytes of memory.
Processor board ID 17531816, with hardware revision 00000002
Bridging software.
X.25 software, Version 3.0.0.
2 Ethernet/IEEE 802.3 interface(s)
System/IO memory with parity disabled
8192K bytes of DRAM onboard
System running from RAM
8K bytes of non-volatile configuration memory.
4096K bytes of processor board PCMCIA flash (Read/Write)

Configuration register is 0x2102
```

Notice the last line produced by the command contains the configuration register. Retain this value before moving on to the next step.

> **Note:** To perform the next step successfully, you will need a terminal emulation program that is capable of transmitting a break character.

The next step is to reboot the router. While the router is coming back online (within the first 60 seconds), send a break to it. This will halt the boot process and enter the ROM monitor (ROMMON) mode, as shown.

```
System Bootstrap, Version 12.0(3)T, RELEASE SOFTWARE (fc1)
Copyright (c) 1999 by cisco Systems, Inc.
C1600 platform with 8192 Kbytes of main memory


monitor: command "boot" aborted due to user interrupt
rommon 1 >
```

Within the ROM monitor you can run the command confreg. This will step you through a configuration dialog.

```
rommon 4 > confreg


     Configuration Summary
enabled are:
load rom after netboot fails
console baud: 9600
boot: image specified by the boot system commands
      or default to: cisco2-C1600

do you wish to change the configuration? y/n  [n]:
```

Answer yes to the first question, "do you wish to change the configuration?" Then answer no to all subsequent questions until the question "ignore system config info?" appears:

```
do you wish to change the configuration? y/n  [n]:  y
enable   "diagnostic mode"? y/n  [n]:  n
enable   "use net in IP bcast address"? y/n  [n]:  n
disable  "load rom after netboot fails"? y/n  [n]:  n
enable   "use all zero broadcast"? y/n  [n]:  n
enable   "break/abort has effect"? y/n  [n]:  n
enable   "ignore system config info"? y/n  [n]
```

Answer yes to this question. Then answer no to the next set of questions, until you see the "change boot characteristics?" question. Answer yes at this prompt, and then press Enter (defaulting to option 2).

You router will ask you again whether you want to change the configuration. Respond no and reboot the router. When your router is back online, it will be in setup mode. You can either follow the setup prompts to run the entire setup dialog, or respond no and set the enable secret password manually.

Being able to configure and manage access to a Cisco router is an important step in learning the product. However, the real heart of the router is found within the functionality of the interfaces. The next section will provide an overview of how to view and configure interface information.

The next section is more of an introduction to the lessons that make up the remainder of the book.

Viewing and Configuring Interfaces

The interfaces of a Cisco router are the physical ports over which data can be routed. Interfaces can be Ethernet, Token Ring, ISDN, AUX, or any other topological port. These physical ports are the direct input and output of the router. Any data being moved by the device will flow through these interfaces.

To keep track of the interfaces, the router numbers them starting at 0. Therefore, the Ethernet ports of the Cisco 1605R are referred to as Ethernet0 and Ethernet1. This point is important when you want to view the properties of a particular interface.

To view the current status of the interface Ethernet0, use the following command.

```
Router#show interface ethernet 0
Ethernet0 is administratively down, line protocol is down
  Hardware is QUICC Ethernet, address is 00d0.58a8.e150 (bia 00d0.58a8.e150)
  MTU 1500 bytes, BW 10000 Kbit, DLY 1000 usec, rely 170/255, load 1/255
```

```
      Encapsulation ARPA, loopback not set, keepalive set (10 sec)
      ARP type: ARPA, ARP Timeout 04:00:00
      Last input never, output 01:39:31, output hang never
      Last clearing of "show interface" counters never
      Queueing strategy: fifo
      Output queue 0/40, 0 drops; input queue 0/75, 0 drops
      5 minute input rate 0 bits/sec, 0 packets/sec
      5 minute output rate 0 bits/sec, 0 packets/sec
         0 packets input, 0 bytes, 0 no buffer
         Received 0 broadcasts, 0 runts, 0 giants, 0 throttles
         0 input errors, 0 CRC, 0 frame, 0 overrun, 0 ignored, 0 abort
         0 input packets with dribble condition detected
         48 packets output, 2880 bytes, 0 underruns
         48 output errors, 0 collisions, 0 interface resets
         0 babbles, 0 late collision, 0 deferred
         48 lost carrier, 0 no carrier
         0 output buffer failures, 0 output buffers swapped out
Router#
```

> **Note:** Running the show interface command without any parameters will display the status of all of the interfaces. Depending on the model of router you have, there could be up to 100 or more interfaces on a single router.

The first line that is displayed, Ethernet0 is administratively down, line protocol is down, is the one we will be concerned with here. Everything below this line is a result (or product) of the protocols bound to the interface.

The first half of the line states that the interface Ethernet0 is administratively down. This means that the interface has not been activated (through the IOS) for the router to use. An interface on a Cisco router is not fully functional until it is administratively up and the line protocol is also up. Let's focus on bringing this interface operational.

To bring an interface administratively up, you need to change its shutdown property. This can be done through the configure command.

```
Router#configure terminal
Enter configuration commands, one per line.  End with CNTL/Z.
Router(config)#interface ethernet 0
Router(config-if)#no shutdown
Router(config-if)#
01:58:38: %LINK-3-UPDOWN: Interface Ethernet0, changed state to up
```

After using the configure command (to enter the global configuration), we tell the IOS that we want to edit the interface Ethernet0. The prompt Router(configure-if)# indicates that we are editing the router's interfaces.

Getting the Router Up and Running

The command that controls whether the interface is administratively up or down is `shutdown`. However, rather than using a different form of the command to bring the interface up, you simply place the `no` keyword before the `shutdown` command. This tells the IOS not to shut down the interface `Ethernet0`.

At this point our interface is now administratively up, but the line protocol is still down (as seen in the excerpt below from the output of `sh int e 0`).

```
Router#show interface ethernet 0
Ethernet0 is administratively up, line protocol is down
  Hardware is QUICC Ethernet, address is 00d0.58a8.e150 (bia 00d0.58a8.e150)
  MTU 1500 bytes, BW 10000 Kbit, DLY 1000 usec, rely 170/255, load 1/255
```

Because the line protocol is still down, our interface is not entirely functional. (In fact, it cannot really do much of anything.) Therefore, our next task is to bring up the line protocol. The first part to bringing up a line protocol is to bind a protocol to the interface. In this example we will be configuring IP.

The first step to bringing up an IP interface is to configure an address.

```
Router#configure terminal
Enter configuration commands, one per line.  End with CNTL/Z.
Router(config)#interface ethernet 0
Router(config-if)#ip address 10.52.189.122 255.255.0.0
Router(config-if)#^Z
Router#
02:16:09: %SYS-5-CONFIG_I: Configured from console by console
Router#
```

The parameters for configuring an IP address on an interface are the address and the subnet mask. The command `ip address` tells the IOS that you want to configure the specified address, with the specified subnet mask, on the current interface.

```
ip address 10.52.189.122 255.255.0.0
```

However, configuring the address alone will not change the interface's status from down to up. The second step to bringing up the line protocol is to give it something to communicate with. The router will keep the protocol down until it has determined that the interface can be used. Just attaching a hub to the interface port will be enough to make the line protocol come up.

Once the router has been attached to a hub through the configured interface, the `sh int` command displays the following status for `Ethernet0`.

```
Router#show interface ethernet 0
Ethernet0 is administratively up, line protocol is up
  Hardware is QUICC Ethernet, address is 00d0.58a8.e150 (bia 00d0.58a8.e150)
  MTU 1500 bytes, BW 10000 Kbit, DLY 1000 usec, rely 170/255, load 1/255
```

To configure any of your other interfaces, follow the previous steps, replacing the `int e0` with the label of the interface you wish to configure.

Now that you have successfully configured your first Cisco router interface, let's take a look at some of the other information you should be familiar with.

Creating a Banner

One of the more fun things you can do on a Cisco router is to configure the different banners that appear at the command prompts. Every line that can be used to access the router can have a message banner configured on it.

For example, to configure a message banner on the console login, you would follow these steps.

```
Router#configure terminal
Router(config)#banner motd ! This is the message of the day !
Router(config)#
```

Any character you want can replace the exclamation points; this character becomes the delimiting character. That is, the router will know that your message is finished because it will reach the delimiting character. Table 4.4 outlines the different banners available in the Cisco IOS and where they appear.

TABLE 4.4 Various Cisco Banner Messages

Banner	Placement
Banner MOTD	The message of the day banner is displayed before any other banners on every line. That is, before the login prompt, the user will always see the MOTD banner.
Banner Exec	The Exec banner is displayed (after the MOTD) for anyone entering the router through a virtual terminal.
Banner Incoming	The Incoming banner is displayed only to users who are accessing the router through a reverse Telnet session.
Banner Login	The login banner is displayed after the MOTD banner to signal a login prompt.

Summary

- Booting a router that has never been configured will initiate the Cisco IOS Setup Dialog.
- The setup dialog will prompt the user for all of the essential information needed to create a functional router configuration.
- The setup dialog is intended only to supply the router with just enough information to be operational. The user should always tweak the router's configuration after using the setup dialog.
- If the router has previously been configured, the setup dialog can still be initiated by running the `setup` command from privilege mode.

Q&A

Q Why does the router user still need to tweak the router's setup after running the setup dialog?

A The dialog prompts only for the essential information concerning the router and its surroundings. That is, the router prompts only for what it needs to get up and running on the network (that is, to have at least one functional, addressed interface). The setup dialog make no concessions for items such as routing protocols and WICs.

Quiz

Questions

1. What is the name of the unique type of Ethernet cable used for console connections?
2. What commands are used to enter line configuration mode?
3. Which banner type is displayed at login on every type of line?
4. What command is used to initiate the setup dialog?

Answers

1. A rollover cable
2. `line` (from global configuration mode)
3. MOTD (Message of The Day)
4. `setup` (from privilege mode)

Exercises

1. A user configures the MOTD banner as follows:

   ```
   Router#configure terminal
   Router(config)#banner motd B This is Sophia's router! So Back Off B
   Router(config)#
   ```

   However, when the message is displayed it looks like this:

   ```
   This is Sophia's router! So
   ```

   Why?

   > **Note**
   >
   > The delimiting character chosen was the letter B. Therefore the router stopped displaying the message at the first instance of that character. However, in this example, that first instance was the B in the word "Back."

2. Given the following two configuration files, what will be the IP address of the interface `Ethernet1` after the router is rebooted?

   ```
   running-config:
   Current configuration:
   !
   version 12.0
   service config
   service timestamps debug uptime
   service timestamps log uptime
   no service password-encryption
   !
   hostname Router
   !
   enable secret 5 $1$Zk7H$Svxp5px.vyLcRg7hDXo8Z1
   enable password enable
   !
   ip subnet-zero
   no ip routing
   !
   !
   !
   interface Ethernet0
    ip address 10.52.189.122 255.255.0.0
    no ip directed-broadcast
    no ip route-cache
    no shutdown
    no cdp enable
   !
   interface Ethernet1
   ```

```
    no ip address 198.56.34.1 255.255.0.0
    no ip directed-broadcast
    no ip route-cache
    no shutdown
    no cdp enable
!
ip classless
!
!
line con 0
 exec-timeout 0 0
 transport input none
line vty 0 4
 password vterm
 login
!
end

startup-config:

Current configuration:
!
version 12.0
service config
service timestamps debug uptime
service timestamps log uptime
no service password-encryption
!
hostname Router
!
enable secret 5 $1$Zk7H$Svxp5px.vyLcRg7hDXo8Z1
enable password enable
!
ip subnet-zero
no ip routing
!
!
!
interface Ethernet0
 ip address 10.52.189.122 255.255.0.0
 no ip directed-broadcast
 no ip route-cache
 no shutdown
 no cdp enable
!
interface Ethernet1
 no ip address 10.75.24.125 255.255.0.0
 no ip directed-broadcast
 no ip route-cache
 no shutdown
 no cdp enable
```

```
!
ip classless
!
!
line con 0
 exec-timeout 0 0
 transport input none
line vty 0 4
 password vterm
 login
!
end
```

> **Note** 10.75.24.125

3. How would you set the password for the Telnet port to goaway?

> **Note**
> ```
> Router#configure terminal
> Enter configuration commands, one per line.  End with CNTL/Z.
> 
> 
> Router#config t
> Enter configuration commands, one per line.  End with CNTL/Z.
> Router(config)#
> Router(config)#line vty 0 4
> Router(config-line)#login
> Router(config-line)#password 0 goaway
> 
>     or
> 
> Router#setup  (and set the virtual terminal password to
> "goaway")
> ```

WEEK 1

DAY 7

Backing Up Cisco Routers

This lesson focuses on helping you protect a Cisco router and its configurations. Although being able to configure a router is important, it doesn't mean anything if you lose it all. That is, your router's configuration is only as good as the last time it was saved (or in some cases, only as good as its backup). A valuable skill in any Cisco user is the ability to recognize where and when backups are needed and implement them effectively.

To examine the processes involved in protecting a Cisco router, we will consider the following topics.

- Physical router backups
- Cisco IOS configuration file backups

The first half of this lesson deals with the design-related aspect to protecting your equipment. Concepts such as utilizing multiple power supplies and hot swappable routers form the basis for physical router backups.

Because there is little Cisco configuration involved in hardware protection, the first few sections of this lesson cover more theory than practice. However, to become a well-rounded engineer, you need to be well versed in both the theory and the practice of creating effective backup scenarios.

The second half of this lesson will focus on backing up the router's data files. Earlier in this book we learned that the bulk of the router's functional configuration settings are retained in two files: `running-config` and `startup-config`. We will discuss ways to save and protect these files in the event of a router disaster.

This chapter not only will teach you how to protect your investment (both monetary and intellectual); it will familiarize you with the internal functions that make Cisco routers work. Understanding these functions is critical to learning Cisco router and routing technology.

Physical Backups

Physical backups protect your Cisco router on the hardware level. That is, physical backups pertain to protecting routers from such events as power loss and interface failure. Such events are not uncommon and can cripple a network.

This form of protection is often cost prohibitive for some environments, while others may not be critical enough to warrant the extra hardware.

If the routing environment you are planning (or working in) can be considered mission critical, you should pay particular attention to these methods for physical router backups. Many enterprises require that their routing environments be backed up to allow the least amount of downtime possible. Such networks typically have multiple routers within multiple subnets, connecting two or more geographic locations. These networks rely heavily on the functionality of their routers, and any downtime can be equated to lost revenue.

> **Note** Different businesses and managers will have different opinions of what is mission critical. Some smaller, remote areas of a particular environment may be able to suffer an outage and not affect the overall revenue stream of the business. These networks are not mission critical.

Several forms of router hardware backup will be examined in this lesson. The most basic (and usually the easiest to implement) is a backup power supply. There are two kinds of basic power supply backups:

- Uninterruptible power supplies (UPS)
- Multiple power units (Cisco Hardware)

Installing an uninterruptible power supply (UPS) will protect the power flowing into the router. A UPS will generally be placed between the router and the building's wall sockets. Such placement protects the routing equipment in two ways.

The UPS will force any electricity flowing to the router to pass through itself first. This allows the UPS to suppress any surges in the electrical current that may damage the routing equipment. Electrical surges (especially during storms) can be extremely harmful and pose a great threat to most devices.

> **Note** Not all UPSs offer surge protection. Check the manufacturer's documentation before assuming your UPS will protect your equipment against electrical surges.

UPSs also function (mainly) to detect a loss of electricity in the building's main power grid. Upon encountering such a loss, the UPS will activate an internal battery that will supply power to the router. One important factor to remember about UPSs is that your network will not be very functional if just the routing equipment is protected. All of the devices and computers need to be protected for your protection plan to have an impact during an emergency.

> **Note** The battery on a UPS is not meant to power the router through daily operation. Most UPSs contain enough energy to power a router for 20 minutes. Most manufacturers' guidelines describe this as enough time to power down safely any equipment that can be affected by the power outage.

If using a UPS is not enough protection for your network, there is another option. Some Cisco devices can accept a second power unit. That is, the router itself can hold more than one power unit so that if one fails, the second will continue to power the router until the first is replaced.

Another means of protection is an offline hardware backup. This usually takes the form of a single router that matches the one in your production environment. These routers normally keep a complete copy of your configuration files. Consequently, the router can stand in when a serious hardware problem incapacitates your main router.

The offline backup router is a good solution for companies large enough to have fairly complex routing environments but in which the router hardware is standardized; in other words, where the same series (and preferably the same model) of Cisco router is prevalent throughout the networking environment.

The last form of physical backup we will cover is an online hardware backup, also referred to as a redundant system. Companies can build dual links between networks, with each link serviced by a separate router. If one router were to fail, the second would still service the route.

Backup Power Supplies

One of the most common hardware failures to affect router functionality is a power outage. Unfortunately, power outages are hard if not impossible to predict. They often happen without warning. UPSs, though not a Cisco-specific product, offer good protection against such a catastrophe.

> **Note:** UPSs are fairly generic in nature and do not relate directly to the overall topic of this book. However, they do provide a good tie-in to the subject of secondary power units.

An uninterruptible power supply stands between your router and the public power grid. The UPS (also called a battery backup) stores a predetermined amount of battery power. In the event of a power failure, the battery will continue to power the router.

However, one thing to keep in mind is that a typical UPS is not meant to run your router for a long period of time. The purpose of a UPS is to give you just enough time to shut down your routers properly, thus reducing the risk of data loss and corruption.

A UPS simply plugs into your company's standard wall outlet. Your router can then be plugged into the UPS to ensure some level of router functionality in the event of a power outage. However, if your backup needs entail more than just allowing enough time to shut down the equipment, you may need a generator.

Enterprises with greater routing needs usually implement power generators to supply their routers with a (potentially) limitless amount of electricity. Many of these generators output direct current (DC). For these systems, some modifications may be required to your Cisco routers.

Most models of enterprise series Cisco routers accept a DC power supply (see Day 2, "Understanding Cisco Hardware,"). DC power supplies are hard-wired from your generator (or larger battery backup) directly to the router. The process for wiring a DC power unit onto a Cisco router is not complicated; however, the unit itself is usually considered an upgrade. Cisco DC power supplies are not an option for everyone; most Cisco routers are not capable of utilizing such hardware.

> **Note:** Even though Cisco DC power units are available only for enterprise (including ISP class) routers, few actually come with them as standard equipment. These routers are for much larger environments than we deal with in this book.

> One form of Cisco-based power backup used on a fairly regular basis is the redundant power supply. Many Cisco routers have up to four bays (located in the rear of the chassis) to accept multiple power units. Most companies take advantage of these open bays by installing secondary and tertiary power units.

Cisco Multiple Power Units

Having multiple power units can protect your routers from two major problems. The first is power unit failure. Such a failure can incapacitate a router for hours until a suitable replacement is located.

The second problem is electrical storms and power surges. Although multiple power units cannot protect a router in the same way a power surge protector can, you do have a greater chance to survive one if you have a redundant power supply.

Because power units have a constant supply of energy flowing through them, they often generate and retain a substantial amount of heat. This heat can wear away at the internal components of the power unit, making the power unit more susceptible to sudden failure than other parts of the router's hardware are.

Having two or more power units present in your router can protect you in the event of such a failure. Cisco routers will take advantage of multiple power units by automatically switching between them if one fails. For this to occur, both units need to be plugged in and turned on.

However, if your network is critical and your routers warrant a little extra protection, you may want to look into offline and online backup routers.

Backup Routers

Backup routers fall into two categories: online and offline. Offline backup routers are generally used in environments where the engineers have agreed on a standardized platform. They generally remain off the network until they are needed to stand in for most of the routers in the environment. Online routers, on the other hand, are always in place and functional within the network. When one router fails, an online backup automatically recovers its routes.

Both offline and online backup methods require additional Cisco IOS configurations (covered later in this lesson). These configurations include processes for porting router configuration files from one Cisco router to another.

> Two of the most useful tools when determining a suitable backup strategy for your routers are a paper and pencil. Diagram as much of the environment as possible and try implementing different solutions on paper before committing resources to the project.

Offline Spares

If your environment uses multiple Cisco routers of the same series, you may be a candidate for using an offline spare as a form of backup. Offline routers are used in environments where router downtime must be minimized but where online backups are cost prohibitive.

The reason for using offline backups in a routed environment is simple: to have one router available that can easily stand in for and perform the functions of any of your other critical devices. Using offline router backups does require more planning at the design phase of the network's construction; however, it's worth it in the event of a router failure.

Let's examine exactly how an offline spare can be used in a routing environment. Figure 7.1 illustrates a routed network in which the main operational routers have all been standardized.

For the sake of the example, let's assume that all of the routers in Figure 7.1 are Cisco 2600 Series routers with two Ethernet ports. The routers are interconnected, and some connect back to a central hub/switch.

Note For simplicity's sake, some design and hardware elements may have been omitted from the figure. These elements have no bearing on the present example.

If router D were to fail, the route between two major segments of the environment would be destroyed. Networks A, B, and C would be isolated from networks D, E, and F. Getting this router replaced would be a critical matter.

If an offline backup were present on the network, it could easily be placed in the network where router D resides. However, as you may have deduced by now, just putting a router in place does not mean it will function.

FIGURE 7.1

A standardized routing environment.

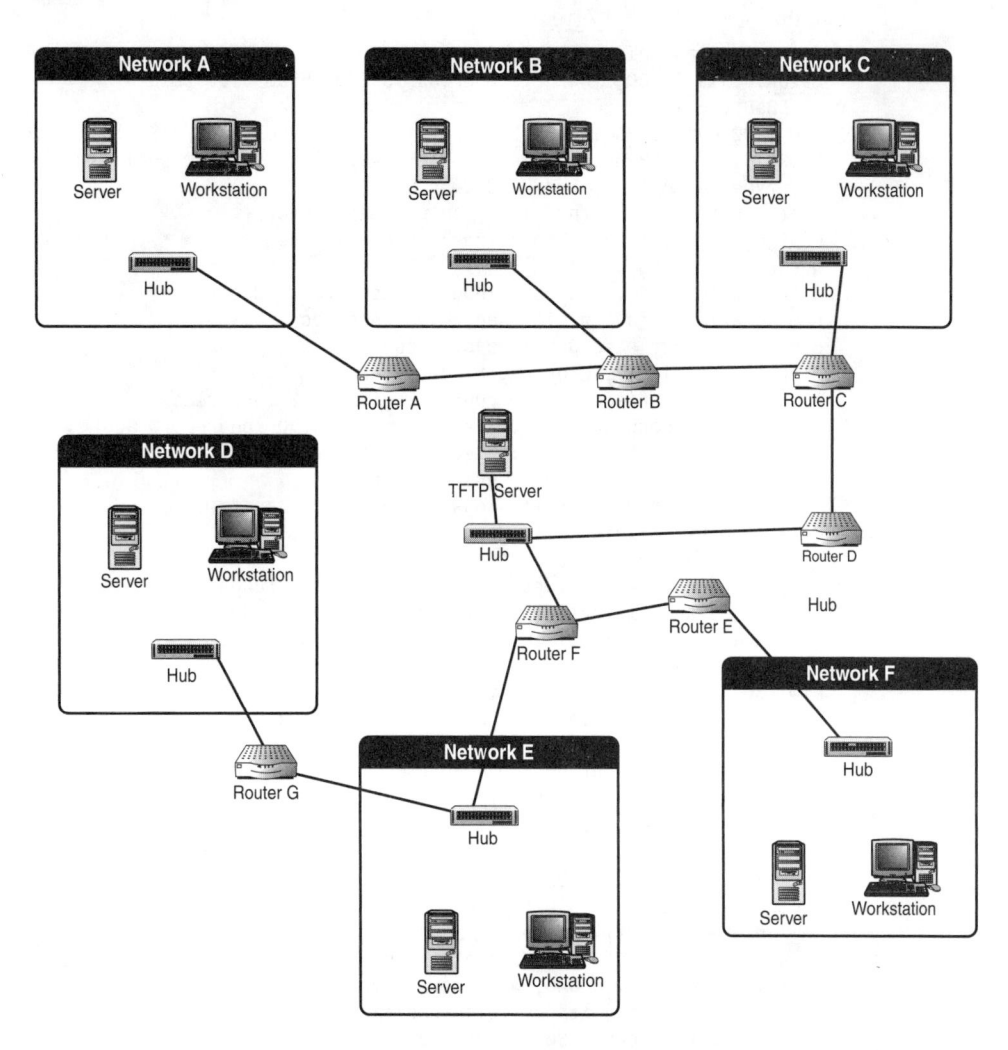

While offline backups can obtain their routing tables from the other routers on the network, configurations for the interfaces need to be done manually. The best way to ensure you have a configuration that matches that of the failed router is to keep configuration backups.

- Confirm that the router has power (30 seconds).
- At the first sign of a communication outage, check the physical cables on the router's interfaces (1 minute).

- Use the show interface command to view the status of the failed router's interfaces. (By doing this you are attempting to confirm that the interfaces affected are "protocol down" and not "administratively down.") A show interface should look like this:

```
Ethernet0 is administratively up, line protocol is down
  Hardware is QUICC Ethernet, address is 00d0.58a8.e150 (bia 00d0.58a8.e150)
  MTU 1500 bytes, BW 10000 Kbit, DLY 1000 usec, rely 252/255, load 1/255
  Encapsulation ARPA, loopback not set, keepalive set (10 sec)
  ARP type: ARPA, ARP Timeout 04:00:00
  Last input never, output 1w0d, output hang never
  Last clearing of "show interface" counters never
  Queueing strategy: fifo
  Output queue 0/40, 0 drops; input queue 0/75, 0 drops
  5 minute input rate 0 bits/sec, 0 packets/sec
  5 minute output rate 0 bits/sec, 0 packets/sec
     0 packets input, 0 bytes, 0 no buffer
     Received 0 broadcasts, 0 runts, 0 giants, 0 throttles
     0 input errors, 0 CRC, 0 frame, 0 overrun, 0 ignored, 0 abort
     0 input packets with dribble condition detected
     3 packets output, 180 bytes, 0 underruns
     3 output errors, 0 collisions, 0 interface resets
     0 babbles, 0 late collision, 0 deferred
     3 lost carrier, 0 no carrier
     0 output buffer failures, 0 output buffers swapped out
Ethernet1 is administratively up, line protocol is down
  Hardware is QUICC Ethernet, address is 00d0.58a8.e151 (bia 00d0.58a8.e151)
  MTU 1500 bytes, BW 10000 Kbit, DLY 1000 usec, rely 252/255, load 1/255
  Encapsulation ARPA, loopback not set, keepalive set (10 sec)
  ARP type: ARPA, ARP Timeout 04:00:00
  Last input never, output 1w0d, output hang never
  Last clearing of "show interface" counters never
  Queueing strategy: fifo
  Output queue 0/40, 0 drops; input queue 0/75, 0 drops
  5 minute input rate 0 bits/sec, 0 packets/sec
  5 minute output rate 0 bits/sec, 0 packets/sec
     0 packets input, 0 bytes, 0 no buffer
     Received 0 broadcasts, 0 runts, 0 giants, 0 throttles
     0 input errors, 0 CRC, 0 frame, 0 overrun, 0 ignored, 0 abort
     0 input packets with dribble condition detected
     3 packets output, 180 bytes, 0 underruns
     3 output errors, 0 collisions, 0 interface resets
     0 babbles, 0 late collision, 0 deferred
     3 lost carrier, 0 no carrier
     0 output buffer failures, 0 output buffers swapped out
```

Both interfaces are "protocol down" but administratively up, which indicates a further problem. By this time, roughly two minutes of router work time have elapsed.

Assuming that you noticed the problem within the first five minutes and then got to the location of the router within three, a total of 10 minutes of downtime have already elapsed.

- By this time a decision has been made to replace the router with the offline spare.
- The failed router is removed from the network (2 minutes).
- The offline spare is put in at the failed router's physical location (2 minutes).
- The Basic Setup dialog is run to enable the functionality of one Ethernet interface (3 minutes).
- The configuration files of the failed router are obtained from the TFTP server (2 minutes).
- The router is restarted, and a network update is kicked off to replicate the routing tables of the neighboring routers.

The entire process for utilizing and configuring an offline router could require as much as 20 minutes of network downtime. For some companies this is an unacceptable amount of business loss. For these environments, online spares may be the key.

Although keeping an offline spare is the scenario we focus on (given the topic of this book), you should be aware of the other options available to protect your routing hardware and environment. Therefore, we briefly cover online spares.

Online Spares

An online spare requires the most planning and configuration, but the reward is well worth it. In many cases, creating redundant routes between locations can save a business both downtime and configuration time in the event of a router failure. This can provide great peace of mind to those who work in environments where router failures are common or router downtime equals a loss of revenue.

Most companies do not create a redundant route for every link on the network. Rather, the most important links are identified and these routers are cloned onto a second set of Cisco routers.

When an online spare is in place, it can serve two functions. First, the router can just sit on the network waiting for a failure. As soon as the primary router fails, the secondary (online backup) immediately takes over and begins managing the failed router's routes. When a router is used in this capacity, it performs no network functions until the primary router fails. The second option available for online spare routers is load balancing, allowing the router to participate in the network while waiting for a failure to occur.

The second function an online spare can perform is as a load-balancing device. That is, the online spare can share the routing duties with the primary router, with each responsible for a certain percentage of the traffic flowing over the route. If one router were to fail, the other would simple pick up the remaining percentage of the traffic.

Let's first examine how redundant routes are designed. Figure 7.2 illustrates the network from our previous example with a redundant route implemented.

FIGURE 7.2

Redundant route.

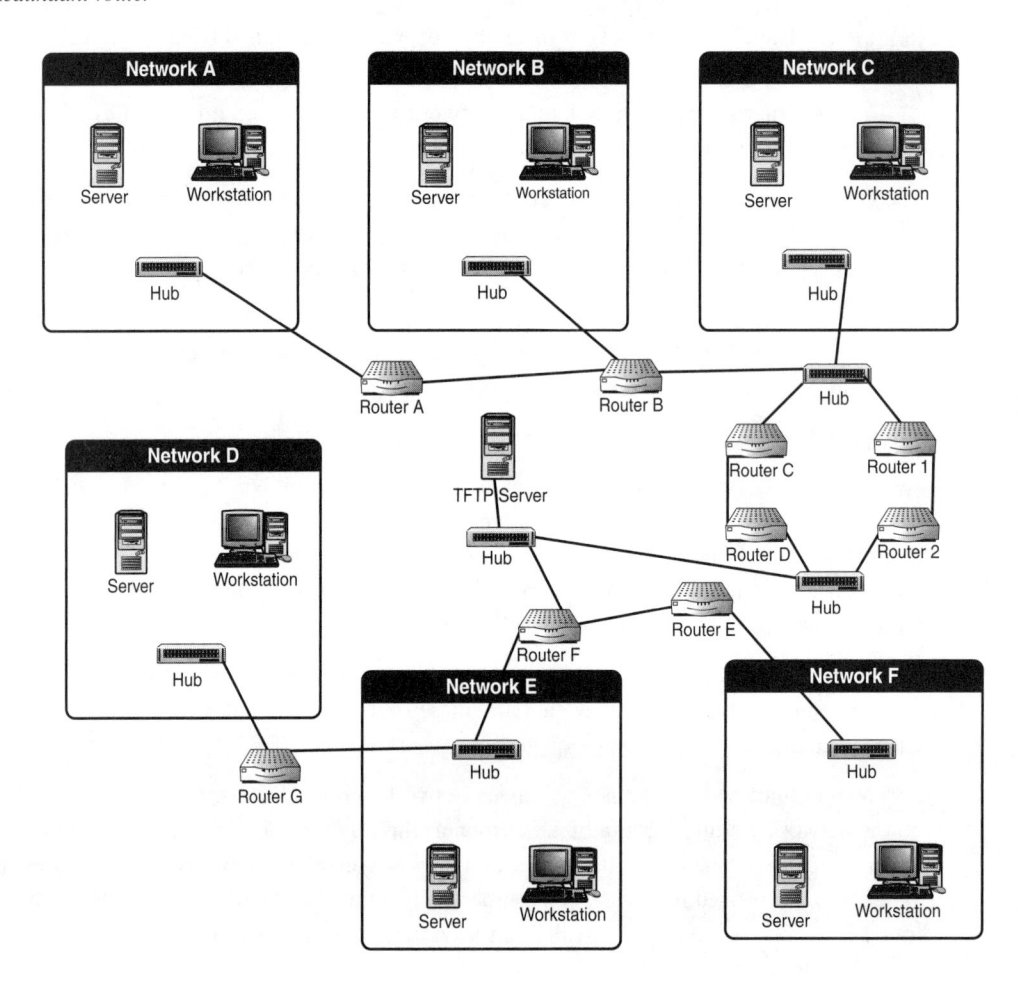

In this scenario routers 1 and 2 serve as online backups for routers D and E. As you can see, hubs/switches feed into both routers. For a scenario such as this, it is highly recommended that you use switches rather than hubs to provide data to the two routers.

> **Note** A hub will generally broadcast information to every port simultaneously. Therefore, you cannot guarantee that one router will be favored over another.

By using switches (especially Cisco switches), you can establish a routing path to the primary router. Thus, within the Cisco switch you could create a static route that would feed only router D. At the point at which router D fails, you could simply deactivate that static route and reactivate one that feeds router 1.

Although this solution may be effective, you may question its worth. If you have the spare routers already sitting in the environment, why not use them?

Load balancing is the most popular form of router redundancy. The configuration required to implement load balancing is fairly complex and can be accomplished only on specific Cisco hardware. Figure 7.3 illustrates the same network scenario we have been working with, with load balancing now implemented.

Notice that the only real change to this diagram is the addition of two links—between router D and router 1, and between router E and router 2. These links help the routers communicate with each other and negotiate the load balancing.

Several configuration changes must be made to the switches that feed these routers as well. Rather than one static route that feeds one router, two routes should be established with equal metrics. Giving the routes equal metrics will ensure that the switch will not favor one path over the other.

> **Note** Although it is outside the scope of this topic, an implementation of Spanning Tree Protocol (STP) may be required on the switches to guard against routing loops.

With load balancing used in the two redundant routes, each router can be assigned a certain percentage of the overall traffic. For example, router D can be configured to handle 40% of the line traffic while router 1 carries the remaining 60%. If either router fails, the other will automatically sense it and take on the remaining traffic.

FIGURE 7.3

Load balancing.

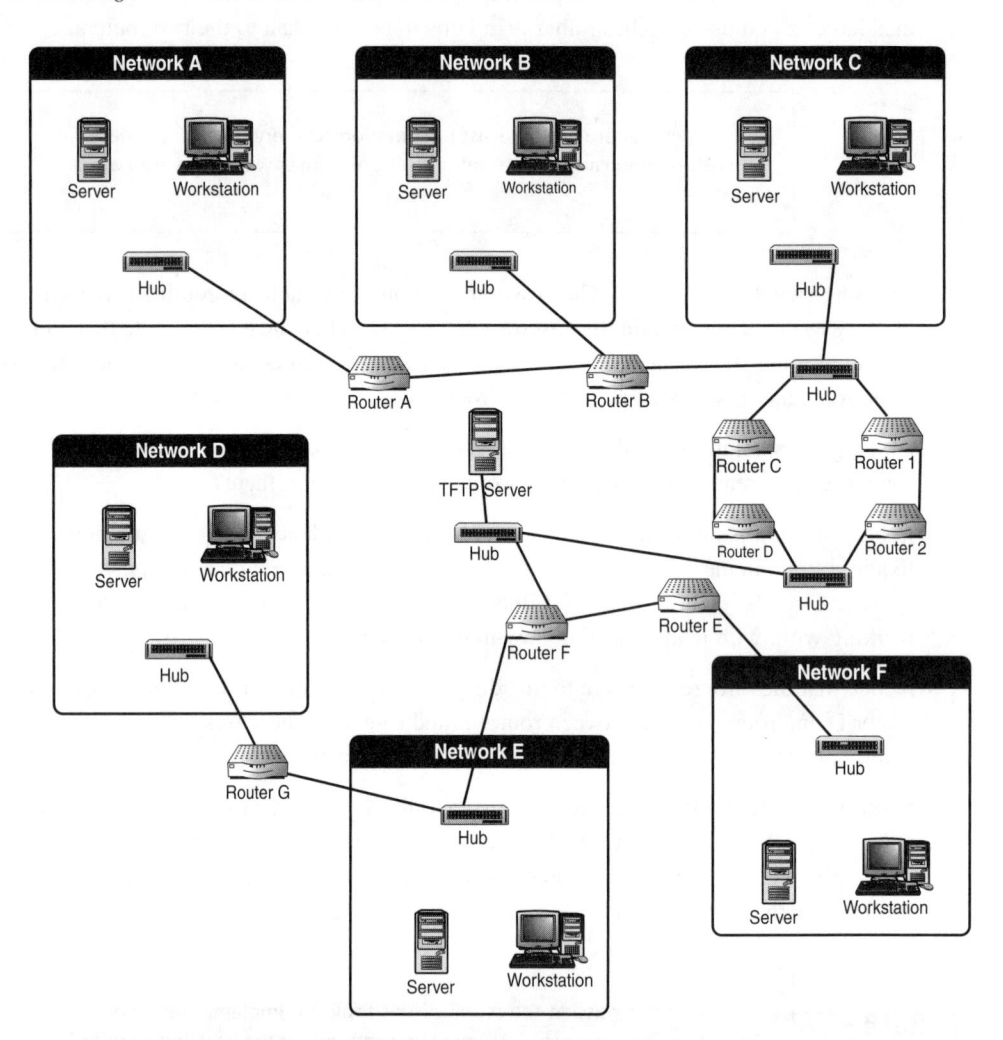

Complex configurations such as this can be achieved only with Cisco's high-end routers, such as the 7000 Series. These routers are built for complicated environments where multiple redundant paths may be present between any two points in a network.

This part of the lesson, though not particularly in-depth, should provide a good overview of the different scenarios available to users of Cisco equipment. However, the real focus remains the process of saving Cisco router configurations.

Cisco IOS Configuration File Backups

The remainder of this lesson will walk you through the processes needed to back up your Cisco router's configuration files. Keeping current backups of your routers' entire configuration is important, no matter how large or small, critical or noncritical, your environment is.

A common adage in the technology field is "You're only as good as your last backup." This is especially true within the realm of routers. Because the majority of Cisco router memory is volatile, one unexpected outage could be devastating to an environment. Therefore, it is a good practice to maintain continual, up-to-date backups of your configurations.

The What and Why of Router Configuration Backups

Deciding what to back up on your router is fairly easy: everything you can. Keep in mind that many of the router's configurations are kept in volatile memory. Therefore, you should keep reliable backups of these files in the event of an emergency.

The first file you need to back up is `running-config`. This file is the most important, because it contains the configuration settings for the router's present operation. If your router were to fail and a current copy of `running-config` were not available, the settings would need to be rebuilt from scratch. The `running-config` file is kept only in the router's RAM, so the file is lost every time the router is shut down or loses power.

The second file you should consider including in your backup plan is `startup-config`. As discussed on Day 6, the `startup-config` and the `running-config` files should be identical. Unfortunately, that is not always the case. Even the best engineers test out settings in `running-config` and forget to copy them to `startup-config`. Therefore, keeping current copies of both files is the best approach.

> **Note**: In almost all instances your `running-config` and your `startup-config` should be identical. However, there are cases where a configuration change in the `running-config` is not copied to the `startup-config` (or an incorrect change *was* copied to the `startup-config`). In either case, saving both files is just an added insurance against problems.

The final file from your Cisco router that should be included in any backup plan is the Cisco IOS image. Although IOS corruption is the least likely cause of router failure, it is a possibility. A copy of your router's IOS image is also useful when you purchase an offline spare (which may come equipped with a newer or older version). After obtaining an offline spare, you can re-image it with your IOS to ensure compatibility.

The first priority of any Cisco engineer implementing a backup plan is to create backups of the `running-config` and `startup-config` files.

`running-config` and `startup-config`

The best way to back up a router's configuration is by copying the configuration files to a TFTP server. A TFTP server can be a great tool for retaining external router data. A TFTP server can hold copies of all of your IOS images and copies of your `running-config` and `startup-config`. Although this is not a foolproof solution, it is a very good way to ensure that you have a backup of your router for emergencies.

> **Note**
>
> Keep in mind that, as with any backup, items stored on a TFTP server are only as good as the last time they were saved. Therefore, if you save your configurations to the server, change multiple settings, and then restore from the server, you will lose all of your changes.

Keeping Backups without a TFTP Server

If you do not have access to or cannot provide TFTP services on your router's networking environment, there are some basic precautions you can take to ensure that your configurations are as secure as possible. Although your best protection is copying the configuration files completely off of your router, simply keeping your `startup-config` as current as possible will take you a long way.

You should get into the habit of using the `copy` command no matter which backup plan you subscribe to. However, this command is even more important if you do not implement a TFTP server.

> **Note**
>
> Copying `running-config` to `startup-config` will keep your `startup-config` as current as possible. Remember that the router will load configuration settings from the `startup-config` file only at boot. Therefore, any settings from `running-config` that are not in `startup-config` will **not** be retained.

To copy your `running-config` to your `startup-config`, use the `copy` command from privilege mode.

```
Router#copy run start
```

This one command will copy any settings currently running on your router to the `startup-config` file. From here, if the router were to fail, the `startup-config` settings would be automatically copied back to `running-config` by the IOS.

No user intervention is required to copy `startup-config` settings to `running-config` at router boot. However, you as the user do need to copy the `running-config` to the `startup-config` to have the latest configuration available at the time of router bootup.

Keeping a copy of your router's current IOS image without a TFTP server is a little less involved. The easiest way to store a good copy of your IOS image is to download one from the Cisco CCO (Cisco Connection Online; see Day 3, "Understanding the Cisco IOS") site. Unfortunately, most Cisco routers do not come with a copy of the IOS image on independent media (it should be preinstalled by Cisco). Therefore, without a TFTP server to copy the image to, you need to obtain an image from Cisco.

> **Note**
> To obtain a Cisco IOS image from Cisco, you have two options. The first is to download it from the Cisco CCO Web site (www.cisco.com). This site requires a secure login and password, which can also be obtained from Cisco.
>
> The second way to receive a Cisco IOS image is to purchase the IOS media from a Cisco reseller.

Once an off-router version of the Cisco IOS is available, there are tools to port that image to the router. The most reliable is the Cisco Remote Software Loader. The Cisco RSL is a Windows-based program that automatically upgrades the IOS on your router without the need of a TFTP server. The RSL contains a TFTP agent; however, it cannot act as a stand-alone TFTP server.

While these scenarios may not represent the best ways to back up your Cisco router's configuration, they are available options if no other methods are at your disposal.

Using a TFTP Server

To back up any of the router's configuration files, use the `copy` command. This command allows you to move files from the router to different areas in the router or to external destinations. If your router (or its configuration) become corrupt, you can again use the `copy` command to copy the files back from the TFTP server to the router.

> **Note**
> The `copy` command is available only with the privilege mode of the Cisco command interpreter.

> **Note:** A TFTP (Trivial File Transfer Protocol) server sends files to devices under a lightweight version of FTP that operates on the User Datagram Protocol (UDP) level. TFTP is incompatible with full-featured FTP.

You may recognize the process from Day 3, "Understanding the Cisco IOS," where we discussed TFTPing a Cisco IOS image from a server to the router. The processes we follow in this section will not differ much from those we covered on Day 3. The use of the copy command persists through both, however, we will cover added functions that allow for the movement of the specific configuration files to and from the server.

First you must identify the files you wish to retain as backups. Generally, you can expect to save only startup-config or running-config, since (if you keep up the router's maintenance) they should be identical.

To copy files to a TFTP server, follow these steps:

```
Router#copy running-config tftp
Address or name of remote host []? 10.4.16.152
Destination filename [running-config]?routera-running-config
```

Notice that the command structure is the same as that used for coping running-config to startup-config. After you specify the TFTP server as the target of the copy, the IOS will prompt you for the server's IP address. Supply the address and destination file name, and the IOS will create a copy of your configuration on the TFTP server.

If the TFTP server is accessible from the router, this one command will supply you with a current copy of the router's configuration.

> **Note:** If you have multiple routers, plan on changing the Destination filename parameter of the copy to reflect the specific router to which the configuration belongs. TFTP servers copy to and from the root directory only. Therefore, if you were to copy the running-config settings from every router to the same TFTP server without changing the file name, you would be overwriting the file every time.

If a router on your network fails, and you implement an offline spare, you need to copy the configuration for the failed router to the offline spare. To do this you first need to configure an interface on the offline router. Normally, you will want to invoke the Basic Setup Dialog to configure one interface quickly (as described on Day 6).

After an interface has been configured, you can copy the configuration file from the TFTP server to the offline router as follows:

```
Router#copy tftp startup-config
Address or name of remote host []? 10.4.16.152
Source filename [startup-config]?routera-running-config
...

Router#reload

...
```

Notice that rather than copy the backup `running-config` back to `running-config`, we send it to `startup-config`. By doing this we ensure that the router will not lose the configuration if something were to happen. However, because `startup-config` is read only during the boot process, we need to issue a `reload` command to tell the router to reboot. Your offline router should now be fully functional

At this point we have covered most of the basic topics needed to understand Cisco routers. It is now time to move on to a more advanced subject. We will begin with Day 8, "Understanding Routed Protocols."

Summary

- One of the most important measures a Cisco router user can undertake is an act of preventive maintenance. You should always try to take the measures needed to back up your Cisco router.
- Cisco router hardware can be protected through the use of UPSs, online or offline spares, or a combination of these.
- The Cisco software can be protected through a combination of TFTP software backups.

Q&A

Q Why should I keep backups of both the `running-config` and the `startup-config` if the router ensures that they are identical during the boot process?

A The answer is that many changes may occur, and unless the engineer performing the changes remembers to copy the `running-config` to the `startup-config`, those changes would be lost during an outage.

Quiz

Questions

1. What command is used to move files from one location to another?
2. What do most enterprise-level Cisco routers have that distinguishes their power supplies from those of other router series?
3. True or False: The `running-config` is copied over the `startup-config` every time the router is shut down.
4. What can a UPS protect against?

Answers

1. `copy`
2. DC (direct current) support
3. False. The `startup-config` is copied to the `running-config` during the boot process.
4. UPSs can protect against power failures. Some models of UPS can also protect your equipment against surges.

Exercises

1. Using the `copy` command, send a router configuration from the IOS to a TFTP server and back again to simulate the failure of a router and its replacement by an offline spare.

Note

```
Router#copy runnning-config tftp
Address or name of remote host []? 10.4.16.152
Destination filename [running-config]?routera-running-config

Router#copy tftp startup-config
Address or name of remote host []? 10.4.16.152
Source filename [startup-config]?routera-running-config
...

Router#reload

...
```

Week 2

Protocols and Functionality

8   Understanding Routed Protocols

9   Learning IP Basics

10 Learning How to Configure IP on Cisco Routers

11 Understanding Segmented Networks

12 Learning How to Configure IPX

13 Understanding WAN Protocols

14 Understanding Routing Protocols

WEEK 2

DAY 8

Understanding Routed Protocols

In this lesson we take a short break from configuring Cisco routers. Routers (in general) need one thing to successfully move data from one location to another: a protocol. Therefore, this lesson explains exactly how protocols work and how they relate to routers. The remainder of this book deals (in one form or another) with configuring the way a router works in relation to the protocols that are in use. For that reason it is important to have a solid understanding of how protocols really work.

In this lesson we will cover the following concepts.

- Protocol categorization
- The OSI model
- Protocol divisions and classifications
- Protocol encapsulation

Protocol Categorization

Protocols can be categorized as either "routed" or "routing." Routed protocols are what most people think of when they picture a protocol. Routed protocols are protocols that can be *routed* by other devices. Common protocols such as IP and IPX are routed protocols.

Routing protocols, on the other hand, are protocols that routers use to communicate with each other (while routing the routed protocols). Routing protocols include RIP and OSPF. These protocols help routers move data in the most efficient way possible.

> **Note**
> To understand Cisco routers fully, you need to have a good grasp of protocols. Therefore, we will cover many protocols over the course of this text. Before the completion of this book, you will be introduced to the following routed protocols:
> - IP (Internet Protocol)
> - IPX (Internetwork Packet Exchange)
>
> You will also be introduced to the following routing protocols:
> - RIP (Routing Information Protocol)
> - IGRP (Interior Gateway Routing Protocol)
> - EIGRP (Enhanced Interior Gateway Routing Protocol)
> - OSPF (Open Shortest Path First)
> - BGP (Border Gateway Protocol)

Throughout this lesson we will examine how protocols work, how routers use them, and why you may want to use one over another. The two protocols we will look at in the most depth are IP and IPX. These are the two protocols you are most likely to encounter while working with Cisco routers.

Keep in mind (especially if you are relatively new to the field of routing) that not all protocols are routable. That is, even though some protocols can be used to move information around a network, routers cannot interact with them. For that reason there are some protocols that you may want to stay away from if you are planning a routed environment. At the end of this lesson we will briefly look at which protocols are not routable and why.

To understand exactly how protocols work, you first need to understand *where* they work. By using the term "where" we are not referring to a physical location; rather, we are describing the way a protocol interacts with a computer or router. Different protocols work on different layers of the OSI model; one device may use a suite of protocols to accomplish a job.

> **Note**
>
> Many protocols are grouped together in "suites" or "stacks." Because most protocols are designed to perform specialized functions, one protocol may do things that another cannot. Together, protocols can complement each other by collectively performing a range of duties.

Two protocols that work together are TCP and IP. These protocols work on separate layers of the OSI model to aid in computer communication. The following sections will help illustrate the role OSI model and how it influences the functionality of Cisco routers.

> **Note**
>
> Knowing the function of all seven layers of the OSI model (even the ones not directly related to routing) will help you better understand the transportation of data. You will also be better equipped to diagnose any problems that may arise. For example, knowing that the World Wide Web operates on the seventh layer can help you determine the source of a Web-related issue. Because the seventh layer of the OSI governs the uses of applications, a problem with the World Wide Web can be traced to the program being used to view your pages.

It is important to understand that protocols serve a specific need, which in fact is not necessarily "routing." One of the many functions of routed protocols is to segment and encapsulate data. Routers take advantage of this function and use it to aid in the routing process. However, it is possible for routed protocols to exist in an environment in which there are no routers. (This is the reason that there are nonroutable protocols.)

Before we can clearly distinguish which protocols will work with Cisco routers and which will not, we need to understand the differences between them. The OSI model will illustrate these differences.

The OSI Model

In the early 1980s the ISO (International Organization for Standardization) developed the OSI (Open Systems Interconnect) model. The OSI model was based heavily on the DoD reference model, but it went a step further. The ISO took the four-layer DoD model and divided it even more. The result was the seven layers of the OSI model. Dividing the OSI model into seven layers helps segregate certain areas of PC communication for more streamlined protocols.

The seven layers of the OSI model are numbered from the bottom up. For information to get from one PC to another, the data must traverse these layers on both the sending and receiving devices. Information originating on layer 7 of one machine will

1. Travel from layer 7 to layer 1 on the machine of origin
2. Be passed to a protocol (possibly for routing) and delivered to the destination device
3. Travel from layer 1 to layer 7 on the recipient machine

Each layer of the OSI has a specific function. Information traveling from one layer is altered slightly to make it readable by the next layer. When the data reaches the receiving device, it traverses the layers in reverse order to undo the alterations made by the originating computer. Therefore, even though a router may be concerned with the data only after it has reached layer 3, if layers 7 through 4 are not functioning correctly, they will have a destructive impact on the router's capability.

The following sections look at each of the layers and their functions to provide a better understanding of the role protocols play in routing. After we have developed a better understanding of the OSI model, we can discuss the concepts behind IP and IPX.

The Application Layer

The application layer (layer 7) is concerned with coordinating communication between applications. This layer of the OSI model synchronizes the data flowing between servers and clients by handling functions such as file transfers, network management, and process services. Other duties of the application layer involve

- The World Wide Web (WWW)
- E-mail gateways
- Electronic data interchange (EDI)
- Chat services
- Internet navigation utilities

The application layer can be viewed as the first step data takes when leaving a PC to be routed. The application layer is routed information's direct access to the program it is bound for. That is, most (if not all) routed information either emanates from or is bound for an application residing on a device, and the application layer of the OSI model creates the rules that govern how this data is treated.

For example, when you view a Web page, you are viewing data at the application layer. The information that makes up the Web page traveled through the seven layers of the OSI model on a remote server. Then, after traversing the Internet, the data climbed up the OSI layers of your PC. Finally, the information is made readable at the application level.

The Presentation Layer

The function of the presentation layer is to translate the information from the application layer into a format that is readable by the other layers. All data encryption, decryption, and compression take place at the sixth layer of the OSI model. The presentation layer also controls all audio and video presentation functions. Services provided by the presentation layer include

- MP3
- RealAudio
- RealVideo
- JPEG
- GIF

Note that all of these services require some form of compression. MP3 needs extraordinary audio compression and GIF utilizes image compression. Without this compression the amount of data reaching the router would be too great to handle without error. The more data that is routed in one session, the higher the likelihood that it will fail to reach its intended recipient intact. Therefore, data compression (along with encryption and decryption) plays a major role in helping data get routed.

The Session Layer

The session layer (layer 5) coordinates communications between network devices. The session layer (working with the session layer of another device) establishes a session between two applications. The two session layers monitor the "conversation" and, when appropriate, terminate communication. Other session layer responsibilities are

- SQL (Structured Query Language)
- X Windows
- NFS (network file system)

The information that is sent (or received) from the three top layers (layers 5, 6, and 7) is known as *user data*. This user data is converted to other forms of data suitable for the remaining layers to handle.

The Transport Layer

The function of the transport layer (layer 4) is to take user data from the upper layers and break it down (or reassemble it, as the case may be) into chunks that can be easily transmitted. The chunks of data formed by the transport layer are known as *segments*. These segments are passed to the lower layers for further processing.

> **Note:** Whether you're working with segments, frames, datagrams, or cells, knowing the terminology behind the layers of the OSI model will help you tremendously. Because each layer deals with a specific data format, you can identify a particular layer (and usually a protocol) by the format of its data. For example, because TCP operates on layer 4, all data passed from TCP will be in the form of a "segment."

The transport layer also provides services for data flow control. Flow control helps this layer ensure the reliable (connection-oriented) transmission of data from one device to another. It does this by taking user data from the upper layers and segmenting it. These segments are then transmitted (one at a time) to the intended recipient. The recipient (after receiving a segment) sends back an acknowledgment. If the sender does not receive an acknowledgment, it retransmits the segment. After several retries, the sending device attempts to re-initiate a connection with the recipient. If the recipient proves to be unresponsive (the receiving device is no longer on the network), an error is generated and the remaining segments are not transmitted. Figure 8.1 illustrates the flow of data from one PC to another via TCP.

FIGURE 8.1

The data flow of TCP.

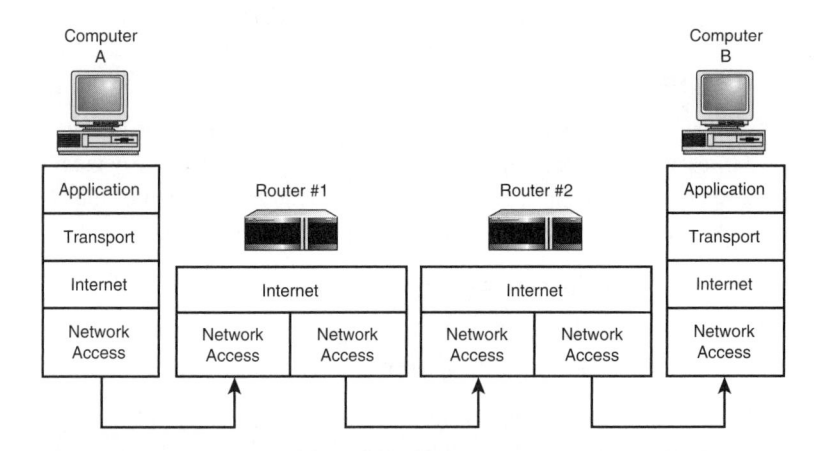

The Network Layer

Although each layer serves a very important purpose, layer 3 is the one over which most routing takes place. Most connectivity devices (routers, layer 3 switches, and bridges) work on the network layer of the OSI model.

To ensure that routing functions correctly, the network layer creates a logical map of the network. This map serves as a guide to route data from one part of the network to another. Although the network mapping functionality of layer 3 serves a major role in the routing process, it is not used exclusively by routers. PCs and other devices also use the services of the network layer to locate routers within an environment. This allows them to send information to the routers for delivery across the network.

Converting transport layer segments into packets is the first step in constructing a network map. These packets are then passed to the data link layer, where addressing information is added.

> **Note** Because routers operate almost exclusively on the third layer of the OSI model, they move data only in packet form. However, when we get to WAN technologies, you will encounter routers that move frames and cells. Remember, the data format depends greatly on the protocol.

When a device receives a packet, the sender's information is stripped from the packet and stored in a table. As this table grows, the network layer builds a clearer picture of the network environment. Other protocols and devices can use this information to route data in a more efficient manner.

> **Note** The data used by the network layer is also stored locally on Cisco routers in a routing table. The specific information contained in the routing table depends on the routing protocol being used. Routing tables will be covered more comprehensively in later lessons dealing with routing protocols.

For example, if a device on network A wanted to send data to a device on network B, it would send a broadcast across its local network (A). This broadcast would act as a scout, searching for the address of the recipient. Because the receiving device is not on network A, no reply to the broadcast would be sent. The device on network A would then assume that the intended recipient is on network B and send the data there.

Before reaching network B the packet travels through router 1. This router searches its own routing table (composed of network layer data) and determines that the intended recipient is truly on network B. Router 1 then forwards the packet to the appropriate networks. The router spanning the two networks will note the situation in its routing table and route all further packets for this device to network B.

One key element of this scenario is knowing the address of the device that you are trying to share information with. Compiling and tracking these addresses is the job of the data link layer.

The Data Link Layer

Whereas the network layer holds the map of the network, the data link layer (layer 2) ensures that the information on the map is correct through addressing. The data link layer accepts packets from the network layer and frames them, thus converting them to data frames. These frames contain the following information:

- Preamble (signaling the start of the frame)
- Destination address
- Source address
- Length field (in a standard Ethernet frame)—indicates the size of the data contained in the frame
- Type field (in Ethernet_II frames)—indicates which protocol will receive the data
- Data
- Frame check sequence (a verification number corresponding to the checksum of the frame)

The data link layer itself provides a lot of functionality, most of which would be wasted on some devices. Therefore layer two has been split in two sublayers: the MAC and the LLC. Each sublayer has its own rules and attributes.

The MAC Sublayer

The MAC (media access control) sublayer is in charge of framing the packets from the network layer. In framing the packets, the MAC sublayer attaches the addressing information to the packet. This addressing information includes the MAC address.

> **Note** Every networkable device has a factory-determined address that uniquely identifies that component on a network. That address is the MAC address.

Another function of the MAC sublayer is to provide connectionless service to the upper layers. Connectionless service takes place when data is sent to a device without a session being open. In other words, the sending device ships the data through the network without alerting the recipient beforehand.

TABLE 8.1 Pros and Cons of Connectionless Service

Pros	Cons
Faster than connection-oriented service. (There is no time spent opening sessions and waiting for responses.)	The delivery of frames is not ensured.
Less network overhead.	Recipient is not informed before data is sent. The machine you are sending may not even be functioning at the time data is sent.

As you will learn in the later parts of this book, the MAC sublayer plays a major part in routing. Because MAC addresses are unique, and they are recognized by almost every protocol, they are found in many aspects of routing.

The LLC Sublayer

One function of the LLC (logical link control) sublayer is to provide connection-oriented service (the MAC is connectionless). Connection-oriented service provides for the establishment of sessions prior to the delivery of frames. By opening a session first, the sender is guaranteed delivery of frames through acknowledgments.

The Physical Layer

The first layer of the OSI model defines the physical connection between devices. The physical layer accepts frames from the upper layers and transmits them as bits over the medium. This becomes more and more evident in dealing with Cisco router interfaces. The physical ports and interfaces that make up the Cisco routing hardware all operate on the physical layer of the OSI model. Figure 8.2 illustrates how the entire process works.

FIGURE 8.2

Data moving through the seven layers of the OSI model.

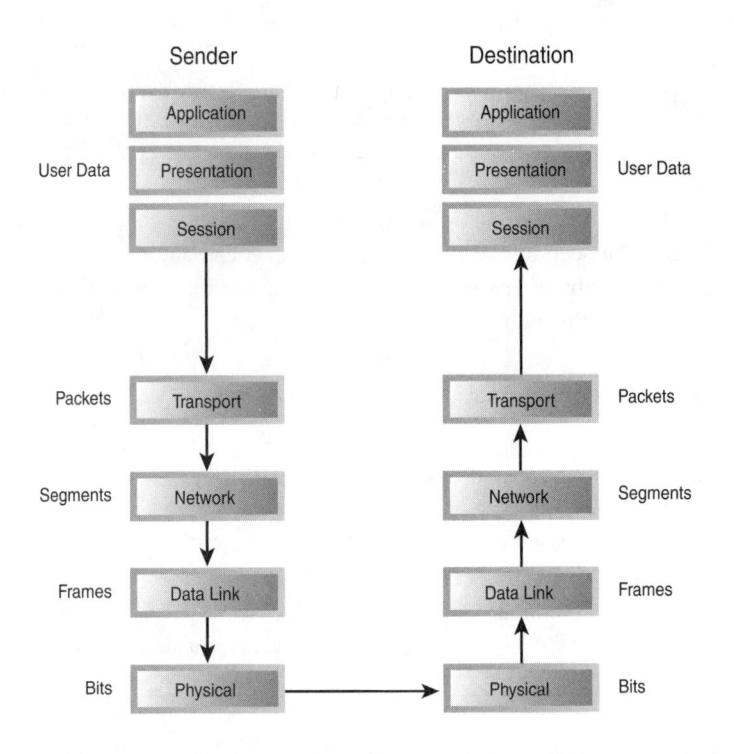

```
                Sender                      Destination
              ┌───────────┐                ┌───────────┐
              │Application│                │Application│
              └───────────┘                └───────────┘
              ┌───────────┐                ┌───────────┐
  User Data   │Presentation│                │Presentation│   User Data
              └───────────┘                └───────────┘
              ┌───────────┐                ┌───────────┐
              │  Session  │                │  Session  │
              └───────────┘                └───────────┘
                                                 ▲
              ┌───────────┐                ┌───────────┐
  Packets     │ Transport │                │ Transport │   Packets
              └───────────┘                └───────────┘
                    │                            ▲
              ┌───────────┐                ┌───────────┐
  Segments    │  Network  │                │  Network  │   Segments
              └───────────┘                └───────────┘
                    │                            ▲
              ┌───────────┐                ┌───────────┐
  Frames      │ Data Link │                │ Data Link │   Frames
              └───────────┘                └───────────┘
                    │                            ▲
              ┌───────────┐                ┌───────────┐
  Bits        │ Physical  │──────────────▶ │ Physical  │   Bits
              └───────────┘                └───────────┘
```

Understanding how the OSI model works will help you understand how protocols function. In turn this will help you master routing concepts that take some people entire careers to grasp.

Having discussed the inner workings of the OSI model, let's take a look at how this information is used by routers to move data from system to system.

Protocol Divisions and Classifications

> **Note**
>
> Because the book focuses on protocol routing with Cisco routers, I do not feel that an in-depth discussion of nonroutable protocols is warranted. However, be aware that just because a protocol exists does not mean that it is routable. One nonroutable protocol is NetBEUI. Entire networks can be built using NetBEUI, and they will work fine as long as there are no routers in use.

Understanding how protocols work and how they transport data from system to system requires an intrinsic knowledge of the inner workings of the protocol. How was the protocol designed to work, what layers of the OSI does it work on, and what can you expect from it? Reviewing the different divisions within the protocols will help you understand how router protocols run and how Cisco routers handle them.

Connection-Oriented Versus Connectionless Protocols

Connection-oriented protocols are designed in a manner that facilitates the opening of sessions between systems. That is, when two systems are using connection-oriented protocols, they establish a session between themselves before passing information.

Connection-oriented protocols, such as TCP (Transmission Control Protocol), work on the transport layer of the OSI model. Given that many routers work on the network layer (which is intrinsically connectionless), connection-oriented protocols are not routable. However, because of their desirable features and their close relation to many connectionless protocols, we will discuss them here, if only to provide a base of comparison with the router-friendly connectionless protocols.

When one system wants to send information to a neighboring system, a session-open request is sent to the desired recipient. The sending system then waits for an acknowledgment to the request, indicating that the system is available to open a session. When the sending system receives an acknowledgment, the session is opened and the two systems can freely exchange data. At the conclusion of the session a "tear-down" packet is sent from the system that initiated the connection. The tear-down packet indicates that the session is over and the resources used to maintain it should be freed. Figure 8.3 illustrates the connection-oriented session process.

FIGURE 8.3

The session process.

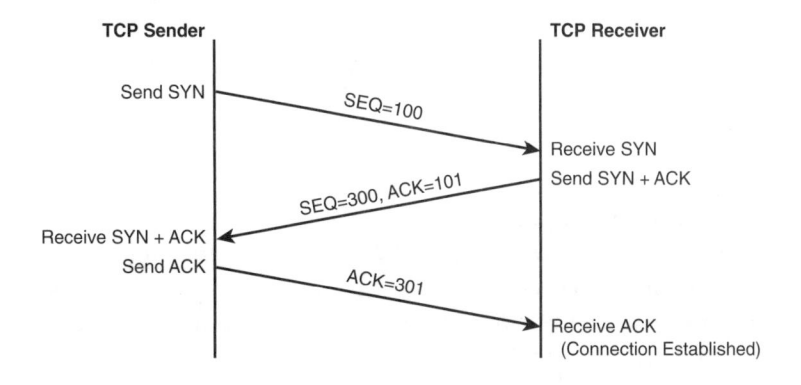

This process in itself (the act of initiating sessions before exchanging information) does not pose many real issues; in fact, it is one of the more attractive aspects of this category of protocols. It is the way the session is maintained that can be problematic for some environments.

When the requester sends out a session-open packet, a record of the path over which it traverses is appended to the packet. By doing this, the packet creates a route for the two devices to continue communicating over. The system that received the packet sends its acknowledgment over the same route the session-open packet took. Therefore, when a session is opened between the two systems, all packets sent between them follow this same path. This results in a guaranteed link between the devices.

However, the resources required for opening and maintaining a dedicated path are fairly substantial. Connection-oriented protocols utilize more overhead than their connectionless counterparts. Also, because of the random nature of routers, dedicated paths cannot be supported.

> **Note** Routers cannot guarantee that two packets will be sent over the same path. A router will always try to choose the "best path" over which to send information. Therefore, given any number of environmental circumstances, this path can change from packet to packet.

Connection-oriented protocols do offer some advantages within a networking environment. Because every packet exchanged between two systems is acknowledged, data delivery is guaranteed. When two systems participating in a session exchange information, an acknowledgment packet is sent confirming the successful arrival of every bit of data. Therefore, one very desirable feature of connection-oriented protocols is the guaranteed delivery of information.

Connection-oriented protocol sessions also travel a set path. That is, every packet is sent over the same route as the last. This allows for easier troubleshooting of connection problems. Using tools such as packet analyzers or "LAN sniffers," an engineer can easily determine the path over which two devices are communicating and thereby diagnose potential problems.

Connectionless protocols such as IP, with few exceptions, work on the network layer of the OSI model. Cisco routers (and all other routers on the market) also work on the network layer. Thus, it can be inferred that all routed protocols are connectionless, and routers support only the connectionless exchange of information.

Connectionless protocols utilize a "best effort" approach to data delivery. When a device attemptss to send information to another system, no dedicated connections are established between the two. Using connectionless protocols does involve a certain amount of risk. The following hazards are associated with connectionless protocols:

- Out-of-sequence packet delivery
- Packet loss
- Increased difficulty in troubleshooting problems

Because there is no dedicated connection between the two devices, each packet exchanged can follow a different path. Therefore, the possibility of packets arriving out of order (or not at all) is much greater with connectionless protocols.

The one major drawback of connectionless protocols is the imminent loss of data due to undeliverable packets. Although in most cases the losses are minimal and barely noticeable, the risks are still there.

Another disadvantage to not using a dedicated route between devices is that troubleshooting connection problems becomes exponentially greater the more routers you inject into the environment. Because packets can utilize different paths to the same destination, it is extremely hard to predict where a problem could fall between any two devices.

One way, within a Cisco router, to control the delivery of data from one system to another is to use static routes wherever possible. Although static routes are certainly not practical for every situation (in fact, they more or less defeat the purpose of routing to begin with), they can help for particularly troublesome systems.

There are definite advantages to using connectionless protocols. They are typically faster and require less overhead than connection-oriented carriers. For these reasons connectionless protocols are perfect for routing. Given the polymorphic nature of routing, connectionless protocols offer a means to quickly move data from one system to another.

Because connectionless protocols do not require the establishment of a session, they can be designed to be fast. The time taken to build and tear down sessions, along with the time needed to send and reply to acknowledgments, adds up over a large network. Therefore, the speed of connectionless protocols is very important in today's routing environments.

Classful Versus Classless Protocols

The best way to explain classful versus classless protocols is to use the example of IP. Understanding IP should be at the top of your priority list when it comes to protocols.

The reason we examine IP as an example of the differences between classful and classless protocols is that in recent years IP has become both. That is, IP can be configured in today's environments to be either classless or classful.

Classful IP

IP is, by nature, classful. When IP was developed (with the first networking environments), it was designed to be a classful protocol. This means that IP can be divided into different classes, each based on the needs of a particular network or client.

Classes are used to determine the ultimate size of an environment based on the relationship of hosts to networks. Each class offers a different number of addressable hosts per addressable network. Whereas one class may offer 127 addressable networks and over 16 million addressable hosts per network, another may supply 2 million networks and 254 hosts per network.

In the case of IP, the protocol is divided into three (commonly accepted) classes. The classes were developed to meet the needs of varying sizes of institutions.

> **Note** Although it is generally accepted that IP is divided into three classes (A, B, and C), there are actually five IP classes. Classes A, B, and C are the most popular for network addressing. However, classes D and E can be used for other purposes such as multicasting.

In a classful protocol, one address is used to specify both the host and network in a variable manner. That is, the portion of the address that is used to determine the network (as opposed to the host) can vary in size depending on the class in use. For example, within a class A IP environment, the address 16.10.20.6 can be split into the network address of 16.0.0.0 and the host address of 0.10.20.6. However, within a class C environment the address 225.198.40.9 can be split into network 225.198.40.0 and host 0.0.0.9.

A router can determine which portion of the address is used for networks by applying a secondary or mask address. Mask addresses (unique to classful protocols) indicate to the routing device which bits of the protocol address represent the network. This determination is key to the functionality of routers.

Classless IP

One problem with classful protocols such as IP is that they are finite. That is, there is a definite limit to the number of addresses that can be assigned over the life of the protocol. For this reason a classless way of utilizing IP has become popular.

Although classless protocols also use one address to represent both the network and the host, they do so in a fixed manner. The host portion of the address is always of a fixed length. Therefore, routing devices can easily and quickly determine the network bits of an address because they never change.

CIDR

CIDR, or Classless Inter-Domain Routing, has become very popular over the last few years. Developed to help ease the growing demand for class B IP networks, CIDR is a classless form of IP.

When routers are configured to use CIDR, IP network addresses are grouped into supernets. Within the IP address structure, bits are transferred from the network portion of the address to the host portion, thus providing a more customized address scheme.

The effect of supernetting is being able to route information to any host within a *group* of networks based on the group's supernet address. A supernet address is used to determine which supernetted networks belong to a particular group.

Protocol Encapsulation

Protocols facilitate the movement of data from one system to another through a process known as *encapsulation*. Through encapsulation, the data being sent from one system to another is packaged in such a way that intermediary connectivity devices can determine where the data is to be moved.

Encapsulation is a process whereby a large data stream is chopped into several small segments of uniform size. These small, uniform packages are easier to send and receive because their size can easily be predicted by all of the systems using the same protocol. Therefore, the network can fine-tune itself to work within the particular size parameters of the segmented data.

During encapsulation, the protocol attaches its own header to each segment or packet.

> **Note** The name given to each smaller package of data varies depending on the protocol being used and the layer of the OSI model it operates on. Some protocols work in packets, whereas other use segments, frames, or cells. However, these are all different names for the same product: a post-encapsulation segment of data ready for routing.

The contents of the header can vary depending on the protocol being used. (As we discuss each protocol in the lesson to follow, we will cover the specific fields of the header; recall that the IP headers were discussed on Day 5, "Understanding How Routers Move Data.") However, there are a few fields that appear in almost every protocol header.

The first two are the origin and destination addresses. These addresses indicate to routers and other connectivity devices where the packet of data came from and where it should be delivered.

The next field is a sequence number. This field is very important to the encapsulation process. Because protocols take large chunks of data and divide them into smaller, manageable pieces, a system must be in place to determine how to reassemble the data stream. (Remember, routers work on the connectionless network layer; therefore, packets will almost always arrive at their intended destination out of order. It is the job of routed protocols to ensure that those packets are reassembled in the correct order.)

Another necessary field indicates the size of the data packet being transmitted.

The final field we will cover here is the checksum. Basically, the checksum represents, in a brief and quickly reproducible way, the contents of the packet being transmitted. After a packet has been received, but before it is reassembled, the target device recomputes the checksum based on the received data and compares it with the received checksum to determine whether the packet has been corrupted during the sending process. Again, this function of routed protocols is essential to the proper operation of routers.

This short yet comprehensive look at routed protocols serves as a good introduction to the remainder of this book, which deals directly with protocols and how Cisco routers use them. We can now dive into configuring our Cisco router to run its first protocol: IP.

Summary

- Protocols are a key factor in the routing process.
- Protocols can be separated on the basis of connection-oriented versus connectionless, classful versus classless, and routable versus nonroutable.
- Connection-oriented protocols use sessions to create dedicated paths between transmitting devices.
- Connectionless protocols offer a quick, low-overhead, routable protocol solution.
- Classful protocols can be divided into classes to fit the specific needs of the environment they are assigned to.
- Classless protocols are more of a "one size fits all" solution to protocols.

Q&A

Q Why do we need routed protocols if routers use routing protocols?

A Routers are not the only devices involved in the transfer of data from one location to another. Other devices use routed protocols to transport and manage information. Routers use routing protocols to carry information between each other. Most of the remaining devices in an environment use routed protocols.

Q Why do routers work only with network layer protocols?

A The network layer is responsible for the mapping of networks and their environments. Therefore, to move information from place to place, routers need the services of the network layer to understand where the data should be transferred to.

Quiz

Questions

1. Is IP a connectionless or a connection-oriented protocol?
2. What layer of the OSI model is concerned with flow control?
3. What is the purpose of protocol encapsulation?
4. What is CIDR and why is it important?

Answers

1. IP is connectionless (TCP, on the other hand, is connection-oriented).
2. The transport layer.
3. Protocol encapsulation helps to segment data streams into manageable pieces and package those segments in a way such that the intermediary devices can understand where they should be sent.
4. CIDR, or Classless Inter-Domain Routing, helps to extend the life of IP schemes by applying supernets to classes.

WEEK 2

DAY 9

Learning IP Basics

TCP/IP (Transmission Control Protocol over Internet Protocol) is by far the most popular suite of network protocols in use today. Therefore, it includes the protocol you are most likely to come across while configuring Cisco routers. Although this lesson will not discuss configuring IP on Cisco routers, it serves as a primer to understanding how IP works. (Configuring IP on a Cisco router is covered in the next lesson, "Learning How to Configure IP on Cisco Routers.")

> **Note** As was discussed in the previous day's lesson, in terms of the OSI model TCP is a transport layer protocol, whereas IP is its network layer counterpart. The two do complement each other, and to get the whole picture you must understand both. However, because IP is the only protocol in the TCP/IP stack that a router deals with, we will not be covering TCP in this lesson.

How does TCP/IP work, and why is it so popular? This lesson will use the following topics to introduce you fully to the basis of IP.

- IP
- Network subnetting
- Supernetting an IP network
- IP and Cisco routers

IP

Everyone is familiar with IP and IP addressing. (You were introduced to it in Hour 6, "Getting the Router Up and Running," configuring the addresses of Ethernet interfaces.) It is almost impossible to work in the computer industry today and not know what IP is. However, do you really understand how it works, or why it is so popular? This section covers how IP works and addresses some common issues such as addressing and subnetting.

> **Note** IP facilitates the network layer's role of mapping the network environment. Through IP's addressing scheme, the network layer can produce a detailed picture of the network around the host. IP operates purely on the network layer.

A standard IP address looks like 128.95.95.178—four sections containing one byte each. An IP address comprises 32 bits or four bytes. Because the bits are binary, the largest achievable value for one byte is 255. This means that the achievable range of IP addresses is 0.0.0.0 through 255.255.255.255. (These numbers are achievable, but they are not all valid.) Therefore, be careful not to use any of the reserved addresses in your routers.

Table 9.1 is a list of IP addresses that are considered reserved.

TABLE 9.1 Reserved IP Addresses

Address	Binary	Reason Address Is Reserved
0.0.0.0	00000000.00000000.00000000.00000000	An address cannot be all 0s. Used by RIP for routing.
255.255.255.255	11111111.11111111.11111111.11111111	An address cannot be all 1s. Used for broadcasts.
127.0.0.1	01111111.00000000.00000000.00000001	Reserved for internal loopback testing.

Depending on the class of the address, anywhere from one to three bytes are used to identify the host, and anywhere from one to three bytes are used to identify the network. The first part of an address is used to identify the network, whereas the second part is used to identify the host. Being able to discern the host from the network is very important in routing.

> **Note** The host address can also be referred to as the node address.

IP addresses are divided into three classes to keep track of the number of addresses being allotted to various sizes of institutions. The classes for IP addresses are classes A, B, and C. There is also a less-known (and even less-used) class D, which we will not be discussing. (Class D is primarily used for multicasting.) Knowing the class of an address will help you correctly identify the proper subnet mask when configuring an interface.

Class A Addresses

For class A addresses the first byte of the address represents the network, and the last three bytes represent the hosts.

Figure 9.1 shows a class A address divided into its network and host parts.

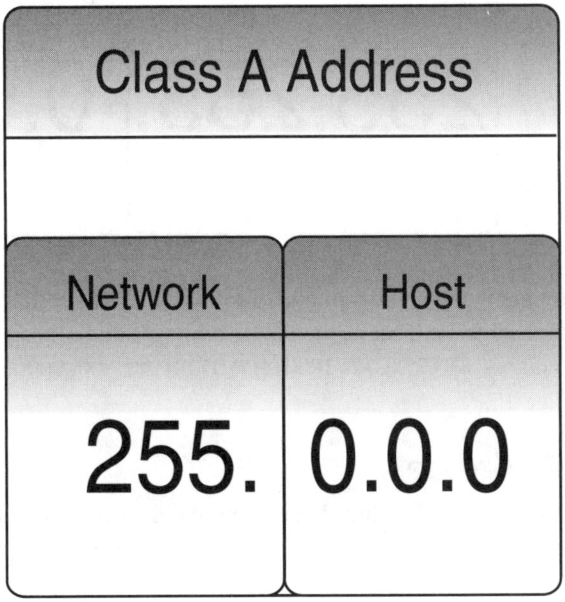

FIGURE 9.1

The host and network portions of a class A address.

Class A Address

Network	Host
255.	0.0.0

Class A addresses have a network range between 1 and 127. Therefore, an IP address starting with a number between 1 and 127 will be a class A address. This can be best illustrated from a binary level. The first bit of the first octet in a class A address will always be 0. For example, the address 127.0.0.0 is 01111111.00000000.00000000.00000000 in binary. Notice the first bit is 0.

Class B Addresses

In class B addresses, the first two bytes represent the network and the remaining two bytes represent the host. A valid range for the first byte of class B addresses is 128 through 191. Figure 9.2 shows a class B IP address divided into its network and host parts.

FIGURE 9.2

The host and network portions of a class B address.

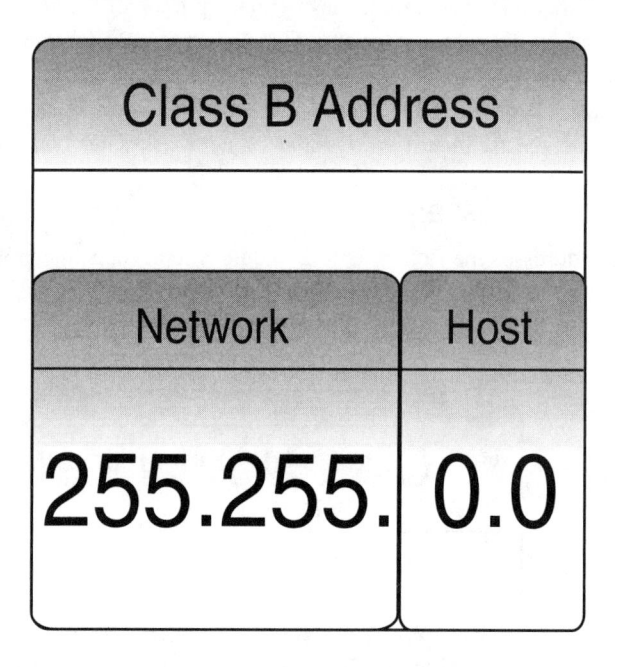

Class B Address	
Network	Host
255.255.	0.0

Again, by examining the address in binary format, we can see that all class B addresses will start with the bits 10. That is, the first two bits of the first octet will always be 10. For example the address 140.75.0.0 is 10001100.01001011.00000000.00000000 in binary. The first two bits are 10.

Class C Addresses

In class C addresses, the first three bytes represent the network and the last byte represents the host. A valid class C range for the first byte of the network address is 192 through 223. Figure 9.3 shows a class C IP address divided into its network and host parts.

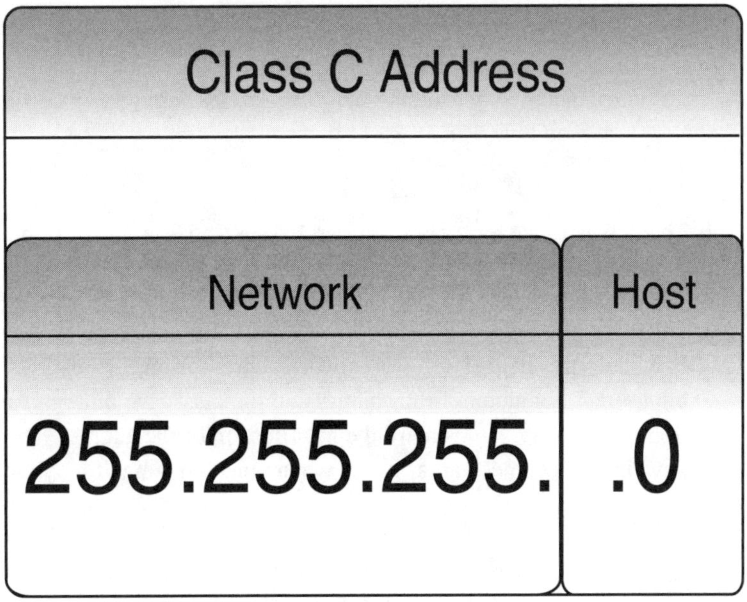

FIGURE 9.3

The host and network portions of a class C address.

Class C Address	
Network	Host
255.255.255.	.0

Let's examine a class C address in binary format. 198.40.50.0 is 11000110.00101000.00110010.00000000 in binary. Therefore, we can see that every class C address will start with the three digits 110.

> **Note**
>
> You may have noticed that the valid range of addresses for class C goes up only to 223, but IP addresses can reach 256. The gap is to leave room for class D (223 through 239) and class E (240 through 255). Don't spend too much time worrying about these addresses; they are not used very often.
>
> However, for troubleshooting purposes it is good to know that these ranges exist. For example, if you are configuring a router's interface for a class C network and assign it an address of 230.230.230.0 with a subnet mask of 255.255.255.0 (the valid subnet mask for a class C network), you may run into problems.
>
> In this particular problem, the device would not be able to communicate with any other devices in the 255.255.255.0 subnet. However, on the surface the address 230.230.230.0 appears to be valid, even though it is actually class D.

The Subnet Mask

The subnet mask is used by IP to distinguish the host address from the network address. To understand how the subnet mask works, let's convert an IP address to binary, such as the class C address 198.68.85.114:

```
11000110.01000100.01010101.01110010
```

The subnet mask for a class C IP address is 255.255.255.0. In binary the subnet mask looks likes this:

```
11111111.11111111.11111111.00000000
```

How does this help IP tell the network address from the host? As you can see from the binary representation of the address and the mask, the binary 1s mark the network portion. Conversely, the 0s mark the host portion of the address. This may seem obvious now, but it becomes harder to see when you start subnetting your networks.

> **Note**
>
> The class of IP addresses you are using will determine the subnet mask you need. Following are the default subnet masks for the three classes of addresses:
>
> Class A = 255.0.0.0
>
> Class B = 255.255.0.0
>
> Class C = 255.255.255.0

Subnetting is one engineering function that you will inevitably encounter over your course of Cisco work. Subnetting is easier to understand the more you do it, but it can be a complicated and, sometimes, mentally trying task. I can only suggest that you plan out subnetting schemes on paper before trying to implement them. However, let's quickly cover the process of subnetting a network here, to help introduce you to the subject.

Network Subnetting

When a network is subnetted, bits are passed from the host portion of an address to the network portion. This allows one IP network license to be used to address more than one network (subnetwork). Figure 9.4 shows a network that would benefit from subnetting.

FIGURE 9.4

A nonsubnetted network.

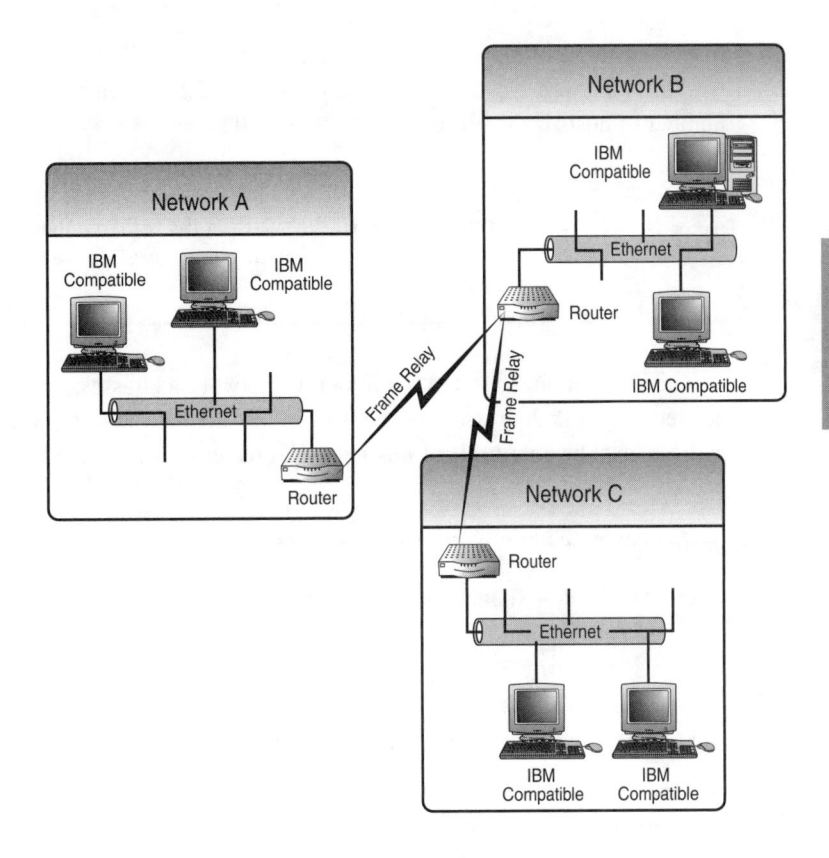

We need to subnet the license 10.0.0.0 to fit three subnets. Where do we start? You should start by looking at the subnet mask. (Even though you are creating three networks, they need to share one subnet mask.) By converting the subnet mask into binary, we can easily see how subnetting is accomplished.

The subnet mask for 10.0.0.0 is 255.0.0.0, which in binary is

11111111.00000000.00000000.00000000.

We then need to determine the number of bits that should be given to the network address to allow for three more networks. For example, suppose we were to pass two bits from the host portion of the mask to the network:

11111111.11000000.00000000.00000000

This subnet mask gives us a new subnet mask of 255.192.0.0.

The following equation can be used when factoring the number of bits needed to supply the required number of networks:

$2^x - 2$ = Number of addresses (where x equals the number of bits in the address)

In the third byte of our example we used two bits for the network. The number of networks is therefore $2^2 - 2 = 2$. There are a total of 22 bits left for the host addresses. The number of hosts is therefore $2^{22} - 2 = 4,194,302$.

> **Note** Why is it necessary to subtract 2 from the total number of addresses? We cannot use all 0s or all 1s as an address; therefore we must subtract those two possibilities.

A second equation is used to figure out the network addresses. The size of the interval between network addresses is equal to 256 less the new subnet mask. Each network address must be a multiple of this interval, greater than zero and less than the subnet mask:

ith network address $y_i = i \times (256 - x)$, $i = 1, 2, \ldots,$ [lt] x

where x is the new subnet mask. In our example, the subnet mask is 192, so

$256 - 192 = 64$

Therefore the valid networks are 10.**64**.0.0 and 10.**128**.0.0 ($128 = 64 + 64$). If we were to add 64 again, we would get 192, which is our subnet mask.

To subnet the example in Figure 9.4 successfully, we need three networks. Two bits added to the subnet mask do not give us enough networks. If we add three bits to the subnet mask to obtain 255.224.0.0 ($224 = 128 + 64 + 32$), we get six networks ($2^3 - 2$), with 2,097,150 hosts each. We would obviously never need that many hosts, but it is the number of networks we are concerned about.

By subnetting the networks, we can direct the traffic better around the three networks. Had we not subnetted the networks, the traffic (produced by broadcasts and CSMA/CD packets) would start to degrade the performance of the network. Now that the networks are subnetted, any traffic whose source and destination hosts are both within the same subnet stays on its particular subnet, creating a less hectic network environment.

Whereas subnetting works by moving bits to the host portion of the IP address, supernetting works by doing the exact opposite. Supernetting is used to define an upper-level "supernetwork" to which all of your other networks belong. Supernetting is used most notably during Classless Inter-Domain Routing (CIDR).

Supernetting an IP Network

With the growing popularity of CIDR it may become necessary to supernet a group of networks. Because the addressing authorities are running painfully low on large classes of IP addresses, a way to extend the life of the remaining addresses has become necessary. The result is supernetting.

When a group of addresses are supernetted, a mask is created to indicate that the individual networks involved belong to one larger supergroup. For example, if an environment is assigned the two network addresses 215.50.25.0 and 215.50.26.0, a supernet can be created to combine and relate the two networks for use within the same physical environment.

The binary form of the subnet mask 255.255.255.0 (the class C mask for both of the assigned network addresses) is 11111111.11111111.11111111.00000000. Whereas subnetting passes bits from the host portion of the address to add more networks, supernetting passes bits from the network portion to reduce the number of networks.

If two bits are passed from the network portion to the host portion, the mask will become 11111111.11111111.11111100.00000000, or 255.255.252.0. When combined with the network address 215.50.25.0, this mask will tell the router that two network addresses are included in the supernet. If you start counting your networks with 215.50.25.0, the two network addresses covered by the new mask are 215.50.25.0 and 215.50.26.0.

Remember, using the same calculations that were introduced in the last section, passing two bits from the host to the network will include two (that is, $2^2 - 2$) networks in your supernet.

> **Note**
>
> If you wonder how the router knows that the new mask of 255.255.252.0 is not a Class B subnet instead of a Class C supernet, the answer is actually quite easy. The first octet of the network address is 215.x.x.x. Only a Class C network can begin with 215; therefore the new mask has to be for a Class C supernet.

Supernetting is easier to understand when looked at in relationship to subnetting. Therefore you should practice (on paper) both supernetting and subnetting to get the hang of it.

IP and Cisco Routers

IP's use is critical to the functionality of Cisco routers. The better you understand IP at an early stage in your Cisco training, the better you will absorb the later subjects of the book. You will soon see that many protocols, both routed and routing, are either based on or rely on IP for their functionality.

All Cisco routers are shipped with the ability to route IP. That is, the "Basic IP" Cisco IOS feature pack is the default for all Cisco routers. Other routed protocols, such as IPX, require a different feature pack to be installed. For this reason, we have spent a little extra time discussing this protocol.

IP is not avoidable in the world of Cisco routers. Not only is it the main protocol in use on the Internet; tools based on IP are an integral part of Cisco router operation. Tools such as ping, traceroute, and telnet are all products of the TCP/IP protocol suite and are very important to router functionality.

The next lesson will walk you through configuring a Cisco router to run IP and IP-related commands and tools. Therefore, let's move on to configuring our Cisco routers.

Summary

- IP is an important element in the functionality of Cisco routers
- Class A IP network addresses can be identified in a binary format by the first bit of the first octet being a 0.
- Class B network addresses are indicated by the first two bits of the first octet being 10.
- Class C network addresses are indicated by the first two bits of the first octet being 110.
- Subnetting is the process whereby bits are borrowed from the host portion of an IP address to the network portion of the address, thus giving the network administrator more networks to work with.
- Supernetting is the process whereby bits are passed from the network portion of the address to the host portion of the address, thus creating fewer networks for the administrator to deal with, but enabling more hosts on each network.

Q&A

Q If TCP and IP are part of the same protocol suite, why do routers work only with IP and not with TCP?

A Even though the two protocols are part of the same suite, they were created to address different needs. TCP was developed to address the needs of the transport layer of the OSI, while IP addresses the network layer, on which routers operate.

Q Why is IP supported in all Cisco IOS feature packs?

A IP is the backbone protocol of all routers. Whether your environment encompasses two small networks or a group of web servers, IP is going to be a protocol you need to route.

Quiz

Questions

1. How many classes have been created for IP?
2. What is the standard subnet mask for a Class C IP address?
3. What class is the IP address 126.45.30.1?
4. What IP address is reserved for loopback testing?

Answers

1. Five (A through E)
2. 255.255.255.0
3. Class A
4. 120.0.0.1

WEEK 2

DAY 10

Learning How to Configure IP on Cisco Routers

On Day 9 we discussed one of the most popular protocols in routing today: IP. However, there are a few other tools and protocols directly related to IP that we have not discussed. The TCP/IP suite of tools and protocols includes more than just the two protocols that are its namesake (TCP and IP). This lesson will discuss two of these additional tools: ICMP (Internet Control Message Protocol) and Telnet. After looking at these tools and discussing the commands needed to configure IP on Cisco routers, we will have developed a complete knowledge of the uses and workings of IP. To achieve this goal we will study the following subjects:

- IP and Cisco interfaces
- ICMP
- Using ICMP tools

- Telnet
- Remote administration using Telnet
- `rlogin`

ICMP is a protocol that is closely linked to IP. Used for diagnostic purposes, ICMP is a powerful tool in the world of routing. Mastering ICMP and its tool set will help you diagnose many of the problems that can occur with Cisco routers, such as end-to-end connectivity problems. A portion of this chapter will deal directly with ICMP.

Another widely used protocol (also directly related to IP) is Telnet. Depending on your computer experience, you may be familiar with Telnet. Cisco routers utilize this protocol for two purposes. First, PCs can use Telnet to communicate with Cisco routers to gain access to the command prompt. The second (and more useful) purpose is that Telnet enables Cisco routers to administer other Cisco routers remotely from within the IOS. That is, one Cisco router, using Telnet, can remotely administer a number of other Cisco routers. As you work in larger and larger routing environments, the ability to administer multiple routers from one location becomes invaluable.

This lesson will serve to wrap up our discussion of IP. The topics covered in this lesson are part of the larger picture that is the TCP/IP suite of tools and protocols. IP is unarguably the most important protocol in routing today, and mastering every aspect of IP is key to understanding the inner functions of routing. You will have a very strong base for your routing knowledge after completing this lesson.

With that said, let's discuss configuring your router to run IP. Then we can dive into its tools and their uses.

IP and Cisco Interfaces

IP as a protocol should be installed on your router already. All Cisco IOS feature packs, with the exception of IPX Basic, include IP. Therefore, no software installation is necessary to obtain the functionality of IP. Using that functionality is what this lesson is about.

All IP configurations are done in the interface configuration mode. Use the following commands to enter the interface configuration mode of the Cisco router.

```
Router>enable
Router#configure terminal
Router(config)#intface ethernet 0
Router(config-if)#
```

The `enable` command will activate the privilege mode of the Cisco Exec. From here we can execute the `configure terminal` command. This will put the router into the global configuration mode. Within the global configuration mode, the command `interface ethernet 0` is used to enter the interface configuration mode of the router for the interface Ethernet 0. Within the interface configuration mode, one simple command can enable IP on your router:

`Router(config-if)#`**`ip address 10.156.4.16 255.255.0.0`**

The `ip` command has a simple list of parameters. The keyword address specifies the IP address for the interface. The address and the subnet mask to be assigned to the interface follow the `address` keyword. This single command will enable IP functionality on one interface on your router. Repeat this command on all of the physical interfaces you need IP functionality for.

After the interfaces have been configured, you can turn on routing with, again, one simple command:

`Router(config)#`**`ip routing`**

The `ip routing` command enables the routing of IP packets between all configured interfaces. However, with a peripheral command, you may need to enable the classless form of IP routing.

If you know that your network will be running a classless form of IP, you will need to enable it on your router. (We discussed classless IP on Days 8, "Understanding Routed Protocols," and 9, "Learning IP Basics.") The command for enabling classless IP is as follows:

`Router(config)#`**`ip classless`**

Notice that the `ip classless` command is executed from within global configuration mode. This is because the functionality of classless IP routing affects all interfaces.

When the router receives a packet, it tries to locate the matching network within its routing table. If no match is found for the destination of the packet, it is forwarded to the supernet address. For example, if a router's defined routes are for networks 128.46.69.0 and 128.45.77.0, and a packet comes in for 128.46.68.15, it will be forwarded to 128.46.68.0 because 128.46.x.x is the closest matching supernet for the packet in question.

Finally, if your router is not the router of last resort for the network, one needs to be defined. That is, the router you are configuring needs to know what to do with any packets for which there are no defined routes. More often than not, these undefined packets should be sent to another network, which requires the use of a gateway. For this reason, routers of last resort can also be default gateways.

> **Note**
>
> The router to which every other router on the network forwards packets with no defined routes is the router of last resort. This router is most often the only direct connection to the Internet.
>
> It can be safely assumed in most cases that any packet for which your router does not have a predefined route should be forwarded to the Internet. Therefore, the router that connects your environment to the Internet should be configured as the router of last resort on the remaining routers on the network.

To configure the address of the default gateway, use the `ip default-gateway` command:

`Router(config)#`**`ip default-gateway 198.2.65.1`**

Notice again that this command is executed in global configuration mode. Therefore, the parameter applies to all interfaces. Finally, to define static IP routes, use the `ip route` command:

`Router(config)#`**`ip route 198.52.2.0 255.0.0.0 Ethernet 0 100 perm`**

The `ip route` command defines, within the router, a direct path to a specific network. By defining static routes, you can control the flow of data out of your router. However, the `ip route` command requires a few parameters. Let's quickly discuss the role of these parameters.

`ip route` indicates to the router that a static route definition follows. The IP address of the network and the subnet mask should immediately follow the `ip route` command.

Because these configurations are made in global configuration mode, you need to specify which of the router's interfaces the route should be defined for. Therefore, the next parameter gives the physical interface to which any packets matching this static route are to be forwarded: `Ethernet 0`.

The next parameter is a fairly arbitrary one and can be left out if you so desire. This parameter, `100`, defines the administrative metric for the route. The administrative metric is used in situations where there may be more than one path defined to a specific network. In such cases the path with the lowest metric is the one that gets used, and the other becomes a backup.

Finally the `perm` option defines the entire static route as being permanent. Therefore, it will be saved to the `startup-config` configuration file. It is possible to define temporary routes by omitting the `perm` option. These temporary routes are not saved to configuration files and are forgotten when the router is reloaded.

Let's walk though some IP routing scenarios. For example, how would the router in the network shown in Figure 10.1 be configured to run and route IP from network A to network B?

FIGURE 10.1

A sample IP network.

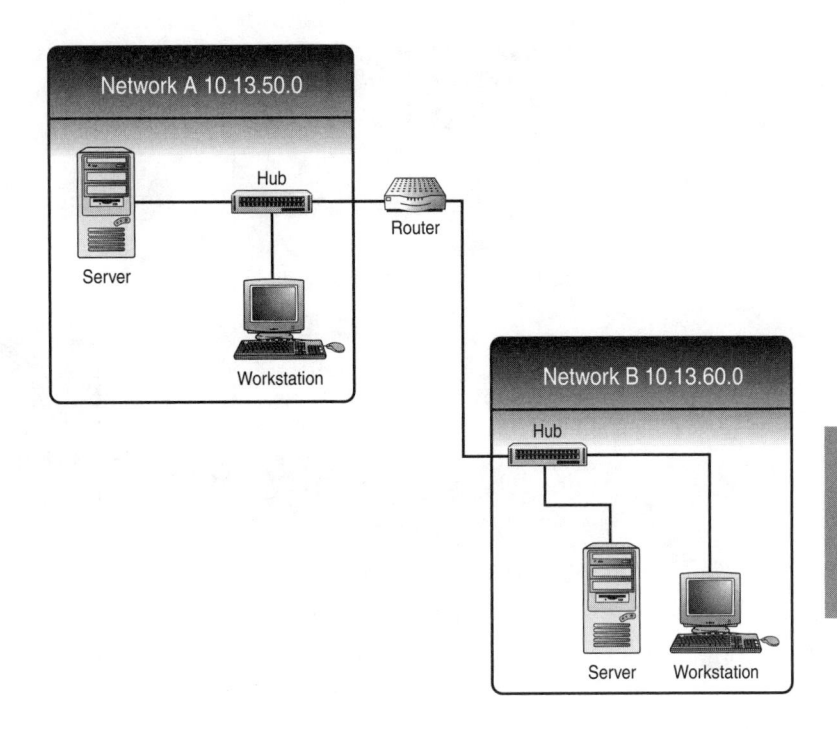

From the beginning we would need to use the following list of commands to enable routing:

```
Router>enable
Router#configure terminal
Router(config)#interface ethernet 0
Router(config-if)#ip address 10.13.50.1 255.255.0.0
Router(config-if)#^Z
Router#configure terminal
Router(config)#interface ethernet 1
Router(config-if)#ip address 10.13.60.1 255.255.0.0
Router(config-if)#^Z
Router#configure terminal
Router(config)#ip routing
Router(config)#ip route 10.13.50.0 255.255.0.0 e0 perm
Router(config)#ip route 10.13.60.0 255.255.0.0 e1 perm
```

Although this scenario may seem simple on an engineering level, every network is essentially a scaled-up version of this basic functional operation.

However, before you assume that you have all of the basic knowledge needed to configure Cisco routers for IP, you should be aware of one more scenario. The next example shows a common occurrence in network environments. Figure 10.2 illustrates three networks merging together.

FIGURE 10.2

A three-subnet network.

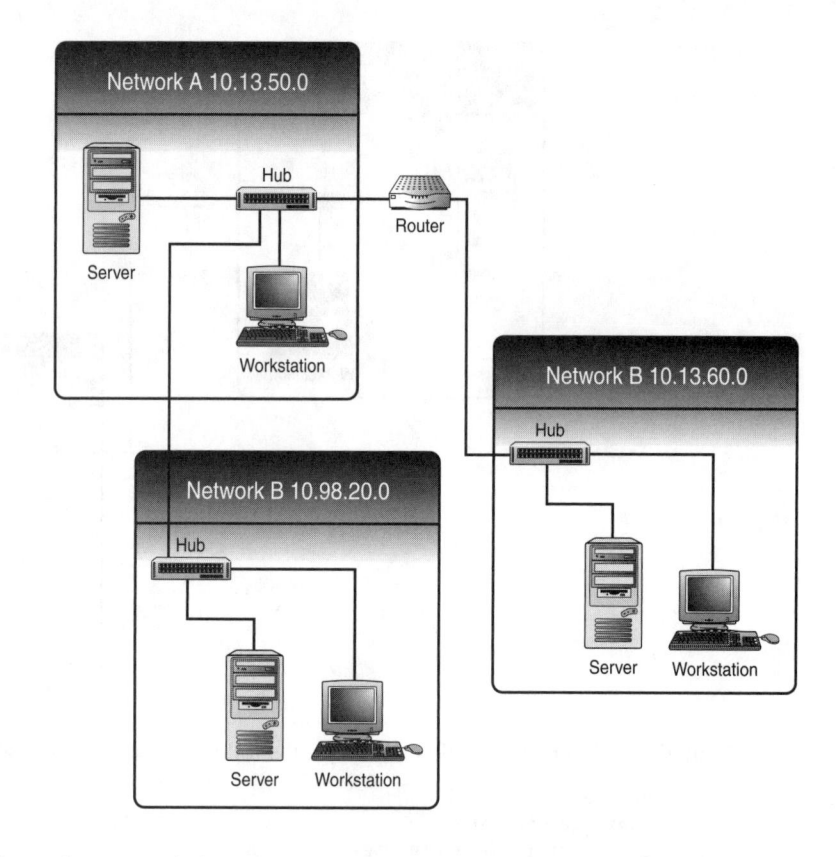

In this scenario we have an existing network acquiring a third, smaller segment. The problem here is that the two physical interfaces of the router are already in use.

The solution is to use the `secondary` parameter of the `ip address` command to specify a secondary IP address on one of the interfaces.

> **Note**
> Interfaces on Cisco routers can be configured with a secondary address to facilitate the routing of packets in situations such as this. However, any packet sent from the router's interface will "originate" from the primary address.

To configure the secondary address for the router in Figure 10.2, use the following command:

```
Router(config-if)#ip address 10.98.20.1 255.255.0.0 secondary
```

Learning How to Configure IP on Cisco Routers

By now you should have a fairly good grasp of the commands needed to configure IP on a router. Therefore, we can safely dive into the discussion of the remaining IP-related tools and functions.

ICMP

ICMP is tied very closely to IP. Many devices use the services of ICMP to monitor network conditions and report on environmental factors. Being so closely related to IP has its upside and its downside. One advantage is that, because of the popularity of IP, many devices are capable of running ICMP. On the other hand, there are still quite a few PCs and other devices that do not use IP, and unfortunately ICMP cannot detect such devices for diagnostic purposes.

Most PCs and other networkable devices have the ability to use tools such as `ping` and `traceroute`. These tools use ICMP packets to test connectivity factors among devices. Knowing how these tools work, and being able to use them to your advantage, will help you keep your network and router in good maintenance.

The remainder of this section discusses the technology and concepts behind ICMP. No extra configuration is required to install ICMP on a Cisco router, but you should be familiar with how to use it.

> **Note** Although no extra configuration is necessary to install ICMP or ICMP services on a router, the router does need at least one functional interface using IP. If you do not have an interface configured on IP, you will still have access to the ICMP commands; they just won't work until the IP line protocol of an interface is brought up.

ICMP tools provide one of the easiest ways to diagnose network problems. Therefore, to learn Cisco router operations you should become familiar with the use of these commands and understand their output.

Using ICMP Tools

ICMP is a protocol that is used almost exclusively for testing and diagnosing network connectivity issues. Because of the complex nature of routing, diagnosing even the simplest problems can be difficult without the correct tools. To understand how difficult it can be to diagnose network problems in a routed environment, let's look at a sample network.

Networking environments today are larger and more complex than ever before. It is not uncommon to have 5 to 10 separate routers within one network. However, most networks do not stop at the office walls. Having connections to the Internet adds hundreds if not thousands of routers to a company's routed environment. Figure 10.3 illustrates a typical routed environment.

FIGURE 10.3

A typical routed environment.

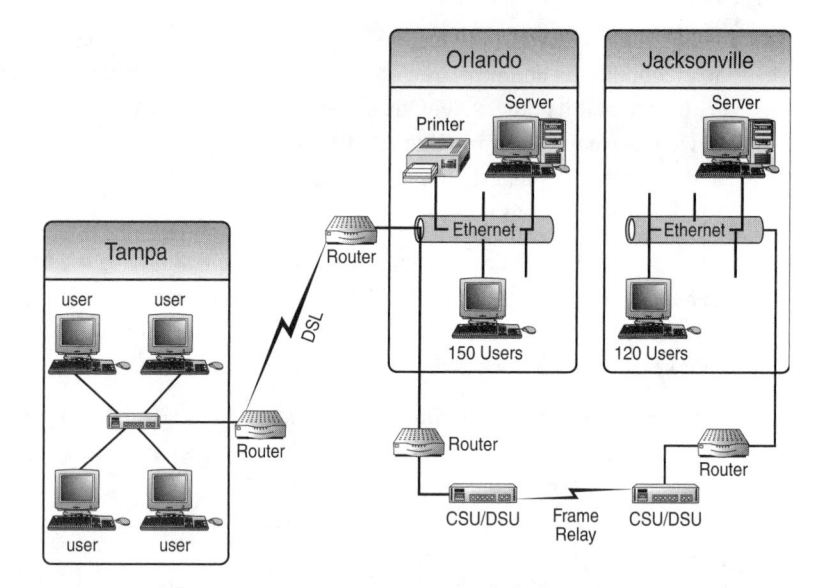

When the number of routers in a network grows, the level of complexity within the environment grows as well. One common complication that arises from adding routers to a network involves tracking packets within the environment. Using ICMP, an administrator can track the routing of packets from end to end. This not only can help engineers and designers determine whether there are connectivity problems on the network, but also helps show whether the routers are using the correct paths.

Cisco routers can use two ICMP tools to determine the overall health of a route. These tools are `ping` and `traceroute`. Both tools offer powerful diagnostic ability.

Ping

The ping utility is used to test for the existence of an end system. For example, let's say you are trying to TFTP a configuration file from a router to a TFTP server and you receive the following message:

```
%Error opening tftp://10.16.4.153/
```

This immediately tells you that the server you are trying to contact is not responding. Obviously there are myriad reasons why the server may not be responding. One way to narrow the possibilities down is by using ping.

The ping tool uses ICMP echo packets to test for the presence of a server just as a submarine's sonar uses sound pulses (which have long been called "pings") to test for the presence of objects in the surrounding water. By "pinging" the server's IP address, you can tell whether the machine is running and whether the protocol is functioning properly. This will allow you to narrow the scope of possible problems.

> **Note** Ping works by sending ICMP echo packets to an IP address you select. When the device at the specified address receives the ICMP packets, it echoes them back to the sender.

However, the only thing you can be assured of by using ping is that a device is on and functioning properly; ping tells you little else. For example (using our previous scenario), if you ping the TFTP server's IP address and you receive no replies, it could indicate many different problems. The server may be powered off, the server may not be configured to run IP, or the router you are pinging from may be configured incorrectly. There is really no way to tell, but at least you have a starting point.

As a Cisco IOS command, `ping` has some features that standard versions of ping may not include. Because of these added features, `ping` is one of the few commands that can be run from both user and privilege mode. Let's examine the user-mode version of `ping`.

> **Note** Keep in mind that, when using any of the ICMP tools, your router needs at least one configured interface that is up (running IP). If you do not have at least one line up, you may see the following error when attempting to run a command:
>
> ```
> % Unrecognized host or address, or protocol not running.
> ```

`ping` (User Mode)

The standard version of `ping` can be accessed from the user-mode command prompt. Entering **ping** at the user-mode command prompt will produce the following results:

```
Router>ping
% Incomplete command.
```

That is, `ping` requires at least one parameter. The list of parameters used by `ping` can be displayed using the Cisco IOS help system.

```
Router>ping ?
 WORD Ping destination address or hostname
 ip   IP echo
 tag  Tag encapsulated IP echo
```

> **Note**
>
> The two advanced options we will not be dealing with are `ip` and `tag`. The first, `ip`, specifies use of IP during the ping. Cisco allows you to ping under other protocols through the options `apollo`, `appletalk`, `clns`, `decnet`, `ipx`, `vines`, or `xns`. We will be focusing primarily on IP as a protocol (because it is the default).
>
> The `tag` option is used to specify the tag encapsulation of the packet. This is used primarily in switching and will not be covered here.

To assemble a fully functional `ping` command, you need to specify the IP address of the device you wish to ping.

```
Router>ping 10.16.4.152
```

A standard `ping` command will produce the following output. At first glance, the output message may seem cryptic and somewhat hard to follow; however, if we take it section by section, it really is easy to understand.

```
Router>ping 10.16.4.152

Type escape sequence to abort.
Sending 5, 100-byte ICMP Echos to 10.16.4.152, timeout is 2 seconds:
!!!!!
Success rate is 100 percent, round-trip min/avg/max = 1/3/4 ms
```

The first line of the output message (`Type escape sequence to abort.`) is actually generated by the IOS before the command runs. It is a status message letting the user know that the command process can be aborted. To abort the ping execution, use the Ctrl+Shift+6 key combination.

The second line, again, is a status message generated by the Cisco IOS. This line reiterates the intent of the ping command. In our example the ping command is going to send five 100-byte packets to the IP address 10.16.4.152. The timeout is set to 2 seconds.

The timeout (also referred to as TTL, or "Time To Live") is a clock used by the devices involved to determine whether a packet can be discarded. When a packet's TTL expires, the packet is discarded by the device holding it. Therefore, the sending device can infer that if no response is received within 2 seconds, the destination address is unreachable. Otherwise the sending device would be waiting indefinitely for a response that may never come.

The next line in the output message is actually a representation of the `ping` execution. Each icon displayed (in this case an exclamation point) represents one packet sent by the router to the destination address. The fact that the icon in our example is an exclamation point ! indicates that the ICMP packets were successfully echoed back to the router. Had the icon been a period ., the packets would have been lost, meaning that the destination address did not echo the ping.

There are eight icons that can appear on this line:

- ! (success)
- . (failure)
- U (end node unreachable)
- N (end node network unreachable)
- P (protocol incompatibility)
- Q (source quench)
- M (packet too big to be routed; it could not be fragmented)
- ? (unknown response)

The final line of the output message is a summary produced by the IOS. The IOS will alert you as to whether the ping was successful and how long the packets took to be echoed back (if the echoes were received).

> **Note**
>
> Although we have not yet discussed the concept of "hops," ping does have a hop limit. Routers on a network are commonly referred to as hops (when describing the number of routers a piece of information must traverse before reaching its final destination). For example, a packet that must go through three routers to reach its destination covers three hops.
>
> The `ping` command (in user mode) will test over a maximum of only nine hops. Therefore, any address you are testing that is more than nine router hops away (even if it is fully functional) will produce a "destination unreachable" response.
>
> We will discuss hops further as they relate to routing protocols in later chapters.

Although this may seem like a lot of useful information, it is actually a very basic usage of the command. To run a more powerful version of ping, you must enter privilege mode.

ping (Privilege Mode)

Offering slightly more power than the standard form of ping, Cisco includes a privilege-mode ping in the IOS. The privilege-mode version of ping lets administrators test more variables than simply whether the node is responsive.

At first glance the user-mode and privilege-mode versions of ping are the same. Using the Cisco IOS help system will even yield the same results concerning the parameter options accepted by the two commands:

```
Router#ping ?
 WORD Ping destination address or hostname
 ip   IP echo
 tag  Tag encapsulated IP echo
```

(For an explanation of these parameters, see the preceding section.) However, executing user-mode ping with no parameters at all produces the following error:

```
Router>ping
% Incomplete command.
```

Executing the privilege-mode version of ping with no parameters will enable the advanced ping dialog. Here is an excerpt of this dialog:

```
Router# ping
Protocol [ip]:
Target IP address: 10.16.5.152
Repeat count [5]:
Datagram size [100]:
Timeout in seconds [2]:
Extended commands [n]:
Sweep range of sizes [n]:

Type escape sequence to abort.
Sending 5, 100-byte ICMP Echos to 10.16.5.152, timeout is 2 seconds:
!!!!!
Success rate is 100 percent, round-trip min/avg/max = 2/3/4 ms
```

Looking at the parameter options line by line, we can better understand what information ping is looking for in privilege mode.

The first question ping asks you is what protocol you want to use during the ping operation. The default is IP and should be accepted. (As mentioned earlier, Cisco's ping can utilize other protocols, but we will not be covering them here.) Accepting the default protocol of IP will bring up the next line of the dialog.

The second piece of information ping prompts you for is the target address. This is the most important prompt of the dialog. If you were to enter only the target address and escape past every other dialog question, ping would still run. (Obviously, you need an address to ping for the test to work.)

Next you are prompted for a repeat count. This allows you to specify the number of echo packets you want sent to the destination. The default value is five; however, there are occasions where you will want to specify more or less. For example, if you are testing for a faulty or loose connection, five packets may not be enough to detect the problem. Therefore, to test for intermittent line problems, you may want ping to send more than five packets. By sending more packets you can ping a target for a longer period of time, thus increasing your chances of encountering an intermittent problem.

The ping dialog then prompts you to specify the size of the echo packet. This is useful in high-traffic areas. Although 100 bytes does not seem like a lot of data, you may want to specify less. For example, if you are testing a very congested line (possibly to find the cause of the congestion), you may not have the bandwidth to echo five 100-byte packets effectively. Therefore, you may want to use a smaller packet size.

The next line of the dialog deals with configuring the time-to-live of the echo packets. Generally you should have no reason to adjust this value from the default of 2 seconds. This gives the router ample time to determine whether a device is responsive or not.

The ping dialog then asks if you want to enable the extended commands. Answering yes will open a new dialog; responding no will continue the current ping dialog. If you continue with the current dialog, you will then be prompted for "sweeping a range of sizes."

When ping sweeps a range of sizes, it will vary the size of the echo packets being sent. This can help you determine whether packet size is a factor in the connectivity of your end systems. Ordinarily the datagram size affects the ping execution by forcing all packets to be the same size, but sweeping creates multiple packets of differing sizes.

At this point the ping command will execute. However, if you chose to enable the extended commands, you would see the following prompts:

```
Extended commands [n]: y
Source address or interface: 10.153.16.4
Type of service [0]:
Set DF bit in IP header? [no]:
Validate reply data? [no]:
Data pattern [0xABCD]:
Loose, Strict, Record, Timestamp, Verbose[none]: Record
Number of hops [ 9 ]:
Loose, Strict, Record, Timestamp, Verbose[RV]:
Sweep range of sizes [n]:
```

```
Type escape sequence to abort.
Sending 5, 100-byte ICMP Echos to 10.153.16.5, timeout is 2 seconds:
Packet has IP options: Total option bytes= 39, padded length=40
```

The extended commands allow you to have even more control over the operation and execution of your `ping` command.

The first extended-command dialog question asks you for the source address for the ping. By being able to specify a source address, you can control what interface the router executes the command from. This is particularly useful if you have multiple interfaces, each with the potential of reaching the same target address. Specifying the source interface address will help you narrow down the potential connectivity issues. In scenarios where you have more than one router interface that has the ability to contact a particular target, you can run an extended ping through each interface. This helps determine whether the path to the device is the problem.

All of the following prompts are advanced prompts. These tend to deal directly with how the ping packets are formatted—in other words, what bit arrangement to use in certain parts of the packet. This is highly granular material, but it is worth discussing.

The DF bit in the IP header specifies that the packet is not to be fragmented. Routers and other IP devices can be configured to move only packets of certain sizes. Therefore, when a packet larger than the configured size comes along, the device simply fragments it into smaller packets that it can move. Usually this is done transparently, and the user is none the wiser. By setting the DF bit, you are telling any other device on the network, "If you are configured to move only packets smaller than this, drop this packet and send me an error." This can be useful if you are trying to locate a device that may be misconfigured to move small packets, but there is generally no need to change this setting.

The next two options are "validate replies" and "set data pattern." Validating the replies can be redundant because it does exactly that: creates a reply to a reply. However, if you have an intermittent problem, this option may be useful in determining whether you are receiving accurate responses.

Setting the data pattern allows you to change the actual bit pattern of the echo packet. If you change the bit pattern of a packet, you can use a packet analyzer to examine the structure of the packet that was sent as opposed to the reply that was received. This can help you check for problems such as noisy lines and cross-talk. If the reply has a different bit pattern than the message that was sent, you are picking up electronic noise from somewhere.

The next prompt you will see can be kind of cryptic. It asks you for one of the following options:

```
Loose, Strict, Record, Timestamp, Verbose[none]:
```

However, it does not really tell you anything about what those options mean. "Loose," "Strict," "Timestamp," and "Verbose" refer to the way you want the router to examine the packet's header. The default is "none." Table 10.1 explains these options.

> **Note**
>
> Keep in mind that the options Loose, Strict, Timestamp, Record, and Verbose are parameters that are inserted into the "options" field of the IP header. There is no guarantee that every router on a network will understand how to process these commands. This is especially true for non-Cisco routers.

TABLE 10.1 Ping Expanded Options

Loose source routing	This option specifies a list of devices that you want the traceroute to include in its operation. In other words, while traceroute may take a packet through multiple routers, the ones indicated with the "loose" option should be included in the path.
Strict source routing	Similar to the "loose" option, this option specifies the *only* devices that should be included in the traceroute path.
Record	This option allows you to indicate a desired number of hops.
Timestamp	This option allows you to indicate a desired number of timestamps.
Verbose	Selecting any of the options (with the exception of "none") puts the packet into verbose mode. This allows the results of the advanced options to be printed to the user interface.

By setting the packet to "Record," you will receive an echo from every device that the packet encounters on its way to the target address. If you choose this option, the packet will produce the following prompt:

```
Number of hops [ 9 ]:
```

Specifying the number of hops you want to record is where traceroute and record differ. Whereas record limits you to ping's maximum of nine hops, traceroute does not. This option allows you specify fewer than nine hops if you wish, but nine is the default.

After this point the privilege-mode version of `ping` should execute just like the user-mode version. Although `ping` is a good tool for determining the availability of an end system, `traceroute` can help you determine whether there is a problem with a path.

traceroute

As we discovered, ping can very successfully determine whether an end system is responding to ICMP echoes. However, it does little to explain *why* a particular node does not respond.

Another IP-related tool is traceroute, which uses ICMP packets to test for end node connectivity. Traceroute not only sends echo packets from the target address; it sends echoes from every device that it traverses to reach the destination address.

Traceroute, like ping, has two versions within the Cisco IOS, one for user mode and one for privilege mode. User-mode traceroute has the same options as (and executes similarly to) user-mode ping. Within user-mode traceroute, you can specify the target to which you want to trace a route. Once executed, traceroute returns the name and address of every device it passed through to reach the target.

```
Router>trace 10.16.4.153

Type escape sequence to abort.
Tracing the route to 10.16.4.153
1 Router.testnode.com (10.16.4.199) 62 msec 82 msec 78 msec
2 RouterB.testnode.com (10.16.4.189) 80 msec 99 msec 117 msec
3 RouterC.testnode.com (10.16.4.177)100 msec 110 msec 124 msec
```

Notice that at the end of each reply are the times it took to receive the echo from the particular device. As you can see, the default number of packets traceroute sends is three (in contrast to the five for ping).

Within the execution parameters, there are few differences between user-mode ping and user-mode traceroute. Both commands allow you to specify a target and a protocol; then they do the rest for you. If you fully understand the user-mode ping command, user-mode traceroute will hold no surprises; therefore we will move on to privilege-mode traceroute.

traceroute (Privilege-Mode)

Just as for ping, all of the powerful configuration features of traceroute are reserved for the privilege mode. This allows routing administrators to retain more control over the routing environment.

Executing the privilege-mode version of traceroute without a target parameter will produce the following output dialog:

```
Router#trace
Protocol [ip]:
Target IP address: 10.16.4.153
Source address:
```

```
Numeric display [n]: n
Timeout in seconds [3]:
Probe count [3]:
Minimum Time to Live [1]:
Maximum Time to Live [30]:
Port Number [33434]:
Loose, Strict, Record, Timestamp, Verbose[none]:
Type escape sequence to abort.
Tracing the route to 10.16.4.153
```

At first glance you should notice many of the same prompts found in the privilege-mode version of ping. Because they serve the same purpose as the parameters of ping, Protocol, Target, Timeout, Probe count, and Loose, Strict, Record, Timestamp, and Verbose will not be covered in this section. To review the possible values and properties of these parameters see the section "ping (Privilege-Mode)."

Let's examine those parameters that are unique to the privilege-mode version of traceroute. The first (although it may seem the same as its ping counterpart) is source address.

In contrast to ping, the source address parameter for traceroute cannot be used to indicate an interface name. Rather, the source address must be a valid protocol address relating to a physical interface. With the exception of this minor difference, the source address parameter is used the same way for traceroute as it is for ping.

The next two parameters, "Minimum Time to Live" and "Maximum Time to Live," both relate to the packet timeout or TTL. Because we are dealing with multiple devices when we use traceroute, the delay time from one device to another can vary. Therefore, rather than set a static TTL that is adhered to by all of the devices, traceroute creates a TTL threshold.

The traceroute utility is capable of covering more router hops than ping is. Thus, traceroute needs to allow more time for packets to reach their destination. So the 2-second TTL that is used by ping may not be adequate for an application such as traceroute. By setting a minimum and maximum threshold, traceroute can allow for delays between router hops. The default threshold is 1 to 30 seconds. This should be ample time to deal with minor network latencies.

The final traceroute parameter is port number. The traceroute utility allows users to specify what IP (protocol) port they want the traceroute packets sent out from. This can be extremely useful for diagnosing possible security problems. By indicating the port over which to send the traceroute packets, you can determine whether ports that should be open are, and conversely, whether ports that should not be open are closed. Because many networks operate through unsecured protocol ports, testing traceroute through different ports can help you tighten your network architecture.

These simple commands (`ping` and `traceroute`) can go a long way in diagnosing and troubleshooting routing issues. Take the time needed to learn these commands and to become familiar with their parameters and output formats. By knowing how `ping` and `traceroute` work, you can greatly cut down on the time needed to test and develop new routing paths and network schemes.

Now that we have covered the ICMP relatives of IP, it is time to look at a native IP tool, Telnet. Even if you have previous IP experience, the next section of this chapter should be quite informative.

Telnet

Depending on the level of your previous PC and networking experience, you have most likely used (or at least heard of) the IP tool Telnet. Especially within the confines of the Unix operating platform, Telnet is a powerful tool used for logging into and executing commands on remote devices.

Cisco routers can utilize the capabilities of Telnet in two ways. First, Telnet can allow administrators to access the routers (command interpreters and configuration files) from remote locations. This eliminates the need for routing administrators to be physically at the consoles of the routers they are working on. The most common form of router administration is Telnetting from a PC to one or multiple routers.

The second (and somewhat similar) use of Telnet is to allow administrators working at the console of a router to access other Cisco routers. That is, Cisco routers themselves are capable of utilizing a Telnet client to administer other Cisco routers remotely. This means that one router engineer can log into one Cisco router and then, from the router's command prompt, log into other Cisco routers.

However, this incredibly useful ability represents one of Cisco's biggest security problems. In much the same way as the Roman system of roads was turned against them by invaders (all roads led to Rome), network intruders who gain access to one router can easily Telnet from device to device. Therefore, be careful to secure your connections fully. Later in this book we will discuss basic Cisco security.

Remote Administration Using Telnet

Telnet does require some extra configuration on the administrative side to be functional. That is, if you want to administer the router remotely with Telnet, it must be configured to do so. If you want only to use the router as a Telnet client (that is, to connect to other routers and administer them), no extra configuration is required.

By default, Telnet server services are disabled on Cisco routers. This is to prevent routers from being exploited because administrators were unaware that the protocol was active. If you want to enable Telnet on your router, thus allowing Telnet clients to administer the router remotely, you need to follow certain steps.

To this point we have been focusing our configuration efforts on interfaces (Ethernet0 or Ethernet1). Telnet, however, needs to be configured on a line. Use the "line" command to configure a line (remember to specify which line or lines you want to configure; line 0 5 will configure lines 0 through 5 at the same time.

Once in line configuration mode, issue a help command on Telnet, and you will see your options for configuring Telnet on your router

```
Router#configure terminal
Enter configuration commands, one per line.   End with CNTL/Z.
Router(config)#line 0 5
Router(config-line)#telnet ?
  break-on-ip         Send break signal when interrupt is received
  ip-on-break         Send interrupt signal when break is received
  refuse-negotiations Suppress negotiations of Telnet Remote Echo and SuppressGo Ahead options
  speed               Specify line speeds
  sync-on-break       Send a Telnet Synchronize signal after receiving a Telnet Break signal
  transparent         Send a CR as a CR followed by a NULL instead of a CR
                        followed by a LF
```

Cisco does a good job here of defining for you what each of these configuration options means. However, the parameter that you actually need to be concerned about is speed. The speed parameter for Telnet should get your router prepared for accepting remote connections.

> **Note**
>
> Be aware that this example uses the line 0 5 command to configure all available lines to accept Telnet connections. Although you can go a step further and configure each of these lines with a separate password, that may be slightly counterproductive.
>
> When you Telnet into a Cisco router, there is really no way of specifying the terminal line you want to use. Therefore, if you configure six different passwords for the six different lines, you may have to try each one before accessing the system. This problem can be compounded by the fact that the Cisco IOS gives you only three tries to enter a correct password (after which it will lock you out).

To finalize your configuration of Telnet issue the following command from the line configuration command prompt:

```
Router(config-line)#telnet speed 9600
```

This command will enable (in our scenario) lines 0 through 5 to accept Telnet connections at 9600 bps. You should now be able to Telnet into any of these lines from either a remote PC or another router.

After your router is successfully configured, you will want to test your Telnet abilities. To do so, be sure that the router has at least one interface connected to a network. Then from a Telnet client try connecting to the router.

Next, from a Telnet client, try to connect to one of your router's configured addresses. You should see the following message:

```
C:\Telnet 10.16.4.153

Line 0
Password required but none set

Disconnecting
```

As you can see, just configuring the lines to run Telnet is not enough; Cisco will not let you utilize an unsecured Telnet connection. Therefore, our final step in configuring our Telnet connection is to set a password for the lines you will be allowing connections through.

```
Router#configure terminal
Enter configuration commands, one per line. End with CNTL/Z.
Router(config)#line 0 5
Router(config-line)#password telnet
Router(config-line)#^Z
```

Now retry your Telnet connection to the router. You should be greeted by a login prompt.

```
C:\telnet 10.16.4.153

login

User Access Verification

Password:   telnet
Router>
```

You have now successfully configured your router to accept incoming Telnet sessions. Now let's take a look at using your router as the Telnet client.

Using your router as a Telnet client requires no additional configuration (your router does not need to be configured to accept Telnet sessions). Telneting from within a Cisco router to another Cisco router is actually very simple and can be accomplished with one of three commands. The commands `telnet`, `connect`, and `rlogin` can all be used to open sessions (for administrative purposes) between routers.

> **Note**
> Keep in mind that `telnet`, `connect`, and `rlogin` are all standard Unix-based commands. As such, their use within Cisco is not limited to connecting to routers. Administrators can Telnet from within a Cisco router to a Unix server (or almost any other Telnet-compatible server). However, we will only be covering Telnet uses relating to Cisco routers.

The `telnet` and `connect` commands both work the same way and can be used interchangeably. To initiate a Telnet session from Router (our scenario example router) to another router named RouterB, you would use the following syntax:

```
Router>telnet RouterB
Translating "RouterB"...domain server (10.16.4.188) [OK]
Trying Server3—RouterB.STYSCisco.com (10.16.4.188)... Open

login: userforRouter
Password:
RouterB)
```

Using the `connect` command should yield the same results. Both commands will bring you to the login prompt of the desired server. If you are familiar with Unix Telnet, you should be aware of one difference between Cisco Telnet and Unix Telnet. Cisco Telnet does not support trusted connections. That is, Cisco Telnet cannot authenticate a Telnet connection based on the credentials of the current logged-in session. Therefore, every Telnet session initiated will produce a login prompt.

You can also initiate a Telnet session using no commands at all. For example, you may have entered an incorrect command at a command prompt and received the following message:

```
Router>RouterB
Translating "RouterB"...domain server (255.255.255.255)
% Unknown command or computer name, or unable to find computer address
```

This error message is actually generated by the Cisco IOS trying to open a Telnet session to the server named (not realizing you were trying to run a command). In this scenario there is no Telnet server named RouterB (and no Cisco command named RouterB);

therefore, an error was generated. Had a Telnet server existed with the name `RouterB`, you would have seen the follow message:

```
Router>RouterB
Translating "RouterB"...domain server (10.16.4.188) [OK]
Trying Server3—RouterB.STYSCisco.com (10.16.4.188)... Open

login:
```

The one caveat here is, if you have a Telnet server with the same name as an existing Cisco command, you must preface the server name with either the `telnet` or `connect` keyword. For example, to connect with a Telnet server named `Enable`, you should use the following convention:

```
Router> connect enable
Translating "enable"...domain server (10.16.4.189) [OK]
Trying Server3—enable.STYSCisco.com (10.16.4.189)... Open
```

After you have successfully initiated a Telnet session, you will see a new prompt. The prompt will consist of the remote router's name and a right parenthesis.

```
RouterB)
```

This prompt indicates that you are issuing commands to a remote device. Every remote router that you connect to will have its own unique command prompt. However, stacking up command prompts can get confusing, and switching between them can be difficult. That's why Cisco created the `resume` command. To move between sessions, use the syntax `resume <connection name>` from any prompt.

```
Router>resume RouterB
RouterB)
```

The `resume` command will bring you to the requested session. To exit a session, use the `exit` command.

```
RouterB)exit
Router>
```

Two other commands exist that can come in very handy if you plan on using multiple Telnet sessions. These are the `notify` command and the `refuse-message` command.

The `notify` command (after being enabled) will alert you when a remote session (other than the one you are working in) has output waiting for your attention. The following example illustrates how to enable the `notify` feature.

```
Router#configure terminal
Enter configuration commands, one per line. End with CNTL/Z.
Router(config)#line 0 5
Router(config-line)#notify
Router(config-line)#^Z
Router#
```

The `refuse-message` command will notify anyone trying to Telnet into a router if the line is already in use.

```
Router#configure terminal
Enter configuration commands, one per line. End with CNTL/Z.
Router(config)#line 0 5
Router(config-line)#refuse-message ! line in use !
Router(config-line)#^Z
Router#
```

The `refuse-message` command has the same parameters as most banner messages.

The `telnet` and `connect` commands can be used to access remote routers (and other Telnet servers). However, another command with a more specialized purpose can also be used: `rlogin`.

rlogin

The `rlogin` command works just like `telnet` and `connect`. The major difference is that rlogin is not supported by every device that supports Telnet. Rlogin is a tool originally developed for BSD Unix. Therefore, if you want to initiate an rlogin session, the server accepting the session must be configured to use rlogin.

The syntax for the `rlogin` command is actually quite similar to that of `telnet`:

`Router>rlogin RouterB`

The advantage to using `rlogin` over `telnet` is that `rlogin` supports debugging of the output. By specifying the connection to be made in debug mode, you have greater control over the flow of the output through `rlogin`.

`Router>rlogin RouterB debug`

Ping, traceroute, Telnet, connect, and rlogin give you much greater control over your routing environment. Learning and mastering these commands will prepare you for the more complex features to come.

Summary

- IP functionality is installed by default on Cisco routers with every Cisco IOS feature pack except the IPX Basic Feature Pack.
- IP addresses are configured within the interface configuration mode of the privilege command interpreter.
- To access the interface configuration mode, use the `interface` command.
- Static IP routes can be written to the `startup-config` file by using the `perm` parameter.

- Several tools provided as part of the TCP/IP protocol suite are the ICMP commands.
- Ping tests the existence of an entity by sending ICMP echo packets.
- Traceroute works similarly to ping. However, traceroute echoes back to the sending device the path it took to the target device.
- Another important IP tool is Telnet.
- Cisco routers can support several Telnet sessions as both clients and servers.

Q&A

Q IP functionality is provided by default on all Cisco routers. Can it be uninstalled?

A No, IP support cannot be uninstalled. If you do not want to use or support IP on your Cisco router, simply do not enable it. (Or, if it is enabled, use the `no ip routing` command.) Even the most basic IPX feature pack includes IP support.

Quiz

Questions

1. If you want to test the path between six specific routers, which type of source routing would you select for your ping statement?
2. How many lines are available for incoming Telnet sessions?
3. What does an M stand for as the result of a ping or traceroute?

Answers

1. Strict
2. 6
3. The packet used to test with was too large to be routed.

Exercises

1. Configure the interface Ethernet1 with the IP address 198.5.42.1 subnet mask 255.0.0.0.

Note

```
Router(configureconfig)#int e1
Router(configureconfig-interface)#ip address 198.5.42.1 255.0.0.0
```

2. What do the following ping results mean?

   ```
   1) Sending 5, 100-byte ICMP Echos to 10.16.5.152, timeout is 2 seconds:
   . . . . .
   2) Sending 5, 100-byte ICMP Echos to 10.16.5.152, timeout is 2 seconds:
   ! ! ! ! !
   3) Sending 5, 100-byte ICMP Echos to 10.16.5.152, timeout is 2 seconds:
   U U U U U
   ```

   > **Note**
   > 1) No ICMP echoes were received from the target address.
   > 2) The ping was successful.
   > 3) The host was unreachable.

3. What is the one major difference between the record mode of privilege-mode ping and traceroute?

   > **Note**
   > Ping can span no more than 9 router hops.

4. What is wrong with the following Telnet connection syntax to the router show?

   ```
   Router>show
   ```

   > **Note**
   > The Telnet connection will not be processed because show is a Cisco IOS command. You need to include one of the following keywords.
   > ```
   > rlogin
   > connect
   > telnet
   > ```

WEEK 2

DAY 11

Understanding Segmented Networks

Today's lesson is going to take us into the realm of network design. Working with Cisco routers entails not only configuring the router and ensuring that it is maintained correctly, but also placing the routers in the most effective places on the network. You should always consider the proper placement of a router to ensure the optimum performance from your equipment.

To this point in the book we have covered all of the basic concepts needed to choose, configure, and maintain a simple IP router successfully. However, the world is not based on the examples provided in the lessons so far. Real-life routing environments are much more complicated and involved than those we have worked with thus far.

The remainder of this book is going to jump right into some of the most prevalent topics and technologies facing Cisco engineers today. One such topic is segmented networks. Segmented networks can be a thorn in the side for many networking and routing professionals, because segmented networks have complexities and intricacies that make them truly difficult to work with.

Note that, although today's lesson deals with routing IP data between segmented networks, it does not consider cases where routing protocols would be involved, because we have not covered routing protocols yet in this book. Within this lesson we will examine only the part IP plays in routing. Understanding routing as a whole requires knowledge of both routed and routing protocols, but for now we will keep to a logical progression, concluding our discussions on IP with today's introduction to IP routing. We will cover the various routing protocols in later lessons.

To cover the subject of segmented networks and segmented network routing thoroughly, we will discuss the following topics:

- Identifying the need for subnetting
- Configuring static routes between subnets

Mastering the segmented networks requires you to expand your understanding of IP and IP routing. To this point we have discussed such topics only in a flat environment—that is, an environment that is fairly static and consists of one path spanning two networks. If you have worked with computer networks before, you know that this is not the case in the majority of companies that use Cisco routers.

The most common type of LAN (WAN) configuration today is the IP segmented environment. In segmented environments, IP networks are subnetted to create dozens of smaller IP networks. Each of these subnets links back to the main network and to the other subnets. This can create a confusing array of paths and addressing schemes that can daunt even the most seasoned professional.

On Days 9 and 10 we briefly covered the binary process for creating an IP subnet and deriving a subnet mask from it. The first section of this lesson expands upon those concepts and shows you the physical side of network subnetting, as well as more concepts to help you segment your own environments.

Identifying the Need for Subnetting

Up to this point, all we have discussed about subnetting is the fact that the bits are borrowed from the host address and given to the network. Although this process increases the number of networks you can address, it decreases the number of hosts in each network. Actually, there are many valid reasons for subnetting an IP network. One of the biggest reasons an administrator would want to subnet a network is to make better use of the ever-dwindling supply of IP addresses. The current IP-4 addressing scheme is finite and quickly drying up.

> **Note:** Although IP-4 is the most widely used version of IP, IP-6 is just over the horizon. IP-6 offers a greater range of addresses and should carry us further into the future of computing.

With the advent of the dot-com age, the static pool of IP addresses is quickly running out. Network administrators, routing engineers, and ISPs need to conserve what few addresses they have.

Subnetting an IP Network

When a network is designed and created, the administrator has the responsibility to formulate a functional *IP scheme*. The scheme must provide an adequate number of IP addresses to meet the needs of the environment. Every device that will communicate on the network needs to have at least one address, from the PCs to the servers and routers. This requires a great deal of planning and foresight to ensure that the environment is properly addressed.

> **Note:** An IP scheme is the set of IP addresses (both network and host) that are assigned to and used within a single operating environment. An IP scheme can consist of a range of addresses all of one class, or it can comprise several ranges from different classes.

For example, Figure 11.1 illustrates a proposed network environment. Within this environment the geographic locations and estimated staffing requirements are defined. From this information an administrator can extrapolate a rough number of IP addresses needed to meet the proposed requirements.

In Figure 11.1 the administrator sees a requirement of 695 IP addresses. To this number the business needs to add more addresses that can be reserved for future expansion, such as for new employees or equipment. In this example, the administrator and the business entity agree that the IP scheme of the network should include at least 750 host addresses and one network address.

To meet this requirement a class B IP license is required. Class B IP licenses are capable of accommodating 65,534 hosts. That may seem like overkill on a network that requires only 750 addresses, but the next smaller option, a class C license, can support only 254 hosts. Therefore, the business unit purchases a class B license and prepares to build its new network.

FIGURE 11.1

A proposed network.

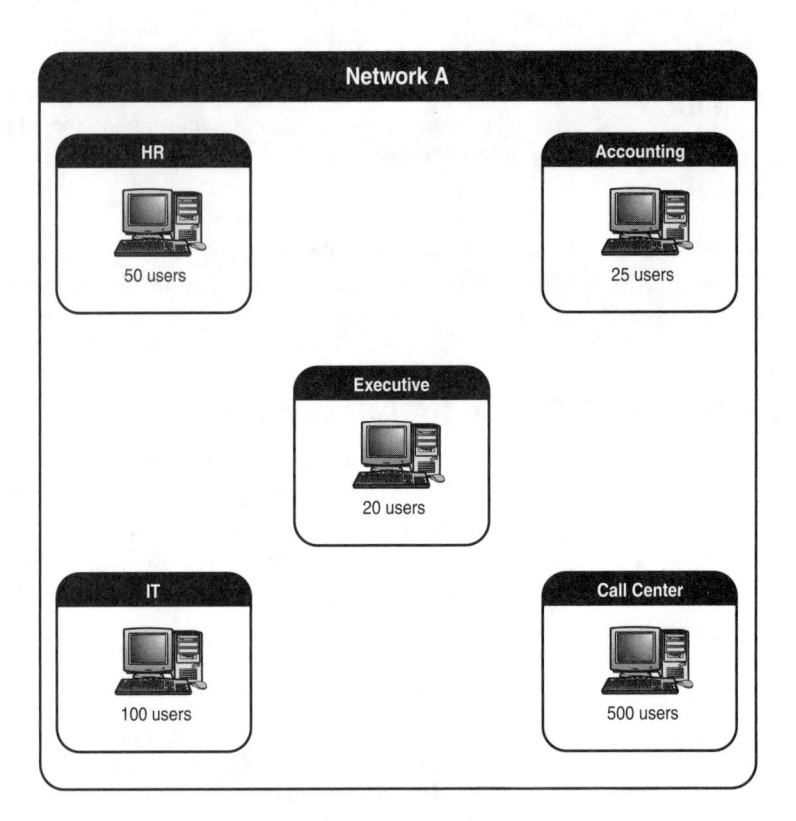

> **Note**
>
> The demand for IP licenses has been growing over the past few years. Because of this overwhelming demand, it is unlikely today that an entity of 750 people would be assigned an entire class B license. In all likelihood, the business in our example would be assigned a subnet of an ISP's class B license. However, to illustrate the process of subnetting fully, we will proceed to assume that the company in our example has been granted the entire license.

The class B license that is assigned to our business is 135.55.0.0, with a subnet mask of 255.255.0.0. Keep in mind this license allows for one network (135.55) and 65,534 hosts (1.1 through 254.254). The administrator applies the new addresses to the proposed network. Figure 11.2 illustrates the new networking environment.

In Figure 11.2, the administrator treated the entire environment as a single entity (which it technically is) and assigned different host addresses based on PC location. The PCs in the HR department were assigned the host addresses 1.1 through 1.51; the IT department

FIGURE 11.2

The networked environment with an IP scheme.

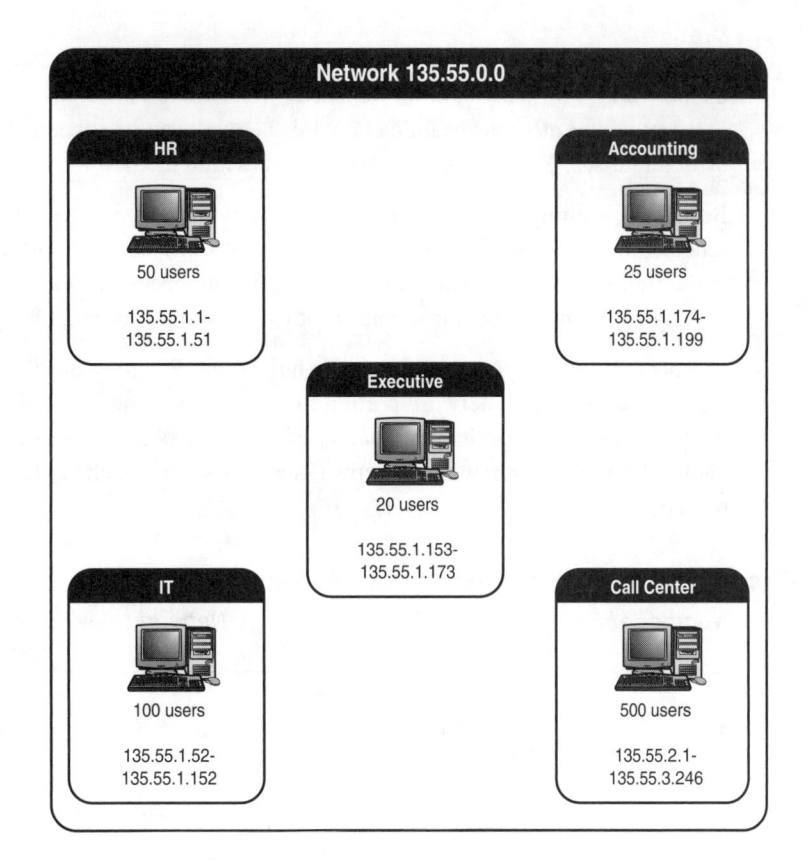

Network 135.55.0.0

- **HR** — 50 users — 135.55.1.1–135.55.1.51
- **Accounting** — 25 users — 135.55.1.174–135.55.1.199
- **Executive** — 20 users — 135.55.1.153–135.55.1.173
- **IT** — 100 users — 135.55.1.52–135.55.1.152
- **Call Center** — 500 users — 135.55.2.1–135.55.3.246

was assigned the addresses 1.52 through 1.152, and so on. However, this is not the most efficient way to have distributed the addresses.

For example, if the company were to add a new office, or acquire another smaller entity, there would be no network addresses left to assign (the only network address, 135.55, is in use). Any new networks added to the environment need to be addressed before they can participate in the environment. The network administrator needs a way to create more network addresses while still having enough host addresses to assign throughout the environment. In other words, the class B license needs to be subnetted.

Subnetting the class B license splits it into multiple networks. By dividing the single network address (135.55) into multiple network addresses, the administrator can use one address for the current network and keep the others for future use. This keeps the environment as scalable as possible.

However, subnetting an IP network address does have its downside. By adding more networks to your IP license, you lose hosts. That is, by creating more network addresses for your environment, you decrease the number of hosts that can be assigned to each of the networks. For many entities, the need for networks outweighs the need for hosts on each network. Let's now examine how this network can be subnetted to maximize its use of IP addresses. Then we can discuss routing within the new environment.

Because subnetting increases the number of network addresses available to the IP scheme, the administrator needs to forecast how many networks the company could need in the future while still maintaining an adequate number of hosts. The administrator already knows that the company needs at least one network and 695 hosts.

The next task is to figure out how many bits of the IP address need to be reassigned from the host portion to the network portion to provide an adequate number of networks. The mathematics for computing the number of hosts and networks was presented on Day 9. Table 11.1 illustrates how many networks and hosts are available for each bit that is passed.

TABLE 11.1 Number of Networks Made Available by Subnetting

Number of Bits	Binary Address	Networks	Hosts per Network
2	11000000.00000000	2	16382
3	11100000.00000000	6	8190
4	11110000.00000000	14	4094
5	11111000.00000000	30	2046
6	11111100.00000000	62	1022
7	11111110.00000000	126	510

If the administrator chooses to pass 6 bits from the host to the network, there would be 62 possible network addresses to use, with 1022 hosts for each. That would be more than enough to keep the environment addressed and working properly.

Now that the administrator has determined how many bits to use for the correct number of network and host addresses, those addresses must be assigned to the network. The first step to assigning the new addresses is to figure out what the usable network addresses are and their related subnet mask.

Figuring out the new network addresses is going to take a little math, which we discussed on Day 9. The formula for determining the network address off subnetted networks is

$$256 - \text{subnet mask} = \text{interval between network addresses}$$

Understanding Segmented Networks

The address of the first network in the subnet is simply the interval between network addresses. All subsequent addresses are determined by adding the interval successively until the sum equals the subnet mask, which itself is not a valid address. This might sound complicated, but it will make more sense after you work through the example in the following text.

The first variable in the equation for determining network addresses is the subnet mask. Accordingly, before you compute any network addresses, you must determine what the subnet mask for the new IP scheme is going to be.

> **Note**
> The subnet mask remains constant throughout the IP scheme. That is, even though we have subnetted an IP address into multiple networks, all of those networks will share a common subnet mask. This will be the thread that ties these networks together.

To figure out the subnet mask, simply convert the network portion of the address (in binary) to all ones. This provides you with a common subnet mask to use across your environment. Table 11.2 illustrates various subnet masks available for Class B addresses.

TABLE 11.2 Class B Subnet Masks

Number of Bits	Binary Mask	Subnet Mask
1	11111111.11111111.10000000.00000000	255.255.128.0
2	11111111.11111111.11000000.00000000	255.255.192.0
3	11111111.11111111.11100000.00000000	255.255.224.0
4	11111111.11111111.11110000.00000000	255.255.240.0
5	11111111.11111111.11111000.00000000	255.255.248.0
6	11111111.11111111.11111100.00000000	255.255.252.0
7	11111111.11111111.11111110.00000000	255.255.254.0

According to this table, the subnet mask for our network should be 255.255.252.0. This is the mask for a class B network in which 6 bits have been passed from the host to the network. If we had decided to pass 5 bits from the host, we would be using the mask 255.255.248.0.

Now that we have determined the subnet mask, we can plug that value into the equation and find out what our network addresses are. Recall that our equation to figure out the network address of our subnetted environment is

256 − subnet mask = interval between network addresses = first network address

Knowing the subnet mask (255.255.252.0), we can now plug that value into our equation:

256 − **252** = 4

By using this formula, we have determined that our first addressable network will be 135.55.**4**.0, with a subnet mask of 255.255.252.0. Using this network address we can begin to readdress our sample network. The first 1022 addresses of the 135.55.4.0 network are 135.55.1.1 through 135.55.4.254. Figure 11.3 shows our sample network with the assigned addresses from our subnet.

FIGURE 11.3

A sample network with subnetted address information.

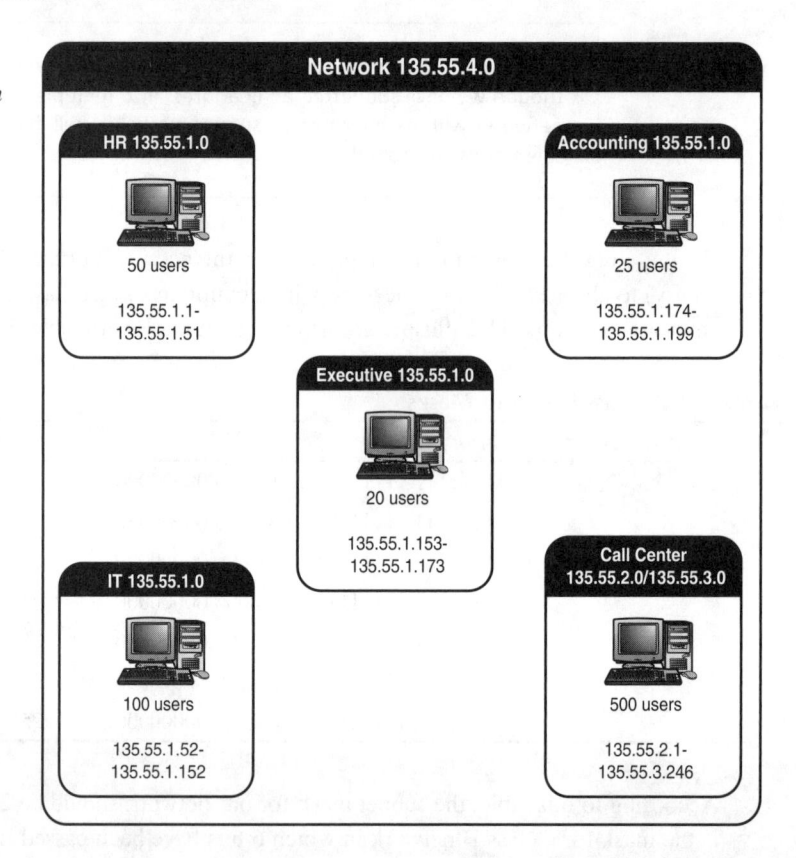

Network 135.55.4.0

- **HR 135.55.1.0** — 50 users — 135.55.1.1-135.55.1.51
- **Accounting 135.55.1.0** — 25 users — 135.55.1.174-135.55.1.199
- **Executive 135.55.1.0** — 20 users — 135.55.1.153-135.55.1.173
- **IT 135.55.1.0** — 100 users — 135.55.1.52-135.55.1.152
- **Call Center 135.55.2.0/135.55.3.0** — 500 users — 135.55.2.1-135.55.3.246

Compare the network in Figure 11.2 with the one in Figure 11.3. The design in Figure 11.2 used the only network address and wasted roughly 64,000 host addresses, whereas the new design uses one of 63 networks and has only roughly 300 spare hosts. This is a much more efficient design, and it is much more router friendly.

Understanding Segmented Networks

Now suppose that after the network is complete, the business expands to a second office. The new network needs to be addressed using the same IP scheme as the first. Finally, a Cisco router must be placed between the two networks to connect them to each other. Figure 11.4 illustrates the new network.

FIGURE 11.4

A second network to be subnetted.

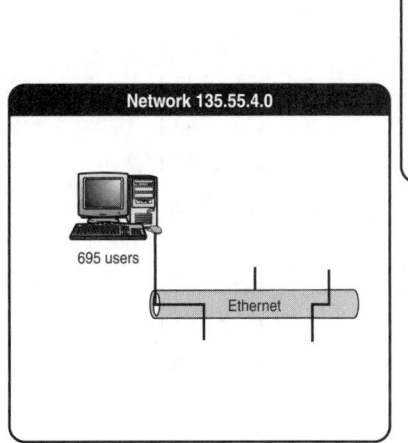

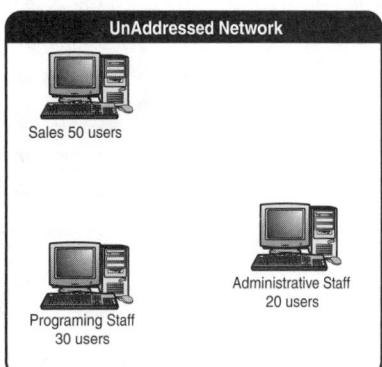

Recall that we determined the first network address for our subnet as

$256 - 252 = 4$ (135.55.**4**.0)

To get the next network address, add the difference of the equation to the first network address. If we take the first network address (4) and add it to the first network address, we have the second network address (135.55.**8**.0). This second network has all of the same characteristics as the first. That is, the second network allows for 1022 hosts and uses the subnet mask 255.255.252.0.

This process of adding the first network address again to obtain the next network address can be repeated until the sum is equal to the subnet mask address itself; that sum is not a valid network address. All of the available networks can be determined this way. Table 11.3 shows the available remaining networks for our class B subnet.

TABLE 11.3 Remaining Subnet Network Addresses

Subnet Mask	Subnet Networks	Start Host Range	End Host Range
255.255.252.0	135.55.4.0	135.55.1.1	135.55.4.254
	135.55.8.0	135.55.5.1	135.55.8.254
	135.55.12.0	135.55.9.1	135.55.12.254
	135.55.16.0	135.55.13.1	135.55.16.254
	135.55.22.0	135.55.17.1	135.55.22.254
	135.55.26.0	135.55.23.1	135.55.26.254
	135.55.32.0	135.55.27.1	135.55.32.254
	135.55.36.0	135.55.33.1	135.55.36.254
	135.55.42.0	135.55.37.1	135.55.42.254
	135.55.46.0	135.55.43.1	135.55.46.254
	135.55.52.0	135.55.47.1	135.55.52.254
	135.55.56.0	135.55.53.1	135.55.56.254
	135.55.62.0	135.55.57.1	135.55.62.254
	135.55.66.0	135.55.63.1	135.55.66.254
	135.55.72.0	135.55.67.1	135.55.72.254
	135.55.76.0	135.55.73.1	135.55.76.254
	135.55.82.0	135.55.77.1	135.55.82.254
	135.55.86.0	135.55.83.1	135.55.86.254
	135.55.92.0	135.55.87.1	135.55.92.254
	135.55.96.0	135.55.93.1	135.55.96.254
	135.55.102.0	135.55.97.1	135.55.102.254
	135.55.106.0	135.55.103.1	135.55.106.254
	135.55.112.0	135.55.107.1	135.55.112.254
	135.55.116.0	135.55.113.1	135.55.116.254
	135.55.122.0	135.55.117.1	135.55.122.254
	135.55.126.0	135.55.123.1	135.55.126.254
	135.55.132.0	135.55.127.1	135.55.132.254
	135.55.136.0	135.55.133.1	135.55.136.254
	135.55.142.0	135.55.137.1	135.55.142.254
	135.55.146.0	135.55.143.1	135.55.146.254
	135.55.152.0	135.55.147.1	135.55.152.254

continues

Understanding Segmented Networks

TABLE 11.3 Continued

Subnet Mask	Subnet Networks	Start Host Range	End Host Range
	135.55.156.0	135.55.153.1	135.55.156.254
	135.55.162.0	135.55.157.1	135.55.162.254
	135.55.166.0	135.55.163.1	135.55.166.254
	135.55.172.0	135.55.167.1	135.55.172.254
	135.55.176.0	135.55.173.1	135.55.176.254
	135.55.182.0	135.55.177.1	135.55.182.254
	135.55.186.0	135.55.183.1	135.55.186.254
	135.55.192.0	135.55.187.1	135.55.192.254
	135.55.196.0	135.55.193.1	135.55.196.254
	135.55.202.0	135.55.197.1	135.55.202.254
	135.55.206.0	135.55.203.1	135.55.206.254
	135.55.212.0	135.55.207.1	135.55.212.254
	135.55.216.0	135.55.213.1	135.55.216.254
	135.55.222.0	135.55.217.1	135.55.222.254
	135.55.226.0	135.55.223.1	135.55.226.254
	135.55.232.0	135.55.227.1	135.55.232.254
	135.55.236.0	135.55.233.1	135.55.236.254
	135.55.242.0	135.55.237.1	135.55.242.254
	135.55.246.0	135.55.243.1	135.55.246.254

Although any network address for this list can be assigned to the new network in our environment, we choose 135.55.8.0. The new addresses from the 8.0 network can now be assigned to the environment. Following the same process used for the first network, the new addresses are assigned by corporate function. That is, "Sales" is assigned addresses 135.55.5.1 through 135.55.5.101, and so on. Figure 11.5 illustrates the fully addressed environment.

The two networks with our environment lack one important feature: the ability to communicate with each other. Because they are addressed as two separate networks, the two networks within our environment cannot exchange data. To facilitate the movement of data we need to place our router in a position that will allow it to serve both portions of the entire environment.

FIGURE 11.5

A fully addressed two-network subnetted environment.

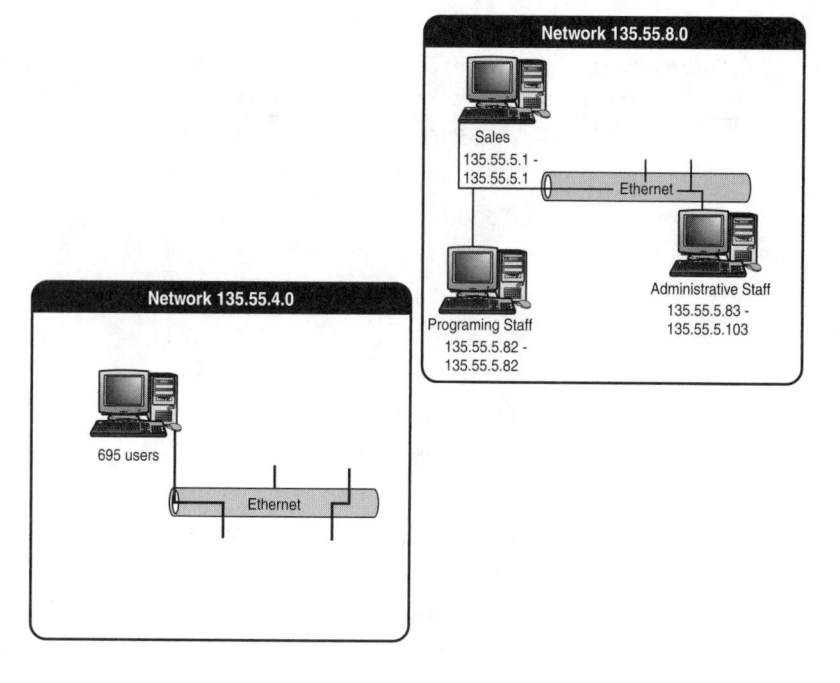

Placing Cisco Routers within Segmented Environments

Many network problems can be avoided during the design phase of the environment. Learning Cisco routers calls for accepting some responsibility for the overall design of a network (be that physical routing hardware or protocol software). In this section of today's lesson, you will learn how to place Cisco routers correctly within segmented networks.

A router that has just been placed with an environment without regard for the surrounding architecture will not function efficiently. Careful attention needs to be paid to elements such as network traffic and the number of available interfaces. When placing a Cisco router between segmented networks, you should consider several factors:

- Keep track of the available interfaces on your router. Most Cisco routers have two LAN interfaces. While one router can span two networks, three networks may require up to three routers to configure the paths you need.
- Place your router where the busiest parts of the network will be served best. For example, you may want to have a separate router for the busiest part of a network, even if you are only routing between two networks.

- If you are connecting critical network segments, place the routers in a way that is conducive to building redundant links.
- Physically locate your routers in a common area close to the other communications devices. This helps you during expansions, especially where the Internet is involved.
- Place your routers with your routing protocol in mind. Certain routing protocols may require that you place routers in certain locations or not exceed specific limitations. (For example, if you plan on using RIP, you cannot reach networks beyond 16 router hops.)

> **Note**
> Although you should always consider the routing protocol to be used in your environment, we do not have that luxury in this lesson, because we have not yet covered any routing protocols. We will therefore consider only the other factors when placing the routers in this lesson. (We will cover routing protocols in the remaining days' lessons.)

With these factors in mind, let's find the best area to place our router. The obvious location is between the two networks in a physical location that is close to both. Figure 11.6 illustrates the logical placement of the router.

When working with only two networks, you can be logical about the placement of your router. Keep in mind that working with routers can (at times) be difficult enough. If a logical solution presents itself, take it. Because there are only two networks in the current scenario, we can easily place the Cisco router between the two.

With the router in place, the last step is to configure it. Let's look at each of the steps required to configure a Cisco router to run between two subnets.

1. Configure each interface with an address from its respective network.
2. Turn on the interfaces.
3. Define the subnet mask.
4. Enable IP routing.
5. Create static paths to connect to two networks.

The first step is to configure each interface to run IP. This means that we need to assign each interface on the router an address that corresponds to the network it is attached to. During this same command sequence, we can define the subnet mask on each interface and turn the interface on, thus performing the first three steps in the foregoing list with

FIGURE 11.6

A Cisco router placed between two networks.

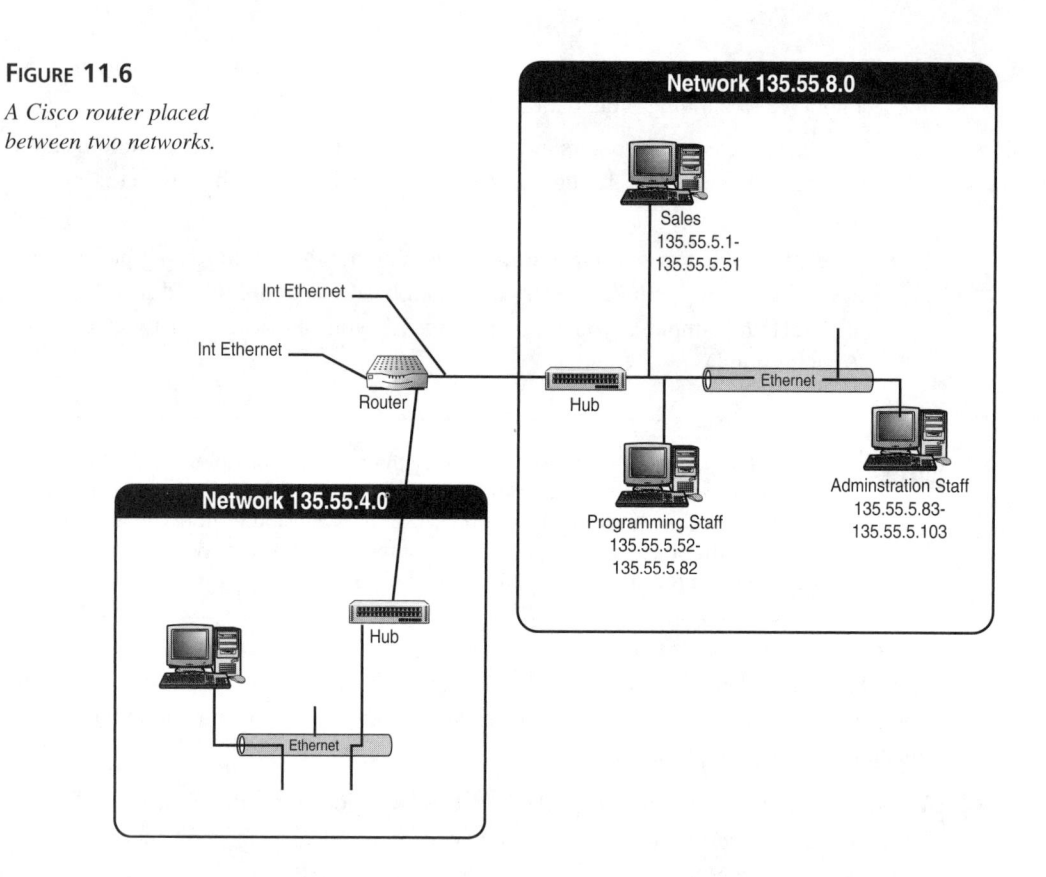

one command sequence. (Remember that every interface defaults to a "shutdown" status, so they must be turned on manually.) The following commands carry out these steps:

```
Router>enable
Router#configure terminal
Router(configure)#interface ethernet 0
Router(configure-interface)#ip address 135.55.4.1 255.255.252.0
Router(configure-interface)#no shutdown

Router#configure terminal
Router(configure)#interface ethernet 1
Router(configure-terminal)#ip address 135.55.8.1 255.255.252.0
Router(configure-interface)#no shutdown
Router(configure-terminal)#^Z
```

Let's examine each command as it relates to a specific step in the foregoing list.

```
The first three lines of the command sequence put the router into the interface
configuration mode. To reach interface configuration mode, you first enter priv-
ilege mode, then into global configuration mode:Router>enable
```

```
Router#configure terminal
Router(configure)#interface ethernet 0
```

> **Note** The number at the end of the `interface ethernet 0` command indicates which interface we want to configure.

Once in interface configuration mode, we can define the IP address and the subnet mask (fourth line) for the desired interface. In this case, interface Ethernet 0 is connected to network 135.55.4.0; therefore, we configure it with the address 135.55.4.1 (step 1 in the list) and subnet 255.255.252.0 (step 3 in the list):

```
Router(configure-interface)#ip address 135.55.4.1 255.255.252.0
```

Now that the address and the subnet mask have been defined, it is time to turn on the interface (step 2 in the list). The following command turns on the interface and saves the configuration to the `running-config` file (the Ctrl+Z on the second line exits from the interface configuration mode):

```
Router(configure-interface)#no shutdown
Router(configure-interface)#^Z
```

Notice the structure of the command. Rather than tell the router to turn on the interface, we indicate to the router not to shut it down. Then pressing Ctrl+Z returns the router to the privilege mode prompt. From there we can repeat the process for the second interface:

```
Router#configure terminal
Router(configure)#interface ethernet 1
Router(configure-terminal)#ip address 135.55.8.1 255.255.252.0
Router(configure-interface)#no shutdown
Router(configure-terminal)#^Z
```

> **Note** It is not necessary to exit interface configuration mode between every configuration set. The Ctrl+Z was used here to illustrate the full process. Normally you can configure both interfaces during one session.

Step number 4 in our checklist is to enable IP routing. This actually enables the passing of packets from one interface to the other. Before we can use our router between the two subnets, we must enable IP routing. The following two commands complete this step:

```
Router#configure terminal
Router(configure)# ip routing
```

Because IP routing affects the router as a whole, the command is executed from global configuration mode. Logically, you cannot enable IP routing on one interface and not another—the data would not move anywhere—so all routing options are considered global configurations.

The final step in our checklist is to configure some static routes to guide the flow of data between the subnets. Because there is no routing protocol present in this design, we cannot take advantage of dynamic routing. Therefore, even though the routing takes place from one interface to another (within the same router), we still need to configure the static routes:

```
Router#configure terminal
Router (configure)#ip route 135.55.4.0 255.255.252.0 Ethernet 0 perm
Router (configure)#ip route 135.55.8.0 255.255.252.0 Ethernet 1 perm
```

These two statements tell the router that network 135.55.4.0 is attached to the interface Ethernet 0 and that network 135.55.8.0 is attached to Ethernet 1. However, the `ip route` command has much more capability than we are using here. As this book progresses (especially after Day 13, "Understanding WAN Protocols"), you will be using the `ip route` command much more.

Configuring Static Routes Between Subnets

A route is a map or rule used by a router to move data from one network to another. Routes define the movement of information on your network. Cisco routers can utilize two different types of routes: static and dynamic. Dynamic routes will be covered in later lessons; static routes will be your focus in this section. Simply stated, static routes are predefined paths for network-to-network data transfers that have been hard-coded into a router's memory.

Keep in mind as you read this section that static routes are a good tool only in certain situations. There are three main network situations that would warrant the use of static IP route definitions:

- The routers in the environment do not use a routing protocol.
- Security elements dictate that only certain traffic pass through certain routers.
- The routing environment does not change.

> **Note** We will cover dynamic routes in a later lesson of this book, because dynamic routes are supported only by routing protocols.

Understanding Segmented Networks

The command for configuring static routes between subnets is actually quite straightforward, although there are several optional parameters (see Table 11.4) that you can supply to perform different tasks. The command string format for ip route is as follows:

`#ip route <Destination Network> <Destination Subnet> <Next Hop | Interface | Null> <Next Hop | perm>`

TABLE 11.4 Parameters for the `ip route` Command

Parameter	Description
`<Destination Network>`	The IP address of the destination network (that is, the path to which data should be sent)
`<Destination Subnet>`	The subnet mask of the destination network
`<Next Hop	Interface	Null>`	A parameter for specifying how to route packets addressed to the destination:
Next Hop	The IP address of the router to which packets for the destination network should be forwarded
Interface	The internal interface to which packets for the destination network should be forwarded
Null	Indication that the Static route is going to be used with another command (this option is used more within routing protocols such as BGP)
`<Next Hop	perm>`	An optional parameter as follows:
Next Hop	The IP address of the router to which packets should be sent as related to the specific interface (optional if the previous position contains an interface parameter)
perm	Indication that the router is to write the route to the `startup-config`, thus making the route permanent

Using Table 11.4 as a guide, let's configure the static routes for a more complicated example network segment. Figure 11.7 illustrates a portion of a large subnetted network.

In this scenario we have four interconnected routers, each serving a smaller segment of a large subnetted network. To make it possible to move data from network 198.10.0.0 to 198.13.0.0, the following routes should be configured:

- Router 198.10.1.1:

    RouterA(configure)#**ip route 198.13.0.0 255.0.0.0 ethernet 1 198.11.1.1 perm**

- Router 198.11.1.1:

    RouterB(configure)#**ip route 198.13.0.0 255.0.0.0 ethernet 1 198.12.1.1 perm**

FIGURE 11.7

A network segment.

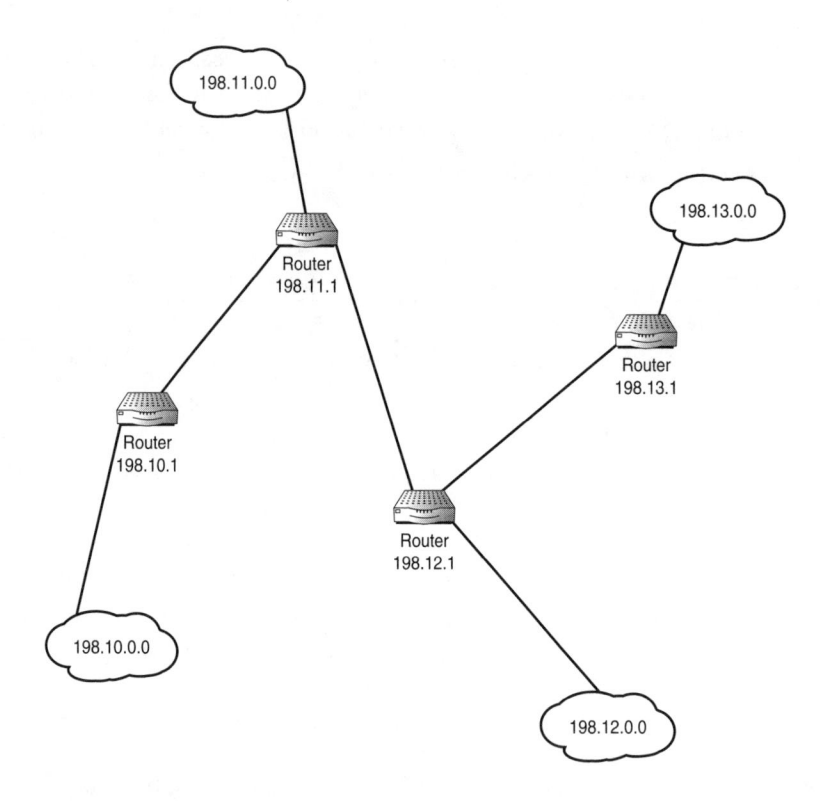

- Router 198.12.1.1:

  ```
  RouterC(configure)#ip route 198.13.0.0. 255.0.0.0 ethernet 1 198.13.1.1
  perm
  ```

- Router 198.13.1.1:

  ```
  RouterD(configure)#ip route 198.13.0.0 255.0.0.0 ethernet 1 perm
  ```

When these four routes are configured, the information is carried from one router to the next until it reaches its destination. The basic language of the command states that information for network 198.13.0.0 should exit the router through a specific interface and (in three cases) be passed to another router.

Keep this lesson in mind when we cover routing protocols such as RIP and OSPF. We will be combining routing and routed protocols to create a fully functional environment. It is possible to combine both dynamic routes (through routing protocols) and static IP routes within the same router. This lesson will be particularly useful in larger dynamic environments.

Now that you have finished this lesson, you should have a fairly comprehensive knowledge of IP routing and IP subnetting. Both IP routing and IP subnetting will be used in the more advanced stages of this book.

Summary

- One of the biggest reasons to subnet a group of networks is to conserve the already dwindling supply of IP addresses available.
- Subnetting is achieved by passing bits from the host portion of an IP address to the network portion.
- Every network within a subnetted environment will share the same subnet mask.
- You should always place your routers in areas that are consistent with the routing protocol you plan to use.
- Static routing definitions should be used only in areas where routing protocols are not used, where security dictates that certain data should be sent to certain places, or where the routing environment does not change.

Q&A

Q If the IP address I subnetted was originally class B, why can't I use the subnet mask 255.255.0.0?

A The subnet mask 255.255.0.0 accommodates only one class B network. To see this better, we can look at the mask in its binary format. The mask 11111111.11111111.00000000.00000000 has two octets reserved for the host addresses on the network. After an address is subnetted, some of these bits are no longer available. Therefore the original mask can no longer be used.

Q Why do I use the `no shutdown` command to turn on an interface?

A To make the Cisco IOS as uncluttered and easy to use as possible, several commands were left out. Rather than create two different commands—one to perform an action and one to negate that action—Cisco decided to have one keyword that could negate any command. The obvious choice for that keyword was `no`. To perform the opposite of any action (not just `shutdown`), simply put a `no` before it.

Quiz

Questions

1. How many networks are available in a class B address with a subnet mask of 255.255.224.0?
2. How many bits need to be passed to the network to accommodate 2000 hosts?

3. What is the static route parameter for saving an IP route to the `startup-config` file?
4. After you configure an IP address on an interface, what command turns the interface on?

Answers

1. Six
2. Five
3. `perm`
4. `no shutdown`

Exercises

1. Subnet the following Class C address to provide at least 20 network addresses: 220.156.50.0

> **Note**
>
> By passing five bits from the host to the network we get a possibility of $2^5 - 2 = 30$ networks with 6 hosts each. Our new subnet mask is 255.255.255.248.

WEEK 2

DAY 12

Learning How to Configure IPX (Internetwork Packet Exchange)

IPX is a lesser-used, but no less important, routed protocol. Used mainly by networks running Novell NetWare, IPX is a crucial technology for anyone planning to work with the Novell operating system. This lesson will both introduce you to IPX as a protocol and walk you through configuration of your Cisco router to use IPX addresses.

The major topics covered by this lesson are:

- Introduction to IPX
- IPX addressing
- IPX routing

By the end of this lesson you will have a fuller understanding of the IPX routed protocol, thus expanding your routing knowledge to include two of the most popular routed protocols in use today. This will give you an edge in your Cisco background that will help you in many situations.

Introduction to IPX

Until the release of Novell NetWare version 5, IPX was the default protocol on Novell networks. IPX (Internetwork Packet Exchange) is a routed protocol similar in design to IP. That is, both protocols operate on the network layer of the OSI model, and both protocols are connectionless.

Novell developed IPX in the early 1980s. IPX was developed as a routing protocol for the Novell NetWare line of server products. IPX (and its transport layer counterpart SPX) would serve as a proprietary protocol that would replace TCP/IP in NetWare architecture.

> **Note:** Novell modeled IPX after an early Xerox protocol, XNS.

Because it is a layer 3 connectionless protocol, Cisco routers have no trouble working with IPX within a routed environment. Cisco routers can freely and easily route IP, IPX, or both within the same network (even the same router).

Unlike IP, IPX is not a default routed protocol on Cisco routers. This means that to utilize IPX routing on your Cisco router, an IPX-enabled feature pack must be installed. For most models, the most basic feature pack that supports IPX is the IPX/IP Basic IOS. This one feature pack supports both IP and IPX, allowing one router to work with both protocols.

If you have never worked with or been introduced to IPX, you will notice a few differences between IP and IPX. The most obvious difference is in the format of the IPX addresses. IPX addresses may appear foreign to anyone who has never worked with the protocol before. The major difference between working with IPX addresses as opposed to IP addresses is adjusting your thinking to hexadecimal as opposed to dotted decimal.

Although IPX is not the most common routed protocol, it is used in a number of production environments—enough environments to warrant a comprehensive discussion of the topic. One of the most common configurations for Cisco routers (involving IPX) deals with connecting IPX networks and IP networks. For example, if an IPX environment needs a connection to the Internet, the IPX packets would need to be converted to IP. This kind of high-level protocol routing can be performed on most Cisco routers.

Learning How to Configure IPX (Internetwork Packet Exchange)

The remainder of this lesson will deal with understanding and configuring the IPX routed protocol on Cisco routers. An important aspect of IPX architecture is the addressing scheme that it employs. We will begin this lesson by taking a look at the IPX address format and how IPX addresses are assigned.

IPX Addressing

IPX addresses are similar to those of IP in that one address is used to identify both the network and the host. Whereas IP addresses have a variable-length network designator (the network portion of the address can be represented by one, two, or three octets of the address, depending on class), IPX addresses are of a set length. An IPX address will always follow the convention: *network.host*.

An IPX address is a 32-bit network address followed by a 48-bit host. This makes IPX addresses a total of 80 bits (10 bytes) in length, which is substantially larger than 4-byte IP addresses. Having a larger address size gives IPX addresses an advantage: many moreIPX addresses are available for device addressing. Figure 12.1 illustrates a typical IPX address.

> **Note:** IPX addresses are always expressed in hexadecimal format.

FIGURE 12.1
An IPX address.

Network	Host
123abcde.	00b0.5ef76.02a6

The network portion of an IPX address is an administrator-assigned value. The network administrator assigns a unique number as an IPX network address for the entire environment. The number assigned must be expressed as 8 hexadecimal digits (4 bytes). This address should remain unique throughout the routing environment to eliminate router confusion.

If you have never worked in hexadecimal, it may take some getting used to. Hexadecimal digits have a base of 16 (binary has a base of 2 and therefore uses two digits, 0 and 1). The hexadecimal digits are listed in Table 12.1.

TABLE 12.1 Hexadecimal Digits

Hexadecimal	Binary	Base 10
0	0	0
1	1	1
2	10	2
3	11	3
4	100	4
5	101	5
6	110	6
7	111	7
8	1000	8
9	1001	9
A	1010	10
B	1011	11
C	1100	12
D	1101	13
E	1110	14
F	1111	15

If an administrator assigns a network address that is less than 8 hexadecimal digits in length, the router automatically prepends the digit 0 to the address until it is 8 digits long. For example, if an administrator assigns the network address 76b8 to an IPX environment, the Cisco router will convert that address to 0x000076b8.

> **Note:** The notation 0x indicates that the attached value is written in hex. If there were no 0x before the value, you can assume it is not written in hex. For example, whereas "bad" is a word in the English language "0xbad" is the hexadecimal number corresponding to decimal 2989.

The host address is not as arbitrary as the network address. One feature of IPX that sets it apart from protocols like IP is that the host address is dynamically set. That is, unless otherwise specified by an administrator, IPX dynamically assigns the host portion of the address for the specific device it is residing on.

The host address for an IPX device is generally composed of the device's media access control (MAC) address. Because MAC addresses are globally unique by design, there is always an IPX address available for any given host. As long as the protocol has access to read the device's NIC, the MAC address becomes the host address.

> **Note:** The MAC address is a number assigned to every network device at the time the device is manufactured. Every network device manufacturer is assigned a group of numbers (from a central control agency) that it can give to the products it manufactures. This address applies to the MAC sublayer of the data link layer of the OSI model. Although some manufacturers allow you to change the MAC address of a device, most are permanent.

It is this uniqueness and global availability that makes the MAC address particularly attractive as a protocol address. Every device has one, and every device's MAC address should be unique. Thus, because IPX uses the MAC as the host address, there are theoretically an endless number of IPX addresses that can be used.

Configuring IPX on Cisco Routers

Before attempting to configure IPX on your Cisco router, you need to determine whether your router has the correct feature pack. The lowest-level feature pack your router can have and still provide IPX functionality is the IPX/IP Basic feature pack. One way to tell what feature pack is installed on your router is to use the `show version` command:

```
""Router#show version
Cisco Internetwork Operating System Software
IOS (tm) 1600 Software (C1600-NY-M), Version 12.0(3), RELEASE SOFTWARE (fc1)
Copyright (c) 1986-1999 by cisco Systems, Inc.
Compiled Mon 08-Feb-99 20:21 by phanguye
Image text-base: 0x02005000, data-base: 0x024A8D24

ROM: System Bootstrap, Version 12.0(3)T, RELEASE SOFTWARE (fc1)
ROM: 1600 Software (C1600-RBOOT-R), Version 12.0(3)T, RELEASE SOFTWARE (fc1)

Router uptime is 57 minutes
System restarted by reload
System image file is "flash:c1600-ny-mz.120-3.bin"
```

This command does not explicitly tell you the name of the feature pack installed, but it does tell you the name of the IOS image. The last line in the output shown above states that the IOS image is named c1600-ny-mc.120-3.bin. If you look on the Cisco Connection Online (CCO) Web site (mentioned on Day 3, "Understanding the Cisco IOS"; you will need to have purchased a service agreement), you will find that this filename corresponds to the IP/IPX Basic feature pack for a Cisco 1600 Series router running version 12.0.3 of the IOS.

However, by the time you had researched all that information, you could have just tried configuring IPX on the router. If the proper feature pack is not installed, the router will tell you so when you try to configure it.

Either way you do it, determining that your router has the correct feature pack should be your first priority. Having determined that your router is capable of supporting IPX functionality, you can begin configuring. IPX functionality is enabled within global configuration mode.

> **Note** Many of these steps will seem similar to those used to configure IP. Cisco purposely made the commands for configuring protocols similar to make the IOS as understandable as possible.

From within the global configuration mode you need to enable IPX routing to enable the IPX protocol. Use the `ipx routing` command to enable IPX on the router. If you use Cisco IOS help on the `ipx routing` command, you will see that it takes one parameter. The IOS allows you to specify a host address to be used by the router.

```
Router(config)#ipx routing ?
  H.H.H  IPX address of this router
```

However, if you enter the command without this parameter, the IOS uses the router's MAC address as the router's host address. To ensure uniqueness, you should use the command without specifying the host address:

```
Router(config)#ipx routing
Router(config)#^Z
```

This command enables IPX routing on the Cisco router. (Keep in mind that IPX routing can be disabled by using the no command, for example, no ipx routing.) Both IP and IP routing can be enabled on the same router. The following command lines illustrate the steps to enable both IP and IPX routing on the same router:

```
Router#configure terminal
Enter configuration commands, one per line.  End with CNTL/Z.
Router(config)#ipx routing
Router(config)#ip routing
Router(config)#^Z
```

One reason for enabling IPX and IP on the same router is to bridge two networks. For example, IPX is not used on the Internet, so any IPX network wishing to communicate over the Internet would need to go through a router. This router would need to have IPX configured on one interface and IP configured on the other.

At this point the Cisco router is ready to route IPX and whatever other protocols you configure. However, before the router can actually begin moving IPX data from interface to interface, some key pieces of information still need to be configured on the router:

- Network number
- Interface addresses
- Encapsulation type

These items of information are all input to the `config-if` interface configuration program, so we must enter the interface configuration mode to finish our IPX setup. Because you can configure only one interface at a time, we will start with Ethernet 0:

```
Router#configure terminal
Router(config)#interface ethernet0
Router(config-if)#
```

The three pieces of information in the foregoing list can all be entered using the same command. The `ipx network` command allows you to specify the network address, the host address, and the encapsulation type for the interface. The command is formatted as follows:

```
#ipx network <network number> encapsulation <encapsulation type>
```

> **Note**
>
> Notice that the command's structure lacks parameters for specifying the interface's host address. Because IPX dynamically assigns the host address based on the MAC address, you do not need to initiate it. However, the host address is not assigned until you complete the `ipx network` command. Therefore, the `ipx network` command indicates to the Cisco router that it can assign a host address to the device.

The first parameter for the `ipx network` command is the network address. This number should be configured on all IPX devices within the same environment. The network address indicates to the router where it should (or should not) route packets.

The network address can be no longer than 8 hexadecimal digits. However, as previously mentioned, if you specify an address that is shorter than 8 digits, the router adds 0s to the front of it until it is 8 digits long. In our example we use the network address 1234. (The Cisco router stores this number internally as 0x00001234.)

Immediately following the network address is the `encapsulation` keyword. This keyword is used to indicate the particular encapsulation method to be used by the router for IPX packets.

The encapsulation type is a very important part of IPX configuration. As discussed in previous lessons, when a piece of data is passed to a protocol, the protocol encapsulates it. In encapsulating the data, fields are added to indicate key pieces of information about that data. However, depending on the type of network in use, the encapsulation may need some changes for the data to be routed correctly.

IPX Encapsulation

One key element in the configuration of IPX on a Cisco router is the selection of an IPX encapsulation method. The encapsulation method specifies the types and order of fields in the protocol's header. There are some important factors in choosing the encapsulation method for IPX. First, the same encapsulation method must be used across the environment. That is, every device that comes in contact with the IPX packets must use the same encapsulation. Second, the encapsulation must correspond to the type of network in place—for example, ethernet encapsulation for ethernet networks. Table 12.2 illustrates the options for IPX encapsulation available to Cisco users.

TABLE 12.2 IPX Encapsulation Types

Network Type	Encapsulation Type
Ethernet	Ethernet II
	Ethernet 802.3
	Ethernet 802.2
	Ethernet 802.2 SNAP
FDDI	FDDI 802.2 LLC
	FDDI 802.2 LLC SNAP
	FDDI raw
Token Ring	Token Ring
	Token Ring SNAP

> **Note** Notice in Table 12.2 that the encapsulation methods are grouped by network type. It is important that you choose the correct network type for your network.

> **Note** The model of router that you use on your network must also match the network type. In other words, if you have a Cisco 1605R (an Ethernet router), you should not choose the Token Ring encapsulation method.

The type of network you run is the primary factor in determining which IPX encapsulation to use. Even though there are four encapsulation types for Ethernet, each one represents a different version of the network. The type of encapsulation you choose determines what fields are attached to the IPX packet (different fields are readable by different network types). To illustrate this, we will examine the fields associated with the Ethernet encapsulation methods.

Ethernet Encapsulation Fields

In the process of configuring IPX routing on a Cisco device, the engineer must select an encapsulation method that corresponds to the type of network in use. Although selections are available for Ethernet, Token Ring, and FDDI network types, we will not discuss them all in detail. The process of encapsulation can be easily illustrated by examining the fields associated with the four different versions of Ethernet.

The most popular type of Ethernet encapsulation for IPX is Ethernet_II. Ethernet version II is the latest incarnation of the widely used network standard. If you do configure IPX for an Ethernet environment, you will most likely use Ethernet_II encapsulation. The following listing shows the Cisco keywords associated with the different methods of Ethernet encapsulation:

```
Router(config)#interface ethernet0
Router(config-if)#ipx network 1234 encapsulation ?
  arpa          IPX Ethernet_II
  hdlc          HDLC on serial links
  novell-ether  IPX Ethernet_802.3
  novell-fddi   IPX FDDI RAW
  sap           IEEE 802.2 on Ethernet, FDDI, Token Ring
  snap          IEEE 802.2 SNAP on Ethernet, Token Ring, and FDDI
```

Notice that the Cisco keyword for Ethernet_II encapsulation is arpa. To configure this interface for Ethernet_II encapsulation, use the following command:

```
Router(config-if)#ipx network 1234 encapsulation arpa
Router(config-if)#^Z
```

This command configures the current Cisco interface for IPX network 0x00001234 and an encapsulation of Ethernet_II. Choosing the Ethernet_II encapsulation method adds certain fields to the IPX packet. These fields are required for packet routing across the specified network type. Figure 12.2 illustrates an IPX packet with Ethernet_II encapsulation.

FIGURE 12.2

Ethernet_II field headers.

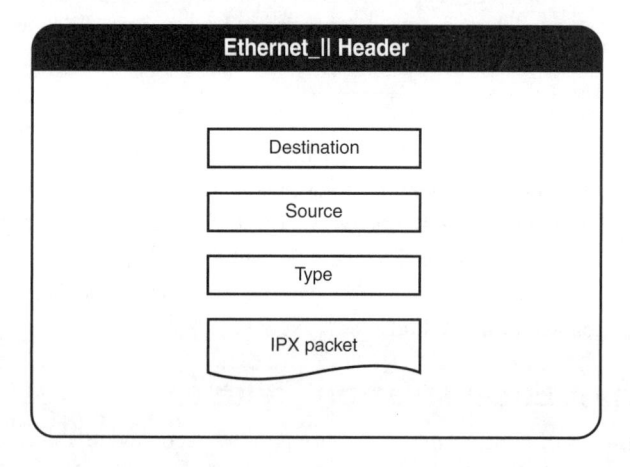

Learning How to Configure IPX (Internetwork Packet Exchange) 243

For comparison, the field headers added to an IPX packet during Ethernet_SNAP encapsulation are shown in Figure 12.3.

FIGURE 12.3

Ethernet_SNAP field headers.

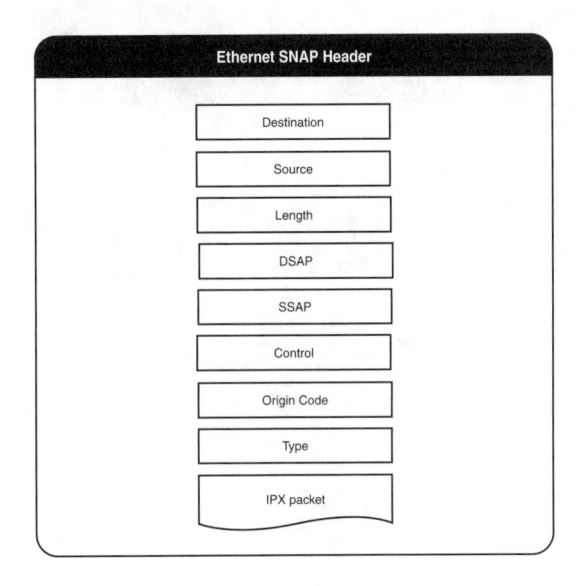

```
┌─────────────────────────────────┐
│      Ethernet SNAP Header       │
│                                 │
│           Destination           │
│             Source              │
│             Length              │
│              DSAP               │
│              SSAP               │
│             Control             │
│           Origin Code           │
│              Type               │
│           IPX packet            │
└─────────────────────────────────┘
```

There are two important things to keep in mind when dealing with IPX encapsulation types. First, the encapsulation type chosen does not change the structure of the IPX packet itself. Rather, it adds fields to the beginning of it. When a device receives the encapsulated IPX packet, it simply strips off the encapsulation fields and leaves the IPX packet intact.

Figure 12.4 illustrates a typical IPX packet. Shown in this figure are the fields of the IPX packet as they would appear prior to any encapsulation.

FIGURE 12.4

An IPX packet.

```
┌─────────────────────────────────┐
│      Ethernet SNAP Header       │
│                                 │
│            Checksum             │
│          Packet length          │
│        Transport Control        │
│           Packet Type           │
│       Destination network       │
│        Destination node         │
│       Destination socket        │
│         Source network          │
│           Source node           │
│          Source socket          │
│         Upper level data        │
└─────────────────────────────────┘
```

When this packet is sent from a device, it is encapsulated for the particular type of network being used. The details of Figure 12.5 show this same packet (shown in Figure 12.4) after encapsulation.

FIGURE 12.5

An IPX packet after encapsulation.

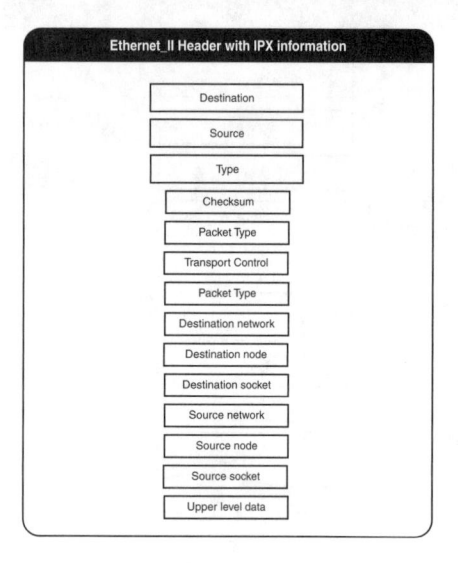

```
Ethernet_II Header with IPX information
         Destination
         Source
         Type
            Checksum
            Packet Type
            Transport Control
            Packet Type
            Destination network
            Destination node
            Destination socket
            Source network
            Source node
            Source socket
            Upper level data
```

Notice that the original IPX fields are intact. When the target device receives the packet, it strips off the fields that were added during encapsulation. What is left is the original IPX packet.

The second thing to keep in mind when dealing with IPX encapsulation is that different encapsulation methods can be defined on the same interface. If one router is connected to multiple networks (each using a different network type), the engineer can assign the correct encapsulation as needed. The next section of this lesson discusses this concept.

IPX Routing

IPX routing can be somewhat more complicated than IP routing. One factor behind this is the multiple encapsulation types that can be found within IPX networks. Although a single encapsulation type must be shared throughout a network, one Cisco router can span multiple networks. To operate successfully within any given IPX environment, a Cisco router may need to be configured for multiple IPX encapsulation types.

To illustrate this, we will look at two different scenarios. The first is a basic IPX environment that consists of two Ethernet networks, each with a different network type. Figure 12.6 illustrates this IPX environment.

FIGURE 12.6

A two-network IPX environment.

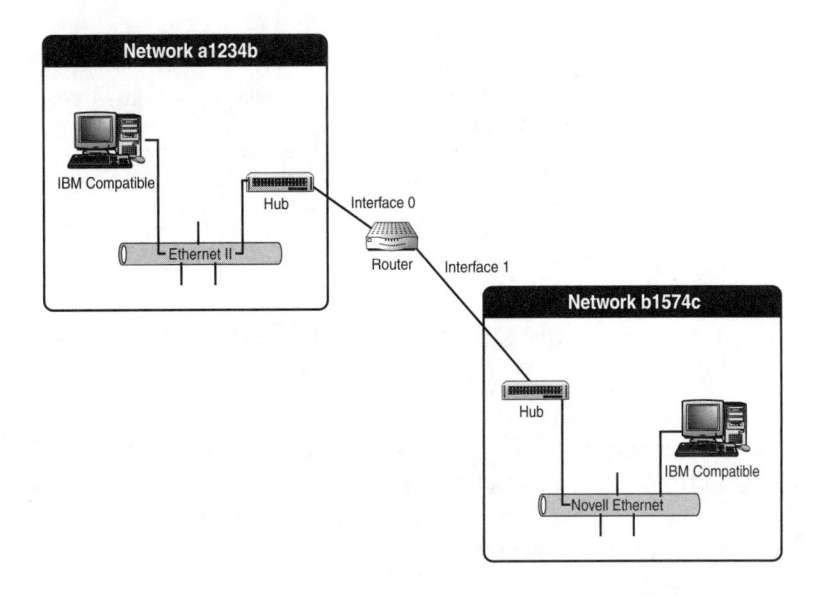

Within this environment (see Figure 12.6) is a standard Ethernet_II IPX network. This network can be thought of as the newer portion of the networking environment. The network was set up to expand the capabilities of the second network within the environment. The second network is an older Novell Ethernet environment that uses the IEEE 802.3 architecture. A Cisco router has been placed between the two networks to allow information to flow from one network to the other.

> **Note**
>
> Because the encapsulation types are different, the two networks in Figure 12.6 would not be able to communicate on their own. The services of an intermediary device are required to enable communications.

The Cisco router in Figure 12.6 would be configured as follows. First, IPX routing needs to be enabled on the router. Then the two interfaces need to be assigned the appropriate network numbers and encapsulation types. The full set of commands needed to configure the interfaces of a Cisco router for this scenario is as follows:

```
Router#configure terminal
Enter configuration commands, one per line.  End with CNTL/Z.
Router(config)#ipx routing
Router(config)#^Z
Router#
```

```
1d00h: %SYS-5-CONFIG_I: Configured from console by console
Router#configure terminal
Enter configuration commands, one per line.  End with CNTL/Z.
Router(config)#interface ethernet 0
Router(config-if)#ipx network a1234b encapsulation arpa
Router(config-if)#no shutdown
Router(config-if)#interface ethernet 1
Router(config-if)#ipx network b1574c encapsulation novell-ether
Router(config-if)#no shutdown
Router(config-if)#^Z
Router#
1d00h: %SYS-5-CONFIG_I: Configured from console by console
Router#
```

Here, interface `ethernet 0` was configured for network 0x00a1234b and Ethernet_II encapsulation. Interface `ethernet 1` was configured for network 0x00b1574c and Ethernet 802.2 encapsulation. At this point the interfaces should be configured correctly and able to move packets between the two networks. However, as with IP, before the router can begin moving data, static routes need to be defined for the interfaces.

The static routes are needed to tell the router which packets can be moved to and from which interfaces. Using the IPX route command, static routes for the router in our scenario would be configured to move data from interface `ethernet 0` to `ethernet 1` and back.

The format for the static route command within IPX is a little different from that for IP. The command structure and parameters for IPX static routes are as follows:

```
#ipx route <network> <network-mask> <destination> | <tick> | <hop count> | <float>
```

Although it may seem that the command has some confusing parameters, they will begin to make sense. The following list explains the purpose of the ipx router command parameters.

- The network parameter is the source address of all packets affected by this static route.
- The network mask (similar to a subnet mask) is used to tell the router how many bits are in the network address. It is very rare that you would have to use anything other than FFFFFFFF.
- The destination is the IPX address (network and host) of the interface you want the packets forwarded to.

Along with the aforementioned required parameters, the `ipx route` command also accepts three optional parameters. The optional parameters give you more control over the way your router uses the routes defined.

- The tick count is the amount of time before the packet expires. In other words, if the packet is not delivered before the "tick" runs to 0, the packet is discarded.

Learning How to Configure IPX (Internetwork Packet Exchange) 247

> **Note**
>
> A tick is a general representation of time in the routing world. Ticks (which got their name from the ticking of a clock, big surprise) do not correspond directly to an actual unit of time. Rather they represent a cycle of the router's processor or (more accurately) the average amount of time the router's processor takes to run a set of commands.

- The hop count indicates the total number of router hops a packet can traverse before being discarded.
- "Floating" indicates that the route (even though it is static) can be overwritten by a dynamically learned route.

Knowing the parameters for the `ipx route` command, we can now establish a static route. The following commands illustrate the establishment of two static routes from our router.

```
Router(config)#ipx route a1234b ffffff b1574c.00d0.58a8.e150
Router(config)#ipx route b1574c ffffff a1234b.00d0.58a8.e150
```

At this point the router in our IPX configuration scenario is fully capable to route packets between the two networks in Figure 12.6. However, there are occasions where you may be presented with an IPX environment like that illustrated in Figure 12.7.

FIGURE 12.7

An environment with three IPX networks.

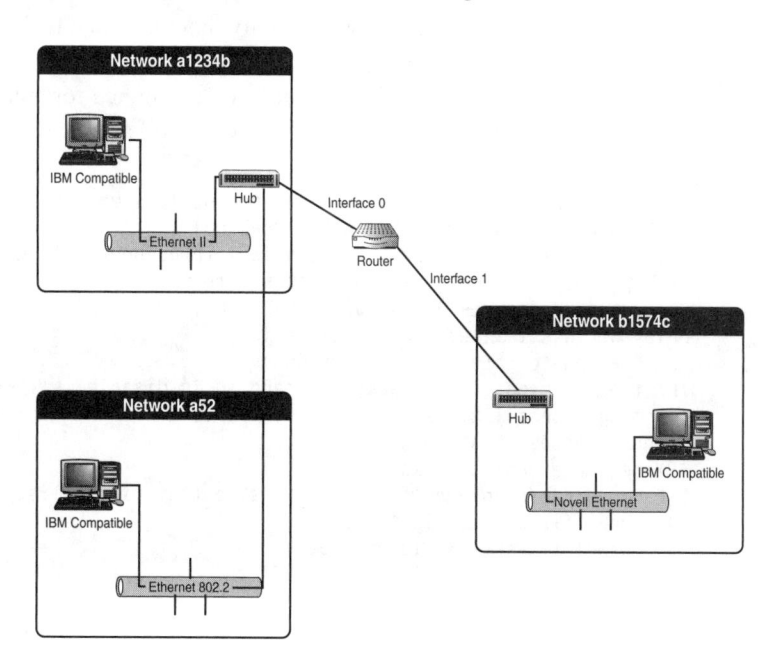

Notice that the two IPX networks attached to interface `ethernet 0` use different encapsulation types. Cisco routers can be configured to use different encapsulation methods on the same interface (as long as each encapsulation type is for a different network number). For example, to configure the second network on interface `ethernet 0`, use the following commands:

```
Router#configure terminal
Enter configuration commands, one per line.  End with CNTL/Z.
Router(config)#ipx routing
Router(config)#^Z
Router#
1d00h: %SYS-5-CONFIG_I: Configured from console by console
Router#configure terminal
Enter configuration commands, one per line.  End with CNTL/Z.
Router(config)#interface ethernet 0
Router(config-if)#ipx network a1234b encapsulation arpa
Router(config-if)#ipx network a52 encapsulation sap secondary
Router(config-if)#no shutdown
Router(config-if)#interface ethernet 1
Router(config-if)#ipx network b1574c encapsulation novell-ether
Router(config-if)#no shutdown
Router(config-if)#^Z
Router#
1d00h: %SYS-5-CONFIG_I: Configured from console by console
Router#
```

The secondary keyword allows you to specify more than one IPX address per interface. If we were to view the IPX configuration for this router (using the `show ipx interface` command, we would see that both interfaces are configured for their respective networks, and `ethernet 0` is configured for two separate networks and encapsulation types:

```
Router#show ipx interface
Ethernet0 is administratively up, line protocol is up
  IPX address is A52.00d0.58a8.e150, SAP [up]
  Delay of this IPX network, in ticks is 1 throughput 0 link delay 0
  IPXWAN processing not enabled on this interface.
  Secondary address is A1234B.00d0.58a8.e150, ARPA [up]
  Delay of this IPX network, in ticks is 1
  IPX SAP update interval is 60 seconds
  IPX type 20 propagation packet forwarding is disabled
  Incoming access list is not set
  Outgoing access list is not set
  IPX helper access list is not set
  SAP GNS processing enabled, delay 0 ms, output filter list is not set
  SAP Input filter list is not set
  SAP Output filter list is not set
  SAP Router filter list is not set
  Input filter list is not set
  Output filter list is not set
```

Learning How to Configure IPX (Internetwork Packet Exchange)

```
    Router filter list is not set
    Netbios Input host access list is not set
    Netbios Input bytes access list is not set
    Netbios Output host access list is not set
    Netbios Output bytes access list is not set
    Updates each 60 seconds aging multiples RIP: 3 SAP: 3
    SAP interpacket delay is 55 ms, maximum size is 480 bytes
    RIP interpacket delay is 55 ms, maximum size is 432 bytes
    RIP response delay is not set
    IPX accounting is disabled
    IPX fast switching is configured (enabled)
    RIP packets received 0, RIP packets sent 0
    SAP packets received 0, SAP packets sent 0
Ethernet1 is administratively up, line protocol is up
    IPX address is B1574C.00d0.58a8.e151, NOVELL-ETHER [up]
    Delay of this IPX network, in ticks is 1 throughput 0 link delay 0
    IPXWAN processing not enabled on this interface.
    IPX SAP update interval is 60 seconds
    IPX type 20 propagation packet forwarding is disabled
    Incoming access list is not set
    Outgoing access list is not set
    IPX helper access list is not set
    SAP GNS processing enabled, delay 0 ms, output filter list is not set
    SAP Input filter list is not set
    SAP Output filter list is not set
    SAP Router filter list is not set
    Input filter list is not set
    Output filter list is not set
    Router filter list is not set
    Netbios Input host access list is not set
    Netbios Input bytes access list is not set
    Netbios Output host access list is not set
    Netbios Output bytes access list is not set
    Updates each 60 seconds aging multiples RIP: 3 SAP: 3
    SAP interpacket delay is 55 ms, maximum size is 480 bytes
    RIP interpacket delay is 55 ms, maximum size is 432 bytes
    RIP response delay is not set
    IPX accounting is disabled
    IPX fast switching is configured (enabled)
    RIP packets received 0, RIP packets sent 0
    SAP packets received 0, SAP packets sent 0
```

You have now been introduced to the commands required to configure a Cisco router for running IPX in a few different (yet basic) scenarios. This concludes the portion of this book dealing with LAN routed protocols. The remaining lessons will address WAN protocols and routing protocols.

Summary

- IPX is a network layer protocol similar to IP.
- The protocol addresses within IPX are represented in hexadecimal format.
- The host portion of an IPX address consists of the MAC address of the host device.
- The `ipx network` command is used to configure IPX on a Cisco interface.
- The encapsulation type must be common throughout your network, and it must match the network type being used.
- A single Cisco interface can accommodate multiple network numbers and encapsulation types.

Q&A

Q Why are there different encapsulation types for IPX?

A IPX was a proprietary protocol for a long time. Therefore, when Novell changed header formation or protocol versions, it really only affected their own devices. As the technology spread, a method was needed to distinguish between the different network types.

Q Can the `secondary` keyword be used with other protocols?

A Yes, most routed protocols such as IP and IPX can use the `secondary` keyword. This allows for a more versatile routing environment.

Quiz

Questions

1. What is the common encapsulation type used on ethernet networks today?
2. What does the `<float>` parameter specify?
3. How many encapsulation types can be configured on a single network?
4. How many hexadecimal digits are used in an IPX network address?

Answers

1. Ethernet_II (`arpa`).
2. It allows a static route to be overwritten by a dynamic one.
3. One. You can have only one encapsulation type per network. (However, you can have more than one network, thus allowing more than one encapsulation type.)
4. Eight.

Learning How to Configure IPX (Internetwork Packet Exchange)

Exercise

1. The following example illustrates the commands used to configure a router spanning two IPX networks. Following the command list is a sample output from the "show ipx interface" command. Assuming the encapsulation methods are correct, why is the router not working?

```
Router#configure terminal
Enter configuration commands, one per line.  End with CNTL/Z.
Router(config)#ipx routing
Router(config)#^Z
Router#
1d00h: %SYS-5-CONFIG_I: Configured from console by console
Router#configure terminal
Enter configuration commands, one per line.  End with CNTL/Z.
Router(config)#interface ethernet 0
Router(config-if)#ipx network ab encapsulation arpa
Router(config-if)#interface ethernet 1
Router(config-if)#ipx network bc encapsulation arpa
Router(config-if)#^Z
Router#
1d00h: %SYS-5-CONFIG_I: Configured from console by console
Router#
```

The command show ipx interface provides the following information:

```
Router#show ipx interface
Ethernet0 is administratively down, line protocol is down
  IPX address is Ab.00d0.58a8.e150, SAP [up]
  Delay of this IPX network, in ticks is 1 throughput 0 link delay 0
  IPXWAN processing not enabled on this interface.
    IPX SAP update interval is 60 seconds
  IPX type 20 propagation packet forwarding is disabled
  Incoming access list is not set
  Outgoing access list is not set
  IPX helper access list is not set
  SAP GNS processing enabled, delay 0 ms, output filter list is not set
  SAP Input filter list is not set
  SAP Output filter list is not set
  SAP Router filter list is not set
  Input filter list is not set
  Output filter list is not set
  Router filter list is not set
  Netbios Input host access list is not set
  Netbios Input bytes access list is not set
  Netbios Output host access list is not set
  Netbios Output bytes access list is not set
  Updates each 60 seconds aging multiples RIP: 3 SAP: 3
  SAP interpacket delay is 55 ms, maximum size is 480 bytes
  RIP interpacket delay is 55 ms, maximum size is 432 bytes
  RIP response delay is not set
```

```
     IPX accounting is disabled
     IPX fast switching is configured (enabled)
     RIP packets received 0, RIP packets sent 0
     SAP packets received 0, SAP packets sent 0
Ethernet1 is administratively down, line protocol is down
     IPX address is BC.00d0.58a8.e151, NOVELL-ETHER [up]
     Delay of this IPX network, in ticks is 1 throughput 0 link delay 0
     IPXWAN processing not enabled on this interface.
     IPX SAP update interval is 60 seconds
     IPX type 20 propagation packet forwarding is disabled
     Incoming access list is not set
     Outgoing access list is not set
     IPX helper access list is not set
     SAP GNS processing enabled, delay 0 ms, output filter list is not set
     SAP Input filter list is not set
     SAP Output filter list is not set
     SAP Router filter list is not set
     Input filter list is not set
     Output filter list is not set
     Router filter list is not set
     Netbios Input host access list is not set
     Netbios Input bytes access list is not set
     Netbios Output host access list is not set
     Netbios Output bytes access list is not set
     Updates each 60 seconds aging multiples RIP: 3 SAP: 3
     SAP interpacket delay is 55 ms, maximum size is 480 bytes
     RIP interpacket delay is 55 ms, maximum size is 432 bytes
     RIP response delay is not set
     IPX accounting is disabled
     IPX fast switching is configured (enabled)
     RIP packets received 0, RIP packets sent 0
     SAP packets received 0, SAP packets sent 0
```

> **Note** The interfaces were never turned on. The command no shutdown is needed to activate the interfaces.

WEEK 2

DAY 13

Understanding WAN Protocols

In this lesson we are going to take some time out to understand wide area network (WAN) protocols. To this point the environments discussed have been (fairly) small local area networks (LANs). The scenarios covered have included a single environment bound together by a single routed protocol. However, especially in today's age of business-to-business (B2B) communication, small LANs are increasingly harder to find.

WAN protocols are specialized protocols that carry data across WAN links. Physical links that connect two or more environments over long distances require special attention when it comes to information transportation. These links utilize protocols specifically developed for one purpose: providing WAN communications.

While examining WAN protocols, this lesson will introduce the following topics.

- ISDN
- X.25
- Frame Relay

The WAN protocols addressed in this lesson provide a good cross section of the technologies you are likely to see in real world situations. From the smallest in capacity, ISDN, to the largest, Frame Relay, each has a particular set of requirements when it comes to routing. However, before we can thoroughly examine the actual protocols, we must discuss the hardware requirements for Cisco routers to use WAN elements.

Some Cisco routers do not ship with the hardware required for supporting WAN communications. For these routers a separate WIC (WAN interface card) is needed for the router. Whether a Cisco router is equipped to handle WAN functionality (or whether it can be upgraded to do so) can vary from series to series (and even between models within a series).

For example, within the 1600 Series some models are equipped with WAN interfaces, whereas others only have WIC slots. Which WICs can be installed in the slots is also dependent on the model of router. Table 13.1 shows which Cisco 1600 Series routers are equipped with WAN interfaces and which WICs they can accept.

TABLE 13.1 WAN Interface Comparison

Model	WAN Interface	WIC Options Available					
		Serial	T1 CSU/DSU	56k CSU/DSU	ISDN dial-in ST	ISDNU	ISDN leased ST
1601	Serial	X	X	X	X	X	
1602	56K CSU/DSU	X	X	X	X	X	
1603	ISDN dial-in ST	X	X	X			X
1604	ISDN dial-in ST / ISDN Phone	X	X	X			X
1605	N/A	X	X	X	X	X	

As Table 13.1 shows, some 1600 series routers are equipped with an on-board WAN interface (and can accept other interfaces through the WIC slot), whereas others (such as the 1605) can only use the WIC.

The remainder of this lesson will discuss these interfaces and the protocols that can run over them. Connecting smaller, independent networks into a larger enterprise is a major part of learning Cisco routing. One of the keys to connecting larger and larger environments is to learn the WAN protocols.

The first WAN protocol we will examine is the Integrated Services Digital Network (ISDN). Although the presence of ISDN is not as large in the marketplace now as it was a few years age, the technology can still be found in existing networks. Following our discussion of ISDN, we will explore the technologies that make up other WAN protocols such as Frame Relay and X.25.

ISDN

ISDN was the first of the consumer-grade broadband products to be widely accepted. Offering digital transmission rates over public lines, ISDN caught on very quickly with the general public (up to that point, 56Kbps modems were the fastest connection devices available).

In the time before ISDN became popular as an "in-home" technology, it was a burgeoning enterprise technology.

One of the main advantages to ISDN was the price. ISDN offered an inexpensive solution for businesses that needed a high-bandwidth connection between sites but did not need the 100% availability of (or as much bandwidth as) a T1. ISDN links could be configured as dial-in pay-per-use. In other words, you pay for what you use. This feature made ISDN a popular choice for WAN links that may not be used as often as other links requiring more up-time.

Another feature of ISDN that makes it popular is that it was designed to work over existing telephone networks. This allows ISDN users to utilize their existing telephony infrastructure. Home users can also receive telephone calls while using ISDN services on the same line.

Few businesses today still utilize ISDN connections, but many SOHO (small office/home office) users still take advantage of the inexpensive access to bandwidth while utilizing the existing cabling. Home offices make the best use of pay-per-use technologies, because they are not in use around the clock. The home user stops paying for the WAN services when the PC is shut down.

One of the most popular uses for ISDN is to connect a home office with a central location, thus providing true WAN connectivity. This is the type of scenario where you are most likely to find ISDN today. This is also the most common ISDN scenario where a Cisco router would be utilized.

ISDN Technology

ISDN is a digital supply link that consists of multiple channels. The most common type of ISDN is BRI (Basic Rate Interface). Most Cisco routers can work with BRI ISDN. Support for ISDN is provided in the Basic IP feature pack of most Cisco IOS revisions.

> **Note:** Before attempting to configure ISDN on your router, confirm that the hardware for ISDN is present.

ISDN BRI service consists of three channels. A standard BRI ISDN line has two B (bearer) channels and one D (data) channel. The two B channels are the digital data links. These two channels are used to transfer data from point to point, while the D channel is used for signaling. The combination of these channels creates a line capable of 144 Kbps of transmission. Table 13.2 shows the bandwidth of a BRI ISDN line.

TABLE 13.2 Bandwidth of BRI channels

Type of Channel	Number of Channels in a BRI Line	Bandwidth
B	2	64 Kbps (each)
D	1	16 Kbps

Because ISDN is a pay-per-use service, most ISDN connections are made through a dialer. Similar to a standard telephone line, ISDN modems are required to dial a central location and initiate service. Most Cisco routers include the functionality of an ISDN modem with the ISDN hardware (whether it is on-board or WIC).

Before ISDN services can be configured on a Cisco router, several key pieces of information required by the router during setup need to be obtained from the ISDN provider. During the setup process, the router will prompt you for information such as the switch type, encapsulation method, and SPID (Service Profile ID); the purpose of these pieces of information is explained in the following sections. Once we have covered the required information for establishing ISDN connectivity, we will review the steps needed for setting up a Cisco router to use ISDN.

Not only does the term "ISDN" mean a type of service used to connect WAN links; "ISDN" also refers to the suite of protocols used to move data across these links. ISDN is a dynamic suite of protocols that address the functional needs of multiple OSI layers. Although the specific function of each protocol within the ISDN suite is beyond the scope of this text, the next section will cover the types of protocols present within ISDN.

ISDN Terminology

Like most protocols, ISDN comes complete with its own set of terminological phrases and abbreviations. These words and phases are used in ISDN literature and Cisco interface properties. The following tables (13.3 and 13.4) illustrate some of the key terminology used in ISDN concepts.

Table 13.3 illustrates the terms used in ISDN documentation for different types of equipment that may appear on an ISDN network. These pieces of ISDN equipment may appear on either the host or the client side.

TABLE 13.3 ISDN Equipment Types

Symbol	ISDN Term	ISDN Equipment Type
TE1	Type-1 terminal equipment	This is a piece of ISDN equipment that contains within itself all of the components necessary for ISDN communication. In other words, there is no need for a separate modem for the router to interface with. Most Cisco routers with ISDN support are equipped with Type-1 terminal equipment.
TE2	Type-2 terminal equipment	This type of equipment uses a separate terminal adapter and modem to establish an ISDN connection.
TA	Terminal adapter	A terminal adapter is an ISDN interface that does not have modem capabilities. That is, a router equipped with a terminal adapter requires the services of a separate ISDN modem to establish an ISDN connection.
NT1	Type-1 network termination equipment	NT1 equipment is used to terminate the ISDN signal at an End System, such as a multiplexer.
NT2	Type-2 network termination equipment	This type of device is used to switch or transport the ISDN signal to type-1 termination equipment.

ISDN equipment types are commonly referred to by their abbreviations or terms, especially in Cisco literature. Although most Cisco routers are equipped with TE1, you should be aware that some scenarios may require the use of TE2 interfaces.

Another range of abbreviations and terms applies to the multiple protocols that form the ISDN suite. ISDN is a suite of protocols that define operations and functionality on the first four layers of the OSI model. That is, the protocols that make up ISDN collectively work on the transport, network, data Link, and physical layers. These protocols are grouped into categories for easy reference as shown in Table 13.4.

TABLE 13.4 ISDN Protocol Categories

ISDN Term	Protocol Category
Q	These protocols deal with the signaling of points in an ISDN connection. Generally, these protocols work on the D channel of a BRI link.
E	Some of the ISDN protocols are used to carry data across the existing telephone network. These protocols serve as standard network protocols (in much the same way that IP and IPX serve as protocols).
I	Some protocols are used only to define certain concepts within the ISDN technology. These protocols also define the terms and services of ISDN connectivity in a WAN environment.

One of the major Q protocols within ISDN is LAPD (Link Access Protocol [for Channel] D). Functioning like many of the protocols discussed thus far, LAPD serves to encapsulate ISDN data for transmission. Whereas ISDN E protocols function on the network layer of the OSI (being routed protocols), LAPD functions within the data link layer.

One of the major functions of LAPD is to maintain the addressing capabilities of ISDN as they relate to the specific devices involved in the ISDN environment. These devices can include Cisco routers on the business end or public telephone equipment on the WAN side.

> **Note** This text is geared to cover network layer protocols, but you should be aware of the role LAPD plays in the ISDN suite.

There are several terms to describe specific points, known as reference points, within an ISDN environment. Reference points are the locations within an ISDN loop related to a specific function of the ISDN protocol. Table 13.5 lists ISDN reference points and the ISDN terms for them.

Understanding WAN Protocols

TABLE 13.5 ISDN Network Reference Points

ISDN Term	(Network) Reference Points
R	The link between a TA and any other unrelated equipment
T	The link between an NT1 and an NT2
S	The link between an end system and an NT2
U	The link between an NT1 and the public network

Now that you have become familiar with the terminology of ISDN, let's discuss how these differently named parts work together. The next section of this lesson will cover the concepts behind ISDN functionality.

ISDN Functionality

ISDN is a WAN protocol, and as such, the daily maintenance of ISDN links (type U reference points) is normally the responsibility of the WAN provider. Regardless, gaining an understanding of how ISDN functions provides insight to what information Cisco routers require when preparing for ISDN connections.

To a business, a type U reference point should appear as a seamless integration between two geographically separated locations. Figure 13.1 illustrates a business's perceived notion of an ISDN link.

FIGURE 13.1

A business's perception of an ISDN network.

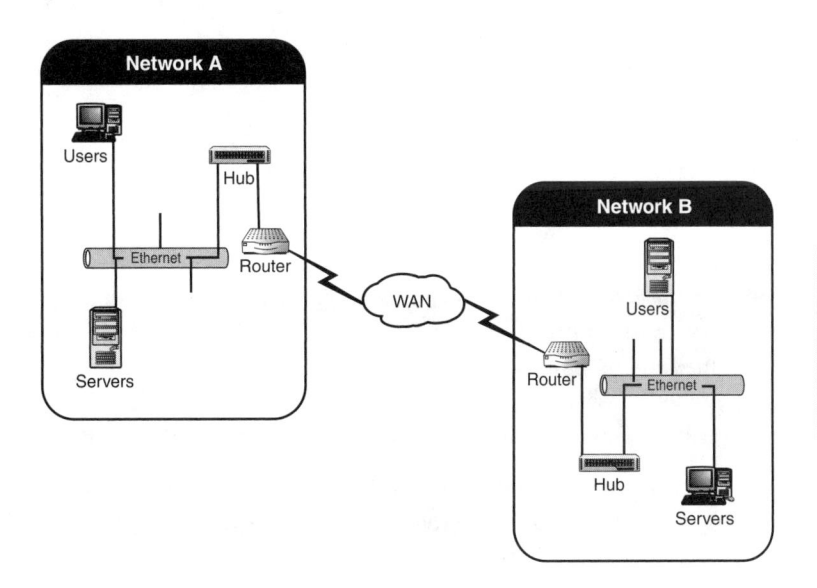

This scenario is accurate not only from the business's perspective but from an engineer's view as well. The network illustrated in Figure 13.1 shows the equipment under the responsibility of a Cisco engineer in an ISDN environment. When you are configuring a router (or pair of routers) for ISDN connectivity, this should be your view of the network. The remaining environment that exists between the two sites is the sole responsibility of the host or carrier.

The carrier, who is responsible for the ISDN environment between the two sites, monitors and maintains the NT1 and NT2 equipment that transport the ISDN signal from each site. Figure 13.2 illustrates the full ISDN environment corresponding to the business environment depicted in Figure 13.1.

FIGURE 13.2

A full ISDN environment with reference points.

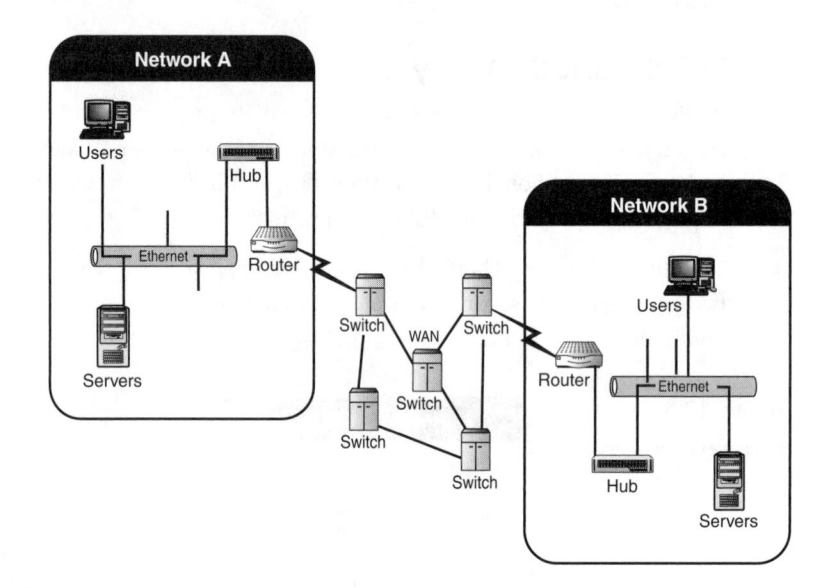

To understand how the environment in Figure 13.2 works, let's trace the path of a data transmission from Network A to Network B. The information originates on Network A in the form of an IP packet. The IP packet is created and addressed like any other IP packet (with no concern for how to reach a destination). The destination IP address (residing within Network B) is affixed to the packet, and it is sent to Router A (a TE1 device).

Router A compares the destination address of the IP packet with its existing route table. This comparison tells the router that Network B can be reached only through the WAN interface (which is configured for ISDN as a type U reference point). The router prepares the IP packet for transportation across the ISDN WAN link. Within Router A the IP packet is "framed"; that is, encapsulated according to the type of switch the carrier is using within its environment. ISDN has been designed to accommodate over 15 different types of public switching networks (PSNs).

> **Note** The term "public switching network" refers to the network of the public telephone companies. Many of these public switching networks greatly pre-date the use of ISDN, and they could not be made to conform to a single later standard. That fact made it necessary to develop the various ISDN protocols (E, Q, etc.) in a way that allows it to accommodate the various types of PSNs that currently exist. In other words, each protocol within ISDN can be configured to work with many different reference points and switch types.

After the packet has been framed, or encapsulated, properly, the TE1's ISDN interface attempts to open a circuit to the carrier's network. The ISDN interface dials the carrier's network, identifies itself, and passes the ISDN frame(s) to the environment (that is, the PSN). The public switching network is then responsible for ensuring that those frames reach Network B (based on the destination ISDN address).

When the frames reach the TE1 on Network B, the framing fields are stripped off, and the data is restored to IP packet form. The IP packets can then be routed to the target system. A Cisco router can be configured to take IP packets (or packets from any other protocol) and convert those packets into frames suitable for ISDN transmission.

The following section of this lesson will cover the process for configuring a Cisco router to handle ISDN. By doing so, you make your Cisco router into a fully functional TE1 or TE2, depending on your specific hardware configuration.

Configuring ISDN

Now that you have a grasp on how ISDN works, we can discuss configuring a Cisco router to participate successfully in an ISDN environment. To be configured as a fully functional TE1 or TE2 device, a Cisco router requires the information listed in Table 13.5. This information includes the SPID and the switch type.

To this point in the book, only basic information has been required in configuring a Cisco router to handle a specific routed protocol. For example, the router needs to know the protocol address assigned to the interface being configured, and in the case of IPX the encapsulation type.

> **Note:** WAN protocols, being forms of routed protocols, do require much of the same information needed to configure other routed protocols. However, because WAN protocols involve connections between networks that have no direct knowledge of each other (for example, a business network and the PSN), more detailed information is needed to establish a successful connection.

ISDN has a more complicated configuration that requires more information to be specified than most other routed protocols need to operate correctly. In fact, the type of information required by ISDN is similar to that needed when configuring other routed protocols. Table 13.6 shows the information required for configuring ISDN.

TABLE 13.6 Information Required for Configuring ISDN

Required Information	Purpose
ISDN switch type	This informs the router what type of equipment the carrier is using on its network. Globally, there can be over 15 ISDN switch types.
SPID	The SPID (Service Profile Identification Number) is used to identify the type of service to be provided to a certain link. Each ISDN link within a network can have up to two SPIDs.
Encapsulation method	Used in conjunction with either Frame Relay or X.25.
Protocol address	Because ISDN links route routed-protocol data, they must be configured with an appropriate address.

> **Note:** Some of the information shown in Table 13.6 should be obtained from your ISDN provider.

Let's begin configuring your Cisco router by entering the global configuration mode. From within global configuration mode, you can specify the switch type. Specifying the switch type in global configuration mode indicates that the setting applies to any ISDN interface that may be installed on the router. Table 13.7 shows the appropriate switch types for North America.

> **Note:** Switch types beginning with `primary` are found only on Primary Rate Interface (PRI) ISDN, which has 23 B channels and one 64 Kbps D channel.

TABLE 13.7 North American Switch Types

Switch Type	Description
basic-5ess	BRI AT&T switches
basic-dms100	BRI DMS-100 switches
basic-ni1	National ISDN-1 switches
primary-4ess	AT&T 4ESS switches (PRI ISDN only)
primary-5ess	AT&T 5ESS switches (PRI ISDN only)
primary-dms100	NT DMS-100 switches (PRI ISDN only)

From global configuration mode, configure the ISDN switch type. You can obtain the specific switch type for your network from your ISDN provider. Use the following command to enter global configuration mode:

```
Router#configure terminal
Router(config)#isdn switch-type basic-ni1
```

After the switch type has been configured, you can configure the interface-specific information. This information includes any protocol addresses, SPIDs, and encapsulation methods. The first piece of information you configure is the SPID. Keep in mind that you may have none, one, or two SPIDs; it depends on the service that is being provided to your site. Confirm the SPID(s) with your carrier. To configure SPID(s), use the following commands:

```
Router(config)#interface bri 0
Router(config-if)#isdn spid 1 123456789
Router(config-if)#isdn spid 2 987654321
```

Next, you configure the encapsulation method. Your choices for encapsulation are PPP (Point-to-Point Protocol) or HDLC (High-level Data Link Control). Again you need to consult your provider as to the encapsulation method you need to configure (PPP is the most common). To configure the encapsulation method for PPP:

```
Router(config-if)#encapsulation ppp
```

Finally, you need to configure the routed protocol addresses on the interface that carries the ISDN data:

```
Router(config-if)#ip address 153.4.16.1 255.255.0.0
```

At this point the interface is configured to run ISDN. Now, as with the other routed protocols we have covered in this book, routes need to be established, connecting the IP (or IPX) packets to the ISDN link. For protocols like IP and IPX, you use the `static route` command to create the mapped routes. For ISDN, on the other hand, you use the `dialer` command, in association with Cisco access lists, to provide the functionality for these "static routes." Let's examine some configuration steps for establishing ISDN routes.

```
Router(config)#dialer map ip 153.4.10.1 name NETWORK_B 234567891
Router(config)#dialer-group 1
Router(config)#dialer-list 1 list 99
Router(config)#access-list 99 permit 153.4.16.0 255.255.0.0 153.4.10.0 255.255.0.0
```

While this list of commands may seem daunting, it is quite logical if examined and followed one line at a time. The first line (`dialer map ip 153.4.10.1 name NETWORK_B 234567891`) states that a mapped route is to be configured where any ISDN frames are to be forwarded to the IP address 153.4.10.1 (presumably not on the local network). The address 153.4.10.1 is then related to the name NETWORK_B at the ISDN address 234567891.

The second line then creates a dialer group and names it 1. The dialer group acts as a package to hold and refer to the dialer map. The third line (`dialer-list 1 list 99`) then creates a link between that dialer group (which has been added to a dialer list) and an IP access list.

Note: One dialer list can represent many dialer groups.

The last line of the command sequence (`access-list 99 permit 153.4.16.0 255.255.0.0 153.4.10.0 255.255.0.0`) actually creates the IP access list that allows the router to accept packets from network 153.4.16.0 (local) and pass them to 153.4.10.0 (not local).

In plain English, the four commands state the following:

Permit this router to take IP packets from network 153.4.16.0 and pass them to network 153.4.10.0 through the ISDN link 234567891 (also known as NETWORK_B)."

ISDN is a protocol that works hand-in-hand with other, higher-end WAN protocols. The most popular of these protocols are X.25 and Frame Relay. Because Frame Relay is based on the technology established in X.25, we will discuss X.25 first.

X.25

X.25 has been in use since the mid-1970s. Like most WAN technologies, X.25 started on the public switched networks used by the telephone companies. The technology that comprises X.25 predates most WAN technologies by a decade. Other WAN protocols, such as Frame Relay, are based on the examples set forth by X.25.

This section of the lesson introduces you to X.25 in a way that makes the next section (Frame Relay) easier to comprehend. X.25 is a large subject that could not be sufficiently covered within a beginner's routing book. Also, given the prevalence of Frame Relay in today's Cisco routing environments, we will examine Frame Relay in much more depth than X.25.

Some technologies introduced in X.25 that are used in other WAN protocols include virtual circuits and packet framing. Both of these technologies would later be adopted by Frame Relay. Although packet framing was briefly discussed in the last section, we have yet to introduce the topic of circuits. Virtual circuits define the path that data takes when moving from one device to another. To ensure that the majority of information being transferred arrives intact, two devices can form circuits between them. The virtual circuits used by X.25 can be described in two categories: permanent or switched.

Permanent Virtual Circuits

Routers, by definition, are designed to choose the best path available to send information for one device to another. When dealing with an environment such as the public telephone networks, this may not be the best way to send data. When electronic data is sent from a PC, it is sent out in short bursts. That is, each packet is injected onto the network one at a time. Because the recipient device is not "listening" to these packets in chronological order, the packets can take any available route to the destination (even if it means arriving out of order).

Imagine if that same scenario were applied to a telephone conversation. Every time you spoke a word into the telephone, it would go down a different path to the receiver. Many of the words would arrive out of order, and the conversation would be garbled. Also, because each word would travel along a different line, many different conversations would stream about the wires at the same time. It would be nearly impossible to determine which words were meant for you.

For this reason, when a telephone call is initiated, the switches that make up the PSN create a static link between the two callers for the duration of the conversation. During the call, every word, sigh, and noise will traverse the same path as the last, thus ensuring that everything arrives in sequence and uninterrupted. More importantly, no other conversations can utilize the same lines involved in the link. This link is known as a `circuit`. WAN technologies that utilize the PSNs have adopted these circuit technologies and learned to use them to their advantage.

A PVC (Permanent Virtual Circuit) defines a set path that data traverses when moving from one location to another. This path never changes. Whenever one device initiates a session with another (on the opposite side of the WAN link), the same path or circuit is used. PVCs can best be thought of as something like static routes. In much the same way static routes can be defined on Cisco routers to use the same path between devices every time, PVCs always use the same circuit between two entities. Figure 13.3 illustrates an X.25 PVC between two networks.

FIGURE 13.3

An X.25 PVC. Any information sent between Network A and Network B will always travel across the circuit "1:2:3".

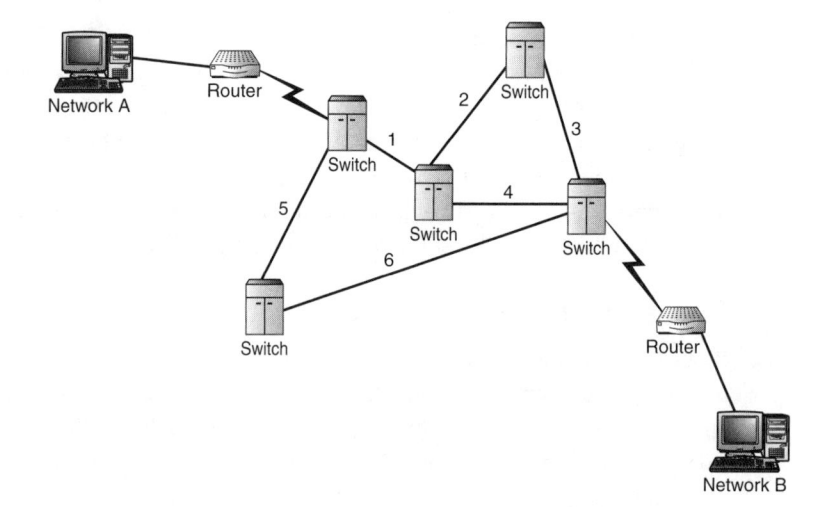

There is one major downside to using PVCs. If one cable were to become unusable (for example, link 2 in Figure 13.3), the whole communication path between Network A and Network B would go down. Where a router would simply choose a new path to the destination (working around the bad line), the PVC cannot stray from the set circuit. One point of failure separates a WAN from an unusable heap of cables. For this reason, SVCs (Switched Virtual Circuits) are an alternative to PVCs.

Switched Virtual Circuits

One difference separates SVCs from PVCs. Whereas a PVC does not change, an SVC can differ with each new session. That is, when a session is initiated between two devices, one circuit is used for the duration of the session. At the conclusion of the session, the circuit is "torn down." The next time a session is established between the two devices, a different circuit may be used.

This method retains the reliability of having a single circuit connect two devices, but it eliminates the vulnerability to a single point of failure. This makes SVCs an attractive alternative to PVCs.

When the Frame Relay protocol was being developed, many of the technologies and advances present in X.25, such as SVCs, were used and adapted to the newer, higher demands of modern networking. Let's move on to discussing the concepts that constitute Frame Relay.

Frame Relay

Frame Relay was developed in the late 1980s as a quicker (more streamlined) version of X.25 geared for the new ISDN networks. Cisco was one of the companies that helped to pioneer the use, development, and implementation of Frame Relay. It stands to reason that nearly all Cisco routers have the capability to maintain WAN links using Frame Relay.

Frame Relay as a WAN protocol operates on the data link layer of the OSI model. This is one major change from X.25, which operates on both the network (routing) layer and the data link (switching) layer. In an effort to streamline the protocol, network layer support was removed from Frame Relay. The rationale here is to let switches do their jobs while routers do theirs.

> **Note** Just as routers operate purely on the network layer of the OSI model, switches operate on the data link layer. This would make Frame Relay a switching protocol. However, the Cisco routers themselves are not involved in moving Frame Relay data. Rather, as with most WAN protocols, the router's job is to pass preformatted data to the switch for transport to another router. When the information reaches the target router, the WAN data is translated back into routed-protocol information.

Frame Relay Technology

The process of configuring a Cisco router to connect Frame Relay involves new keywords and technology that we have yet to cover. This short section introduces you to some of the technology and terminology that you are going to encounter when establishing a Frame Relay connection using a Cisco router.

The hardware required in maintaining and completing a Frame Relay connection is grouped into two categories: DTE (Data Terminal Equipment) and DCE (Data Circuit Terminating Equipment). The DCEs are the switches that make up the PSN. A DCE should never be a part of a business-level Frame Relay network. A DTE, on the other hand, is the Frame Relay equipment that resides on the consumer side of the WAN. A Cisco router would be considered DTE. In contrast to ISDN, most Cisco routers do not have an interface for Frame Relay. To accommodate a Frame Relay connection, added equipment would be needed. The type of equipment required is known as a multiplexer.

A multiplexer takes a T1 (or other larger telephone pipeline) and splits it into separate channels. These channels are then sorted into those that contain Frame Relay data and those that do not. The channels that do contain Frame Relay data are then sent (serially) to the Cisco router. You must use a Cisco router equipped with a serial interface to connect to a multiplexer to implement Frame Relay.

> **Note**
>
> A large-bandwidth line such as a T1 is actually composed of channels, or what we would consider telephone lines. T1 lines contain 24 separate channels. These channels can be used for data or as telephone connections; one T1 line could carry any combination of data and voice. Multiplexers are used to separate these channels from the trunk of the T1.
>
> Equipment such as multiplexers will generally be supplied by either the T1 or Frame Relay provider.

Another term commonly used in Frame Relay configurations is DLCI. The DLCI (data link connection identifier) is the number assigned to the Frame Relay circuit. This number is unique and used by the routers at each end of the WAN to establish a connection. A Frame Relay DLCI is similar to the ISDN SPID. When configuring a Cisco router for Frame Relay, you need to know the DLCI assigned to your particular circuit.

A Cisco router can learn the DLCI through updates with the Frame Relay carrier, called LMI (Local Management Interface) updates. These allow the DLCI to change periodically without the intervention of the router administrator. For example, if the provider uses SVCs, the DLCI can change each time a connection is established. Using the LMI update to carry the DLCI information allows the router to receive the proper DLCI for its connection. The only time you will need to know the DLCI is during the configuration of static Frame Relay route maps.

> **Note**
>
> As far as the circuit is concerned, Frame Relay can handle both PVCs and SVCs. However, it is generally the decision of the carrier as to which will be used.

One piece of optional information you may need is known as an LMI (local management interface). There are several LMI options that can be configured into your router; however, your specific carrier needs to support the LMI you want to use. One popular LMI is known a virtual circuit status.

The virtual circuit status LMI provides an alert back to the routing equipment should a PVC link become unavailable. Referring back to the section on X.25, PVCs are vulnerable to a single point of failure. Should one link in a PVC fail, the entire circuit is useless. By using the virtual circuit LMI, the PSN can notify the router in the event of such failures. Let's use the information we have discussed to now configure a Cisco router for basic Frame Relay service.

Configuring Frame Relay

After the external equipment has been connected to the serial interface of the Cisco router, the IOS configuration can begin. Frame Relay is one of the few protocols not initiated from the global configuration mode of the Cisco IOS. Because much of the functionality is addressed by external equipment, the majority of the configuration is performed at the interface level.

The first piece of information supplied to the interface is the encapsulation method of the Frame Relay network. Cisco has a proprietary encapsulation method that can be used only by Cisco equipment. If you know (from the Frame Relay provider) that the equipment used in the PSN is Cisco-based, the encapsulation method can be left as `default`.

If the PSN equipment is not Cisco-based, or you are unsure, specify the IETF (Internet Engineering Task Force) encapsulation method. IETF encapsulation is a commonly used cross-platform encapsulation that all hardware vendors have implemented. In short, before configuring the encapsulation mode, you need to consult with your Frame Relay provider.

Configuring a Cisco router for Frame Relay differs slightly from the processes used to configure other protocols. Use the following configuration samples as a guide when establishing a Frame Relay connection.

```
Router#configure terminal
Router(config)#interface serial 0
Router(config-if)#encapsulation frame-relay ietf
Router(config-if)#no shutdown
```

Because the Cisco router communicates through one interface (serial) to a multiplexer, it is conceivable that one Cisco serial interface may be the communication point for multiple Frame Relay links. There is no rule that says every channel of the T1 (in the multiplexer) can't be a separate Frame relay circuit. To handle this challenge, Cisco serial interfaces support subinterfaces.

> **Note:** A subinterface is a division of a single interface. One physical interface can be divided into multiple logical subinterfaces, each with a unique address and configuration.

You can configure any number of subinterfaces on one serial interface. If your configuration calls for using multiple Frame Relay circuits, use the following syntax to configure the subinterfaces:

```
Router#configure terminal
Router(config)#interface serial 0.1 point-to-point
Router(config-if)#encapsulation frame-relay ietf
Router(config-if)#no shutdown
```

The subinterface number is separated from the interface number by a decimal point. By requesting `interface serial 0.1`, we are configuring the first subinterface of serial interface 0. (The third subinterface of serial 2 would be 2.3, and so on.) The keyword `point-to-point` indicates that the circuit is a point-to-point circuit. You should use this keyword unless otherwise indicated by your provider. The remaining steps should be repeated for all interfaces.

At this point in the configuration the DLCI (provided by the Frame Relay carrier) should be configured into the router. Although the majority of these steps can be performed in any order, the DLCI is also needed when establishing Frame Relay route maps, so you should supply the DLCI next.

Along with the DLCI, you need to configure the routed protocol address of the interface. This step is the same as that you used to configure ISDN earlier in this lesson. The interface's (IP or IPX) protocol address will be used to route data to and from the interface. Keep in mind that WAN protocols, such as Frame Relay, connect networks. That means the networks participating in the Frame Relay connection need a way to identify each other. By using either an IP or IPX address, networks can communicate transparently of the WAN connecting them. Use the following commands to link an addressed router interface to a Frame Relay link.

```
Router(config-if)#frame-relay interface-dlci 56
Router(config-if)#ip address 198.156.82.1 255.255.255.0
```

With all applicable addresses configured, you can configure the static mappings. You should recognize the format of the command as being similar to that used for the `dialer-map` in ISDN. The command used to create the Frame Relay static maps is `frame-relay map`. This command relates an IP addressable network to a specific frame link. Notice the syntax of the `frame-relay map` command in the following example.

```
Router(config)#frame-relay map ip 198.156.81.0 56
```

In plain English the command states, "Route all IP data from network 198.156.81.0 to Frame Relay circuit (DLCI) 56." In general, this command takes parameters as follows:

`#frame-relay map <protocol> <protocol address> <dlci number>`

With that you have completed a basic Frame Relay configuration. You should take some time before the next lesson to complete the exercises at the end of this lesson. They will help you retain what we have covered in today's topics.

Beginning with the next lesson and continuing through the end of the book, the focus will shift to routing protocols. Routing protocols are the heart of Cisco routers, and the final lessons of this text are geared towards discussing them in detail.

Summary

- ISDN service is divided into two categories, the most common of which is BRI.
- A BRI line consists of two bearer (B) channels and one BRI data (D) channel.
- ISDN is a suite of protocols that collectively addresses the needs of the lowest four layers of the OSI model.
- X.25 introduces the concept of virtual circuits.
- Frame Relay is a streamlined version of X.25 for the existing ISDN networks.
- Frame Relay drops the layer 3 support that was present in X.25.

Q&A

Q If most of the WAN protocols work on the data link (switching) layer, how can they run on a Cisco router?

A Keep in mind that the Cisco router is not routing Frame Relay or ISDN data; rather it takes routable data, encapsulates it in a format corresponding to the WAN protocol, and passes that data to a switch. The Cisco router does not need to understand how to switch data from location to location—it simply passes correctly formatted information to the PSN.

Quiz

Questions

1. What is the total bandwidth of an ISDN BRI line?
2. What is the purpose of a BRI D channel?
3. What is ISDN TE1?

4. What layer(s) of the OSI model does X.25 operate on?

5. What is the identifying number assigned to Frame Relay circuits?

Answers

1. 144 Kbps: 64 Kbps for each of two B channels and 16 Kbps for the D channel.
2. The D channel is used for network signaling.
3. In ISDN, TE1 is Type-1 terminal equipment.
4. Network, data link, and physical.
5. DLCI (Data Link Connection Identifier).

Exercises

1. One command line is missing from the following configuration. Insert the correct command.

```
1>    Router#configure terminal
2>    Router(config)#isdn switch-type basic-nil
3>    Router(config)#interface bri 0
4>    Router(config-if)#isdn spid 1 56342
Router(config-if)#isdn spid 2 98654
Router(config-if)#no shutdown
7>    Router(config-if)#encapsulation ppp
8>    Router(config-if)#ip address 198.37.134.1 255.255.255.0
9>    Router(config)#dialer map ip 198.37.135.0 name NETWORK_B 42156987
10>   Router(config)#dialer-group 1
11>   Router(config)#access-list 108 permit 198.37.134.0 255.255.255.0
198.37.135.0 255.255.255.0
```

Note Between lines 10 and 11, insert the following line.
    Router(config)#dialer-list 1 list 99

2. Configure subinterface 14 (IP address 198.52.62.1) of a Frame Relay interface to route IP network 198.52.63.0 to DLIC 130.

Note
```
Router#configure terminal
Router(config)#interface serial 0.14 point-to-point
Router(config-if)#encapsulation frame-relay ietf
Router(config-if)#no shutdown
Router(config-if)#frame-relay interface-dlci 130
Router(config-if)#ip address 198.52.62.1 255.255.255.0
Router(config)#frame-relay map ip 198.52.63.0 130 cisco
```

Week 2

Day 14

Understanding Routing Protocols

This lesson focuses on introducing you to routing protocols. To this point in the book, we have covered two different types of protocols, WAN and routed, neither of which is actually used by routers. Rather, these protocols are the objects of the router's function. Routers simply move these protocols from location to location. Routing protocols are the tools that routers rely upon to perform this task.

Routers in general use routing protocols to perform the day-to-day operation of transporting data from one network to another. WAN protocols and routed protocols (such as IP) are merely the recipients of the operations performed by routed protocols. The remainder of this book will get increasingly technical as more emphasis is put on Cisco configuration and the configuration of routing protocols.

Today's lesson will introduce to you the concepts behind the workhorses of the routing world: the routing protocols. The job of protocols such as RIP, IGRP, OSPF, and BGP is to compute the best path over which to send routed protocol data and to ensure that the data reaches that destination. The topics examined in this lesson include:

- Routing algorithms
- Protocol routing
- Dynamic updates

Let's examine the job of routing protocols in two parts. The first part of a routing protocol's job is to determine the best path over which to send data. The router uses complex calculations to determine precisely how to move the data to the target network. The responsibility of performing this calculation is delegated to the *routing algorithm*.

The next part of the routing protocol's job is to ensure that every router on a network is working from the same overall "picture" of the networking environment. That is, every router must have the same information about the presence or absence of all network links.

The remainder of this lesson will discuss both of these functions pertaining to routing protocols in more detail. We'll begin by examining the topic of routing algorithms.

Routing Algorithms

A routing algorithm, regardless of type, is a mathematical formula that a routing protocol uses to calculate the desirability of the different paths between devices and destination networks. The algorithm is stored within the router's memory and called out whenever a routing decision needs to be made. Two major categories of routing algorithms can be used by routing protocols: distance vector and link state. Although routing protocols can utilize either distance vector or link state algorithms, each protocol can implement them in slightly different ways. However, there are general terms with which to describe the purpose and function of routing algorithms.

> **Note** Although the implementation of distance vector and link state algorithms can differ slightly from one routing protocol to another, each protocol implements the algorithm identically from one routing platform to another. For example, both RIP and IGRP are distance vector routing protocols. RIP may implement an algorithm slightly differently than IGRP, but RIP as a protocol is implemented the same regardless of the brand or model of router.

The routing protocol gathers certain information about networks and routers from the surrounding environment. This information is stored within a routing table in the router's memory. The information contained in the table is plugged into the routing algorithm. The result of the calculation performed according to the algorithm is used to determine the best path in a particular scenario. Table 14.1 is an example of a routing table (for a fictitious routing environment).

TABLE 14.1 Example of a Routing Table

Router Link	Metric
Router A to router B	2
Router B to router C	3
Router A to router C	6
Router C to router D	5

> **Note** Table 14.1 has been simplified to make a discussion of routing algorithms possible without focusing on one particular protocol.

Our sample routing algorithm states that the "best" path to any destination is the one that has the lowest "metric" value. When router A is presented with a packet bound for router C, the routing table shows two possible paths to choose from. The first choice is to send the packet from router A directly over the link to router C. The second option is to send the packet from router A to router B and then on to router C. The routing algorithm is used to determine which option is best.

Using the "metric" numbers in Table 14.1 associated with each possible link, we see that the path from router A to router B to router C has a metric value of 5, while the direct link to router C has a value of 6. The algorithm selects the A-B-C path and sends the information along that "best" path.

Although simplistic, this example demonstrates how routing algorithm functions as the true decision engine within the router. The specific information that is stored in the routing table, and how the algorithm uses it, depends on the protocol. Distance vector protocols may require different metrics to make a decision than link state protocols do. In the upcoming sections we will examine the differences between these two algorithmic types.

Distance Vector

Distance vector algorithms are similar to the simple algorithm used in our example in Table 14.1. A distance vector algorithm uses metrics known as costs to help determine the best path to a destination. The path with the lowest "total cost" is the one that is chosen as the "best" path.

When a network utilizes a distance vector algorithm, different "cost" amounts are gathered by each router. These costs can be completely arbitrary. Routing administrators can assign any value to a particular cost, based only on their own scale of priority. For example, if the cost is "5," the number 5 may not be of any significance to an outside observer, but the administrator may have assigned it to a particular link to represent the link's reliability.

Costs can also be dynamically gathered values, such as the amount of delay experienced by the router when it sends packets over one link as opposed to another. All of the costs (assigned and otherwise) are compiled and placed within the router's routing table. The cost values are then used by the algorithm to calculate a best path for a given network scenario.

A single router can collect costs to populate its own routing table, a mechanism is needed for enabling multiple routers to share the values they collect. This process is known as a routing update. When distance vector protocols update each other, all or part of the routing table is sent from one router to another. By this process each router is exposed to the information contained within the other routers' tables. This gives each router a more complete view of the networking environment and enablesit to make better routing decisions.

Note All routing protocols, regardless of algorithm, partake in some form of routing update. Although the information, size, and frequency of the updates may vary form protocol to protocol and from algorithm to algorithm, the purpose is the same: to share routing information with neighboring routers.

Examples of distance vector algorithms are Routing Information Protocol (RIP) and Border Gateway Protocol (BGP), two of the more popular protocols in use in Cisco environments. Other popular protocols, such as Open Shortest Path First (OSPF), are examples of link state protocols. Link state protocols function in a slightly different manner than their distance vector counterparts.

Link State

Link state protocols work within the same basic framework as distance vector algorithms, in that they both favor the path with the lowest cost. However, link state protocols work in a somewhat more localized manner. Whereas a router running a distance vector protocol computes the end-to-end path for any given packet, a link state protocol computes the best path as it relates to the most immediate link.

For example, a distance vector protocol may calculate that the best path from router A to router E is A-C-D-E and then send the packet to router E over that exact path. A link state protocol, on the other hand, would determine that the best path from router A to router E would be through router C,. The protocol would then send the packet to router C and let router C calculate the next step.

This process is best for larger environments that may change fairly often. In such environments the routing tables can be quite large. For this reason, each router's table contains only a small piece of the network pie. When a particular link becomes unavailable (changes state), the router sends an update through the environment alerting the network to the one link state change.

Link state and distance vector protocols handle routing situations quite differently. As we discuss each protocol in the remaining lessons of this book, we will address the topics of distance vector and link state as they pertain to particular protocol routing situations.

Dynamic Updates

The first part of a routing protocol's job is to determine what the best path for a data flow should be. The second part of every routing protocol's job is to update routing devices with the most current routing information.

Most routing protocols implement some form of dynamic update. In other words, these protocols have in place some mechanism that allows them to share information with other routers that pertains to a select area or group. Although several parameters vary from protocol to protocol, such as the number of hops an update can traverse and what information can be included in the update, there are some general rules that apply to all routing updates. The following list describes some general rules for how routers and routing protocols utilize dynamic updates:

- Update routing table information for the routing protocol's algorithm to use while making decisions.
- Ensure that each router has an accurate view of the network.
- Facilitate network transactions by allowing routers to collect smaller copies of tables.

Let's examine how routing updates utilize these rules to complete successful transactions. As we begin discussing individual protocols, we will look at the rules more specifically.

Most routers gather only the information that pertains directly to their interfaces. In other words, a router has first-hand knowledge of only the links that are directly connected to its interfaces. Figure 14.2 illustrates a linked routing environment.

FIGURE 14.1

A linked routing environment.

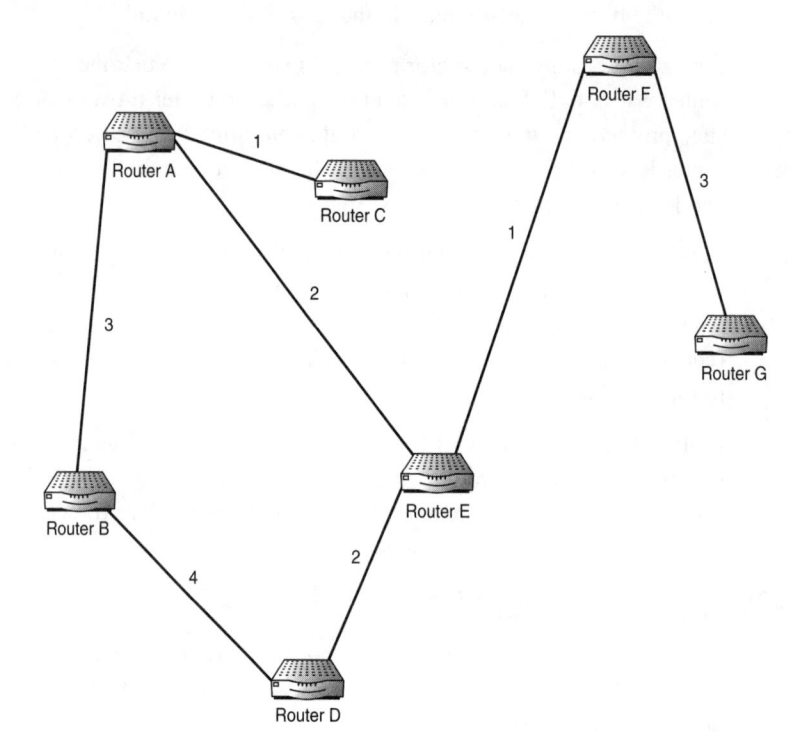

The environment depicted in Figure 14.2 shows seven routers with assigned (arbitrary) metrics. Figure 14.2 is typical of what a network environment might look like. Tables 14.2 through 14.8 show the routing tables for each router in Figure 14.2 as they would appear before any routing updates.

TABLE 14.2 Routing Table for Router A

Link	Metric
A–C	1
A–B	3
A–E	2

TABLE 14.3 Routing Table for Router B

Link	Metric
B–A	3
B–D	4

TABLE 14.4 Routing Table for Router C

Link	Metric
C–A	1

TABLE 14.5 Routing Table for Router D

Link	Metric
D–B	4
D–E	2

TABLE 14.6 Routing Table for Router E

Link	Metric
E–A	2
E–D	2
E–F	1

TABLE 14.7 Routing Table for Router F

Link	Metric
F–E	1
F–G	3

TABLE 14.8 Routing Table for Router G

Link	Metric
G–F	3

From looking at each of the routers' tables it becomes obvious that not every router knows a path to every other router. In fact, every router sees only its direct neighbors. If a packet were to be presented to router A destined for router F, router A would have no way to determine which path is best. (If router A were using a distance vector protocol, it would know the complete path to router F. If router A were running a link state protocol, it would have no way of knowing whether any links beyond its own were still functional.) Each router needs to update the others as to what the rest of the environment looks like.

After a larger-scale update, where every router told its neighbor what information its routing table was holding, the new collective table would look like that in Table 14.9.

TABLE 14.9 Updated Table for Router A

Link	Metric
A–B	3
B–D	4
A–C	1
A–E	2
D–E	2
E–F	1
F–G	3

After the update is complete, it is much easier for router A to send a packet to router F. After examining its table, router A can see that router F lies beyond router E, which can be reached either directly or through the link A–B–D–E.

Routing updates like those used in the preceding scenario can occur in one of two ways. They can be triggered by an event, or they can occur at a set interval. Some protocols initiate the update process at a set time around the clock, for instance, every 30 seconds. In that case as soon as the interval expires, each router sends out an update containing the information from its table. This information may contain vital network changes, or it may have no information at all.

Some protocols use a triggering event to initiate a routing update. For example, if the link between router A and router E goes down, it triggers an update to notify the other routers immediately not to rely on that link.

Ether way, the product of routing updates remains the same: convergence. Network convergence occurs when all of the routers in an environment are working from the same picture of the network. Speedy network convergence is highly sought after and is a major selling point for any protocol.

Convergence

When it comes to routing, convergence is the magic word. Convergence is the condition in which every router within a given environment is operating from the same view of the network. For example, if one link in a network becomes unavailable, a routing update begins. From the time when the link fails until every router's table has been updated, the routers are out of convergence. Any packet sent over a network that is not in convergence risks being misrouted or lost.

Convergence is harder to achieve in larger environments with complicated paths. Therefore, the type of protocol chosen for a certain environment is critical. In very large environments, link state protocols achieve convergence more quickly than distance vector protocols do. However, in small networks, distance vector protocols can route information more quickly.

Summary

- Routing protocols are the heart of a router's functionality.
- Routing protocols use algorithms to calculate the best path from one network to another.
- The two major types of routing protocols are distance vector and link state.
- All routers maintain only a portion of a routing table.
- Updates are used to allow routers a means of building a picture of the entire network.
- Convergence is the point at which all routers within an environment are working from the same picture of the surrounding environment.

Q&A

Q Why are there different types of routing protocols? Why not make one that works in larger environments and routes quickly?

A Routing environments, by nature, are very dynamic. Therefore, it is impossible to anticipate every network environment or condition. Choosing which protocol will best serve your particular network is a tough yet important task that faces nearly every routing engineer.

Quiz

Questions

1. Which type of routing protocol would work best in a large routing environment?
2. What is the term used to describe a router within a routing environment?
2. What is the arbitrary value assigned to router links?

Answers

1. Link state.
2. Hop.
3. A metric (or cost).

Week 3

Cisco Routing Advanced Topics

15 Learning How to Configure RIP

16 Using IGRP and EIGRP

17 Configuring OSPF

18 Understanding Border Gateway Protocol (BGP)

19 Learning IS-IS

20 Introduction to Basic Cisco Security

21 Understanding Cisco Catalyst Switch Routing and PNNI

WEEK 3

DAY 15

Learning How to Configure RIP

To this point we have discussed all of the topics one should understand to learn Cisco routing. We have covered Cisco hardware, the Cisco IOS, simple routed protocols, and WAN protocols. These concepts constitute the base of knowledge that a prospective routing expert should possess.

With the main topics introduced, it is now time to dive into more specific areas of knowledge. Some topics and technologies require more in-depth coverage than others, and one of those technologies is routing protocols. Today's lesson focuses on the first routing protocol you will learn: RIP. The topics we will cover in this lesson include:

- An overview of the Routing Information Protocol (RIP)
- The RIP routing algorithm
- How RIP works
- Configuring RIP
- Maintaining RIP

An Overview of the Routing Information Protocol (RIP)

Introduced in the last lesson, routing protocols are the heart of the routing process. The routing protocol is responsible for the successful transfer of data from one location to another over the best possible path; therefore, engineers generally spend more time designing for and implementing routing protocols than they spend on any other router maintenance duty—which is understandable, considering the tremendous responsibility placed upon these routing protocols in general.

RIP (Routing Information Protocol) was one of the first routing protocols used in widescale environments. Originally released in 1982 for Unix environments, the technology behind RIP can actually be traced back to a Xerox protocol called PUP (PARC Universal Protocol) GWINFO. RIP as a routing protocol can be classified as an IGP (Interior Gateway Protocol). In other words, RIP is designed to work within one homogeneous environment.

> Routing protocols can be classified either as IGP (interior gateway protocols) or EGP (exterior gateway protocols). IGPs are routing protocols that move data within one specific, defined environment. IGP protocols tend to lack the addressing ability to provide interenvironmental connectivity.
>
> EGPs are routing protocols that span multiple, nonrelated networking environments. Loosely meshed networks, such as those that form the Internet, are bound by exterior gateway protocols.

Although one environment may consist of several networks, RIP cannot be used to span multiple environments. However, the definition of a single homogeneous (multiple-network) environment can be blurry and rather abstract depending on the protocol(s) being used. A good rule of thumb for identifying a single routing environment suitable for accommodating RIP is the presence (or lack) of a WAN connection. A single networking environment will generally lack a WAN connection that uses a public access environment, such as a PSN (public switched network). If your environment spans two or more WAN connections, it may not be suitable for RIP.

Because RIP was designed during a time when routing environments were not as large as they are today, it cannot handle some of the more complex environments that are often found in use throughout enterprises. However, because of the protocol's focus on small to midsized networks, it remains extremely popular today.

One reason for RIP's continued popularity was achieved quite by accident. When RIP was introduced, it was not presented as a "small- to medium-network routing protocol." Rather, RIP was meant to handle the more robust needs of the latest in networking technology. As technology continued to improve, networks grew larger, and RIP was left behind. However, as environments grew larger, engineers soon discovered that very few protocols worked better in smaller environments than RIP.

The Technology That Built RIP

RIP was designed during the early 1980s by one of the innovating companies in networking technology, Xerox. The protocol was originally designed to run on PCs, Unix servers, and other computing devices. Using the early versions of RIP, these devices could be networked together in a single environment resembling a bus network.

> **Note:** A bus network is a simple form of network that consists of computers connected to a single backbone. Rarely used now, bus networks were popular in areas with few devices and limited space or resources.

Because RIP was designed to run on computers (rather than routers), the engineers developed it so as to allow the sharing of processor time. In other words, the same processor that handles requests from the protocol also had to handle requests from the computer. This meant that RIP had to be streamlined enough not to use all of the available processing time.

The computers that ran RIP also had very limited resources (memory and drive space). To work around this limitation, RIP needed to be very lightweight. RIP does not take up as much memory as other, modern routing protocols. This makes it a quick protocol that does not require a lot of overhead.

The initial designers of RIP also tried to build in some safety features to protect networks from potential routing problems. One of those common problems is known as a routing loop. A routing loop occurs when devices are connected in such a way that protocols become confused and continue around in a never-ending journey across the environment. Figure 15.1 illustrates a simple routing loop.

In Figure 15.1, if device A sends a packet to device D, the packet gets caught in a routing loop. The link to device D has become unavailable; however, each device still thinks device D is accessible through the remaining devices. The packet moves from device A to device B to device C looking for the target. Device C (lacking access to device D) forwards the packet to the next hop (device A). This loop continues indefinitely.

FIGURE 15.1

A simple routing loop.

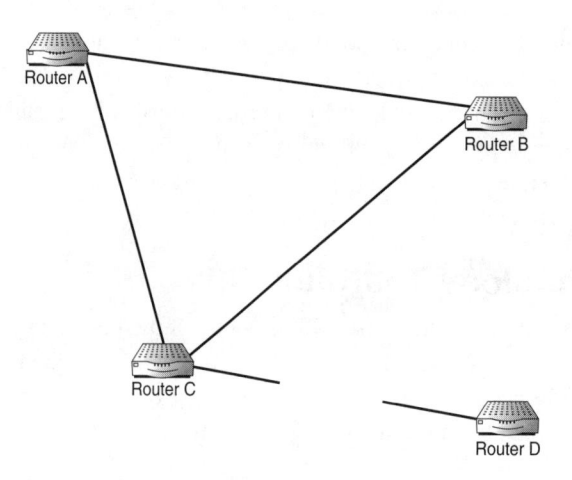

To remedy such loops, the original designers of RIP wrote into the protocol a type of kill switch: a limit to the number of hops that, if exceeded, would cause the packet to be labeled undeliverable and be dropped. This feature of RIP is known as the "hop count limit." It is one of four technological routing advances introduced with RIP. These four technological advances include:

- Hop count limit
- Route poisoning
- Split horizon
- Hold-down timers

Each of these items is used (in one form or another) in most routing protocols today. They are important features for engineers to understand, because they can greatly affect the overall routing process. Learning these widely used routing protocol concepts also aids in future troubleshooting processes. Each of these features is prevalent in the functionality and operation of RIP, so we will take time now to cover each of them. However, before we can discuss these RIP features, we need to introduce the RIP routing table, on which they all depend.

The RIP Routing Table

The routing protocol produces a routing table that stores all of the information a Cisco router needs to move data from one location to another. This table is normally stored within the router's RAM (rather than flash memory). This allows the router to access the table quickly and make changes as needed.

> **Note**
>
> Recall that the RAM of a Cisco router is volatile; that is, it is not retained when the router is powered off. Files such as `running-config` are also stored in the RAM memory. If a Cisco router is powered off (regardless of the routing protocol), the routing table is lost.
>
> Unlike `running-config`, the routing table is a dynamic file that cannot be copied to the flash memory for saving.

The contents of the routing table differs depending on the routing protocol being used. Table 15.1 illustrates a typical routing table on a Cisco router running RIP (the router that the table belongs to is router D).

TABLE 15.1 A Sample Routing Table

Network	Next Hop	Metric	Timer	Flags
153.19.88.0	Router A	2	30–180-240	
198.63.35.0	Router B	6	30-180–240	
153.19.89.0	Router C	1	30-180–240	

> **Note**
>
> In Table 15.1, the column headed "Flags" is optional. Commonly a routing table will not including any information in the flags field. The Flag data varies with the protocols being used, because each protocol has its own parameters and options that can be configured for it.

The table holds the information needed to make informed routing decisions. These fields are described in the following list.

- *Network:* The destination network address.
- *Next hop:* The address of the router that is the next direct link to the destination.
- *Cost:* Also known as "metric," the cost represents the number of hops after the "next hop" required to reach the destination.
- *Timer:* The "timer" field actually represents three different timers used by RIP. The routing update timer is used to mark the interval between routing updates. RIP generally sends a routing update every 30 seconds. The second timer is the route timeout. If a routing update is not received from a particular network within 180 seconds, the route is marked as inaccessible. The final timer is the route

removal timer. The route removal timer deletes any route in the routing table that has not been updated in the last 240 seconds.

- *Flags:* The flags field holds any optional RIP features (not commonly used).

From the routing table illustrated in Table 15.1 we can deduce that router D is 2 hops away from network 153.19.88.0 through router A, 6 hops away from network 198.63.35.0 through router B, and 1 hop away from network 153.19.89.0 through router C. When router D receives a packet addressed to network 153.19.88.0, the router uses RIP to examine the routing table and conclude that the packet should be sent through router A.

> Router hops are an important concept in routing. Each router through which a packet of data must pass before reaching its final destination is considered another "hop." The number of hops between a source and its destination greatly affects the following routing elements.
>
> - TTL (Time to Live) time expiration
> - Signal corruption. (Just as in the old school game "Telephone," the more times a message is passed, the greater the chance it can be corrupted.
> - Network size limits. Many routing protocols limit the size (in hops) a network can span.

Cisco routers running RIP send copies of their routing tables to their neighbors every time the routing update timer expires. This allows routers to keep abreast of changes in the network's topology.

Note A router's neighbor is any router that is directly linked to it. In other words, two routers that are directly linked to each other are considered neighbors; however, routers that are separated by a third router (or other connectivity device) are not considered neighbors.

The purpose of the routing updates is to allow each router an opportunity to inform its neighbors as to the current number of hops from one location to another. However, one problem that can arise from this process is when routers incorrectly report the state of networks of which they do not have direct knowledge. The cure for many common routing problems can be found in the four added features of RIP: hop count limits, route poisoning, split horizon, and hold-down timers.

Hop Count Limits

The most debated feature of RIP is the hop count limit. When the protocol was designed, a limit of 15 hops was imposed on all RIP environments. This feature is viewed as a dual-edged sword. Although hop count limits are an effective tool against routing loops, they also severely limit the size of environments using the protocol.

Through the fields in the packet's routed protocol header, the number of hops a packet has passed through can be tracked. For example, IP packets contain the Time to Live (TTL) field, mentioned on Day 5, "Understanding How Routers Move Data." Packets that are sent from a PC under RIP begin with a TTL 15. Each time the packet passes through a router, the TTL field is decremented by 1. When a packet has made its 15th hop, the TTL is zero, and the device discards the packet as unreachable. If a loop occurs, it could last for no more than 15 passes, because after 15 passes from hop to hop, the router discards the packet and moves on to other routing responsibilities. In the same way, an IPX packet header contains a "transfer control" field that is incremented at each hop; when this field reaches 16, the packet is discarded.

Every time a packet reaches a RIP router, the routed protocol header is stripped off. The router determines the best path for the data to traverse, and then the RIP-adjusted protocol header is reapplied. When the header is reapplied, a field that keeps track of the number of hops taken, such as the TTL (Time to Live) field on an IP packet, is adjusted to indicate that the packet has encountered another hop. Therefore, when a packet reaches a router and the header is examined, the router can immediately see whether the packet has reached the hop count limit. Any packet that has reached this limit can be discarded.

At the time that RIP was developed, its designers could barely imagine a single environment that would encompass more than 15 hops. Many of the larger environments at the time did not have even 10 networked devices. A path that could surpass 15 routing hops seemed far-fetched.

As routing technology progressed and networks became larger, it grew evident that routing environments would quickly surpass the RIP hop limit of 15. It would have been easy to abandon the old RIP routing protocol in favor of an up-to-date version. However, instead of redesigning RIP to meet the needs of modern networks, new protocols were developed based on the architecture of RIP (without the limitations). Routing protocols such as OSPF were created to meet some of the enterprise needs that RIP could not address.

RIP was not redesigned to remove hop count limits because they are a valuable tool in combating routing loops. Although imposing hop limits does limit the size of your routing environments, they are more of a help to administrators than a hindrance. Keep in mind that most routing loops are created unintentionally; you may not notice them right away. The hop count limit within RIP is one more tool that engineers rely on to help control these common problems.

Route Poisoning

RIP has also implemented a tool known as route poisoning. Route poisoning occurs when a particular path in a routing table is assigned a hop count of 16. With the assignment of a hop count of 16 to a path within the routing table, the path becomes invisible or unreachable. Poisoning a route can quickly prevent routing loops.

The following scenario describes a situation in which a router would choose to poison a path. If a router continuously receives updates in which a particular path's metric is incrementing, the router deduces that a routing loop has occurred. The router then sets the route's metric to 16 in its own routing table and triggers a routing update. This update alerts all neighboring routers that the path is poisoned and should not be used. Figure 15.2 illustrates a network where route poisoning has occurred.

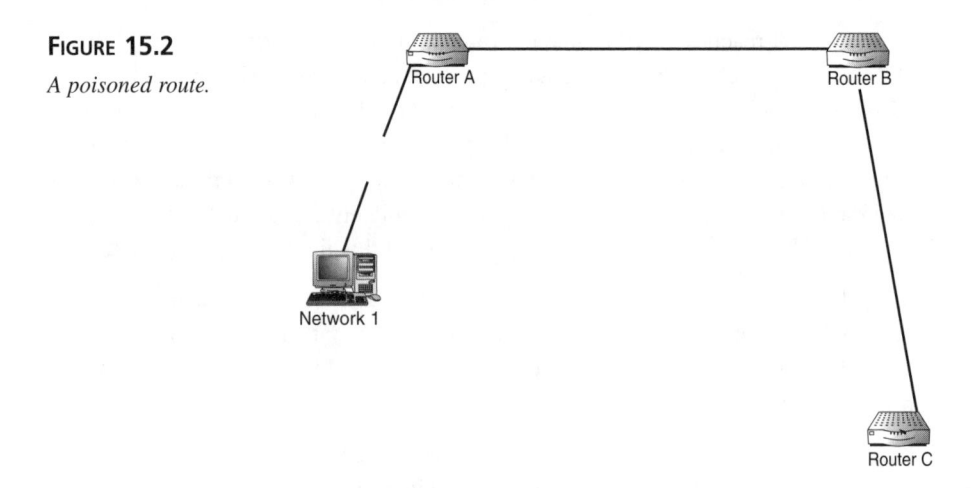

FIGURE 15.2

A poisoned route.

In Figure 15.2 the link between network 1 and router A has become unavailable. Router B, during an update, tells both router A and router C that it can reach network 1 in 2 hops. Router A, realizing that it can no longer reach network 1 itself, changes the metric for network 1 on its own routing table to 3—1 (itself) plus 2 (the metric from router B)—and sends out an update. Router B receives the update, notices that router A has changed its metric from 1 to 3 and adjusts its routing table to reflect a metric of 4. This is a classic routing loop.

To eliminate this problem, Router C (receiving the update from router B) realizes that the loop has occurred and immediately sets the path to 16. When router A and router B receive the update, the path is poisoned and becomes ignored.

Split Horizon

The concept of split horizons is another tool to help prevent routing loops. The rule of split horizon states that a router cannot send an update back to the device it was received from. Through elimination of these "redundant" updates, routers are not misled into believing links that do not exist are actually fully functional.

For example, Figure 15.3 illustrates an environment where the split horizon rule could make a difference.

FIGURE 15.3

An example of the split horizon rule.

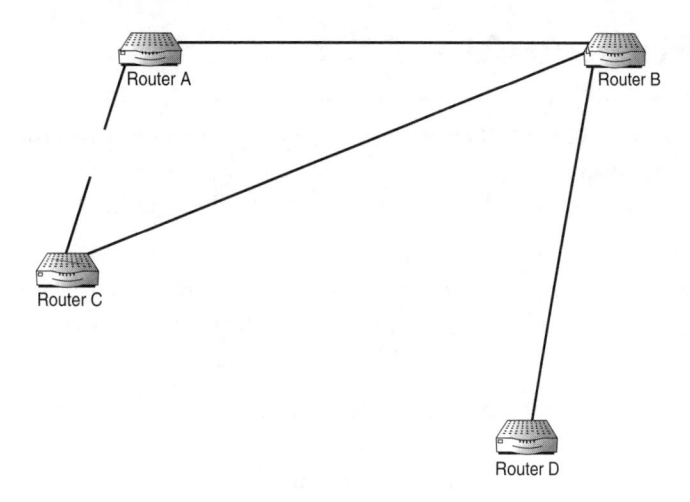

The scenario depicted in Figure 15.3 shows four routers (A, B, C, and D). To demonstrate split horizon, let's say that the link between routers A and C fails. Router A adjusts its routing table to show that it no longer links to router C. Router A sends an update to router B notifying it of the unavailable link. However, before router B can send out another update, it receives an update from router D stating that the link from router A to router C is still operational. Router B then corrects its routing table and notifies router A that the link between router A and router C is now functional (even though it is not). This creates a routing loop between router A and router B.

In an effort to combat this, the split horizon rule states that a router cannot send an update to a router it has received an update from until it has updated its remaining neighbors. By doing this, the router can be assured that the correct information will be sent to all of the routers involved.

Hold-Down Timers

Hold-down timers are used in conjunction with other RIP features such as split horizon. A hold-down timer is used to indicate the amount of time during which a particular path cannot be updated. For example, in a split horizon scenario a hold-down timer would be used to prevent an inactive route from becoming improperly reactivated.

When a router detects an unavailable link, a routing table update is initiated. Then the router places a hold-down timer on the route. The hold-down timer prevents the router from reupdating its own routing table with potentially false information from a neighboring router (which may not have received the update yet). After the hold-down timer expires, the router is free to update the unavailable path as needed.

RIP Routing Algorithm

RIP remains a lightweight, efficient protocol that is specifically suited for the needs of small to medium-sized environments. Although the structure of routing networks has changed over the years, RIP has simply moved from "a routing protocol for any environment" to "a premier routing protocol from small to midsized environments."

One key to RIP's enduring success is that it is a distance vector routing protocol. In other words, the protocol utilizes a form of routing algorithm known as distance vector (also known as a Bellman-Ford algorithm). This algorithm dictates how the protocol makes routing decisions and where table updates are sent.

Simply stated, a distance vector algorithm calculates the distance between router links (vectors) and then forwards information across the shortest path. The values or metrics attached to these vectors (used by the algorithm to calculate the path) can be purely arbitrary numbers assigned by router administrators, or they can represent real values such as the amount of packet delay time on a specific link. (In the next section, we will see how the RIP metric information is gathered from the routed protocol header.)

> **Note** A protocol's header is the portion of a packet that contains the protocol-specific information. Each routed or WAN protocol (but not routing protocol) adds its own header information to every packet.

When a router receives a RIP packet containing routing table update information, the algorithm for RIP uses two major pieces of information from the RIP packet header and compares them with the router's present routing table. The result of this comparison is the path or paths that a packet can use to reach its target. In the event multiple paths are returned, the algorithm uses the metric for each route to decide which path is "best."

The next section of the lesson uses scenarios to show the beginning-to-end process of routing a packet with RIP. In that discussion the topics of algorithms, updates, and packet headers are covered in detail. When we have a more complete understanding of how RIP works, we can examine the commands and procedures needed to configure RIP on a Cisco router.

How RIP Works

RIP functions like any routed or WAN protocol. RIP is a common language that all routers within a single environment can speak to facilitate the movement of data from one network to another. When dealing with routing protocols such as RIP, it is important to recognize that all of the routers within a given environment need to use the same routing protocol.

> **Note** Although all of the routers within a given environment need to use the same routing protocol, they do not necessarily need to use the same *routed* protocol. Routers can connect networks that use dissimilar routed protocols. However, for information to be passed from one router to another, the routers do need to share a routing protocol.

When a packet of data reaches a router, it has already experienced a few changes. (Referring back to the discussion of routed protocols, the packet has been segmented and encapsulated with the data representing the routed protocol being used.) The router receives the data and begins to read the protocol header information. To this point the routing protocol has yet to be used.

> As we discuss how RIP utilizes packets and packet headers, keep in mind that RIP (being a routing protocol) does not encapsulate data. This means that there is no such thing as an RIP-encapsulated packet. RIP, as a routing protocol, simply acts on packets prepared by other, routed protocols such as IP.

The router looks first at one field within the protocol header: the destination field (the fields of the routed protocol header—in this case IP—are illustrated in Table 15.2). The router then compares the routed protocol destination data with the entries in its routing table (which is a product of the routing protocol). Keep in mind that the router has not even made a decision to route this packet; no protocols, routing or otherwise, have been called into use by the router. At this point the router is simply determining where the packet is trying to go.

After the router determines that the packet is addressed for a destination that is reachable through one of the its interfaces, the router hands the packet over to RIP. RIP then takes a closer look at the router's routing table to determine exactly what path the packet needs to be sent down. Still working from the packet's original protocol header (usually IP) destination, RIP compares that value to a list of possible known destinations. If more than one path is returned as a matching destination, RIP then looks to the routing table metrics. Table 15.2 shows a sample IP packet header. Within this sample header the information needed by RIP is clearly available. Table 15.3 illustrates a sample routing table. Using these two tables, we can easily follow the process RIP uses to route data.

TABLE 15.2 An Incoming IP Header

Field	Value
Version	4
Header length	6
Type of service	0
Total length	16
Segment ID	1
Flags	0
Fragment offset	0
TTL	15
Protocol	17
Checksum	1024
Source address	153.85.23.15
Destination address	153.85.26.85

The data in the packet header is compared with the router's routing table illustrated in Table 15.3. After the destination address of the header file is compared with the networks listed in the routing table, two possible matches are produced: Router C and Router D.

TABLE 15.3 A Sample Routing Table

Network	Next Hop	Metric	Timer	Flags
153.85.23.0	Router B	4	30–180–240	0
153.85.24.0	Local	0	30–180–240	0
153.85.23.0	Local	0	30–180–240	0
153.85.26.0	Router C	2	30–180–240	0
153.85.26.0	Router D	3	30–180–240	0
203.152.0.0	Router C	2	30–180–240	0

The router now has a choice to make: which path to send the packet over to reach the network 153.85.26.0? The router (according to the routing table) can reach network 153.85.26.0 either through router C or router D. The router looks to RIP's routing algorithm to decide which path to use. The algorithm takes the metrics for both, the path to router C (2) and the path to router D (3), and determines that the packet should be sent through router C.

Now RIP's job focus shifts from determining the best path to moving data across that path. The IP protocol header is reattached; however, some of the fields are changed. Table 15.4 shows the fields of the reattached IP header.

TABLE 15.4 The Reattached Protocol Header

Field	Value
Version	4
Header length	6
Type of service	0
Total length	16
Segment ID	1
Flags	0
Fragment offset	0
TTL	14
Protocol	17
Checksum	1024
Source address	153.85.23.15
Destination address	153.85.26.85

To sum up what we have covered so far, RIP as a routing protocol acts on packets sent from routed protocols. When a router receives a routed protocol packet, the packet is handed over to RIP. Examining the packet's header, RIP extracts the key routing information: the source and destination addresses and the routing metrics. The RIP routing algorithm then calculates the best path for transmission of the packet, reattaches an updated routed protocol header, and forwards the packet onto the network.

This scenario is repeated on every router the packet comes into contact with. This means that the RIP routing tables on each of these routers must be identical to ensure routing accuracy. The next section explains how RIP keeps routers updated and ensures the integrity of the networking environment.

Routing Updates within RIP

Aside from its duty to move data around the network, RIP is also responsible for updating the routing tables of the routers it runs on. RIP facilitates the updating of routing tables and the successful convergence of the environment through automated updates.

RIP updates are sent every 30 seconds by every router on the network. However, unlike most link state protocols, RIP routers send updates only to their neighboring routers. These updates (depending on the update trigger) can contain either the entire routing table or a portion of the table.

> **Note** An update trigger is an event that either starts or requests a routing update.

Three events can trigger a RIP routing update. These events are the expiration of an update timer, the state change of a link, or a direct RIP update request. The first event, the expiration of an event timer, tracks a field within RIP's routing table. The routing update timer expires by default every 30 seconds. When this timer expires, the router sends a copy of its routing table to each of its directly connected neighbors. These neighbors use the information to update their tables and produce their own routing updates.

The second event occurs if a link between two routers (or one router and a network) fails, the directly attached router updates its table and sends out an immediate update. During an update that is triggered by a network change, only the affected portion of the routing table is sent to the neighboring routers. The neighboring routers update the related portions of their own tables and continue to propagate updates.

Finally the third event happens when a Cisco router running RIP requests an update from a specific router. This is typically done after the expiration of a hold-down timer. When a router receives a request for an update, the entire routing table is sent back to the requesting router.

Regardless of the event that triggered the update, routing tables are sent out in the format of RIP header information. The only routing-protocol-generated packets are those used to publish routing table updates. An update packet generally consists of just the protocol header (with no data). Keep in mind that routing updates are not the product of protocol encapsulation; rather, they are a means to send data from one router to another. Table 15.5 is the header for a routing table update packet. Table 15.6 illustrates the fields used by RIP to disseminate routing update information.

TABLE 15.5 RIP Update Message Header Fields

Field	Purpose
Command	Indicates whether the packet is a request for an update or a response to a request
Version	Indicates the version of RIP being used, typically version 2
Zero	Two bytes populated with zeros

TABLE 15.6 RIP Table Entry Fields

Field	Purpose
Address family identifier	Represents the address family, typically IP
Route tag	Populated with zeros
Address	The protocol address of the route
Zero	Populated with zeros
Zero	Populated with zeros
Metric	Metric associated with address

In the RIP header the fields listed in Table 15.6 can be repeated multiple times to represent an entire routing table. (The limit is 25 addresses within a single update.) If the packet represents a link change, the packet contains only one entry.

RIP continues to send updates to each of its neighboring routers until convergence is achieved. Convergence is that point at which all routers within the same environment have the same routing information. If the network is ever out of convergence, serious problems such as routing loops can occur. If, when using RIP on your Cisco router, you find you are not achieving convergence cleanly or quickly enough, certain elements such as timers can be adjusted to help meet the overall network goals.

Now it is time to take the concepts we have covered (relating to RIP) and apply them to Cisco routers. Moving forward, we will now examine how to configure a Cisco router to run RIP.

Configuring RIP

The commands used to configure a Cisco router to run RIP should appear similar to the commands used for other protocols, and RIP, like most protocols we have covered thus far in this book, needs to be enabled before it can be configured. To begin the process of configuring RIP, the router must be in global configuration mode. From this mode, the `router rip` command can be run to enter the routing protocol configuration mode on the Cisco router.

```
Router#configure terminal
Router(config)#router rip
Router(config-router)#
```

> **Note:** We will be using the `router` command often throughout the rest of this book. The `router` command is used to enable almost all routing protocols.

Now you can begin setting the parameters that are required to run the protocol. To enable RIP functionality on a Cisco router, set the router's network. This gives the router a point of identity on the network and informs it as to its location within the environment. Use the following `network` command to specify the router's network location.

```
Router#configure terminal
Router(config)#router rip
Router(config-router)#network 198.124.0.0
Router(config-router)#^Z
```

> **Note:** The specific interfaces of the router should still be configured (following the examples throughout the first half of this text) to run an appropriate routed protocol. Even with RIP enabled correctly, it does little good if the individual interfaces are not configured.

These simple commands enable RIP on a Cisco router. Because these commands are executed in global configuration mode, you should assume that the commands apply to all of the router's interfaces. No other configuration is required at this point to produce an active RIP router. Still, there are several optional parameters that you should know about. These parameters make administering and maintaining a Cisco router running RIP much easier. Parameters such as those used to set RIP timers and configure RIP neighbors are covered in the next section.

Maintaining RIP

Cisco allows engineers to be extremely flexible with their implementations of RIP. They offer several optional parameters to customize the performance of RIP. Many of the features and parameters associated with RIP can be manually configured to suit the needs of almost any environment. As mentioned in the last section, some of these adjustable parameters include:

- RIP timers
- Addresses of a router's neighbors
- The version of RIP to be compatible with other vendors and implementations

Becoming familiar with the syntax and uses of these options can help you to better manage routers and maintain clean, efficient routing environments.

Setting RIP Timers

One set of optional parameters Cisco allows users to adjust is the RIP timers. RIP uses four timers over the course of normal routing: the routing update timer, hold-down timer, route timeout, and route removal. All four timers relate to the manner and interval in which a router deals with table updates. Each of these timers, while having default values, can be manipulated to fit the specific needs of any network. Use the `timer basic` command to set the RIP timers. The structure of this command is as follows:

```
#timer basic <routing update timer> <route timeout> <hold-down timer> <route removal>
```

For example, to set specific times with the `timer basic` command, you would run these commands from within the routing protocol configuration mode:

```
Router(config)#router rip
Router(config-router)#timers basic 30 180 45 270
Router(config-router)#^Z
```

> **Note** Use caution when executing the `timer basic` command. Not only can you seriously affect the performance of the network, but, because the command updates all four timers at once, you may inadvertently set a timer incorrectly.

In the previous example the routing update timer was set to 30 seconds, which means this specific Cisco router sends its table updates every 30 seconds. The route timeout was set to 180 seconds, meaning that any router for which an update is not received within

180 seconds is marked. The hold-down timer was set to 45 seconds. Because the hold-down timer specifies the amount of time during which a router cannot apply any updates, it should be staggered so as not to correspond to any existing update timers.

Finally, the route removal timer was set to 270 seconds. Any router for which an update is not received within 270 seconds is considered to be unavailable and is removed from the routing table. Because these timers control updates that are sent to a Cisco router's neighbors, you may want to manually inform the router as to the location and address of its neighbors.

Manually Configuring RIP Neighbors

Another configuration option on Cisco routers is the ability to specify RIP neighbors. RIP is configured as a global router setting. Because of this, it is active on every interface by default. However, Cisco realizes that some environments may not require RIP to be run on every interface—for example, one router may connect to more than one network. One of these networks may run RIP, but the other might not. For that Cisco router to send RIP updates over both of those links would be a needless generation of network congestion.

A Cisco router auto-detects its neighbors. However, in an environment of mixed router types, you may not want to run RIP with every router you interface with. Or you may want more control over the routing process. If either of these instances are the case, you can use the `neighbor` command.

The `neighbor` command is used within the Cisco IOS to specify neighboring routers to which the RIP sends table updates. Conversely, the `passive-interface` command specifies interfaces over which RIP should *not* send updates. The combination of these commands allows engineers to have more control over how RIP operates within a particular environment.

To use the `neighbor` command, put the routing into the routing protocol configuration mode. The syntax for running the `neighbor` command is as follows:

```
#neighbor <protocol address>
```

Using this command, configure a RIP router to recognize the router 198.53.10.1 as a RIP neighbor:

```
Router#configure terminal
Router(config)#router rip
Router(config-router)#neighbor 195.53.10.1
Router(config-router)#^Z
```

Learning How to Configure RIP

The `neighbor` command can be used to specify as many neighbor routers as needed. To view which neighbor router has been configured on your system use the `show running-config` command.

```
Router#show running-config

!
router rip
 network 153.5.0.0
 neighbor 153.5.86.2
 neighbor 153.5.46.1
!

(output abbreviated)
```

> **Note:** Keep in mind that all router changes and configurations are sent only to the `running-config` file. You must manually copy those settings to the `startup-config` file to save them.

The `running-config` file displays the two routers that have been manually configured as neighbors on the Cisco router. To remove any of the manually configured neighbors, use the no keyword:

```
Router#configure terminal
Router(config)#router rip
Router(config-router)#no neighbor 153.5.86.2
Router(config-router)#^Z
```

Whereas the `neighbor` command ensures that a particular router is recognized as a neighbor, the `passive-interface` command restricts RIP from sending updates over selected interfaces. The syntax of the `passive-interface` command is as follows:

```
#passive-interface <interface> <interface number>
```

To restrict RIP from sending updates over the interface Ethernet 1, use the following set of commands:

```
Router#configure terminal
Router(config)#router rip
Router(config-router)#passive-interface ethernet 1
Router(config-router)#^Z
```

Mastering the `neighbor` and `passive-interface` commands gives Cisco users a broader range of control over how RIP operates on their routers. Another useful configurable command provided by Cisco allows the user to specify which version of RIP to use on a router.

Cisco routers are capable of (and installed with support for) both version 1 and version 2 of RIP. The next section will explain how to choose which one you use on your router.

Working with Multiple Versions of RIP

Using RIP in an environment where multiple router hardware vendors are used may cause some problems. For example, Cisco routers send RIP version 1 as the default version of the RIP protocol. Some brands of router may only receive RIP version 2.

Cisco provides a set of commands that allow users to specify, either globally or by interface, which version of RIP should be used. The global command is simply `version`. This command specifies which version of RIP is used on the whole router.

> **Note** Versions 1 and 2 of RIP are incompatible. If you have a Cisco environment and change one router to use RIP 1, that router will not work (the rest of the Cisco routers default to RIP 2). Ensure that all of your routers are using compatible versions of RIP before changing settings.

One common application of the `version` command is to use a Cisco router as a protocol translator—that is, using RIP 1 on one interface (to interface with equipment using RIP 1) and configuring RIP 2 on another (to bridge to equipment using RIP 2). The syntax of the version global command is simply `version <version number>`:

```
Router#configure terminal
Router(config)#router rip
Router(config-router)#version 2
Router(config-router)#^Z
```

For configuring RIP versions on the interface level, Cisco gives users a little more flexibility. On the interface level a user can specify which version of RIP to use for both the send and receive attributes of the interface.

This flexibility is useful if you are participating in a route redistribution. When participating in route redistribution, you can choose to only receive updates from RIP 1 routers while redistributing those updates to RIP 2 routers. Specifying the send and receive RIP versions of a particular interface will be an incredibly useful tool for you as you experiment with different network configurations.

> **Note** The RIP interface `version` commands are available only if you are running IP on the particular interfaces.

To specify the send or receive properties of an interface, the router must be in interface configuration mode. The command syntax is as follows:

`#ip rip <direction> <version number(s)>`

The following example of the interface version command configures the interface Ethernet 1 to send only RIP version 1 updates, while Ethernet 2 is configured to receive both version 1 and version 2:

```
Router#configure terminal
Router(config)#interface ethernet 0
Router(config-int)#ip rip send version 1
Router(config-int)#interface ethernet 1
Router(config-int)#ip rip receive version 1 2
Router(config-int)#^Z
```

The commands we have discussed thus far are very useful to any user running RIP in a Cisco environment. However, these commands only set the properties of RIPs. Many times you may encounter a router with an existing installation of RIP. The last section of this lesson examines the commands used to view the statistics of RIP routers that are already configured.

Viewing RIP Stats

Configuring a Cisco router to run RIP is an important step in learning the mechanics behind Cisco routing. However, configuring RIP does you little good if you cannot monitor how the router is performing once you have finished. Among the several key pieces of information that Cisco allows you to view concerning RIP routers, the most important for you at this point is the RIP routing table.

> **Note** The show command (which we will use to view the RIP routing table) can be used to list hundreds of individual pieces of information. Everything from the IP sockets that are in use to the version of the IOS installed can be summoned using the show command.

Ensuring that your router is both sending and receiving accurate updates is an important issue in maintaining RIP routers. You can view the contents of the routing table to determine whether the routes are active or failed and whether failed routes are being used. Viewing the RIP table is also one way you can confirm that the router is actually functioning and configured correctly. To view the router's RIP table, use the show command as follows:

`Router#show ip route rip`

The output for this command should look similar to this:

```
Codes: C - connected, S - static, I - IGRP, R - RIP, M - mobile, B - BGP
       D - EIGRP, EX - EIGRP external, O - OSPF, IA - OSPF inter area
       N1 - OSPF NSSA external type 1, N2 - OSPF NSSA external type 2
       E1 - OSPF external type 1, E2 - OSPF external type 2, E - EGP
       i - IS-IS, L1 - IS-IS level-1, L2 - IS-IS level-2, * - candidate default
       U - per-user static route, o - ODR
       T - traffic engineered route

Gateway of last resort is not set

R 153.16.4.0 [90/1] via 153.16.4.1, 00:00:10 Ethernet1
C 198.56.0.0 is directly connected, Ethernet2
```

Viewing the contents of the RIP routing table on a fairly regular basis can help Cisco users adjust RIP configurations as needed to keep their environment running smoothly. For example, if a link becomes unavailable but you still notice it in the router's table, you can adjust the routing timers to help close that loop.

Summary

- RIP was one of the first routing protocols developed.
- Features that help RIP control routing loops are split horizon, hold-down timers, poison routes, and hop count limits.
- RIP is capable of serving only environments of 15 hops or less.
- Routing table updates inform the other routers in a RIP environment as the to current status of the network.
- A RIP router shares its entire routing table with its neighbors every 30 seconds.
- Cisco routers use RIP version 2 by default.

Q&A

Q Why is RIP still used if it is limited to 15 router hops?

A Because RIP is limited to 15 router hops within a single environment, it is great for smaller environments. As demonstrated in this lesson, there are very few commands needed to configure RIP. Therefore, it is a good protocol for users who do not have a lot of time to devote to router management.

Quiz

Questions

1. By default, how long will a Cisco router wait (after failing to receive an update) to delete a current route?
2. What command is used to view the RIP routing table?
3. A sample routing environment consists of five routers, two of which are connected to router A. Every 30 seconds, how many routing tables will router A receive during updates?

Answers

1. 240 seconds
2. `show ip route rip`
3. Two, one from each directly connected neighbor

Exercise

1. Configure a router connection to network 10.0.0.0 for RIP. The router should run RIP only on the interface Ethernet 0 (of the two interfaces Ethernet 0 and Ethernet 1). Also, the updates being received from the rest of the network are from both version 1 and version 2 devices, but this router should only send RIP version 2 updates. (IP has already been configured on the router.)

> **Note**
>
> ```
> Router#configure terminal
> Router(config)#router rip
> Router(config-router)#network 10.0.0.0
> Router(config-router)#passive-interface ethernet 1
> Router(config-router)#^Z
> Router#configure terminal
> Router(config)# interface ethernet 0
> Router(config-int)#ip rip send version 2
> Router(config-int)#ip rip receive version 1 2
> ```

WEEK 3

DAY 16

Using IGRP and EIGRP

For the first few, and most experimental, years of computer internetworking, RIP was the king of routing protocols. However, as computer networks began to grow in size, new demands were placed on routing equipment. Networks required quicker, more stable convergence and looser environment restrictions (networks were beginning to reach the 15-hop limit imposed by RIP). Also, businesses were beginning to interconnect environments (something that was not even possible with RIP).

The Internet age was looming on the horizon, and a new breed of routing protocol was needed to meet the growing demands of corporate infrastructures. As routing was still a burgeoning technology, the new routing protocols needed to be as easy to understand, maintain, and configure as RIP. However, the core technology of RIP could not withstand being tweaked to the extent necessary to handle the accelerating traffic.

As the Internet began to take hold, the need to find a routing protocol that expanded on the capabilities of RIP was becoming more obvious. Cisco began developing a new routing protocol, IGRP (Interior Gateway Routing Protocol), in the mid-1980s. IGRP expanded on the core technology of RIP to take the job of routing to a new level within the environment: the gateway. Not long after the introduction of IGRP, its successor, EIGRP (Enhanced Interior Gateway Routing Protocol), would be introduced. Together, the two protocols would become a key factor in interdomain routing.

This lesson introduces you to Cisco's implementation of IGRP and EIGRP. We will cover the technology behind these two routing protocols and the commands needed to configure them on Cisco routers. The topics discussed in today's lesson are

- IGRP and EIGRP versus RIP
- IGRP technology
- Configuring IGRP
- EIGRP technology
- Configuring EIGRP

IGRP and EIGRP have a specialized purpose within routing environments. Whereas their predecessor (RIP) worked to connect devices within a single, limited environment, IGRP and EIGRP function to connect larger environments known as autonomous systems. The key to understanding how IGRP and EIGRP work is to understand how they compare (and contrast) with RIP.

Each of the two interior gateway routing protocols covered in this lesson was derived from RIP; however, similarities among the three are not always apparent. On the surface it seems that the only thing these protocols have in common is their use of the Bellman-Ford distance vector routing algorithm. With some simple investigation, however, we will uncover and discuss a few other common elements among the protocols.

Studying the similarities and differences among the three protocols will help you to better understand how each works. In general, protocols are not easily interchangeable; they tend to have their own specialized functions in the routing world. Where you use one, you may not necessarily be able to use another. This is the case with RIP, IGRP, and EIGRP.

IGRP and EIGRP Versus RIP

Recapping the previous lesson, RIP is an interior gateway protocol (IGP). As such, RIP's purpose is to move data within a single networking environment. That is, the technology that lies behind the functionality of RIP was not designed to handle the addressing and operational needs of routing data among multiple environments.

Because RIP was designed to be quick and lightweight as well as functional, some compromises had to be made. RIP's designers chose to narrow down the amount of add-in parameters and options for the protocol. This resulted in a fairly fast and lightweight protocol that was easy to maintain. It also lacked many features that later administrators would look for in routing protocols.

It is nearly impossible to design a protocol that is everything to everyone, and as time progressed, network administrators and designers needed protocols that could grow with them and their networks. Cisco (along with a few key organizations) quickly began work on IGRP. This protocol would pick up where RIP left off.

IGRP still maintains the title of an IGP; however, IGRP works on a much larger scale than RIP, allowing multiple environments to share data seamlessly among their individual devices. IGPs such as RIP, IGRP, and EIGRP work within the networking environments without being able to move data between them. Interior and exterior gateway protocols work hand in hand to provide routing functionality for large, multinetwork environments. IGRP, and later EIGRP, introduced a few new terms into the vocabulary of routing and network engineers. A large, common-purpose environment would now be referred to as an autonomous system (AS). An AS can be viewed as a collection of networks or environments with a common routing element. These environments were grouped into a separate category for addressing purposes. Autonomous systems can be addressed as individual entities, allowing data to be easily routed to entire networks at a time.

Another term that would be introduced into the routing lingo was *gateway*. Gateways are devices that route information from within a specific, addressed network to devices belonging to and addressed by environments not residing within the origin network. In other words, gateways are usually routers that sit on the border of a network and route data into and out of that network. Figure 16.1 illustrates an environment with a gateway.

Gateways, as conceptual devices, become increasingly important in the choice of a routing protocol as we move into the later lessons of this book. The use of, or interaction with, gateways defines the functionality of many routing protocols. Therefore, it is best that we define what constitutes a gateway.

The most common gateways in environments today are those that link corporations with the Internet. The Internet is, on a fundamental level, a large routed environment. Thus, any router that connects a local environment to the Internet is a gateway. We're going to take a step back from this broad definition of a gateway and look at it from more of a local level.

FIGURE 16.1

An example of a gateway.

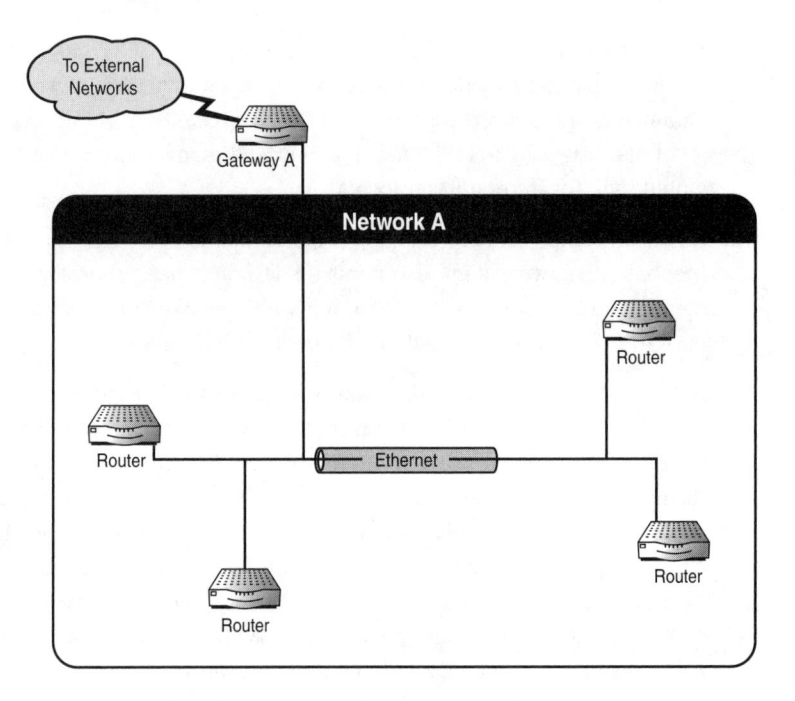

A simplistic multinetwork environment consists of two networks (each with a certain number of routers) and two gateways. (The two networks could exist within the same building or across the country; either way a gateway on each side if the environment would connect them.) The routers within each network would route information around the network just as we have seen throughout the earlier lessons of this book. When the routers within one of the networks discover a packet for which they have no address information, the packet is forwarded to the gateway. The gateway examines the packet and sends it to the corresponding gateway at the other network. The packet is then passed to the routers within the other network, and the process continues.

When environments are connected through the use of gateways, they can be categorized into two elements: the interior and the exterior. The portion of the environment that contains the network (and the routers within that network) is considered the interior, and the portion of the environment that connects the gateways is known as the exterior. The interior and the exterior each have their own specialized routing protocols. IGPs such as RIP, IGRP, and EIGRP are used to route information within the interior portions of the environment, and exterior gateway protocols (EGPs) are the backbone protocols that connect the gateways with each other.

Enhanced IGRP, or EIGRP, improved on the changes made within IGRP. Whereas IGRP improved on basic features such as hop count and environmental placement, EIGRP greatly enhanced the convergence times and algorithm calculations. The following sections will discuss the technology behind IGRP and EIGRP and examine the commands used to configure Cisco routers during an IGRP or EIGRP implementation.

IGRP Technology

IGRP, the Interior Gateway Routing Protocol, was based strongly on the base technology behind RIP. Many core elements were not changed, but the capacities of the elements were increased. This section will discuss those elements that were expanded upon in the design of IGRP.

The major elements of RIP that were modified in IGRP are the metrics used in the distance algorithm, the number of achievable hops, and unequal-cost load balancing technology. When Cisco was designing the standards for IGRP, they had one luxury that the designers of RIP did not: the ability to design the protocol for specific routing hardware. Whereas RIP was adapted to routers, IGRP would be written directly for them. Therefore, some elements needed to be adjusted in ways that would accommodate the new hardware platform.

Some small changes were also made to the way routing table updates are sent and processed. We will examine how the RIP updates were changed for use with IGRP.

IGRP Metrics

IGRP employs metrics used by an algorithm to calculate the best path from one network to another. Keep in mind that RIP allows only one metric: the hop count. IGRP abandoned the hop count as a metric in favor of more definitive and accurate variables. We will discuss each metric as it relates to the calculation of routes within IGRP. IGRP uses the following metrics:

- Internetwork delay
- Bandwidth
- Load
- Reliability

The Bellman-Ford distance vector algorithm that is used by RIP is still used in IGRP, only the parameters that factor into the calculation have changed. Although hop count is still used in cases where the overall network medium is the same (which leads to similar numbers for the remaining metrics), some new metrics have been added. IGRP weighs delay, bandwidth, load, and reliability as factors when considering the best possible path for information to travel.

Internetwork delay describes the amount of time from when a packet is released by a router to when it reaches its destination (another router). As a value, delay can be represented by any number from 1 to 16,777,216 (tens of microseconds). The delay factor of a path represents a more abstract value compared with the other metrics. There are many reasons for one particular line having more delay than another. One possible reason is an abundance of traffic. While the source of delay cannot be pinned to any one factor, keeping delay under control can drastically affect the performance of a network.

Bandwidth is the cumulative speed of a link, ranging from 1200 bits per second to 10 gigabits per second. The concept of the bandwidth of a link is a little less abstract than the delay. Most administrators should have a good idea of the bandwidth of their lines. If a particular link has a low bandwidth, the chances of that line being chosen as the best route are slightly diminished.

The load of a line is a value ranging from 1 to 255 that represents the current use of the line. If a line is being used very heavily, the load on that link will jump and may increase the cost metric associated with the route. This use of load as a metric is different from load balancing. Load balancing distributes the number of packets sent to a given destination between the available paths according to their costs so that none is used too much or too little.

The last metric, reliability, has a value of 0 to 255. The reliability of a line represents how often packets are lost when using the line. A metric value for reliability of 255 indicates that the line is 100% reliable and never drops a packet.

All of the metrics used by IGRP are combined to produce a more accurate way of calculating the best path over which to transmit data from one network to another. Each line connected to a router running IGRP has these metrics associated with it. Therefore, IGRP needs a place to store the expanded base of metrics used during route calculation. To accommodate the new data load, the routing table was expanded in the change from RIP to IGRP. The IGRP routing table has the field space to track delay, bandwidth, load, and reliability.

Increased Hop Count

Another improvement to the RIP core technology made by the designers of IGRP was an increase in the RIP hop count limit. In a move to decrease the number of unintentional routing loops while maximizing the available processing memory, the creators of RIP implemented a 15-hop limit within the protocol. By the time Cisco began work on IGRP, it was obvious that the 15-count limit was too restrictive to support the needs of growing environments.

Using IGRP and EIGRP

The hop count limit for IGRP was increased from 15 to 255. Increasing the hop count limit vastly increased the potential for IGRP as a routing protocol. Environments that could not be serviced by RIP could easily be routed using IGRP.

> **Note**
> Do not confuse a hop with a node. A hop refers specifically to a router (or a PC running routing software), whereas a node is any device within an environment.

Load Balancing

The final, most notable improvement made to the older RIP technology was the ability for IGRP to load-balance across lines that have unequal cost. That is, IGRP can be configured to send data between different links based on the overall traffic in those links.

Most routing protocols automatically alternate the sending of packets across lines that have the same metric value. IGRP, on the other hand, allows for the configuration of load balancing across lines with unequal metric values. Figure 16.2 illustrates a networking environment where unequal-cost load balancing can be implemented.

FIGURE 16.2

An example of unequal-cost load balancing.

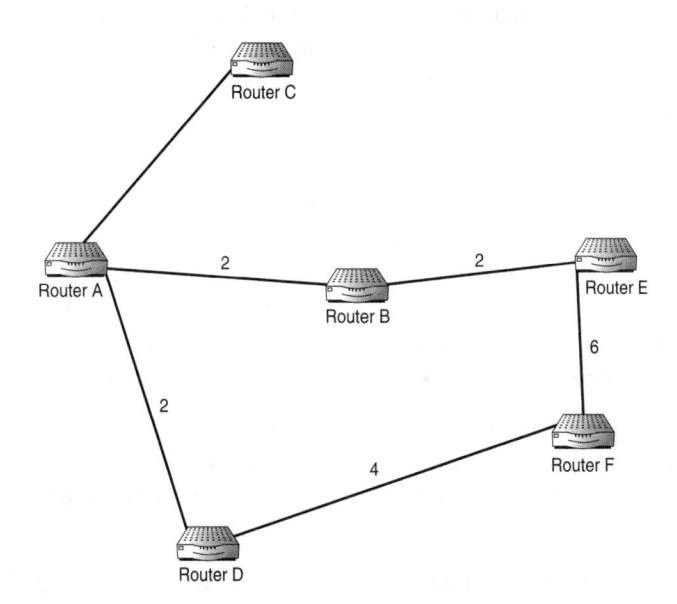

In Figure 16.2, router A has two possible paths to router E. Because the path A–B–E has a better metric combination than the path A–D–F–E, that path will always be chosen over the other. However, this can create problems. Fundamentally, the network is left with one link that is overused and one link that is not used at all.

The way to ensure that one link is not overused simply because it has better metrics is load balancing. IGRP can be configured to say, "Both paths A–B–E and A–D–F–E reach router E; use the two paths in turn when sending information from router A to router E."

In the configuration of unequal load balancing, one line is configured as a variance multiplier of another. That is, path A should be used x times more than path B. In this way, every x number of packets is shared over the load-balanced lines.

> **Note** IGRP is capable of defining four lines for one load-balanced path.

IGRP Updates

IGRP routing table updates contain the same basic information as those used by RIP. That is, with the exception of the added fields used by the IGRP metrics, the update information did not change. IGRP routers, like RIP routers, send local updates of their routing tables to any directly connected neighbors on a periodic basis. The timing of IGRP updates differs significantly from that of RIP. Also, a new type of update was introduced: the flash update.

IGRP routing updates are sent every 90 seconds. This is a big jump from the 30 seconds used for RIP. The reason for the extra time is simple. IGRP can handle much larger networks than RIP and must allot enough time to ensure that every router in the environment is updated before another update is begun. Due to this increase in time between updates, the amount of time used to discard unused routes was increased as well.

If an update pertaining to a specific router is not received within 270 seconds, the route is marked inactive. Inactive routes are not used; however, they remain in the routing table for future use. After 630 seconds with no updates, the routes are removed from the routing table.

Routing updates from IGRP tend to be more extensive (due to the number of fields) and they tend to take longer (due to the number of hops). For this reason, the designers of IGRP decided to expand the amount of time used in dictating the intervals between key IGRP update functions.

One IGRP update feature not carried over from RIP is the flash update. IGRP's routing updates are sent out every 90 seconds; however, some of the metrics used by IGRP can change in real time. Consequently, a mechanism was put in place to allow IGRP to notify its neighbors in the event of a drastic metric change.

If an IGRP metric changes, IGRP can initiate a flash update. During a flash update the new metric values for the affected route are sent to the router's direct neighbors. Flash updates help keep IGRP tables current while avoiding the traffic caused by full updates.

On the subject of IGRP updates, we should mention the elements that did not change in the move from RIP to IGRP. The loop prevention features present in RIP, such as split horizon, hold-down timers, and poison routes, are still present in IGRP.

Configuring IGRP

Because IGRP was developed by Cisco, it stands to reason that the protocol should be fairly easy to configure yet offer a great amount of control. Configuring IGRP is very straightforward, and Cisco provides an ample selection of optional parameters that allow the configuration of IGRP to be adjusted. Parameters such as those used to configure load balancing (examined later in this chapter) make IGRP a very versatile routing protocol.

Like RIP (and all other routing protocols), you must configure IGRP within the router configuration mode of the Cisco IOS. As you enter the router configuration mode, the first parameter the IOS asks you for is the ASN (autonomous system number), a number used to differentiate one autonomous system from another. A valid ASN is any number from 1 to 65535. Unless otherwise indicated, the ASN can be any number you deem appropriate. The syntax required to begin configuring a Cisco router for IGRP is

`#router igrp <asn>`

> **Note** Some routing protocols, such as BGP, use ASNs that are assigned from a central agency, much the same way IP addresses are assigned. You should always check with the appropriate governing bodies before assigning ASNs.

After you have assigned the autonomous system number, the network address needs to be assigned. The network address is the valid IP network address for the router being configured. This address is used for all routing table updates. The syntax for the `network` command is

`#network <ip address>`

The ASN and network address specifications are the only required configuration tasks for implementing IGRP. The following code segment shows the process required for implementing IGRP on a Cisco router:

```
Router#configure terminal
Router(config)#router igrp 210
Router(config-router)#network 198.10.0.0
```

These commands should successfully configure a Cisco router to participate in an IGRP network. However, there are several optional parameters that can be configured to modify the performance of IGRP. These optional parameters include configuring unequal-cost load balancing, modifying update timers, and disabling features such as split horizon.

Establishing Unequal-Cost Load Balancing

As discussed in the previous section, unequal-cost load balancing is a process where routes that have different metric values, yet pass between the same origin and destination points, can share the traffic load of a busy path, so that one link is not overwhelmed with traffic just because it has the more desirable metrics.

To use a path as a load-balancing path, use the `variance` command. Rather than specify which path should be used for load balancing, you use the `variance` command to indicate a "range" in which any potential paths should fall. The Cisco router uses any path that falls within the "variance" as a load-balancing path. The syntax of the `variance` command is as follows:

```
#variance <multiplier>
```

The variance is a multiplier of the "best path" metric. That is, any path that is to be considered as a load-balancing path must have a total metric that is less than or equal to the multiplier times the metric for the best local path. For example, if the best local path has a metric of 6 and the variance on the router is 2, any path that is to be considered for load balancing must have a metric of 12 or less (to the same destination).

Another guideline for considering a path for use in load balancing is that the next hop from the local router needs to have a smaller metric. In other words, if router A has a metric value of 4 to destination D, router B needs to have a metric value of 3 (to the same destination) to be considered as a load-balancing route.

Although these may seem like stringent guidelines for creating and using load-balancing paths, they help to maintain the integrity of the algorithm that makes IGRP as versatile as it is. The only step you need to take in configuring a Cisco router to use unequal-cost load balancing is to use the `variance` command:

```
Router#configure terminal
Router(config)#router igrp 51
```

```
Router(config-router)#variance 3
Router(config-router)#^Z
```

As you can see, the `variance` command is easy to use. It simply indicates the value that the Cisco IOS can use to determine which routes are feasible for load balancing. By indicating a variance rather than an absolute path, the router can adapt dynamically to changes in the environment. If a load-balancing path suddenly becomes unavailable, it simply falls out of the range of the variance and is no longer used. Conversely, if a new route is brought online that falls within the range of the variance, it is immediately used to share the traffic.

Modifying Update Timers

IGRP uses four timers to initiate and track certain events related to routing updates. These timers are the route update timer, the route timeout, the hold-down timer, and the route removal timer. Each timer has a default value. However, the default values are configurable for the purposes of modifying a particular routing environment. Table 16.1 shows the default values of the IGRP update timers.

TABLE 16.1 IGRP Timer Default Values

Timer	Default Value
Route update	90 seconds
Route timeout	270 seconds
Route removal	630 seconds
Hold-down	Three times the route update timer value plus 10 seconds

You use the `timers basic` command to change the default timer values within the Cisco IOS. You can change a timer to achieve quicker updates or to remove failed routes more rapidly from the routing table. The overall goal of adjusting any IGRP timer is to achieve a quicker and more reliable convergence. Use the following Cisco syntax to modify an IGRP timer (all timer values are in seconds):

`#timers basic <update timer > <timeout timer > <hold-down timer > <removal timer >`

In an attempt to achieve a greater convergence rate for the network as a whole, you can adjust the timers to yield more favorable results. You must be careful when adjusting any timers, as any changes may cause longer, more inaccurate updates just as easily as they can create faster ones. Use the following commands for the `timers basic` command:

```
Router#configure terminal
Router(config)#router igrp 51
Router(config-router)#timers basic 75 200 76 550
Router(config-router)#^Z
```

These commands change the Cisco router's update timer from 90 to 75; the timeout from 270 to 200; the hold-down to 76; and the route removal from 630 to 550.

Enabling/Disabling Split Horizon and Hold-Down Timers

A convenient feature of IGRP is the ability to enable or disable the features used by the router for preventing routing loops. In small environments with very little dynamic change, these features may not be needed. In another scenario, you may want to use only one feature rather than all of them.

Cisco built in the ability to enable or disable split horizon and hold-down timers. You need to configure each from different locations within the Cisco IOS. The first of the features we will examine is the hold-down timer.

The router uses the hold-down timer to mark suspect routes. A route can be placed into hold-down if the router has recently learned it or if it fails unexpectedly. In either case the router would not use the route for the period of time that the route is in hold-down. When the route comes out of hold-down, the router can forward packets over it as usual.

> **Note:** When a router "learns" a route, the information pertaining to that route is acquired during an update. In other words, the router has no direct knowledge of the route; it learns the route through updates from other routers.

You can disable the hold-down timer through the use of the *no* keyword. Using the keyword within the router configuration mode allows you to disable the hold-down timer:

```
Router#configure terminal
Router(config)#router igrp 51
Router(config-router)#no metric holddown
Router(config-router)#^Z
```

> **Note:** The use of the command no metric holddown must be standardized across all routers within the same environment. That is, every router running IGRP within the same networking environment must have hold-down timers either enabled or disabled.

The split-horizon feature is treated a little differently within the Cisco IOS. The split-horizon feature forbids routers from sending updates to routers that updates were received from. For example, router A receives an update from router B. In this update, router B informs router A that one of router B's links has failed. With split horizon, router A cannot send an update of its own to router B. This reduces the risk of router A learning (from a third router) incorrect information about router B's link and passing it back to router B.

> Having split horizon either enabled or disabled will affect how your router sends routing updates if you have more than one RIP interface on your router. (If you have only one RIP interface on your router, you can disable split horizon without consequences, most likely saving yourself some processor speed.)

You can either enable or disable split horizon at the interface level. That is, Cisco allows the feature to be used on a per-interface basis. To disable the feature, you must specify an interface in interface configuration mode:

```
Router#configure terminal
Router(config)#interface ethernet 1
Router(config-int)#no ip splithorizon
Router(config-int)#^Z
```

Thus far in this lesson we have covered the concepts and technology behind IGRP. However, in the mid-1990s Cisco began working on an enhanced version of the routing protocol. Aptly named EIGRP (Enhanced Interior Gateway Routing Protocol), the newer version of IGRP would improve upon some of the features within IGRP.

EIGRP Technology

Cisco made multiple changes to IGRP when designing its successor, EIGRP. The first point that designers chose to work on was faster convergence times. However, the designers felt that the current update technology, developed for use with RIP, had been stretched to its limits in IGRP. To accommodate EIGRP, a new modification of IGRP's distance vector algorithm was developed.

DUAL (Diffusing Update Algorithm) utilizes intensive processor usage to achieve an extremely quick convergence time. At the time the router learns a new path, DUAL computes the path to determine whether (within a good degree of certainty) the path can be considered "loop-free." From that point on, only updates pertaining to changes within that environment are processed and applied.

The route calculations for DUAL are very intensive, which is why EIGRP routers do not perform them every update. Because EIGRP routers do not recalculate every route on every update, they achieve much quicker convergence times.

> **Note** DUAL route calculations are processed only when the route being used has changed (which in an optimal environment is very rarely). This is the only processor-intensive task in EIGRP. Therefore, the router is extremely processor efficient during normal daily business.

The other major enhancement made to IGRP in the EIGRP design process was the addition of the hello packet. Many routing protocols use specialized routing packets, known as hello packets, to "discover" their neighboring routers. Hello packets are normally protocol independent and are used to keep dynamic environments under control.

EIGRP routers send hello packets (also known as hello messages) to their direct neighbors at set intervals. The purpose of these messages is to determine the validity of the local routing table. This is easily accomplished because the hello packet is a specialized form of broadcast message.

> **Note** Broadcast messages are packets that are not addressed to any one destination. Therefore, they are processed by every device they reach.

The local router broadcasts the hello packet at a set interval. Each of the routers that are directly connected to the local router responds to the hello with an acknowledgment. The local router then compares its routing table with the list of acknowledgments. If the router detects any discrepancies, a flash update is created.

Configuring EIGRP

The Cisco IOS commands you will use to configure EIGRP are almost identical to those used for IGRP. Logically, none of the command-driven configurations changed from one protocol to the other. Rather, most of the changes occurred "under the hood." Although a few of the optional parameters did change, the basic commands you use to enable EIGRP will remain the same as with IGRP.

The following code sample shows the commands you need to execute to enable EIGRP on a Cisco router:

```
Router#configure terminal
Router(config)#router eigrp 578
Router(config-router)#network 10.0.0.0
Router(config-router)#^Z
```

EIGRP routers still require the specification of a network address and an autonomous system number. These parameters are used by both IGRP and EIGRP. In other words, the same basic command structure can be used to enable either IGRP or EIGRP on a Cisco router.

One optional parameter that you can configure within EIGRP dictates how much bandwidth EIGRP can utilize on any given line. By default, EIGRP uses 50% of the available bandwidth of every link in a route. Cisco allows you to adjust this percentage on an interface level.

If you know that a particular line has very low bandwidth (and losing half would render the link unusable), you can adjust the bandwidth usage within the interface configuration mode. Use the following syntax to adjust the usable bandwidth percentage:

```
#ip bandwidth-percent eigrp <percentage>
```

Within the configuration mode of the particular interface to be adjusted, run the `ip bandwidth-percentage` command followed by the specific amount of the link bandwidth to be used. The router will then allow EIGRP to use only the specified amount of bandwidth.

```
Router#configure terminal
Router(config)#interface ethernet 0
Router(config-int)#ip bandwidth-percent eigrp 25
Router(config-int)#^Z
```

As is apparent from this rather brief treatment of EIGRP commands, most of the differences between EIGRP and IGRP lie beneath the surface. The majority of the commands and concepts used to configure one also apply to the other.

Summary

- IGRP was developed to expand on the capabilities of RIP.
- IGRP is capable of spanning 255 hops.
- IGRP and EIGRP environments are known as autonomous systems.
- Autonomous systems are marked by router gateways.

- IGRP and EIGRP are capable of load-balancing traffic across links with unequal costs.
- Rather than process an entire update every "update period," IGRP and EIGRP routers process only updates that conflict with the local routing table.
- EIGRP uses hello packets to test for the existence of neighboring routers.

Q&A

Q Why was EIGRP developed if IGRP was already an improvement over RIP?

A By the time EIGRP was developed, technology had advanced to a plateau where a quicker, more reliable version of IGRP could be designed. EIGRP made such an improvement to convergence times that the protocol was quickly accepted by companies who had previously adopted IGRP.

Quiz

Questions

1. The specification of what two numbers is required to configure both IGRP and EIGRP?
2. What is DUAL?
3. True or false: To be considered for load balancing, a path metric must equal the product of the local metric times the variance.
4. What three features are used by IGRP for loop resolution?

Answers

1. The ASN (autonomous system number) and the network address.
2. Diffusing Update Algorithm, used by EIGRP for loop-free route calculation.
3. False. The path metric must be less than the product of the local metric and the variance.
4. Split horizon, hold-down timers, and poison routes.

Exercise

1. Configure a router in autonomous system 20 (network 198.32.98.0) for IGRP. Split horizon should be disabled on interface Ethernet 0, and the update timer should be changed to 25 seconds.

> **Note**
>
> ```
> Router#configure terminal
> Router(config)#router igrp 20
> Router(config-router)#network 198.32.98.0
> Router(config-router)#timers basic 25 270 90 630
> Router(config-int)#^Z
> Router#configure terminal
> Router(config)#interface ethernet 0
> Router(config-int)#no ip splithorizon
> Router(config-int)#^Z
> ```

Week 3

Day 17

Configuring OSPF

Distance vector routing protocols are a specialized form of routing protocol that thrive in a specific environment. Many engineers have shied away from them for one reason: the algorithm they use. Distance vector protocols, such as RIP, IGRP, and EIGRP, have relatively slow convergence and routing times—relatively slow, that is, in comparison to their closest counterpart, link state protocols.

Today's lesson will focus on one such link state routing protocol, OSPF (Open Shortest Path First). OSPF is a link state IGP that can work in similar environmental conditions as IGRP or EIGRP. That is, like RIP, IGRP, and EIGRP, OSPF is used to route data within the boundaries of border gateways. OSPF is extremely popular because of its natural ability to converge networks rapidly. This lesson will examine the technology behind OSPF and the Cisco-based commands that are used to configure it. The following topics are covered in this lesson:

- OSPF technology
- OSPF updates
- Configuring OSPF

Introduction to OSPF

OSPF was developed in the late 1980s by the IETF (Internet Engineering Task Force) as a replacement for RIP (at this time Cisco was also working on IGRP.) Rather than using the same core technology as in RIP, the IETF chose to start from scratch. This led the IETF to realize that a link state routing protocol would be a better choice for intragateway routing than a distance vector protocol.

Today, OSPF continues to be one of the most popular IGPs for large environments. The following list describes some of the key points that make OSPF such a popular routing protocol:

- Link state protocols have quicker convergence times.
- Even though OSPF is an IGP, it can send and receive routes to other autonomous systems through an EGP.
- OSPF can route based on IP subnet addresses.
- OSPF can perform load balancing across equal-cost links.

There are many features of OSPF that are not present in other routing protocols. OSPF was designed to meet a need within the routing world (a need that was not fulfilled by distance vector protocols) and was not "based" on any particular existing platform. The next section of this book outlines the technology that makes OSPF one of the leading large-environment IGPs today.

OSPF Technology

The first topic that should be discussed in examining OSPF is the terminology used with regard to the functionality of the protocol. For the most part, the protocols we have examined to this point use a common set of terms and functions. OSPF, on the other hand, introduces a new technology, and with that comes a new set of terms. The first such term is *autonomous system* (AS).

> **Note** Some texts refer to OSPF autonomous systems as *domains*. Many link state protocols operate within domains; however, Cisco uses the term AS. Therefore, for the purpose of this book we will refer to OSPF domains as ASs.

Figure 17.1 illustrates a sample OSPF domain or autonomous system.

FIGURE 17.1

An OSPF autonomous system.

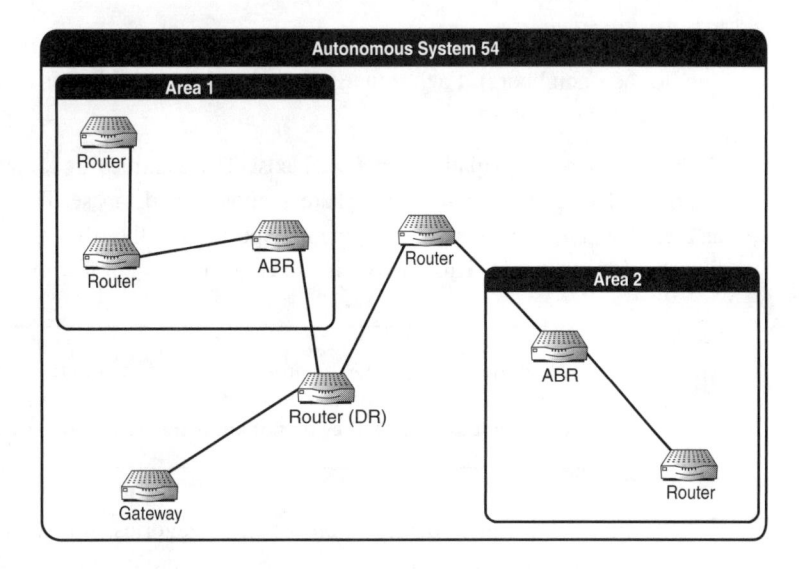

The largest routable area within OSPF is an autonomous system. An autonomous system is a group of networks that use the same IP addressing scheme. One AS contains one or several smaller networks. The end of an AS is defined by the placement of the border gateway routers.

> **Note:** OSPF was designed to work implicitly with IP. For that reason, OSPF network addressing is always in IP form.

A border gateway router is used to connect autonomous systems with other entities, such as the Internet or other ASs. OSPF is an interior gateway protocol, meaning that it can run only on routers contained within a single AS.

Although OSPF runs on the border gateway router, the router does not use it to communicate with other gateways. That is the job of exterior gateway protocols such as BGP. Rather, the gateway uses OSPF to collect route information about the AS. Then, using an EGP, the gateway redistributes those routes to other OSPF autonomous systems.

One OSPF AS can contain many border gateway routers. Regardless of the number of gateways within an AS, however, they all serve the same role. Gateways are used by OSPF to distribute routes to external locations that OSPF itself has no knowledge of.

These routes are distributed through the AS using LSAs (link state advertisements). An LSA contains the portion of a router's routing table that indicates the state of its directly connected links. These LSAs are sent to every router on the network through a process called *flooding* (in contrast to distance vector protocols, in which routers send updates only to their neighbors). Each router takes these LSAs and builds a database of the network's current state.

Within an AS, several smaller entities can exist. These entities are known as *areas*. An area is a network or group of routers that share a topological database. That is, all routers within an area share the same view of the remaining portions of the AS. Each area in an AS is configured with an area ID. This number is used to identify all of the routers within that area.

> **Note** All of the routers within an area are allowed to hold topological data relating only to that area. Although they know what addresses lie outside the area (through LSA floods), they do not know the exact topology of those addresses.

Areas within OSPF can be placed in one of two categories: stub areas and NSSAs (not-so-stubby areas). Both stub and not-so-stubby areas are used only in ASs that have connections to external routes. That is, a specialized area can be used only if your AS connects to other ASs and receives redistributed routes from those ASs.

A stub area is an area within an AS that does not allow external routes to be redistributed into it. To keep down the amount of network traffic, an administrator may choose not to allow external LSAs to enter some areas. Stub areas must originate off the backbone of the AS. Figure 17.2 illustrates an area that could be a stub.

FIGURE 17.2

A stub area.

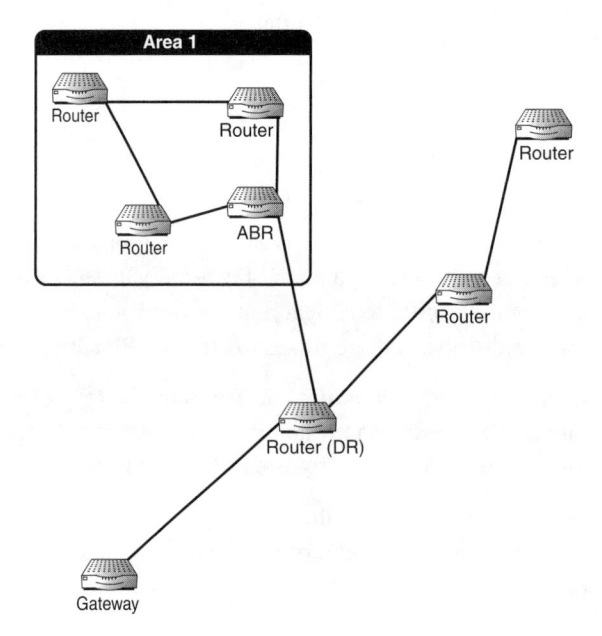

The routers that connect the areas with other parts of the environment are known as ABRs (area border routers). To qualify as a stub area, the area's ABR must connect directly to the backbone of the AS (as shown in Figure 17.2). Area 19 in Figure 17.3, for example, could not be a stub area, because the ABR for the area is attached to another area, not to the AS backbone.

FIGURE 17.3

An area that cannot be used as a stub.

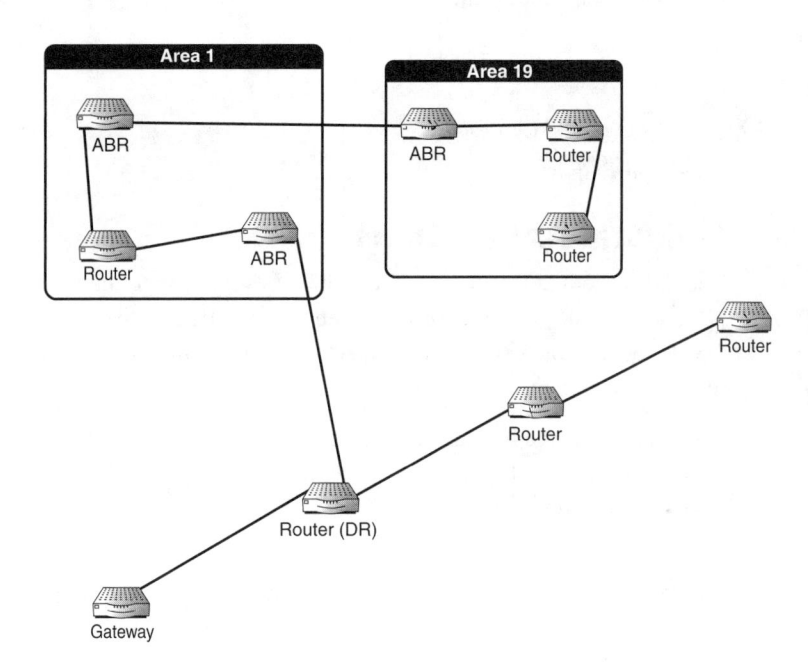

An NSSA, like a stub area, does not allow external LSAs. Whereas stub areas must forward all of their externally targeted packets to the backbone, NSSAs can use default routes to reach certain destinations. This allows for a more versatile area while reducing LSA traffic.

Finally, within an OSPF autonomous system, one router is voted to be the DR, or designated router. This router oversees the LSA flooding process and is the only router that keeps an entire routing database. That is, the DR has the topographical database for the entire AS.

> **Note**
> When the routers in the AS elect a DR, they also choose a backup DR. If the DR fails, the backup DR already has a complete database. This eliminates the need for a massive LSA flood to populate the DRs database.

It is important for you to understand the basics of OSPF terminology, because much of that terminology is shared by other protocols. Having defined some of the terms that are used in OSPF, let's examine exactly how the technology works. The remaining sections of this lesson describe the functionality of the following features:

- Link state algorithms
- Stub areas
- NSSAs
- Route redistribution
- OSPF updates

Link State Algorithms

The theory behind the link state algorithm is very easy to understand. The algorithm simply computes the shortest path between two points. The link state algorithm used by OSPF operates on a custom metric. This metric allows OSPF's algorithm to determine the shortest path through an AS.

An algorithm is the formula used by a protocol to calculate the metrics in a way that produces a definitive "shortest path." The most common algorithm used on IS-IS networks is Dijkstra's algorithm.

As a mathematical function, Dijkstra's algorithm is used to simultaneously compute the shortest path to every point on a grid. Given a starting point, Dijkstra's algorithm calculates the distance (based on preset metrics) between the starting point and every other point on the network.

The following is a plain-terms explanation of how Dijkstra's algorithm works (for now the labels A, B, C, and D are arbitrary):

1. From the starting point (A), identify all neighboring routers (B and C).
2. Calculate the distances between the starting point and the neighboring routers.
3. Mark the router with the shortest distance to the starting point (C).
4. Identify all neighbors of the newly labeled router, and the remaining neighbors of the original starting point (B and D).
5. Go to step 2.
6. Repeat until all routes have been calculated.

Step 1. From the starting point, identify what routers are directly connected to it. Thus, starting from a particular router, Dijkstra's algorithm looks at the routing table and sees what routers are directly connected to it.

Step 2. The algorithm looks in the routing table and finds the metrics assigned to the routers that are directly connected to it.

Step 3. The algorithm then compares the metrics and labels (in its memory) which neighbor has the lowest metric.

Step 4. Similar to step 1, the algorithm looks for more directly connected neighbors. However, this time the algorithm uses whatever neighbors are left over from the last step, and the neighbors of the router that was just labeled as having the lowest metric.

Step 5. Dijkstra's algorithm returns to step 2.

Step 6. The process continues until all possible routes have been marked.

In short, this algorithm calculates from point to point the shortest path and labels the paths accordingly. Let's run Dijkstra's algorithm against the network illustrated step by step.

Step 1. Identify the neighboring routers to the starting point. Figure 17.4 shows the identified neighbors of router A.

FIGURE 17.4

Router A's neighbors.

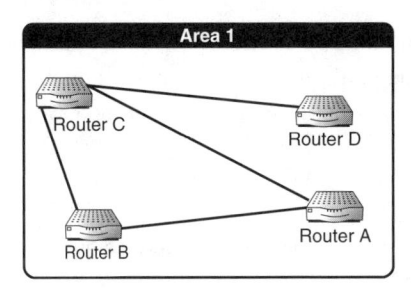

Step 2. Calculate the distances between the starting point and the neighboring routers. Router A's neighbors are B, C, and D. Notice the costs assigned to the links connecting A to its three neighbors. The link with the lowest cost is A-C; therefore, the A-C link is the shortest path.

Step 3. Mark the router with the shortest path to the starting point.

Step 4. Identify the remaining neighbors. The algorithm now identifies the remaining neighbors to A (B and D) and the neighbors of C (D).

Step 5. Recalculate the paths. The remaining paths are recalculated, and the process is repeated until the entire network is finished. Notice that the path A-B has a cost of 3 and C-D has a cost of 2. Because we are running the algorithm from A, the cost of C-D is actually 3 (A-C + C-D). In this case the costs from A-B and A–D are the same.

As you can imagine, as the number of routers on a network expands, this algorithm becomes quite complicated. However, in routing terms, Dijkstra's algorithm takes a few hundred milliseconds to calculate an entire network, making it a very quick and efficient formula.

The process of simultaneously calculating every route within an area at once does have its downside: It is very processor intensive. This means that routers running OSPF tend to use more processing power than routers using other protocols do.

Like all routing algorithms, the link state algorithm requires the use of a metric to determine the shortest distance between two points. OSPF uses a metric that is set by the local router. Using the detected bandwidth of its interfaces, the local router applies a calculation to determine the metric for a particular link. The equation used by routers running OSPF to determine the metric cost for a link is:

Metric cost = 10^8/link bandwidth

Using this formula, the links with the highest bandwidth have the lowest cost. For example, a 128 Kbps line has a cost of 781, whereas a T1 has a cost of 64. This ensures that the links with the most available bandwidth are chosen over those that may not be able to handle the traffic.

Just having the most bandwidth, however, may not make a particular link the best choice. For example, the highest-bandwidth link to a destination may be a leased line that is charged out per byte. The routing engineer would want the OSPF router not to use this line as often as a free link to the same target.

> **Note** Because the metric used by OSPF is calculated automatically by the router, there is less intervention by the administrator, so the administrator is better able to focus on other tasks.

In situations where you do not want the link with the highest bandwidth to be chosen first, you can assign a value and use it to override the router's metric manually. You can give the leased line a higher metric than the free (lower-bandwidth) line, ensuring that it will not be used as often. This kind of metric override is also useful when a designer needs to sculpt or influence the flow of data through a specific area. Trouble areas can be avoided and more favorable ones exploited while the dynamic nature of the protocol is maintained.

The information required for the algorithm to calculate the shortest path is distributed through the use of updates. These updates are shared among the routers within an area and help the devices to create an overall picture of the environment at any one time.

OSPF Updates

Updates in OSPF networks are sent on a periodic basis to all routers within the same area. Unlike distance vector updates (in which the entire routing table is included in every update), the OSPF update includes only the portion of the table that deals with the sending router's direct neighbors.

There are five types of updates in an OSPF area. Each of these updates types has a specific purpose. The five different updates are:

- Hello message
- Database description
- Link state request
- Link state update
- Link state acknowledgment

OSPF routers use a combination of updates to create the most accurate picture of the network possible. Updates, regardless of type, are sent from router to router as OSPF packets. The packet's header contains information pertaining to the type of packet. Figure 17.5 illustrates the fields of an OSPF packet.

FIGURE 17.5

An OSPF packet.

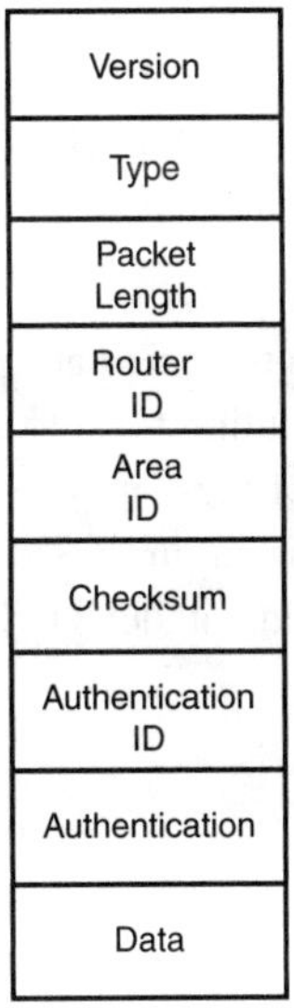

Version
Type
Packet Length
Router ID
Area ID
Checksum
Authentication ID
Authentication
Data

> **Note:** As seen in Figure 17.5, there are many fields in the OSPF update packet. Because this is a beginner's text, we will not explain them all in detail. Rather, we will cover only the fields that have a direct impact on the situations in our examples.

The second field of the packet header indicates the type of update packet. From this field the receiving router can immediately determine whether the packet is a hello message or another type of update.

OSPF routers use the first message type, hello messages, to determine the current state of their links. Routers send hello messages to each of their directly connected neighbors on a regular basis. When a router receives a hello message from a neighbor, it can assume that the link between itself and that router is functioning. However, if a router does not receive a hello packet within a specified amount of time, the link is marked for removal.

The second message type is a database description. A database description is a specialized update used between two routers known as *adjacencies*. When two routers within an area have identical topographical databases, the DR can mark them as adjacencies. When two routers are linked as adjacencies, they pass database descriptions between themselves to ensure that their databases stay in sync.

Routers use the third type of update, a link state request, to initiate a link state flood before the update timer has expired. Some routers send out link state requests when they are powered on. This causes an update flood that helps the new router build its routing tables.

The fourth type of update is the link state update. This is the type of update used to flood the network with topographical data. Every router within an OSPF network uses the link state update to maintain the most accurate view of the environment.

The final update type is the link state acknowledgment. All link state updates sent over a network require that an acknowledgment be sent to the originating device. The router then compares its list of acknowledgments to the routing table to confirm that all of the routes being reported are actually working. Many of these updates are only sent intra-area. Keep in mind that there can be many areas within one AS. Therefore, to understand the flow of OSPF packets through a network, we must understand the formation of areas.

OSPF Areas

OSPF autonomous systems are subdivided into areas. Areas are small networks within an AS that share the same topological database. These areas are addressed (by the protocol) independently of the AS they belong to and of each other. There are three types of areas that can be formed within an OSPF AS:

- Standard area
- Stub area
- NSSA (not-so-stubby area)

> **Note** A fourth type of "area" is known as the *backbone*. The backbone of an OSPF AS is actually not an area in the sense that as the three main area types are. Rather, the backbone is made up of the remaining routers that are not in a particular area. The purpose of the backbone is to connect the areas of the AS with each other and any external networks.

Before we discuss what each type of area does and how they related to the overall performance of an OSPF network, you need to have a fuller understanding of the purpose of areas in general. An area dictates the overall functionality of the devices that are contained within it. Routers in an area can share information only with each other. At least one router within an area functions to connect that area with other areas or with the backbone (the collection of routers that lie in the areas outside of the main areas). This router is known as the ABR (area border router).

The routers within an area have direct knowledge only of each other. If they need to send information to another area, they can forward packets to their ABRs for delivery outside the area, giving them indirect knowledge of the routing environment outside the area. Using this information, the area routers can properly address packets targeted to other areas within the AS.

If an area needs to be connected to the AS backbone but is behind another area, a virtual link can be established. A virtual link is a connection from an ABR to an intermediary ABR that terminates at the backbone. (There are a few important guidelines for the establishment of virtual links that will be covered in the section "Configuring OSPF") Figure 17.6 illustrates a virtual link.

FIGURE 17.6

A virtual link.

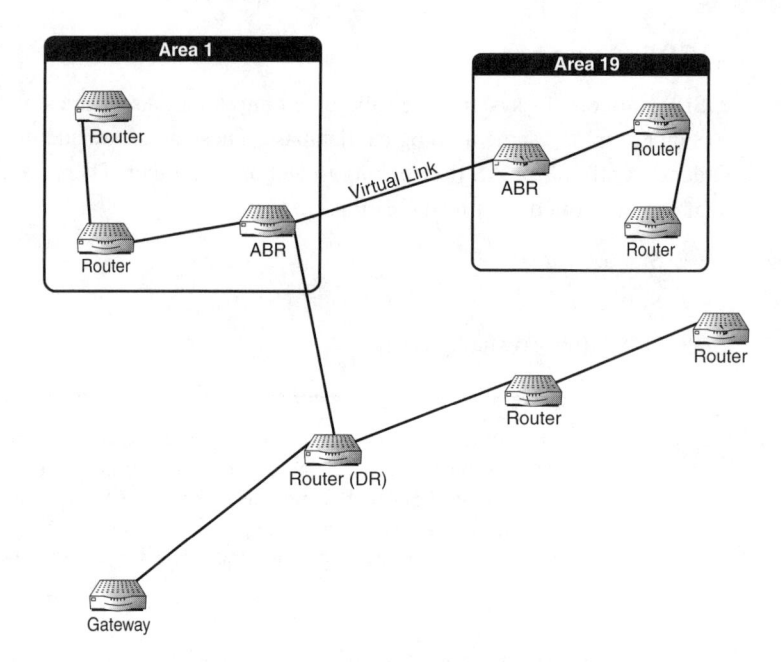

In Figure 17.6 area 19 has established a virtual link to the backbone through area 1. This can allow routers in area 19 to send packets directly to the backbone.

> **Note:** In the configuration of a virtual link, the transit area cannot be a stub.

The routers within an area receive information concerning external routes through a process known as route redistribution. During route redistribution, the AS gateway (using an EGP) gathers the LSA information for external autonomous systems. The AS gateway then forwards this information through the backbone to the ABRs. The ABRs broadcast the redistributed routes to the routers within each area. This information is used by the area routers to send data outside the AS.

Route redistribution can burden areas with extra traffic and LSAs. Therefore, if an area is directly connected to the AS backbone, it can be shielded from the extra traffic of route redistribution by becoming a stub area.

Stub Areas

A stub area is an area that is specifically designated not to receive redistributed routes from areas external to the AS. Creating stub areas can help reduce the amount of traffic in an area and free up resources that would otherwise be needed to process the extra updates. The key criterion to forming a stub area is that the area needs to be directly attached to the AS backbone.

The routers on the AS backbone have implicit knowledge of routes outside the AS. Therefore, the routers within the stub area can still send information to external routes by forwarding those packets directly to the backbone. This process can place added burden on some of the busiest routers in an AS.

NSSA

An NSSA is a stub area that has been programmed with direct routes to external autonomous systems. As for a stub area, the routers within an NSSA are shielded from the added traffic of route redistribution. However, they can still reach some external routes through predefined paths. The routers are configured with the information needed to reach certain routes external to the AS.

NSSAs do not need to be directly connected to the AS backbone. Because the routers have the information needed to properly address packets, these packets can be forwarded through other areas. However, the downside to NSSAs is that they may not be able to reach every external route. The routers within an NSSA can reach only the routes for which they have predefined information.

> **Note:** Even though it is possible for areas not to be directly connected to the backbone and still to function, it is not recommended. In fact, many Cisco documents highly advise against it.

What separates NSSAs and stub areas from other areas is their lack of ability to receive and process redistributed routes. Autonomous systems communicate their internal structures to other autonomous systems through a process of route redistribution. This process enables AS intercommunication.

Route Redistribution

Route redistribution occurs when a border router advertises routes externally. These routes can be static routes, routes learned from other routers, or routes obtained from other IGPs (such as RIP). Redistributing an AS's routes allows devices in neighboring ASs to communicate directly with devices in the local AS.

The process of moving the redistributed routes is assigned to the EGP (exterior gateway protocol) connecting the two or more autonomous systems. The next lesson focuses on one such EGP: the Border Gateway Protocol (BGP). Within that lesson the route redistribution process will be covered in more detail.

Within OSPF, users have the ability to configure which routes they wish to redistribute to external sources and where they wish to send them. Border gateways can advertise all, part, or none of their local routes to external sources. The next section will discuss configuring a Cisco router to participate in an OSPF AS. During this discussion the topic of configuring route redistribution will be examined.

Configuring OSPF

Configuring a Cisco router to use OSPF is not a difficult task. The process of enabling the protocol on the router (as with the that of other protocols we have discussed in this book) involves a few simple command executions. Learning the parameters that Cisco provides to allow the protocol to run in a manner that optimizes the environment may take some time. OSPF contains several peripheral commands that allow the protocol to be tailored to the needs of most networks.

Compared with IGRP or EIGRP networks, OSPF autonomous systems can be quite complicated and quite involved. It is strongly suggested that you have a diagram or sketch of the finished environment before you begin configuring routers. Depending on the role of the router within the AS, the configuration can take different paths. Area routers are configured differently than backbone routers, which are all configured differently depending on the type of areas being used. The point is that you should have a precise idea of exactly how the environment is going to look, and where the router you are configuring fits into that environment, before you begin configuring.

When enabling OSPF you are prompted for some familiar information. As with most of the IGPs we have covered thus far, a process ID is required to lend uniqueness to the environment. The ID can be a number ranging from 1 to 65535. The ID number is used as a parameter option in the following `router ospf` command.

```
Router#configure terminal
Router(config)#router ospf 349
```

> **Note**
>
> You must have IP configured on the router before you begin configuring OSPF. If you do not have at least one interface running IP, you receive the following error:
>
> ```
> Router(config)#router ospf 349
> OSPF: Could not allocate router id
> ```
>
> The router's OSPF ID is based on its IP address.

At this point the router enters the router configuration mode. The next configuration step differs depending on whether you are configuring the router to participate in an area or on the backbone. If you are configuring the router to participate in an area, you need to supply the area ID and the IP scheme for the area.

The command used to configure this information is network. The syntax for the network command is as follows:

```
#network <ip address> <wildcard bits> area <area address>
```

In the syntax for the network command notice that after the IP address for the network, the router requests a set of wildcard bits. These wildcard bits act as a reversed subnet mask. When combined with the network IP address, the wildcard bits indicate the range of addresses available to the area. For example, a class C IP network address of 225.65.34.0 uses a wildcard mask of 0.0.0.255 to include all of the IP address in that network.

In the following command example, you will establish an area with an area number of 1 and a class B addressing scheme.

```
Router(config-router)#network 198.56.0.0 255.255.0.0 area 1
Router(config-router)#^Z
```

To configure a router as a member of the OSPF backbone, you must use area 0. Also, to ensure that the backbone routers can handle all of the potential traffic for your network, the IP range should be 0.0.0.0 255.255.255.255 (the IP broadcast range). The following command example illustrates establishing an IP range.

```
Router(config-router)#network 0.0.0.0 255.255.255.255 area 0
Router(config-router)#^Z
```

> **Note**
>
> The backbone of an OSPF network will always be area 0.

Any ABRs you configure must have at least one interface configured to the backbone and one interface configured to the area. For example, an ABR for area 3 (a sample area directly attached to the backbone) would have one interface configured with an IP address in the acceptable range for area 3 and one interface addressed to the backbone. This ensures that the entire area will have proper communication with the backbone. The following code sample illustrates the commands needed to configure an ABR for area 3:

```
Router#configure terminal
Router(config)#interface ethernet 0
Router(config-if)#ip address 198.109.1.1 255.255.0.0
Router(config-if)#no shutdown
Router(config-if)#interface ethernet 1
Router(config-if)#ip address 197.85.1.1 255.255.0.0
Router(config-if)#no shutdown
Router(config-if)#^Z
Router(config)#router ospf 45
Router(config-router)#network 198.109.0.0 0.0.255.255 area 3
Router(config-router)#network 0.0.0.0 255.255.255.255 area 0
Router(config-router)#^Z
```

The interface ethernet 0 would be attached to area 3, whereas interface ethernet 1 is connected to the backbone. This creates an ABR that functions by moving packets between the area and the backbone.

To configure a stub or NSSA, additional commands must be used. The `area` command is use to create both NSSA and stub networks. The `area` command is executed on the ABR that separates the area from the backbone. The structure of the `area` command is:

```
#area <area number> <area type> <area specific params>
```

If you wanted to configure the ABR from our backbone configuration example to make area 3 a stub, we would use the following code:

```
Router#configure terminal
Router(config)#interface ethernet 0
Router(config-if)#ip address 198.109.1.1 255.255.0.0
Router(config-if)#no shutdown
Router(config-if)#interface ethernet 1
Router(config-if)#ip address 197.85.1.1 255.255.0.0
Router(config-if)#no shutdown
Router(config-if)#^Z
Router(config)#router ospf 45
Router(config-router)#network 198.109.0.0 0.0.255.255 area 3
Router(config-router)#network 0.0.0.0 255.255.255.255 area 0
Router(config-router)#area 3 stub no-summary
Router(config-router)#^Z
```

Let's examine some of the command parameters for the commands used in this example. The `no-summary` parameter indicates that no IP route summaries are to be sent into the stub. This keeps the traffic as low as possible within the stub area. The only parameter that can be used in NSSAs but not stubs is the `no-redistribution` option.

The `area` command is also used to create virtual links between areas and the backbone. Virtual links allow areas to communicate directly with the backbone, through a transit area. The ABR of one area is virtually linked to the ABR of the transit area (which is directly linked to the backbone). This creates a transparent virtual link to the backbone. The syntax for creating a virtual link is:

`#area <local area ID> virtual-link <neighbor ABR address> <optional parameters>`

Using this command syntax, the following code sample configures a virtual link in area 3:

```
Router(config)#router ospf 45
Router(config-router)#area 3 virtual-link 123.1.1.2
Router(config-router)#^Z
```

On some routers the need may arise to change the default metric of a particular link. OSPF automatically computes the metric of a route as 10^8 divided by the bandwidth of the link. Be aware that this calculation may not always produce the desired results.

The largest bandwidth an OSPF metric can accommodate is that of an FDDI link. An FDDI link always produces a metric of 1. If a router has more than one FDDI interface, or if technology has surpassed the FDDI bandwidth, the calculation used to figure the metric may need to be expanded. You should use the `auto-cost` command (in the following example) to change the value used to calculate the default metric.

```
Router(config)#router ospf 45
Router(config-router)#auto-cost reference-bandwidth 4294967
Router(config-router)#^Z
```

> **Note** The value specified in the auto-cost calculation is a representation of the maximum number of bits per second. This value can range from 1 to 4294967.

Although there are many more optional parameters that can be used to configure OSPF, this chapter covers those that a novice Cisco administrator should be familiar with. These commands are the key commands needed to enable and establish functionality.

Summary

This lesson introduced the concepts and commands behind one of the most popular routing protocols in use on larger networks: OSPF. OSPF offers a great amount of flexibility for configuring areas and sculpting traffic flows. The following specific topics were covered in the lesson:

- OSPF is a link state protocol.
- Link state protocols offer quicker convergence times compared with distance vector protocols.
- OSPF environments are autonomous systems (ASs).
- An OSPF AS is subdivided into areas.
- OSPF areas can be classified into stubs and NSSAs.

Q&A

Q **Why do link state protocols allow quicker convergence than distance vector protocols?**

A Link state protocols maintain detailed routing information only for their directly connected neighbors, whereas distance vector protocols share table data across all of the routers in an environment. Because link state protocol updates are limited, the router can converge more quickly.

Quiz

Questions

1. What is a stub area?
2. What is the formula for computing the OSPF default metric?
3. What parameter is required for enabling OSPF?

Answers

1. An area that does not receive redistributed routes.
2. Cost = 10^8/link bandwidth.
3. Process ID (which requires IP to be configured).

Exercise

1. Configure OSPF on a router that servea as an ABR between an NSSA (area 1) and the backbone. The IP scheme of the area is 10.0.0.0, and the interface addresses are 10.1.1.1 and 10.20.1.1.

> **Note**

```
Router#configure terminal
Router(config)#interface ethernet 0
Router(config-if)#ip address 10.1.1.1 255.0.0.0
Router(config-if)#no shutdown
Router(config-if)#interface ethernet 1
Router(config-if)#ip address 10.20.1.1 255.0.0.0
Router(config-if)#no shutdown
Router(config-if)#^Z
Router(config)#router ospf 572
Router(config-router)#network 10.0.0.0 0.255.255.255 area 1
Router(config-router)#network 0.0.0.0 255.255.255.255 area 0
Router(config-router)#area 1 nssa
Router(config-router)#^Z
```

Week 3

Day 18

Understanding Border Gateway Protocol (BGP)

By this point you should feel fairly confident in your basic Cisco abilities. Therefore, this lesson focuses on a more advanced topic, BGP (Border Gateway Protocol). One of the most popular (and arguably the most important) routing protocols in use today, BGP is a very robust protocol that has become the backbone of the Internet. The main purpose of BGP is to advertise a network's presence (and structures) to other (BGP) routers on the Internet—more specifically, the routers of an ISP (Internet Service Provider).

In today's routing landscape, engineers who are well versed in configuring and maintaining BGP environments are highly sought after. These routing experts literally make the Internet move. Therefore, the better you understand the Internet and how it works with Cisco routers and BGP, the better prepared you will be for real-world engineering.

The Internet is a giant mesh of unrelated systems, architectures, and protocols. Think of a large party whose guests come from many different countries, each speaking its own language, just as the Internet includes many different types of computers and several different networking systems. During the party the phone rings. A waiter writes out a message, puts the intended recipient's name on the front of it, and passes it to someone in the crowd (hoping it will reach its destination). If no one in the crowd can speak the language of any of the other countries, the message will not get very far. The note may well be discarded by the first person it is handed to.

The message would have a higher chance of successful delivery if there were an interpreter who spoke enough of each of the various languages to represent names between one group and another. A message given to any one attendee could easily find its way through the crowd of partygoers to its intended destination. Even if the person currently holding the message did not recognize the recipient's name, he or she could get help from the interpreter to give it to someone who might know the recipient. On the Internet, BGP serves as that interpreter.

BGP has become the link that breaks the language barriers that exist among the dissimilar systems of the Internet. The Border Gateway Protocol allows systems and networks to recognize (and be recognized by) unrelated systems. Systems running BGP can advertise their routes and structures to other systems, regardless of the internal architecture of the networks involved.

> **Note** The protocol commonly known as BGP is actually BGP4 (which is the subject of this lesson). This fourth incarnation of the Border Gateway Protocol is very different from all previous versions. BGP4 has been adopted by Internet service providers and is now the most popular form of BGP, however, so it has become commonly known simply as BGP.

As we have seen, most routing protocols route data within a given networking environment. Protocols such as RIP are used to route data internally in networks and systems. This enables users on a network to exchange data with other users in the same area. BGP, on the other hand, routes data between different networks, known as ASs (autonomous systems).

An AS has no inherent knowledge of any other system in the world. This is only logical, because for every network in the world to know automatically the topology of every other network in the world would require some very hefty technology—technology that does not exist yet. Because no system knows the topology (or, for that matter, the existence) of any other system, exchanging data between systems can be very difficult.

BGP (BGP4) as a protocol allows systems with no knowledge of each other to communicate freely. However, if it were that simple, this lesson could end here. BGP is considered an advanced topic because there are so many variables and parameters that make BGP what it is. As you work with Cisco routers, you need to recognize and understand all of these intricacies.

BGP actually comprises two separate protocols: EBGP, or Exterior Border Gateway Protocol, and IBGP, or Interior Border Gateway Protocol. EBGP is used to route data between autonomous systems (what most people think of when they envision a BGP system), whereas IBGP is used to route data within a particular AS.

Before we jump right into configuring a Cisco router to run BGP, we need to discuss and understand the terms and parameters of BGP environments. Configuration examples will be given throughout the rest of this chapter to help you visualize how BGP functions.

Autonomous Systems

Autonomous systems (ASs) are the heart of BGP networks. The AS is the main routing unit of the BGP protocol.

> **Note** An autonomous system can be a single network or a group of related networks (such as a WAN).

> **Note** Every routing protocol works with a standard base unit. For example, PNNI uses domains (see Appendix A), and IS-IS uses peer-groups (PGs) (see Day 19). Essentially these units or groups are all the same. Therefore, do not let the changes in terminology catch you off guard. The different conglomerations of machines that protocols work within are fancy terms for the same network environments.
>
> Protocols may treat the network, AS, PG, or domain differently; however, the unit itself remains the same.

To understand autonomous systems, first let's look at how they are physically formed. Then we can see how BGP differentiates between them. An AS is a related group of systems. That is, just like a local or wide area network, an AS is an environment. Figure 18.1 illustrates a typical AS.

The network shown in Figure 18.1 is a fairly small LAN divided into a couple of subnets. These subnets are in different geographical areas and communicate back to the main office. The only outside access from the network is through the main subnet.

Because the small, external subnets do not have a separate connection to the Internet (they gain their connection through the central office), they are considered part of the same AS. That is, all three subnetworks pictured in Figure 18.1 form one autonomous system.

FIGURE 18.1

An autonomous system.

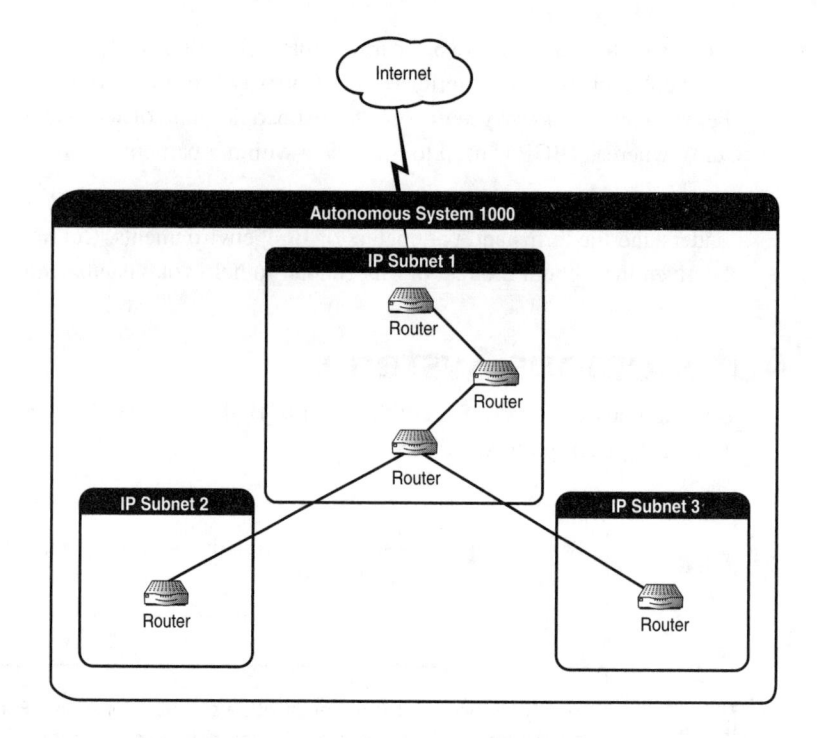

Autonomous systems can be even more basic than the one illustrated in Figure 18.1. A small network such as a POP (point of presence) may have no more than one or two heavy-duty routers (most likely, enterprise-series Cisco routers). Figure 18.2 shows a small one-router network as an AS.

The network in Figure 18.2, though small, is still a valid autonomous system. The one router connecting the servers of the POP to the central office qualifies the POP as an AS.

What makes an AS? Routers alone do not turn a network into an autonomous system. If that were the case, almost every LAN, WAN, and SOHO in the country would be an AS, which is simply not true. There are a couple of requirements that determine whether a network is an autonomous system or not.

FIGURE 18.2

An autonomous system with one router.

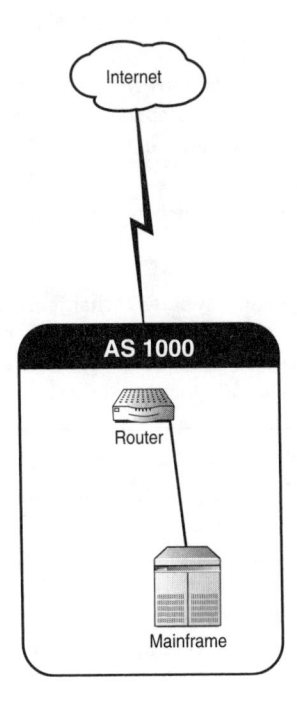

The first requirement is a connection to the Internet. For most companies this means a link to an ISP. Given that BGP enables effective communication between systems, there must be a carrier in place to connect them. This condition is pretty logical and elementary, but it ties into the next requirement.

The other requirement for an autonomous system is an ASN, or autonomous system number. A network's autonomous system number is its identity on the Internet (among other BGP systems). The ASN can range from 1 to 65535.

Once you begin working with and designing large-scale Cisco environments, you may be faced with the task of obtaining and assigning an ASN for a BGP network. The process is not very difficult, but it warrants some coverage in the following section.

Obtaining an Autonomous System Number

An autonomous system number, like an IP network address, must be assigned from a governing body (assuming you will need to communicate to the outside world using EBGP). In most cases your ISP assigns you an ASN as a subset of its own number. Obviously, because autonomous system numbers range only from 1 to 65535, there is a limited number of ASNs that can be assigned. For that reason a smaller range of addresses has been set aside for private use.

> **Note:** The use and assignment of autonomous system numbers is closely related to that of IP addresses. Both types of numbers are assigned by governing bodies, both have public and private ranges, and (unfortunately) both are finite in range.

> **Note:** In the United States, the governing body in charge of registering and releasing autonomous system numbers is ARIN (the American Registry for Internet Numbers). A list of the assigned autonomous system numbers and the entities who own them can be found at http://rs.arin.net/netinfo/asn.txt.

Private ASNs range from 64512 to 65535. Like private IP addresses, private ASNs cannot be advertised to the Internet. Rather, these numbers are used for IBGP routing within a larger BGP network. The numbers in the private ASN range can be used freely by anyone.

There are three classifications of autonomous systems. Whether or not your network qualifies for a public ASN depends on which type of AS you have. The three types of AS are:

- Stub
- Multihomed
- Transit

To be eligible to obtain a public ASN, a network must be a multihomed AS.

A stub AS is a network with only one connection to the Internet. Stub autonomous systems are usually treated as extensions of a larger AS. That is, because there is only one path to and from the stub AS, no further policies are required. It is also not logical to host a massive list of BGP routes on a gateway with only one available path. Figure 18.3 shows a stub network attached to an ISP.

> **Note** Most autonomous systems qualify only as stubs. However, a larger network may have stub sites that are attached to it but are considered to be part of the same autonomous system. These stub autonomous systems do not require their own private ASNs. They can be considered part of the larger AS and therefore share its ASN.

FIGURE 18.3

A stub AS.

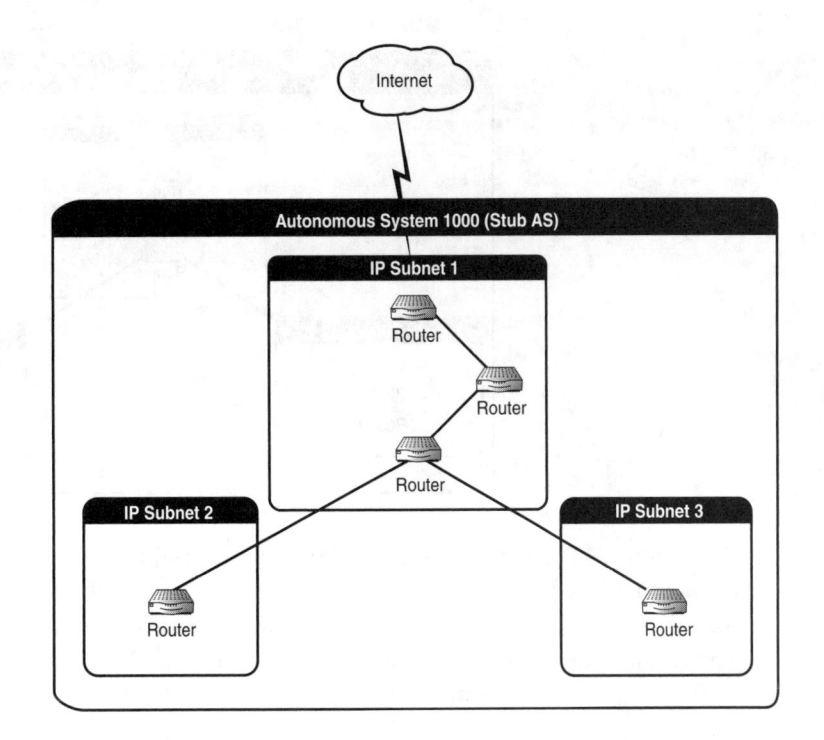

Multihomed systems are networks with multiple links to external autonomous systems. The multihomed AS accepts routed information from all of the systems linked to it, but it routes only internal data. Figure 18.4 illustrates a multihomed autonomous system.

FIGURE 18.4

A multihomed AS.

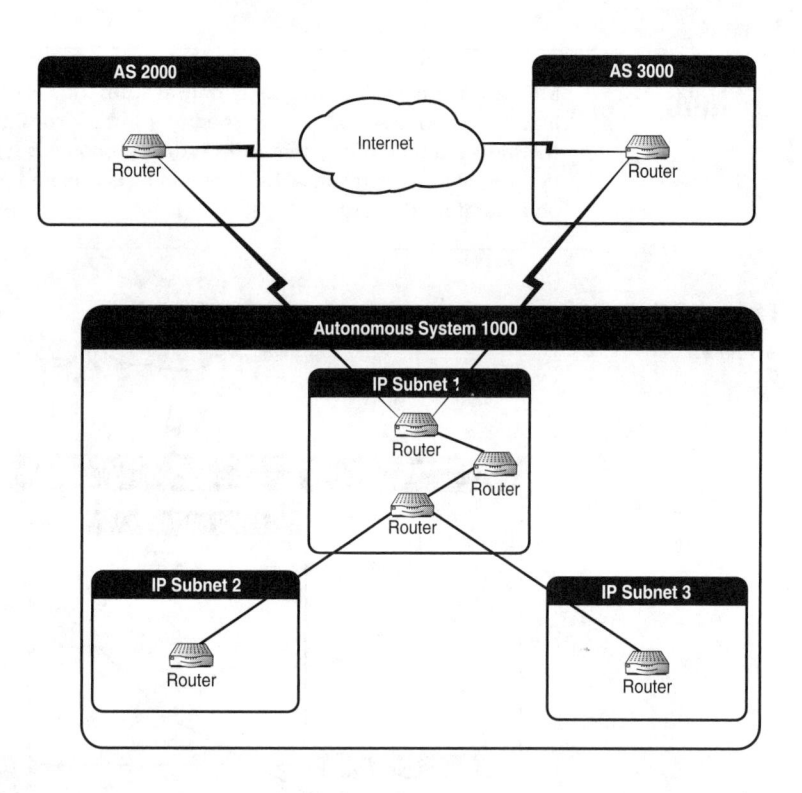

In Figure 18.4 autonomous system 1000 is multihomed because it connects to both AS 2000 and AS 3000. Because a multihomed AS routes only internal data, AS 2000 would not be able to send information to AS 3000 through AS 1000. (AS 1000 accepts and routes only data bound for its internal network.) For AS 2000 to communicate with AS 3000 (in Figure 18.4), it would need its own link to AS 3000.

The third type of autonomous system is a transit AS. Transit autonomous systems are multihomed systems that accept and route information from other external autonomous systems. If the multihomed AS in Figure 18.4 were a transit AS, then AS 2000 would be able to send data to AS 3000 via AS 1000.

> **Note** The uses and ranges pertaining to autonomous system numbers are outlined in RFC 1930.

ASNs and IP Addresses

The link between autonomous systems and IP addresses goes deeper than the regulations on how the two are utilized. IP plays a big part in the operation of BGP and the formation of autonomous systems. An ASN is directly linked to the IP addresses of the autonomous system it belongs to. In other words, an ASN needs to be associated with the IP address segments of the network to which it is attached. This ensures that the proper traffic gets routed to the proper autonomous system.

Figure 18.5 illustrates a network that will soon be an autonomous system. In this figure, all of the IP segments are labeled with their appropriate addresses.

FIGURE 18.5

A segmented IP network.

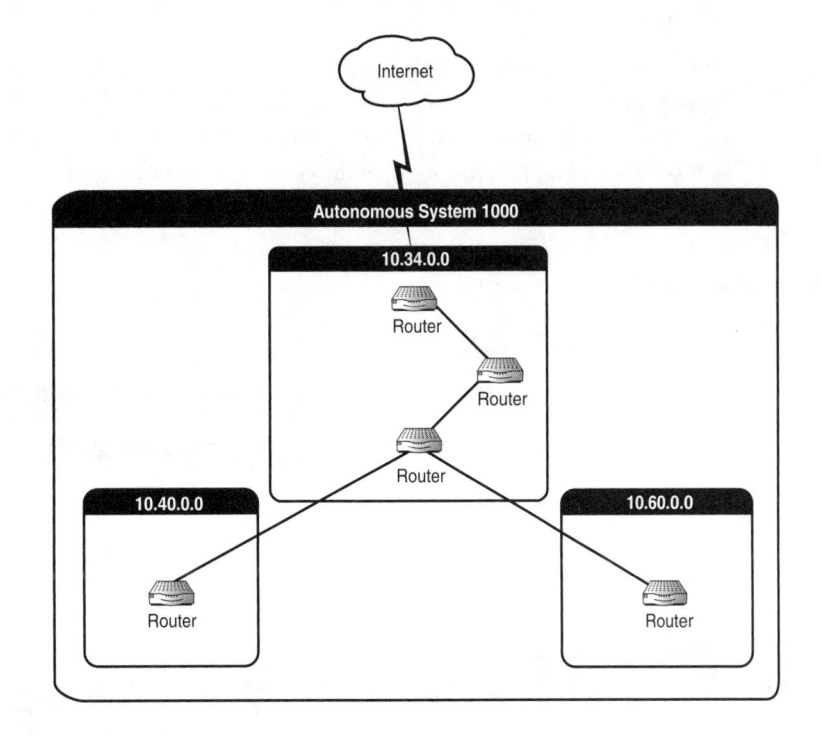

Only IP addresses specifically assigned to the ASN will be routed from the gateway. Having the proper IP address configured for the particular ASN will ensure that any external autonomous systems route the correct data to your border gateways. (This rule is true for all AS types.) If you leave out a subnet or change schemes without modifying your ASN, your network will not reliably receive data bound for it.

Now that we've discussed what autonomous systems are, we can dive into the subject of how they work. The remainder of this section will identify and discuss the parts of an autonomous system. The three major parts of an autonomous system are the BGP speaker, the border gateway, and the BGP peer.

BGP Speakers

All of the routers with an AS (that are configured for BGP) are known as BGP speakers. BGP speakers need to be configured with the ASN of the autonomous system they belong to. If the AS is composed of more than one IP subnet, all of the IP networks must be associated with the ASN.

If a BGP speaker in an AS has an IP address that is not associated with the ASN, the speaker cannot participate in the AS. Consequently, any other systems or BGP speakers that are behind the nonparticipatory speaker are also unable to receive data from the rest of the AS. Figure 18.6 illustrates an AS with one speaker that is not a member of the assigned IP scope.

In Figure 18.6, the two BGP speakers (and the end systems linked to them) located behind speaker 10.50.34.1 cannot participate in the AS. Even though the IP scopes that they belong to are associated with the ASN of the system, no data can pass through speaker 10.50.34.1 because its IP address is not associated with the ASN.

FIGURE 18.6

An AS that is not fully functional.

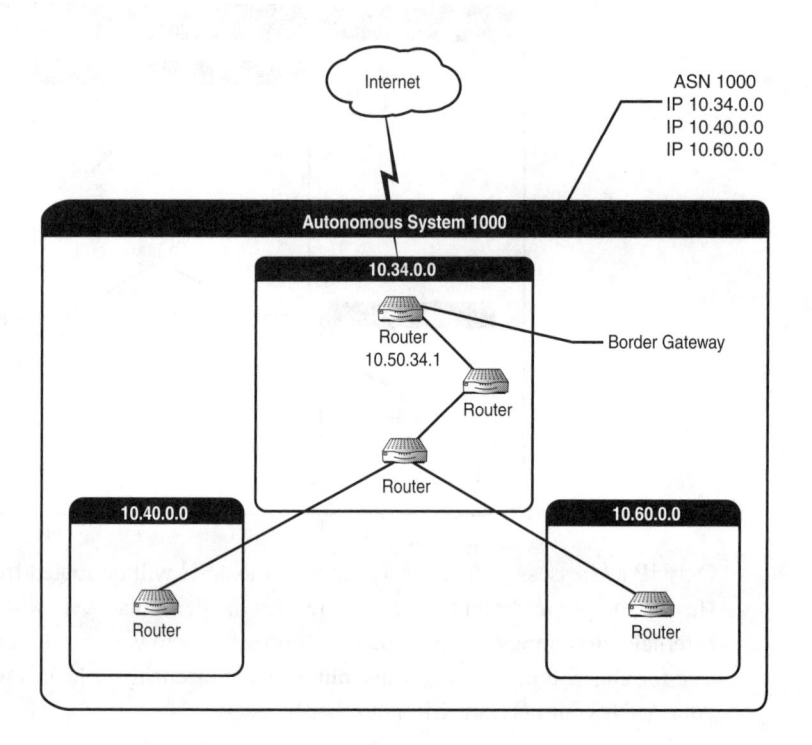

The command to enable BGP on a router (creating a BGP speaker), as in the other router protocols we have covered thus far, is a parameter of the `router` command.

```
Router(config)#router bgp
```

However, this is an incomplete command. When initiating a BGP speaker, you need to assign it an ASN. A more adequate command structure would be as follows:

```
Router(config)#router bgp 400
```

Although there are other commands to enable a functional BGP speaker completely, the router BGP command is the first (we will cover others as you progress through the following sections).

Border Gateways

BGP speakers that are located between two or more autonomous systems are known as border gateways. Border gateways act as bridges from one AS to another and are the other path for information between two autonomous systems. Figure 18.7 illustrates an autonomous system with a border gateway.

FIGURE 18.7

An autonomous system with a border gateway.

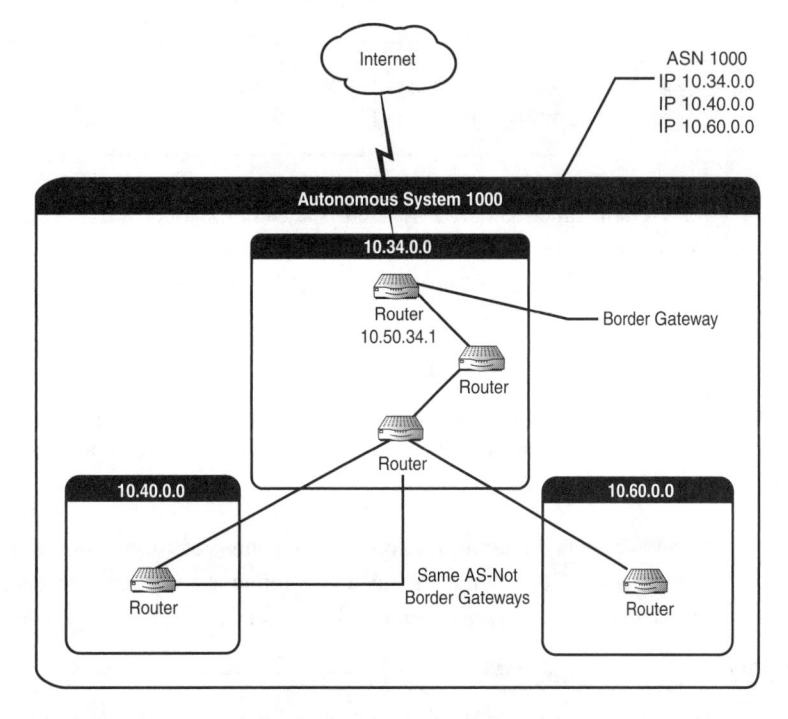

Autonomous systems do not necessarily require a border gateway. A border gateway is needed only if the AS uses EBGP to communicate with other autonomous systems on the Internet. Conversely, any one autonomous system can have multiple border gateways. If an autonomous system interfaces with more than one external AS on more than one BGP speaker, then the AS has multiple border gateways.

The job of the border gateway is to advertise the autonomous system (and any other routes it has knowledge of) to any external BGP speakers that it can contact. This may seem like a pretty broad job description, but it will make more sense later in this chapter.

BGP Peering Sessions (BGP Peers)

Like all other routing protocols, BGP works by sharing routing information among the network's participants. That is, every BGP speaker in an environment needs to exchange routing information (topographical and metric) with other BGP speakers to route network data successfully.

This exchange of routing information takes place during BGP *peering sessions*. When a BGP router is ready to exchange routing data with another BGP speaker, it opens a BGP peering session with the second speaker. The two BGP speakers involved in the peering session are now BGP peers.

> **Note** Because BGP uses TCP as its native protocol, all peering sessions are established and run on TCP port 179.

For BGP to function correctly, BGP speakers must be BGP peers with all other speakers in their autonomous system. That is, they need to form a logical *routing mesh*. Depending on the number of BGP speakers in your AS, this mesh can get rather large and hard to control or keep track of.

> **Note** A logical routing mesh is a configuration where all routers in an environment have a logical (not necessarily physical) link to each other.

The BGP peers do not need to be directly connected to each other (if they are using EBGP rather than IBGP), but they do need to communicate.. Therefore, a standard path of communication must exist between two BGP speakers for them to initiate a peering session.

> **Note** BGP can establish a peering session between two routers that are not directly connected. This is known as *EBGP multihop peering*. Using the external peering capabilities of EBGP, a BGP speaker can initiate a peering session with speakers that are multiple router hops away.
>
> However, the most common (and least complicated) form of peering is that between two directly connected speakers.

To establish a connection between two BGP speakers, use the `neighbor` command:

```
Router(configure)#router bgp 65000
Router(configure-router)#neighbor 10.115.48.1 remote-as 100
```

These two commands collectively configure the current router as a BGP speaker in AS 65000 and establish a BGP peering session with router 10.115.48.1 in AS 100. To create a fully operational link between the two routers, the same commands would need to be run on 10.115.48.1 pointing to your router.

The commands in the foregoing example illustrate the peering process if two IBGP routers are physically connected. If you are attempting an EBGP multihop connection, on the other hand, use the following commands:

```
Router(configure)#router bgp 65000
Router(configure-router)#neighbor 10.115.48.1 remote-as 100
Router(configure-router)#neighbor 10.115.48.1 ebgp-multihop
```

After running the commands on the peer router, you should have two peering EBGP speakers. These speakers are now permitted a full exchange of information. The two peer speakers will update each other and pass routing data from their internal systems to each other.

> **Note** Keep in mind that because the two routers in the EBGP scenario are not physically connected, they need to be running an IGP between them. Any suitable IGP, such as OSPF or IGRP, will complete the communication.

Upon initiation of a peering session, BGP speakers exchange their entire routing tables. This can make the process of convergence rather lengthy. Depending on the number of advertised routes on any given router, the initial update exchange can be very intensive. BGP routers can hold hundreds to thousands of advertised routes. During the first update for a new BGP speaker, each one of these routes must be transferred.

> **Note** BGP peers exchange full routing tables whenever they peer for the first time. This includes restarts. Every time a router is restarted, it exchanges full copies of its routing tables with all of its peers.
>
> Minimizing the number of router reloads alleviates the burden placed upon the network by the heavy traffic of full BGP table exchanges.

However, all future updates between existing BGP peers consist only of changes made to the routing table. The longer a router has been functioning in the autonomous system, the less intensive the table exchanges are.

After a BGP speaker has its routing configuration, it is ready to begin sending and receiving data. Depending on the needs of the network, the speaker uses one of two protocols: IBGP or EBGP. We examine the specifics of EBGP routing and configuration in the next section (IBGP is explained later in the chapter).

Configuring the Exterior Border Gateway Routing Protocol

In this section we cover EBGP, Exterior Border Gateway Protocol. EBGP establishes communication between BGP speakers in different autonomous systems. Situations where EBGP is used include communication between an ISP and a POP or a large enterprise and multiple communications vendors. Functionally there are few differences between EBGP and its counterpart, IBGP; however, the differences are profound enough to warrant separate discussions. (IBGP will be covered in the next section.)

BGP routers learn about their surroundings from other BGP routers. That is, during peering sessions BGP routers tell each other about the routes they know. These routes are the backbone of BGP operation, especially for speakers in different autonomous systems. The key to the (sometimes) smooth and quick operation of the Internet is BGP's ability to communicate and exchange routes with speakers in dissimilar networks.

For any BGP speaker outside of your AS to be able to route data to you successfully, it needs to be aware of your location and what address you represent. However, a route can mean more than "here are the addresses of the networks within my AS." Often a BPG speaker advertises routes it knows to other autonomous systems (that is, paths to autonomous systems other than its own).

A BGP route simply states, "I know how to get information bound for XXX.XXX.XXX.XXX from here to there." The routes specify an IP network address, or a "next hop" router address if the network is not within the sending device's AS. The "next hop" router address is the location of the border gateway that must be used to reach the destination. This information allows BGP speakers to advertise routes they are not directly connected to. This enables data from different autonomous systems to reach virtually anyone.

Understanding Border Gateway Protocol (BGP)

> **Note**
>
> One (unfortunately) common error is advertising a route incorrectly. For example, if an administrator keys in a network incorrectly and ends up advertising someone else's IP, no traffic will flow to the advertised network.
>
> The BGP router advertising the route will receive all of the traffic meant for the address. The router does not actually know how to send data to the address, however, and nothing within the AS actually matches the address either, so all information received will be discarded. On the other hand, all data bound for routes that the router is correctly advertising will be distributed without interruption.

When a BGP speaker has information about a route that needs to be sent (as an update) to other BGP speakers (internal or external), it advertises the route. Advertising (as one may expect) is a way for one speaker to offer routes or routing updates to other speakers.

The most common form of BGP route advertisement is BGP route redistribution. Let's take a look at how BGP route redistribution works. Figure 18.8 illustrates four autonomous systems connected through EBGP.

FIGURE 18.8

Four autonomous systems connected with EBGP.

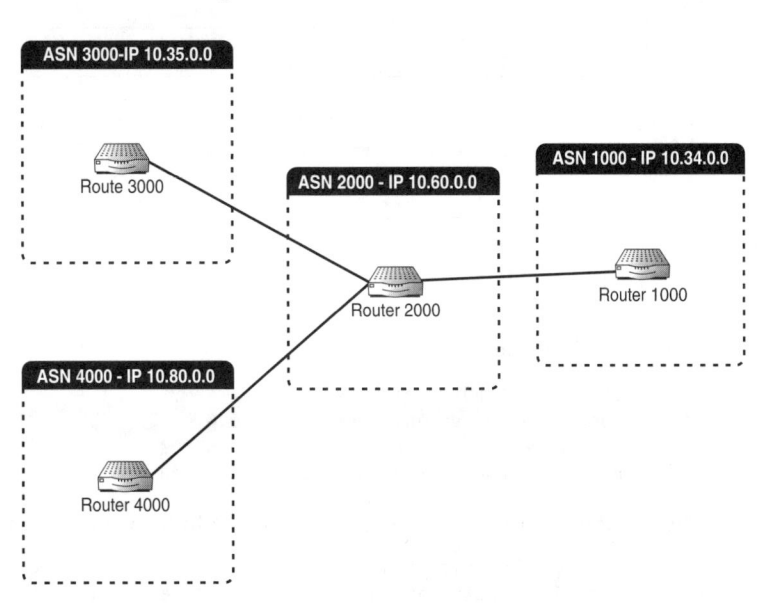

In Figure 18.8, router 2000 advertises (to autonomous systems 3000 and 4000) that it knows to route all traffic for IP network 10.34.0.0 to AS 1000 and all traffic for IP network 10.60.0.0 to AS 2000 (itself). It also advertises (to router 1000) that it can route all traffic for IP networks 10.80.0.0 and 10.35.0.0 to autonomous systems 3000 and 4000, respectively. Router 2000 thereby "redistributes" the knowledge of these routes to router 1000, router 3000, and router 4000.

Now, if router 3000 receives any data for IP network 10.34.0.0, it knows that if it forwards the data to router 2000, the information will get to the intended recipient (AS 1000).

Route advertisements help BGP speakers learn about each other and the networks they represent. Routes advertised by BGP speakers can be one of two kinds: dynamic or static.

A dynamic BGP route is one that the speaker learns about through IGP updates with other routers. In our example (Figure 18.8), the routes that router 3000 and router 4000 learn (through EIGRP updates) are considered dynamic routes.

> **Note**: EIGRP is a common IGP used for communication between border gateways.

> **Note**: The act of redistributing a dynamically learned route is known as BGP dynamic route redistribution (as opposed to BGP static route redistribution, which requires some involvement on your part).

Let's configure a BGP router for dynamic route redistribution. First we must configure the IGP to allow redistribution of its routes, and then we must configure BGP to pass along those redistributed routes:

```
Router(configure)#router eigrp 40
Router(configure-router)#network 10.153.0.0
Router(configure-router)#redistribute bgp 65100
Router(configure-router)#redistribute connected
```

Then, within the BGP configurator, execute the following commands:

```
Router(configure)#router bgp 65100
Router(configure-router)#neighbor 10.154.0.1 remote-as 65100
Router(configure-router)#distribute-list 1 out
Router(configure-router)#redistribute eigrp 10
```

> **Note**
>
> The `distribute-list` command refers to an access list that resides on the router. Although we examine access lists in greater detail in Day 21, you should understand that they are an intricate part of EBGP routing.
>
> For the routes to redistribute successfully, they must be pointed to a local access list. These access lists contain the IP network addresses of hosts to which the router has access.

Alternatively, an administrator can program a route into a BGP speaker. These routes are known as static routes. Using our previous example in Figure 18.8, we could say that router 2000 knows about the networks within AS 1000 through a statically defined route. When router 2000 redistributes that information to router 3000 and router 4000, it is considered a BGP static route redistribution.

To configure a BGP router for static route redistribution, we first need to define the static route:

```
Router(configure)#ip route 10.153.40.0 255.255.0.0 null 0
```

> **Note**
>
> Notice that we set the interface to `null 0`. Normally this would discard any packets for the defined network. However, the inclusion of the BGP redistribution statement will intercede before the packets are discarded.

After configuring the static route through IP we can configure BGP for static redistribution. To configure BGP, use the `redistribute static` command:

```
Router(configure-router)#neighbor 10.153.60.1 remote-as 700
Router(configure-router)#redistribute static
```

These simple commands allow routes to be distributed between speakers. However, problems can arise when you do not want all routes to be distributed. In this case you need to configure route maps.

BGP Route Maps

BGP route maps are used to filter the redistribution of BGP routes from AS to AS. Imagine the number of BGP routes that are exchanged on the Internet every day. If every BGP speaker redistributed every path it learned about, the traffic alone would bring the Internet to a halt. Route maps give you a way to determine what learned BGP routes you want your speaker to redistribute to the Internet.

> **Note:** Route maps work only on the update level. That is, any route maps that may be in place will affect only routes being sent from the router, not those being received.

A route map can consist of a list of criteria that, if met, will permit or deny a route's advertisement or reset a particular metric of the route. For example, using the networks from Figure 18.8 as our guide, an administrator could create a route map on router 2000 that states, "Do not redistribute any routes learned from AS 2000." (The actual technical language of the route map will vary with the brand of router being used.)

With this route map in place, router 1000 would still receive updates from router 2000. However, it would run the route map against it and determine that it should not redistribute that route to router 3000 or router 4000.

However, let's suppose that AS 3000 is also connected to AS 1000, as illustrated in Figure 18.9.

FIGURE 18.9

Four interconnected autonomous systems.

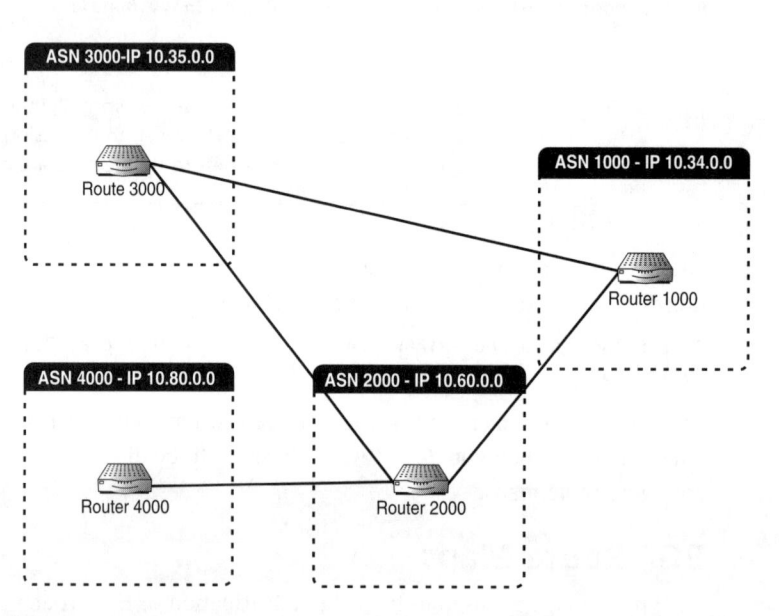

In Figure 18.9, after all of the BGP updates have been processed, router 3000 has two possible routes to select from for sending data to AS 1000. It could send the data through router 2000 or send it directly to router 1000. When faced with a choice like this, the routing algorithm would decide which route to use based on the lowest cost or metric value.

The administrator of AS 2000, knowing that router 2000 is one of the possible paths to AS 1000, could create a route map that would ensure that the direct route (router 3000 to router 1000) will be used before the indirect route (router 3000 to router 2000 to router 1000). Assuming that the route updates from router 1000 are sent out with a default metric of 4, the route map on router 2000 could say, "Redistribute any routes learned from router 1000 with a metric of 10." Then after router 3000 has received all of its BGP updates, it would have two choices for sending data to AS 1000. The data could be sent either directly to router 1000 for a cost of 4 or through router 2000 for a cost of 10. Ninety-nine times out of 100 the routing algorithm goes with the direct route.

Conversely, if your site uses the biggest and best in technology, and you want your border gateway to be the preferred route to another AS, you can create a lower metric value. By implementing a route map that changes another autonomous system's metric to a lower value, you virtually ensure your site's preference as a path to that AS.

This may be valuable during an acquisition of a company. If one company purchases another and wants the larger site to be the preferred route to the small one (before actual network changes can be made), it can implement a route map. To configure a route map, you need to follow a few steps. First an access list must be created to define the rules:

```
Router(configure)# ip as-path access-list 1 permit ^65000$
```

This command creates an access list that permits access to any packets from AS 65000. Next you must create the route map:

```
Router(configure-router)#route-map MYMAP permit 10
Router(configure-router)#match as-path 1
Router(configure-router)#set weight 30
```

The `match as-path 1` command tells the route map to find matches pertaining to the rules established in access list 1. The `set weight` command tells the route map to set the weight metric of any packet that meets the rules to 30.

Finally, you can configure BGP to use the route map:

```
Router(configure-router)#neighbor 10.153.50.1 route-map MYMAP in
```

This line of commands tells BGP to apply the route map MYMAP to any incoming updates from address 10.153.50.1.

The preceding sections have introduced the basics of BGP connections within an EBGP environment. However, as we are all aware, the world is not a perfect routing environment. Not everything works on the first try. Despite even the best configuration and planning you may experience a BGP issues known as route flapping.

BGP Route Flapping and Flap Dampening

If a BGP speaker fails to connect to any of the routers in its BGP table (through a peering session), this route is said to be *flapping*. That is, if router A learns about router B (illustrated in Figure 18.10) through a dynamic BGP route redistribution and cannot open a peering session to it, the route to router B is flapping.

FIGURE 18.10

A flapping route.

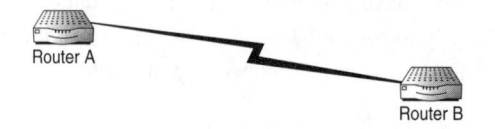

The cause of a route flap could be anything from a T1 line becoming temporarily dislodged to an entire network going belly up. Either way, route flaps can be a processor-clogging hassle. If one route were to flap and every BGP speaker connected to that route continued to redistribute it around the Internet, a lot of information would clog the routers. Such informational traffic congestion could bring the Internet to a standstill.

To combat this, a failsafe was put into place known as *flap dampening*. Flap dampening works by "blacklisting" any route that flaps for x amount of time (usually in relation to BGP updates). When a route is dampened, it is removed from its peer's BGP route tables. Then any further updates won't include the route. The consequence of this is that the route is erased from the collective consciousness of the Internet. The affected route is made invisible, until such time as any communication problems between it and the other peers can be resolved.

> **Note**
> In many instances, routes that are down temporarily must wait a certain amount of time (after coming live again) before they can be readvertised, resulting in a longer downtime than necessary. This is one of the downsides of flap dampening.

Flap dampening is not something that needs to be configured by an administrator; it is simply a feature of the protocol. However, understanding that it exists is key to understanding BGP as a whole.

It is always best to check with your provider if you suddenly lose connectivity. Often a problem on the provider's side (such as a cable coming loose) can cause the routes to your site to be dampened, making your site invisible for up to a few hours.

BGP, like most routing protocols, relies on the use of metrics to aid in the route decision process. We have already discussed how the use of route maps can allow you to change a metric to a higher or lower value (depending on the desirability of a particular route). Now we will discuss how the BGP header collects and stores these metrics. BGP is an involved and complicated subject; we need to explain BGP headers before we can logically continue with the chapter.

BGP Headers

There are four different BGP headers that can be attached to a BGP message. Each header contains information specific to the type of message being delivered: open, update, notification, or keep-alive. However, a common header precedes each of the four message headers. The BGP common header introduces the message and indicates to other systems that it is intended for BGP routers.

The BGP Common Header

The BGP common header, also known as the BGP protocol header, is found on all routing information packets sent from a BGP router. The common header designates the packet as BGP and indicates what type of information is contained within. Figure 18.11 illustrates the fields of the BGP common header.

FIGURE 18.11
The BGP common header.

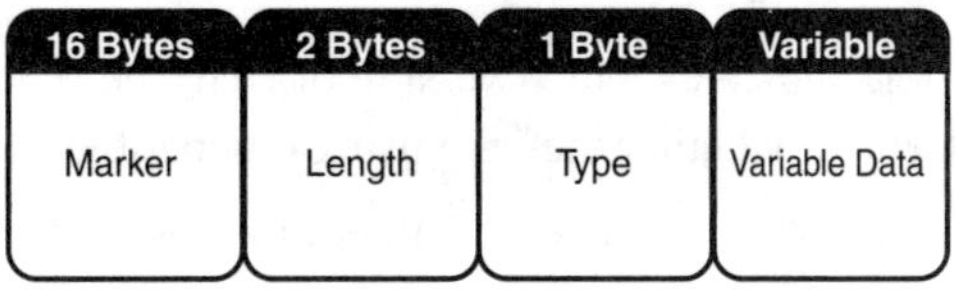

16 Bytes	2 Bytes	1 Byte	Variable
Marker	Length	Type	Variable Data

The four fields of the BGP common header are:

- Header Marker: The header marker is a 16-byte field that identifies the message as a BGP message. A receiving BGP router uses an internal calculation to predict what the marker field should be. If the router receives a packet and the marker field is different from the field predicted, the router knows that the packet is being sent out of sequence and should be discarded.

- Length: The length field, consisting of 2 bytes, is the total length (in bytes) of the BGP packet (not the length of the header).
- Type: This 1-byte field indicates whether the message type that follows is open, update, notification, or keep-alive.
- Variable Data: The variable data field is the message itself. A message-specific header precedes the data in the variable data field. This field can vary in size depending on the type of message.

The BGP Open Message Header

An open message is sent between routers when a BGP session is established. After the routers establish a session using TCP, they exchange open messages to begin the session formally. Figure 18.12 illustrates the fields of an open message header.

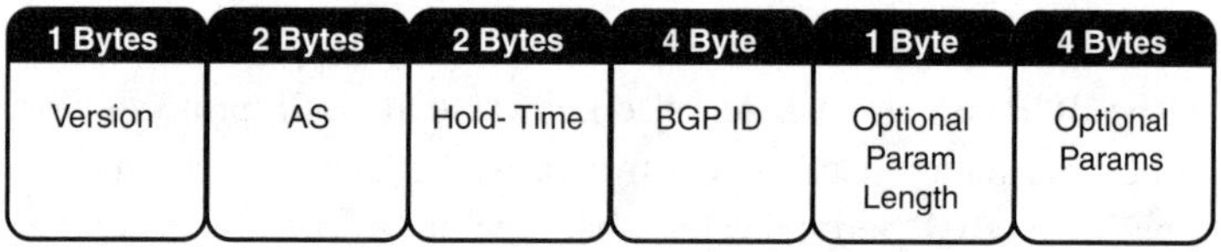

FIGURE 18.12

An open message header.

1 Bytes	2 Bytes	2 Bytes	4 Byte	1 Byte	4 Bytes
Version	AS	Hold-Time	BGP ID	Optional Param Length	Optional Params

The fields of the open message header are:

- Version: This field indicates which version of BGP the sender is using. This helps the routers determine whether they are using compatible protocols.
- AS Indicator: This 2-byte field is the autonomous system number of the router sending the message.
- Hold-time field: The sending router uses the hold-time field to determine whether the recipient is online. If the router that sent the open message does not receive a reply within the time indicated by the hold-time field, the recipient is assumed to be offline.
- BGP Identifier: The BGP identifier is a 4-byte field that refers directly to the sender of the message. The BGP identifier usually consists of the sending router's MAC address and ASN.

The remaining two fields are optional.

- Optional parameter length field: This 1-byte field contains the length of the "optional parameters" field. If the optional parameters are not set, this field is set to 0.

  The "optional parameters" field contains any parameters that the sending router wants to pass on to the recipient. Currently (in BGP4) there is only one optional parameter that can be sent in an open message.

- Authentication information: The "authentication information" parameter is used in cases where the packet must be authenticated before use.

The BGP Update Message Header

An update message is distributed between BGP routers to amend the routing table information. A five-field header precedes these messages within the variable data portion of the common BGP header. Figure 18.13 illustrates the fields of the update message header.

FIGURE 18.13

A BGP update message header.

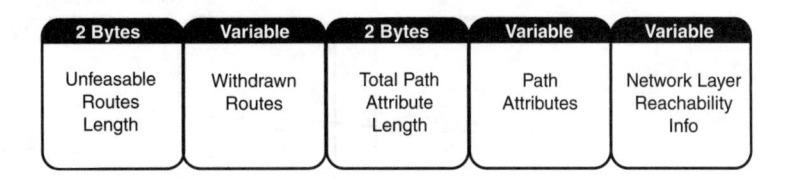

2 Bytes	Variable	2 Bytes	Variable	Variable
Unfeasable Routes Length	Withdrawn Routes	Total Path Attribute Length	Path Attributes	Network Layer Reachability Info

The fields of the update message are as follows. The first two fields in the update message header concern any paths that should be removed from the recipient's routing tables. These paths are known as withdrawn routes.

- Unfeasible route length: This 2-byte value indicates the length of the withdrawn routes field. If there are no withdrawn routes, the unfeasible route length is set to 0.

- Withdrawn routes: The withdrawn routes field is a variable-length field that contains the IP prefixes of any routes that should be deleted from the routing table.

- Total path attribute length: This field that immediately follows is the path attribute field. The path attribute field contains the metrics used by BGP to assign values to particular paths (explained later in this section).

- Update message header: This field contains network layer reachability information. This variable-length field contains the IP prefixes of the paths that are to be added to the routing table.

The BGP Notification Message and Keep-Alive Message

A BGP notification message is exchanged between BGP routers when an error occurs. When one router experiences a problem it sends a three-field notification message and then disconnects any open sessions. The three fields consist of an error code, an error subcode, and the error data.

A keep-alive message is sent when a hold-time is about to expire. The keep-alive message is composed of one field that lets the recipient know to override the expiration of any hold-times.

AS-Path and AS-Set

The AS-Path is an attribute that is attached to a BGP route update. The AS-Path gives a cumulative account of the autonomous systems that a BGP update passed through before reaching its destination (see Figure 18.14).

FIGURE 18.14

An AS-Path cycle.

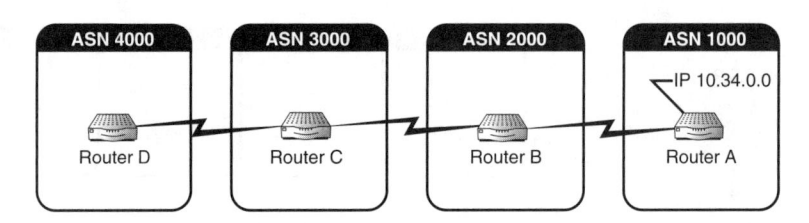

In Figure 18.14, router A advertises that network 10.34.0.0 belongs to ASN 1000. When router B processes the update, the AS-Path that the update came from is added (as a prefix) to the update. The update message now states, "AS 1000 says that 10.34.0.0 belongs to ASN 1000."

Next, router B advertises the same route to router C. After router C processes the update, the advertisement would read, "ASN 2000 says that ASN 1000 says that 10.34.0.0 belongs to ASN 1000." Finally, when the update reaches router D the AS-Path would include "ASN 3000–ASN 2000–ASN 1000."

> **Note** A complete AS-Path is known as an AS-Set.

Now when router D has a message for IP network 10.34.0.0, it just needs to look at the AS-Set on the update. The AS-Set gives the router the AS-Path to the destination. In our example, Router D would forward any data for 10.34.0.0 to the first AS-Path (ASN 3000). Router C would forward that data to what it sees as the first AS-Path, ASN 2000, and so on until the information reaches ASN 1000.

Next Hop

The "next hop" attribute functions similarly to the AS-Path; however, it specifies the IP address of the router port used to reach a particular AS. Using our example from Figure 18.14, just telling router D that the AS-Path for data going to 10.34.0.0 is ASN 3000 is not sufficient if router D doesn't understand how to get to ASN 3000. Router D must also be configured to understand where ASN 3000 is.

The "next hop" attribute on router D needs to be set to the IP address of the physical router port that router D can access router C on (ASN 3000). When you configure the "next hop" attribute, you designate a set path for data to reach a particular destination. BGP networks can get very complicated; simple tools such as the "next hop" help eliminate some of the confusion.

Origin

The origin can be one of three values:

- IGP
- EGP
- Incomplete

> **Note**
> Do not confuse IGP and EGP with IBGP and EBGP. Whereas IBGP and EBGP are specific protocols, IGP and EGP are designators that stand for interior gateway protocol and exterior gateway protocol. These protocols do not need to be IBGP or EBGP. In fact, often you will find other protocols being used to aid in the transportation of BGP data. Protocols such as IGRP and EIGRP (Interior Gateway Routing Protocol and Enhanced Interior Gateway Routing Protocol) can also be used to route IBGP data.
>
> Therefore, the BGP origin attribute specifies (generally) which type of protocol the route was forwarded with.

An origin of IGP indicates that the route was learned from an internal protocol such as IBGP. The BGP speaker will assume that any path with an origin of IGP is within its own AS. An origin of EGP indicates that the route was learned through an external update. This would cause the BGP speaker to use EBGP to reach any route with an origin of EGP. Finally, an origin of incomplete means that the route was obtained through a process other than internal or external learning. In most cases an incomplete origin represents a route that was obtained through route redistribution.

Local Preference

The local preference is a metric used to determine the desirability of one path over another when there are two paths to a particular destination. When a router is presented with two (seemingly equal) paths to the same destination, it compares the local preference attributes of the paths to determine which to use. The higher a path's local preference, the more likely it is to be used. If no local preference is defined, the default value is 100.

Configuring Interior Border Gateway Routing

One of the major differences between the routing logic for IBGP as compared with EBGP is the use of a loopback address. As shown in the preceding section, BGP operates by opening a peering session between two routers on specific physical and logical IP ports. That is, BGP peering sessions will always be established between two routers on IP port 179, on which the physical ethernet port (IP address) is defined. In EBGP this process poses one problem. If the specified physical port is unavailable, the peering session cannot be established. IBGP fixes this problem by using a loopback address.

A loopback address is an IP address that represents a cluster of physical router ports. By representing more than one physical port, a loopback address ensures that a BGP neighbor will gain connectivity regardless of the availability of the physical ports.

Loopback addresses are found only in IBGP because of the reachability of the routers. More often than not, routers connected through EBGP are connected on only one physical port, whereas routers connected by IBGP normally share an entire networking environment.

BGP Confederations

As we discussed earlier in this lesson, all BGP speakers in an IBGP AS need to be fully meshed to communicate successfully. That is, every BGP speaker (running IBGP) in a specific AS needs to have a physical connection to every other IBGP speaker. Figure 18.15 illustrates a large, fully meshed AS.

FIGURE 18.15

A fully meshed autonomous system.

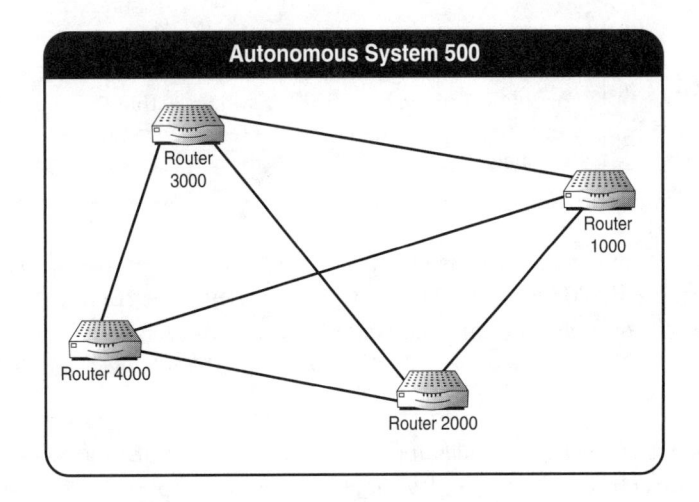

It is quite obvious from Figure 18.15 that as the number of IBGP speakers increases, the number of physical connections increases exponentially. Utilizing, tracking, and administering such a large number of connections can be trying, even for the most seasoned of network professionals. You need a method for reducing the number of physical router connections without limiting the number of IBGP speakers. One way to do so is to configure multiple BGP confederations.

A BGP confederation is a subgroup within an AS. That is, one larger AS can be divided into multiple smaller ASs, retaining the same ASN yet reducing the number of physical connections between speakers.

The function of BGP confederations can be compared to that of IP subnets (Day 11). Whereas IP subnets break down the physical size of an IP network while retaining its identity as a larger entity, confederations create smaller sub-ASs that retain all the outward characteristics of the original, larger AS.

To divide an AS into several confederations you need to do a bit of planning. Map out on paper where your confederation borders will be. This will help you visualize how you should configure the speakers within the confederations. After you have decided where you will be dividing the AS into confederations, you need to assign confederation identifiers to the new AS subgroups.

> **Note:** A confederation identifier is a number assigned to a confederation that distinguishes it from other confederations within the same AS. Confederation identifiers act as, and follow the same conventions as, autonomous system numbers.

Keep in mind that a confederation is a small AS. In other words, IBGP peers within a confederation do need to be fully meshed. However, the IBGP peers within a confederation do not need to be fully meshed with the IBGP peers of another confederation (even if they are within the same AS). This lack of meshing between confederations creates a more manageable environment.

Once the confederation identifiers have been assigned, the interconfederation physical links can be broken down. You should now have completely self-contained confederations within an AS. However, how do the confederations communicate with each other? To enable intraconfederation communication, thus creating a fully functional autonomous system, you need to define IBGP confederation peers.

Confederation peers are routers that communicate from confederation to confederation. They act as BGP speakers for the individual confederations. Defining confederation peers can be confusing because of one small aspect of the process: Confederation peers speak EBGP to each other.

Because confederations have different confederation identifiers, EBGP speakers are needed to enable communication between two or more confederations. However, because these EBGP speakers are contained within an IBGP environment, they follow all of the rules of IBGP speakers. That is, confederation peers share routes like IBGP peers and not EBGP speakers (even though they are technically running EBGP).

Once the confederation peers are defined, connecting all of the confederations within your AS by a single physical link should produce a fully functional group of confederations that appear as one large AS from the outside world. Figure 18.16 illustrates an AS divided into multiple confederations.

FIGURE 18.16

A group of confederations.

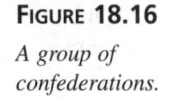

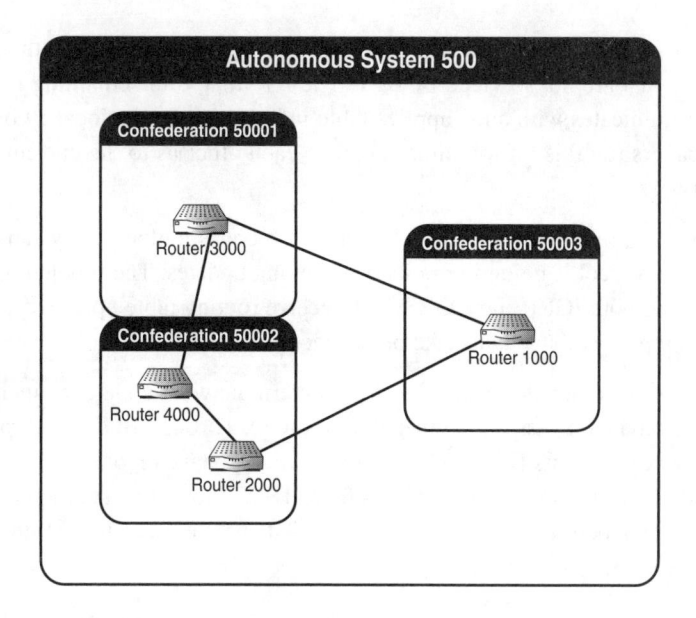

Configuring a Confederation

As a subset of the bgp command, the confederation parameter allows the creation of confederations on Cisco routers running BGP. To create a confederation of three routers (10.198.56.1, 10.198.56.2, and 10.198.56.3) that communicate with one router outside the confederation, use the following commands:

```
Router(configure)#router bgp 65000
Router(configure-router)# bgp confederation identifier 500
Router(configure-router)# bgp confederation peers 65100
Router(configure-router)# neighbor 10.198.56.2 remote-as 65000
Router(configure-router)# neighbor 10.198.56.3 remote-as 65000
Router(configure-router)# neighbor 10.198.56.7 remote-as 65100
```

This code shows that a BGP router was set up in AS 65000. The router was added to the confederation (ID 500) with two other routers. After the confederation routers were added, the neighbor command was again used to establish communication with the BGP router 10.198.56.7 outside the confederation.

BGP Synchronization

Within a BGP environment you may have more than one protocol being run through your routers. That is, all routers not running BGP should be running another routing protocol to facilitate the delivery of packages. Keep in mind that BGP is a border gateway routing protocol; your environment needs an IGP (interior gateway protocol) to route data through the rest of your network.

Your routers may be running OSPF, IS-IS, or any other IGP on the portions of the network that are not serviced by BGP. The IGP that your remaining routers are running communicates with and supplies table information to the local BGP speakers. BGP speakers use this information to update each other as to the current condition of the network.

However, running two or more routing protocols simultaneously can pose a big problem. Each protocol is going to run its own routing updates. The problem is that if one router is running both IGRP and BGP, which receive routing table updates from different sources, which protocol's updates take precedence?

BGP synchronization helps the router determine what updates to include in its routing table (and then pass on to other BGP routers). Through BGP synchronization a BGP router can hold its BGP updates until all routers have reported receiving updates from the IGP. For example, the network in Figure 18.17 shows two autonomous systems. Each AS is running both BGP and OSPF. Notice that some routers are running both protocols while others are running only OSPF.

FIGURE 18.17

An AS running two routing protocols.

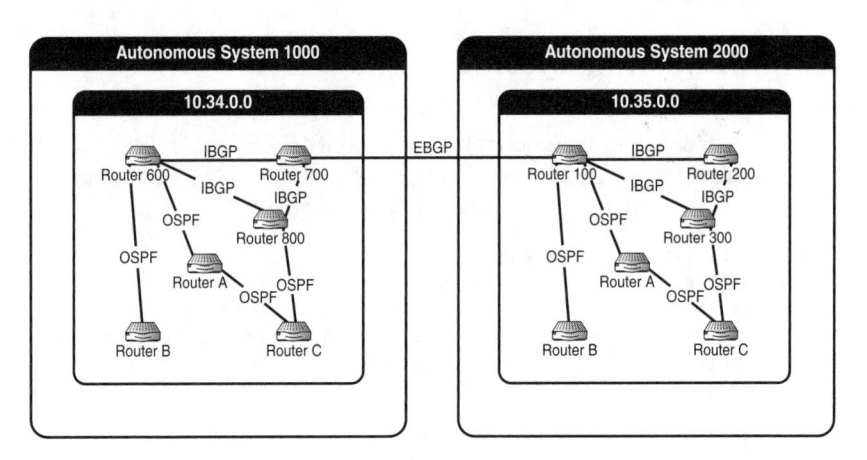

Before the BGP can begin its routing updates, it needs to wait for each router to receive an OSPF update (see Figure 18.17). This ensures that each router is receiving the most accurate information.

To disable BGP synchronization, use the no command:

Router(configure-router)#**no synchronization**

One topic that ties in closely with BGP synchronization is BGP route reflection. We briefly discussed route maps and filters earlier in this chapter. Now we can touch on a more complex issue, route reflection.

BGP Route Reflection

As we have discussed, within an autonomous system all IBGP peers must be fully meshed. One of the reasons for this is that an IBGP peer cannot distribute routes learned from one IBGP peer to another. IBGP peers propagate only updates that relate directly to their own routes. This allows IBGP routers to send out updates that the routers know about first-hand, reducing the number of incorrect or outdated routes. However, the obvious problem is that every IBGP peer must be physically linked to every other IBGP peer. The solution to this problem is BGP route reflectors.

IBGP peers that are configured as BGP route reflectors can distribute, or reflect, routes learned from one BGP peer to another BGP peer. In other words, a BGP router can send an update to another BGP router without being physically meshed to that router. Figure 18.18 illustrates route reflection.

FIGURE 18.18

An AS with a route reflector.

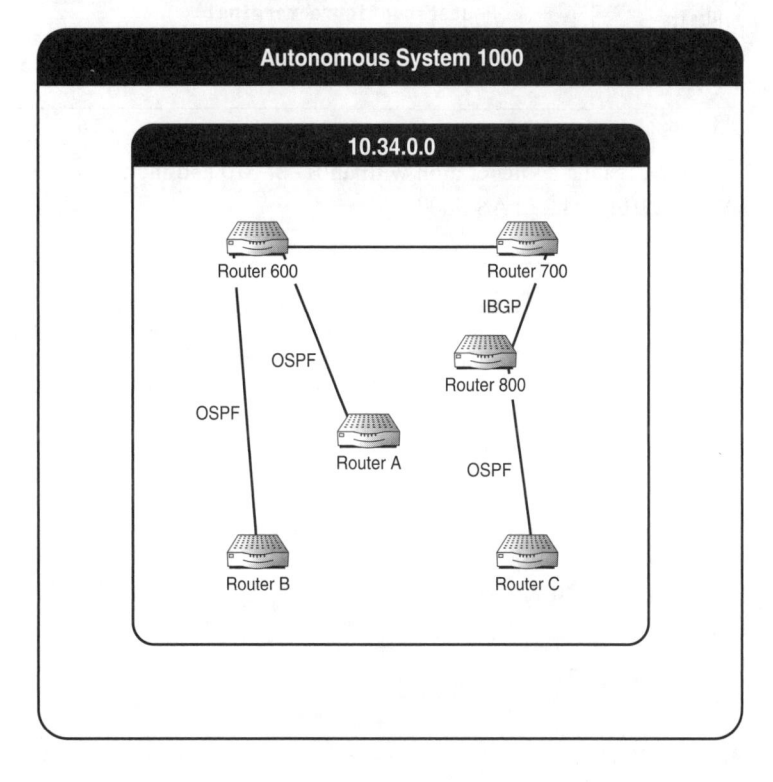

In Figure 18.18, router 700 can reflect routes from router 600 to router 800. Route reflectors are a great tool that administrators can use to help reduce the number of physical links needed between IBGP peers. However, the use of route reflectors does require more router overhead than a standard BGP router.

Exercises

1. Configure router 10.198.24.1 for BGP as part of AS 200.

    > **Note**
    > ```
    > Router#configure terminal
    > Router(configure)#router bgp 200
    > Router(configure-router)#^Z
    > ```

2. Establish a static route redistribution pointing to router 10.16.4.1 (a member of AS 700).

    > **Note**
    > ```
    > Router#configure terminal
    > Router(configure)# neighbor 10.16.4.1 remote-as 700
    > Router(configure-router)#redistribute static
    > ```

3. Create a confederation with an ID of 670 and including the routers 10.156.4.1 and 10.156.4.2 in AS 5000.

    > **Note**
    > ```
    > Router(configure)#router bgp 5000
    > Router(configure-router)#bgp confederation identifier 670
    > Router(configure-router)#neighbor 10.156.4.1 remote-as 5000
    > Router(configure-router)#neighbor 10.156.4.2 remote-as 5000
    > ```

WEEK 3

DAY 19

Learning IS-IS

The IS-IS (Intermediate System to Intermediate System) protocol is a link state routing protocol. IS-IS was developed by the ISO (based on DECnet Phase V) to work with the CLNP (Connectionless Network Protocol). However, because of the protocol's great flexibility, it could work with OSI and DNA architectures and provide a type of protocol bridge between DECnet's proprietary DNA model and the widely accepted OSI.

This lesson focuses on configuring Cisco routers to run IS-IS. Unlike the other protocols discussed in this book, IS-IS was originally developed for a proprietary topology known as DECnet. Therefore, it did not necessarily conform immediately to the same OSI standards as protocols such as IGRP and BGP. As a result, some of the structures and concepts within IS-IS may seem foreign.

The topics we will examine in discussing IS-IS are:

- IS-IS and DECnet
- How IS-IS relates to CLNP
- IS-IS link state routing
- IS-IS metrics and algorithms

- IS-IS addressing, areas, and domains
- IS-IS packets
- IS-IS routing
- Configuring IS-IS

IS-IS and DECnet

The Digital Equipment Corporation developed DECnet as a protocol suite in 1975 for their popular VAX line of computers. Each release, or version, of DECnet is known as a phase (Phase I, Phase II, and so on). Like all protocols, DECnet needed to follow a specific architecture to move information from one system to another. A protocol model was put in place to illustrate how data would move from the user interface of one system, through the PC, over the transmission medium, and into the destination system. Most protocols today adhere to the OSI model architecture. The first four phases of DECnet followed Digital's own proprietary architecture for moving data.

> **Note** IS-IS was based on DECnet Phase V; however, much of what made DECnet Phase V work was actually implemented in DECnet Phase IV.

DECnet was (and still is) a proprietary system used to enable communication between DEC equipment. Because of this, the first four phases of DECnet did not adhere to the OSI model, but rather were based on the DNA (Digital Network Architecture) model. Digital would later develop an OSI-compliant version of DECnet known as DECnet Phase V or DECnet OSI/DNA. DECnet Phase IV DNA comprises eight layers that correlate (more or less) to the seven layers of the OSI model. Figure 19.1 shows the eight layers of Phase IV DNA and how they relate to the OSI model.

> **Note** All phases of DECnet are designed to be backward compatible. Therefore, DECnet Phase III is backward compatible with Phase II. When DEC began developing (OSI-compliant) DECnet Phase V, they realized that the protocol needed to be implemented in such a way as to be backward compatible with the DECnet DNA architecture. This would later become a very important feature of IS-IS.

FIGURE 19.1

The eight layers of the DECnet Phase IV DNA architecture.

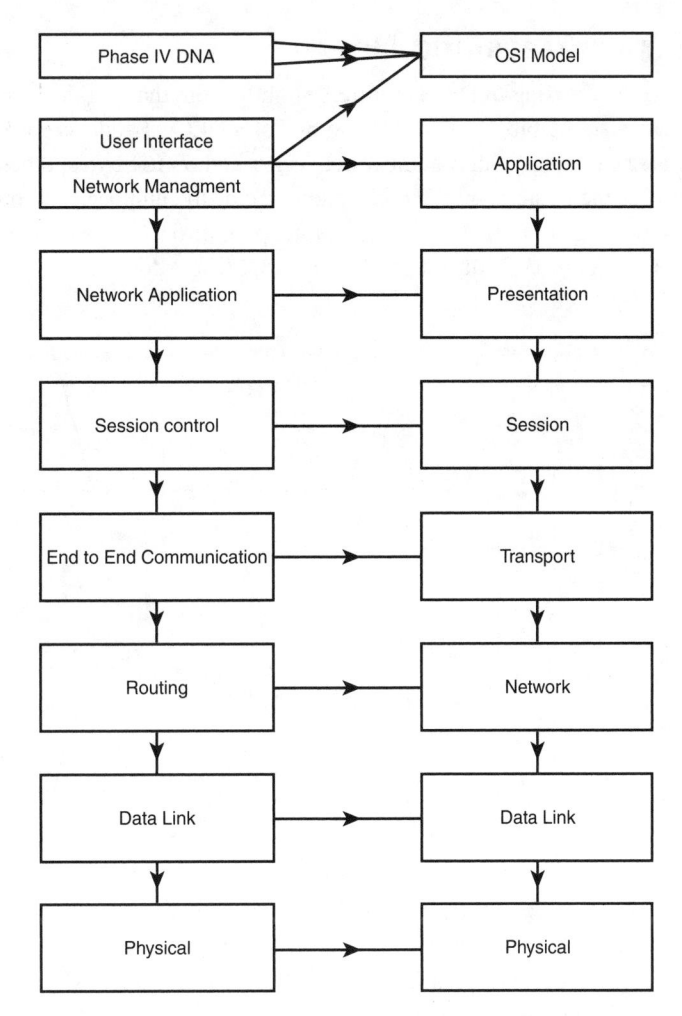

Phase IV DNA	OSI Model
User Interface / Network Managment	Application
Network Application	Presentation
Session control	Session
End to End Communication	Transport
Routing	Network
Data Link	Data Link
Physical	Physical

If you are familiar with the OSI model, you'll notice some small difference between Digital's DNA and ISO's OSI. The main difference is in the upper layers of the two protocols. Many of DNA's upper layers span multiple OSI layers. However, the lower layers (those crucial for routing) are relatively the same (this would help Digital make an easier transition from DNA to OSI).

Because of the differences in the upper and lower layers between the DNA and OSI architectures, DECnet addresses are structured differently than those from other protocols. DECnet addresses are composed of two parts: an area and a node (a concept that would be carried over to IS-IS).

DECnet Areas and Nodes

Protocol addressing in DECnet differs slightly from that of other protocols. DECnet addresses are 16 bits long. The first 6 bits of a DECnet address are known as the *area*. The area can be any valid number between 1 and 63 (64 bytes, 0 being invalid). The last 10 bits of the address are the *node*, addressed as the numbers 1 through 1023 (1024 bytes, 0 being invalid). This creates a total pool of 64,449 possible nodes on a DECnet network. Figure 19.2 illustrates a common DECnet address.

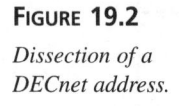

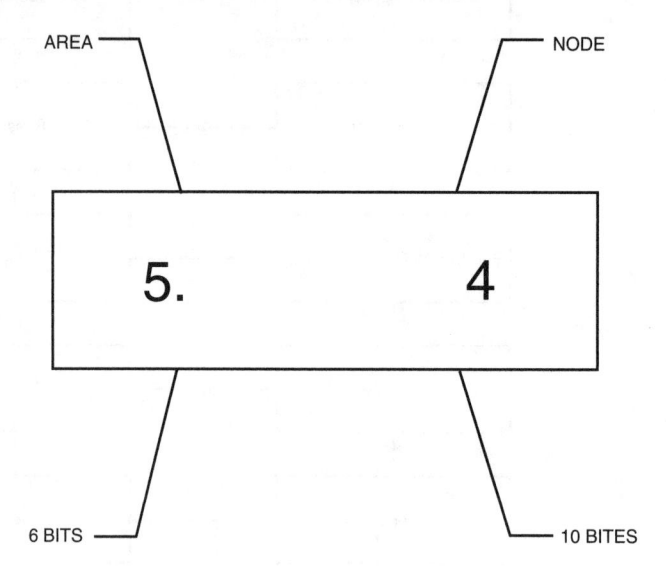

FIGURE 19.2

Dissection of a DECnet address.

```
         AREA                        NODE
    ┌─────────────────────────────────────┐
    │      5.                  4          │
    └─────────────────────────────────────┘
         6 BITS                   10 BITES
```

For example, if one DECnet network is composed of three areas (5, 6, and 7) and each area has four nodes (1, 2, 3, and 4), the network would be addressed as shown in Figure 19.3. Figure 19.3 illustrates a DECnet network with multiple area and node addresses.

Another feature of DECnet addressing that would need to be ported to IS-IS is the manner with which DECnet deals with media access control (MAC) addresses. Systems on a DECnet network have MAC addresses dynamically assigned to them based on their area/node address. For example, the MAC address for an end system (ES, covered later) with an area/node address of 4.2 would be AA-00-04-00-02-10. To arrive at this address DEC follows this convention:

1. First the DECnet address is converted to binary:

    4.2 = 000100.0000000010 (remember, the address format is 6 bits and 10 bits)

FIGURE 19.3

An addressed DECnet network.

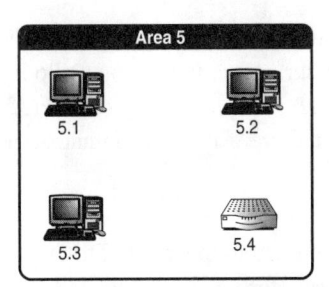

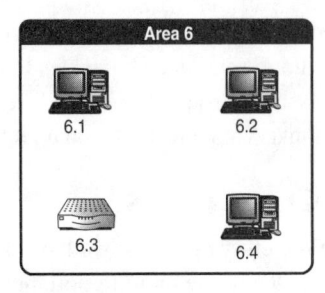

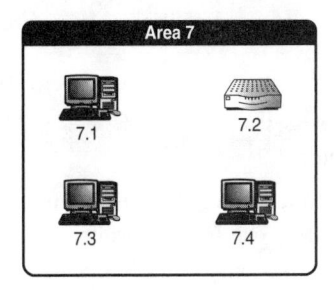

[Figure 19.3: Three areas labeled Area 5 (nodes 5.1, 5.2, 5.3, 5.4), Area 6 (nodes 6.1, 6.2, 6.3, 6.4), and Area 7 (nodes 7.1, 7.2, 7.3, 7.4).]

2. MAC addresses are essentially a series of 8-bit segments; therefore, our new binary area/node address needs to be divided into two 8-bit sections:

   00010000 00000010

3. These sections are then flipped:

   00000010 00010000

4. The flipped binary sections are then converted to hexadecimal format:

   02 10

5. Finally, the new hexadecimal pairs are appended to the DEC Ethernet MAC vendor code AA-00-04. (The null pair 00 is placed between the vendor code and the area/node to fill out the address.)

The end product is the MAC address AA-00-04-00-02-10.

> **Note**
>
> The MAC address, or burned-in address, is a (generally) static number assigned by an Ethernet vendor to ensure uniqueness in large networks. It is possible (however, rarely necessary) to change this number manually to fit the needs of certain networks.

These dynamic MAC addresses are used by DECnet (and IS-IS) both to route information and to send update packets to other nodes. For anyone who has experience with IP addressing or routing, the DECnet address scheme may seem (at first) to be a bit unconventional. This unconventional architecture is the key to understanding how IS-IS works.

DECnet Nodes

Like the other protocols we have discussed in this book, DECnet has its own set of terms. One of the more important terms for you to understand is *node*. A DECnet node can be defined as one of three entities:

- An end system (ES)
- A level 1 router (L1)
- A level 2 router (L2)

An end system is defined as anything that is not a router. The most common ES node is a user's PC; however, ESs can include printers, scanners, and other networked devices. The key to an ES is that it has only one addressable interface and can communicate only with level 1 routers. In a common network environment there should be more ESs than any other type of node on the network.

Logically, a PC on a network cannot send data to any other PC without some assistance. Whether the data flows through a hub or a router, another device is required to enable communication between more than two PCs. (The exception to this is when you want to provide communication between only two PCs. In that case you can connect the two devices with a crossover cable.) PCs do not provide routing capabilities, so they are ESs.

An end system can be considered the destination on the network. The majority of data being routed around the network either starts at or terminates at an ES. Even though they perform no routing duties, ESs are a very important part of the routing process in a DECnet environment.

The second category of node on a DECnet network is known as an L1 (level 1 router). A level 1 router is an intra-area router, which means that a level 1 router can route only within its own area. In routing terms, L1s have no knowledge of any network topology outside their own areas. This is a very important feature that was later ported to the IS-IS protocol. By not routing outside their own area, L1s dramatically cut down on the amount of network traffic in any given environment.

Broadcast messages can hinder a network's performance. By dictating that L1s can serve only one area each, DECnet eliminates the overflow of broadcast messages. When a router is charged with routing between multiple networks, complex factors need to be taken into consideration. If a router has multiple interfaces for multiple networks, it has to send multiple broadcast messages to complete certain tasks. For example, if a router has four network interfaces (A, B, C, and D) and receives a message for network C, the router generally sends a broadcast message to each interface. This message asks each interface what network it is on. Once the router receives an answer from network C, it sends the message along. This process can result in an abundance of broadcast messages.

The routers depicted in Figure 19.3 (area/node addresses 5.4, 6.3, and 7.2) would be considered level 1 routers. Being a level 1 router, router 5.4 can route data only around area 5.

Another important feature of L1 routers is in the way they are addressed by DECnet. Level 1 routers may have multiple interfaces, but they will have only one area/node address. This means that every node interface, or port, on an L1 router will generally have the same address. Therefore, if L1 5.4 has four ports and each is connected to a different ES, each port will be addressed as 5.4. To illustrate this, let's take a detailed look at area 5. Figure 19.4 illustrates the connections within area 5.

FIGURE 19.4

Router 5.4, with multiple connections and one address.

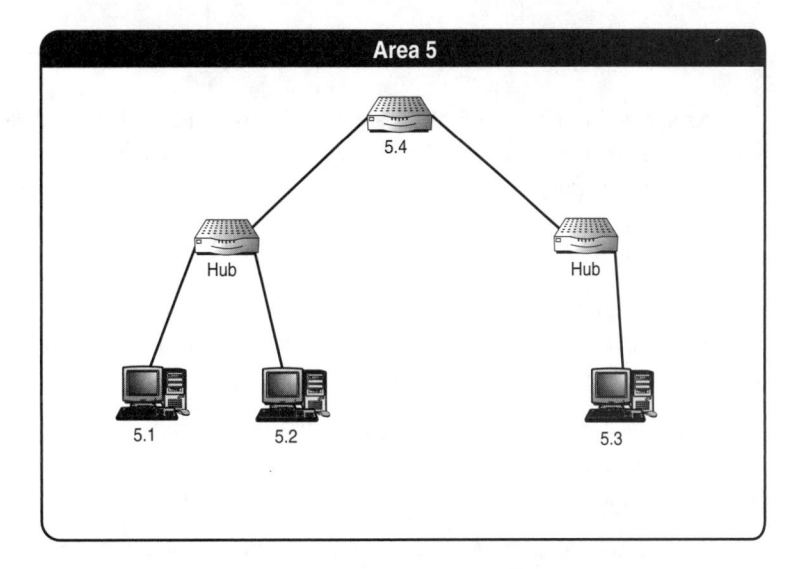

In Figure 19.4, notice how each hub in area 5 is connected to a different interface on router 5.4. However, each interface is still addressed as 5.4. Router 5.4 can communicate only to end systems 5.1, 5.2, and 5.3. If ES 5.2 wanted to send data to ES 7.4, that would require the services of level 2 routers.

Level 2 routers are routers that can communicate with other level 2 and level 1 routers in different areas. To transmit information between two different areas, you need at least two L2s. Figure 19.5 illustrates the different paths that information can take when traveling from system to system across two areas.

FIGURE 19.5

Data flow across areas.

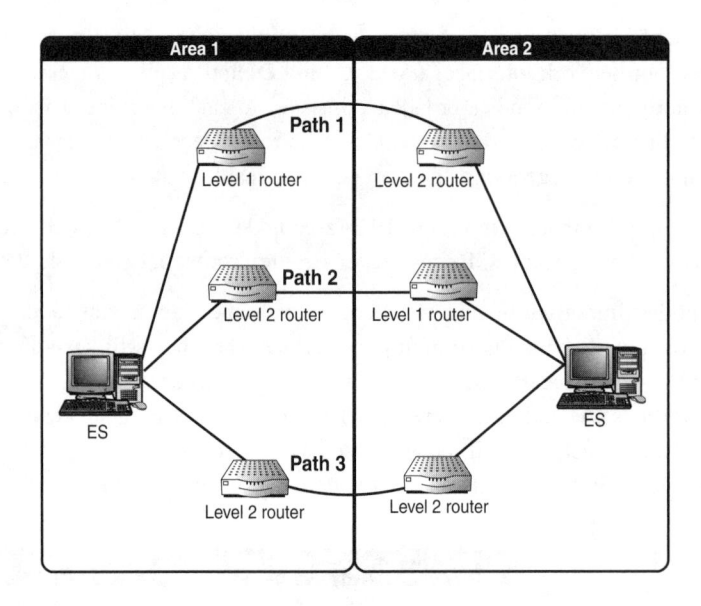

As shown in Figure 19.5, there are three possible paths that information can take when being routed from ES to ES across areas. The first option is to send the data from the ES to a level 1 router in the same area. The level 1 router then routes the packets to a level 2 router in the target area. The level 2 router can then pass the packets to the intended recipient.

The second option is essentially option 1 in reverse. The data leaves the ES and is sent to an L2 in the ES's home area. The L2 then forwards the data to a level 1 router in the target area. Finally, the data is sent along to the receiving ES.

The final option is to have the data be transmitted from the ES to an L2 in the same area. The L2 then forwards the information to another L2 in the intended recipient's area. The recipient L2 then sends the data along to the final ES.

As you can see, level 2 routers can also interact with end systems (giving them the added capabilities of a level 1 router). Also, like level 1 routers, a level 2 router has only one address, which is shared across all of its interfaces. Figure 19.6 illustrates a fully addressed, routable, DECnet network with three areas.

DECnet Routing Basics

The precursor to IS-IS was DECnet Phase IV's DRP (DECnet Routing Protocol). DRP worked by routing packets between systems in an orderly manner. At the heart of DRP is the hello message (HM). Hello messages are Ethernet packets that are routinely sent from system to system as a way of updating each to the status of the others.

Learning IS-IS

FIGURE 19.6

A routable DECnet network.

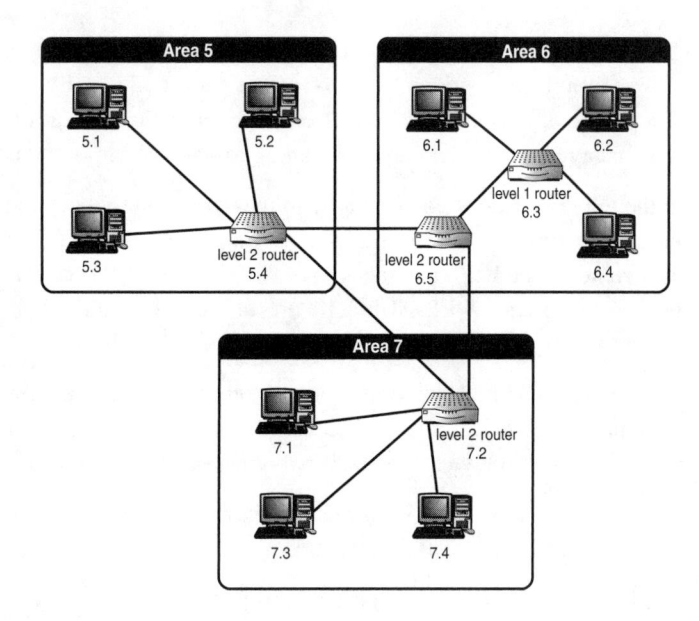

By passing around these hello messages, routers can learn the status of the links and routers around them. An ES sends a hello message to any L1 or L2 it interfaces with. Figure 19.7 illustrates the life cycle of an intra-area HM.

FIGURE 19.7

The life cycle of a hello message.

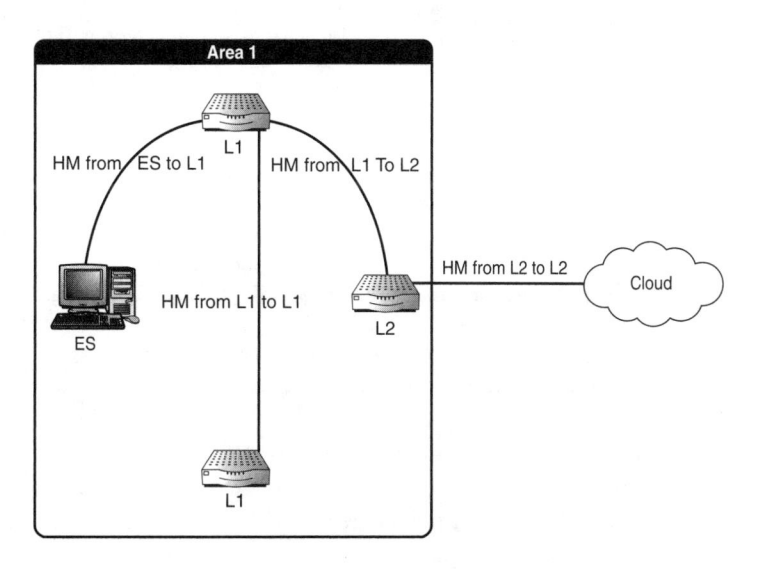

An ES sends a hello message to an L1. This hello message signals to the L1 that the ES is functioning on the network and able to receive packets. The L1 uses this information to build a picture of its home area. By assembling the hello messages from the ESs and the other L1s, any particular L1 can create an up-to-date picture of the network's topology.

Even though the L1 does not send a hello message directly back to an ES, the ES listens to the L1-to-L1 messages to formulate its own picture of the current network topology. Level 1 routers send hello messages to other L1s and L2s. These HMs serve the same purpose as those sent by ESs. The L1 alerts all other L1s and L2s in the same area as to its current state on the network.

Level 2 routers send hello messages only to other level 2 routers (remember, L1s and ESs can have knowledge only of their own areas, and because L2s have routing information for other areas, they cannot share hello messages with either).

End systems, like L1s and L2s, have steps they must follow when sending information onto a DECnet network. These steps are:

1. Most protocols (DECnet being no different) allow PCs to keep a routing cache. An ES always checks its own routing cache before releasing a packet onto the network. This routing cache contains a table relating a destination address with the address of the router that can get the packet there.

2. If the ES cannot find the router it needs in its cache, it adds the destination MAC address (see the formula in "DECnet Areas and Nodes") to the packet and forwards it to the closest L1 (or L2) router.

> **Note** A routing cache is a portion of memory on a PC that has been set aside for storing the addresses of devices that packets are frequently sent to. In other words, every time a PC successfully sends a packet to another device, the destination address and the address of the router that the packet had to be sent through are recorded in the PC's routing cache. Then the next time a packet needs to be sent to the same destination, the PC needs only to look in its cache to find out where to forward the data.

3. The receiving router digests the destination information and, using its routing table (formulated from various hello messages), forwards the packet to its final target. If that target is in a different area, the L1 sends the packet to an L2 that can reach the foreign area. In some cases this process may involve more than one L2.

If a packet needs to be sent from an ES across multiple areas, it will first reach an L2 in its own area. Once the data reaches this L2, the router looks in its routing table for the location of the L2 attached to the target area. (Because level 2 routers can share information across areas, the L2 in the home area should know the location of the L2 in the target area regardless of the number of areas between them). The data can then be forwarded along to its intended recipient.

DECnet Phase V

When DECnet Phase V came along, DEC decided to adopt the OSI model as a base for its protocol. Remember, because all phases of DECnet are backward compatible, DECnet Phase V had to adhere to both OSI and DNA standards.

Because the two architectures were very similar, DEC was able to port DECnet successfully to the OSI model. However, they now needed a routing protocol that could route in either OSI or DEN architectures and route the DECnet protocol (as well as IP). The solution was IS-IS. The Intermediate System to Intermediate System routing protocol, an OSI-compliant routing protocol, was adopted as the routing protocol of choice for DECnet Phase V networks.

How IS-IS Relates to CLNP

Before DECnet Phase V was being developed, ISO was developing the Connectionless Network Protocol. CLNP is a pure OSI routed protocol that allows for the connectionless transfer of data between two end systems. CLNP is quick, is relatively limited in size (using little network overhead), and is the OSI equivalent of IP.

> **Note** A connectionless protocol, as opposed to a connection-oriented one, does not require the acknowledgment of packet receipt. Because of this, these protocols tend to be faster than their connection-oriented counterparts (however, they are also considered somewhat unreliable). IP is a connectionless protocol.

When DEC began developing DECnet Phase V OSI/DNA, they needed a fully OSI-compliant routed protocol to work on the third layer of the OSI model. The protocol they were looking for was CLNP. However, there was one drawback to using CLNP in the backward-compatible, OSI- and DNA-based DECnet environment. At that time there was no routing protocol flexible enough to handle the mixed architectures of OSI and DNA yet robust enough to work in a large connectionless environment.

> **Note:** The third layer of both the OSI and DNA models is the layer used for routing network data. In the OSI model this is the network layer; in DNA this is the routing layer. Such similarities made the transition from DNA to OSI fairly easy for DECnet.

This is where the two histories of IS-IS merge. DEC needed a flexible routing protocol to route the new OSI-compliant DECnet Phase V. ISO had already developed the routed protocol used in the connectionless environment. So DEC helped ISO develop IS-IS in the DECnet OSI (CLNP) environment.

> **Note:** Keep in mind that a routing protocol is the protocol used by routers and other connectivity devices to carry routed protocols across the network media. Routed protocols (such as IP and IPX) are used to encapsulate data for transmission to other devices.

IS-IS proved to be ideal for routing the OSI and DNA networks. ISO developed IS-IS as a quick, portable link state routing protocol for CLNP. As a routing protocol, IS-IS filled the gap in the DECnet Phase V environment. Because CLNP was OSI based and, by definition, connectionless, with minimal adaptation IS-IS would be able to route IP also (keep in mind that IP is also a connectionless protocol).

There was some discussion (every once in a while the subject still comes up) about making CLNP the default protocol of the Internet. However, after a couple of years it became clear that IP has a stronghold on the Internet. Therefore, support for IP was added to IS-IS, completing the protocol.

IS-IS does not support IP by itself. When ISO started to rework IS-IS to support IP, many people were still using it to route pure OSI protocols. For this reason, to distinguish the two implementations of IS-IS, the newer version would be officially named Integrated IS-IS. Integrated IS-IS offers simultaneous support for multiple routed protocols, such as CLNP and IP.

IS-IS Link State Routing

Routing protocols are separated into categories based on the algorithms they use to route data. One common category is link state. Almost every router on the market today can use one of the many link state protocols to move information around a network. Both IS-IS and Integrated IS-IS are link state routing protocols.

Routers running link state protocols update each other periodically. These updates, known as LSAs (link state advertisements), let each router know the status (state) of every other router (link) in the environment. These updates have their advantages and disadvantages; however, before we discuss them, let's define what sets IS-IS and other link state protocols apart from other routing protocols.

IS-IS, like all link state protocols, goes through a process known as flooding, in which a router sends a large amount of LSAs (Link State Advertisements) across the network. The neighboring routers receive these advertisements, update their own tables, and send the updates to their neighboring routers. Figure 19.8 shows an example of an LSA.

FIGURE 19.8

A sample LSA update.

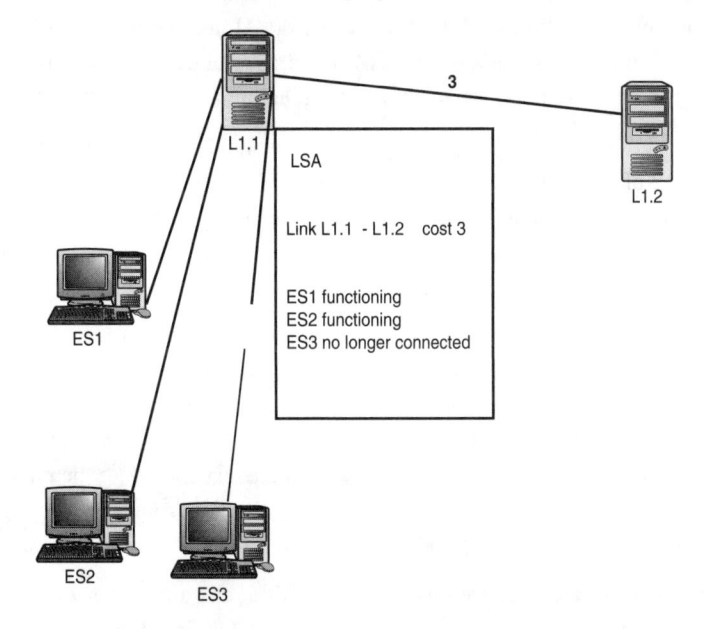

Flooding is the necessary process IS-IS routers go through to build an accurate picture of the environment around them. (A router uses the information contained in the LSA to create a dynamic table. The router then runs its routing algorithms against this table to calculate the shortest path for every packet.) The amount of time an LSA flood lasts depends on the number of updates, or changes, in the routing environment, as well as the convergence time.

> **Note** In routing, convergence is the amount of time it takes for routers to agree on a particular set of changes. In other words, it is the time the routers need to sync up with each other (resulting in all routers working from the same picture of the environment).

Flooding, however, can cause traffic havoc on some networks. The heartiest networking environments may not feel the effects of a large-scale convergence; however, most networks will experience some network latency during a flood. The environments that will be affected the most by a flood are larger networks that already have some bandwidth issues.

Larger networks with plenty of bandwidth, and smaller networks with fewer routers, may not have much trouble during an LSA flood. Large networks will have plenty of available bandwidth to handle both LSAs and normal daily traffic, and in the smaller networks there are not enough routers to generate a massive amount of advertisements.

In a network of any size, having enough available bandwidth before you implement IS-IS is one of the keys to getting through an LSA flood with no noticeable latency. If you are contemplating implementing IS-IS on an existing network, make sure you have the bandwidth to deal with LSA floods. This will save you many headaches down the road.

Floods actually affect networks in two ways. The first, most obvious way is by drowning the network in LSA packets (also known as LSPs). The LSA updates cause a large amount of traffic, and "normal" network data may have trouble getting through. Keep in mind that every router on the network needs to tell its neighboring routers (in the same area) what changes were made to its table. Then the routers that received the LSA information need to send out more LSAs telling everyone about the changes they just received from the first round of LSAs, and so on until every router has the same picture of the network (that's a lot of packets).

Another drawback caused by LSA flooding is the amount of memory and processing power needed by the router to digest the updates. Depending on the number of LSAs on the network and the number of updates in each one, a router may devote the majority of its available memory and processor time to crunching LSAs (in an attempt to converge as quickly as possible). LSA packets always have (processing) priority over a routed protocol packet. Therefore, those network packets that do make it through the traffic jam of LSAs may not get processed.

The reason a link state router will always process an LSA before a routed protocol packet is simple. You want the environment to converge as quickly as possible; therefore, the more quickly an LSA can be processed and applied, the more quickly a router can resume its normal daily function.

As far as protocol downsides go, this one really isn't that bad. Generally, link state protocols have shorter convergence times than other protocol types. Therefore, the network latency experienced during a flood may not last very long. This can be very good news for administrators implementing IS-IS on a larger network with minimal bandwidth.

Controlling Link State Floods

IS-IS does have a few built-in mechanisms for controlling the amount of LSAs sent out during a flood. The first control is a form of poison path. That is, an IS-IS router can never send an LSA out on the same link it received it on. This keeps the same update information from looping infinitely between two routers. Figure 19.9 illustrates this concept.

FIGURE 19.9

An IS-IS router sending and receiving LSA updates.

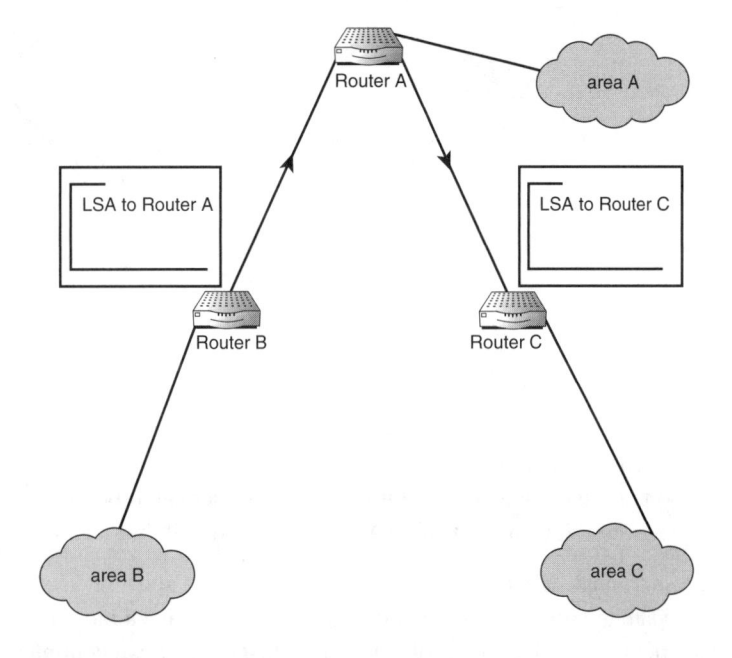

In Figure 19.9, notice that router A received an update from router B on port 1. L1A used that information to update its routing table and sent its own LSA to router C on port 2. However, router A did not send its own updated information back out on port 1 to router B. Because router B started the flood, and the only information in the update pertained to its own links, it doesn't need to receive router A's updated table information.

If we were to follow this example to the end of the update flood, we would see that router C would then block the path between router A and itself. Then any routers receiving an update from router C would block their ports as well. By blocking (also known as killing or poisoning) the link between two routers after an update has been sent, IS-IS ensures that the minimum amount of LSAs are flooded onto the network during an update.

However, what if the router is using multiple ports? Does the theory still hold true? Figure 19.10 illustrates a router with multiple ports to receive the same update. How would the router handle this information?

FIGURE 19.10

A router with multiple receiving ports.

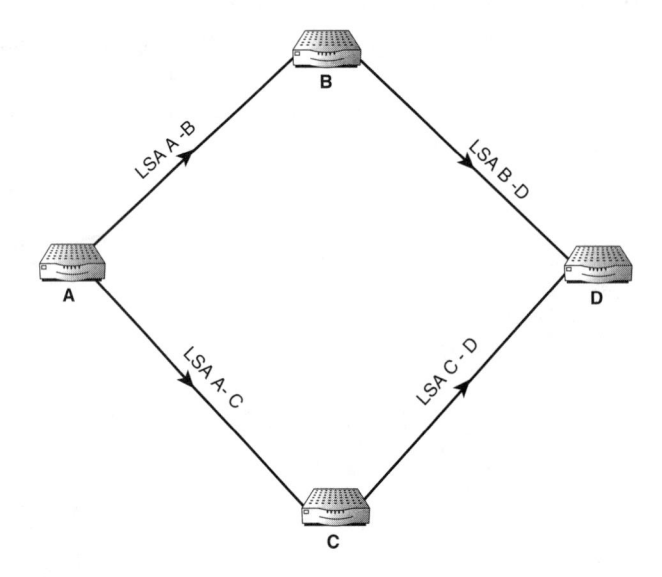

In Figure 19.10, router A sends its update to routers B and C. Both of these routers are connected to router D. So what happens when router D receives two LSAs on two different ports for the same update? Obviously the router can process only one of the updates. However, will it then send an LSA to the router that it didn't receive the update from first?

The short answer is that router D processes the first update it receives, but does not send an update to either router. To understand why, let's take a look inside an LSA packet. Two fields in the LSA control whether an IS-IS router can continue receiving updates and whether the updates are valid: *remaining life* and *sequence*.

The remaining-life field is a time setting used by the router after the LSA is processed. When the router examines the LSA, a timer is set corresponding to the value indicated in the remaining life field. Then, until that timer expires, the router cannot process an LSA pertaining to the link(s) involved in the last LSA.

For example, referring back to Figure 19.10, router D receives an LSA from router B stating that the link between router A and router B is down. Router D processes the LSA, sets the remaining-life timer, and updates its table. However, before router C receives the same update, it sends out its normal periodic LSA. This LSA (in route to router D) still states that the link between router A and router B is fine.

Because the remaining-life timer has not yet expired, router D (recognizing that the LSA pertains to a previous update) ignores the update. Eventually router C gets the updated LSA, and convergence can occur. Also, the remaining-life timer restricts router D from sending any updates pertaining to the link between routers A and B until it expires. In this way, routers are not needlessly receiving conflicting information about a link's status, and they do not send out multiple LSAs for the same problem.

The second control field in an LSA packet is the sequence field, which is used by the receiving router to identify the update contained in an LSA. A router does not process any LSA update that is out of sequence. By using the remaining life and sequence fields, IS-IS can control the sometimes-overwhelming LSA floods.

Another piece of good news for network administrators (who are adept at keeping network changes to a minimum) is that they too can control LSA flooding, to an extent. The control method implemented on link state protocols (to limit the number of unnecessary floods) is as follows: Keep the number of administrative network changes to a minimum.

Although this does not eliminate floods altogether, it does minimize their frequency. LSA floods are sent out periodically to detect nonadministrative changes, and they are triggered after a change. So by limiting the administrative changes, the number of floods can be reduced. This may not be a very practical way to keep traffic down, but it is effective.

An administrator really has no authority over the periodic LSA updates; they are going to happen no matter what. However, administrative updates are triggered by a change in the networking environment. This change could be the reassignment of a metric, a down line, or anything that would change a possible path for data. Figure 19.11 illustrates the events leading up to an LSA flood.

Notice that all of the routers stayed online through the process shown in Figure 19.11; however, an update was triggered anyway. What triggered the update was the changing of the metric assigned to the link between router A and router C. This administrator (arbitrarily) assigned metric is the key calculation used by IS-IS's routing algorithm to figure out the shortest path between two objects.

FIGURE 19.11

The start of an LSA flood.

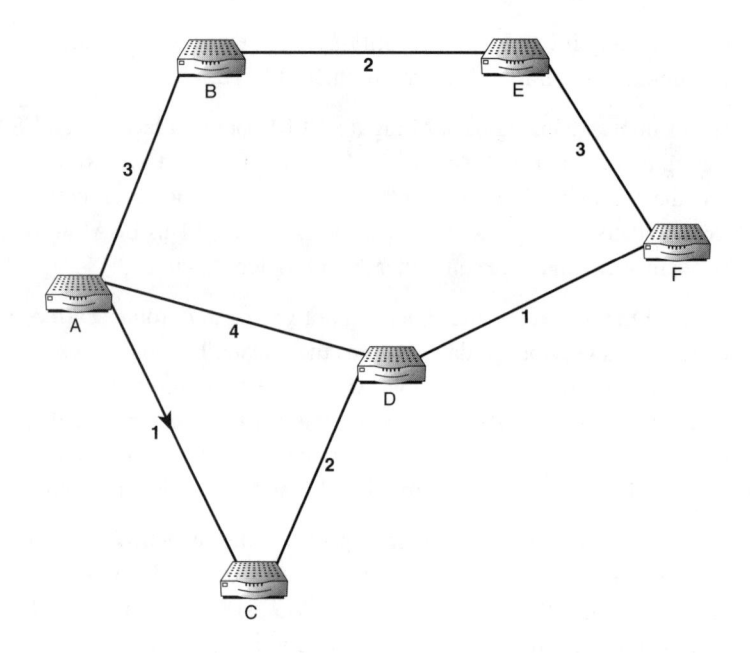

IS-IS Metrics and Algorithms

The protocols installed on your router do not automatically know the shortest route to every possible location on the network. Rather, they must consider certain elements of the environment; then these elements must be acted upon to produce a definite result. Metrics and algorithms help IS-IS decide which path is the shortest to a particular destination.

Metrics are the network variables used in deciding what path is shortest. For link state algorithms these metrics are values assigned by a network administrator. Many routing protocols use multiple metrics including bandwidth, priority, cost, and other dynamically or statically assigned factors. IS-IS simplifies the process by using only one metric: cost.

> **Note**
>
> There are actually three other "optional" metrics that can be defined by the administrator for a line. However, the current implementation of IS-IS recognizes only the default metric of cost. The other metrics are:
> - Delay—the amount of delay on a particular line
> - Expense—the value associated with operating a particular line
> - Error—the relative number of errors associated with a particular line
>
> Expressing values for these metrics will not affect your algorithm in any way. Future versions of IS-IS may make use of these values.

In an IS-IS environment the most important job of an administrator is to assign a cost metric to every link for every router. Figure 19.12 illustrates an IS-IS network with all of the metrics assigned.

FIGURE 19.12

An IS-IS network showing all assigned metrics.

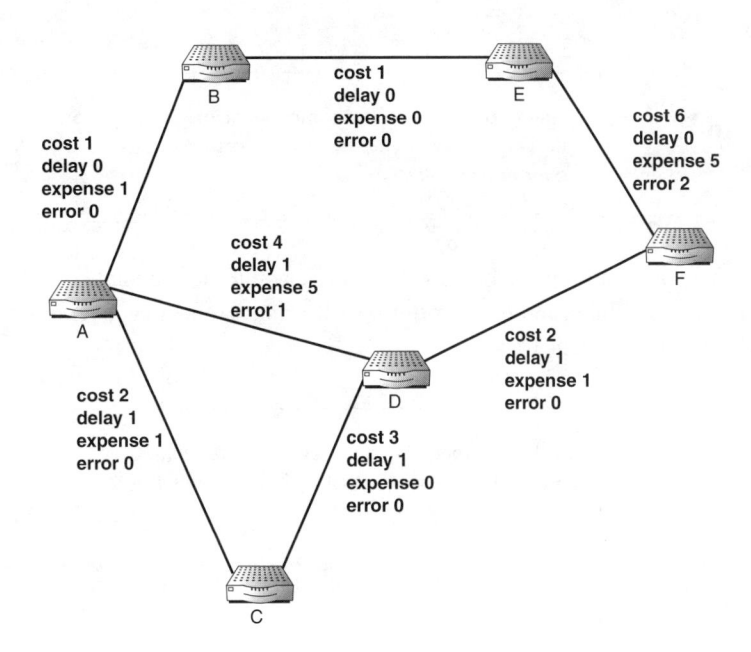

```
            B ──cost 1──── E
           /  delay 0        \
          /   expense 0       \
   cost 1/    error 0      cost 6
   delay 0                  delay 0
   expense 1                expense 5
   error 0                  error 2
        /                      \
       A ─── cost 4 ──────      F
        \    delay 1      \    /
         \   expense 5     \  /
          \  error 1        \/
           \                D
    cost 2  \              / cost 2
    delay 1  \            /  delay 1
    expense 1 \          /   expense 1
    error 0    \        /    error 0
                \  cost 3
                 \ delay 1
                  \expense 0
                   \error 0
                    C
```

As far as an IS-IS administrator is concerned, the metric of cost is totally arbitrary. There is no formula or science to choosing a cost for a particular link. Here are some guidelines to keep in mind when assigning a cost to a link:

- When IS-IS applies its algorithm to all of the metrics on the network, the *lowest* metrics form the shortest path.
- Reliable lines, such as those that are newer or not prone to interference (such as fiber), should always have a lower cost.
- Less expensive lines (such as those owned by the company installing the routers) should always be assigned a lower cost than leased lines such as ISDN.
- Higher-bandwidth lines (such as T3s) should be assigned a lower cost than a low-bandwidth line.

The assigned cost metrics, whatever you decide they should be, will govern what path is chosen as the shortest path between two endpoints. Before you go off and assign metrics to all of your links, however, be aware that there is a limit to the cost metric.

A cost for a specific link cannot exceed 64. Any line assigned a cost of 65 is not recognized as a valid path. However, there is no law against using duplicate values for different links. So if you have a router with more than 64 ports, you may have to double up on costs.

> **Note** Any two links with the same metric originating from the same router weigh equally when run against the algorithm. In this case IS-IS distributes packets over either link.

The other limit placed on the cost metric applies to the total cost of a path (once it is calculated by the routing algorithm). IS-IS cannot route data over any path that has a total cost greater than 1024.

> **Note** If the numbers 64 and 1024 sound familiar, they correlate directly to the amount of memory used by IS-IS to store the routing information.

Some planning is required before you establish your IS-IS costs, especially on a larger network. Fully map out your routes and links before you begin implementing your IS-IS routers. Then assign all of your values on paper, add them up, and confirm that they are in line. When you have done this, you can implement your routers and let the algorithm take over.

IS-IS Addressing, Areas, and Domains

IS-IS, like every other protocol, addresses devices based on their location within an environment. IS-IS identifies devices using a two-part location identifier. These identifiers specify the areas and domains a device can belong to. To understand IS-IS addressing, let's define the divisions of IS-IS networks: the areas and the domains.

By dividing IS-IS networks into areas and domains, administrators have greater control over the flow of data in an environment. This concept can be better visualized in terms of a state road map. Apply the following logic to networking, and you see the reasoning behind assigning areas and domains to IS-IS environments.

Let's use the state of Texas as an example. There are hundreds of thousands of roads and highways in Texas. Each road has a name assigned to it, and each highway has a number. Because there are multiple cities in the state, road names can be reused and recycled in different cities, and county highway numbers can be reused between counties.

The cities serve as geographic markers within the counties (and the counties within the state). For example, if you are looking for a road in Dallas, not only do you immediately know what part of the county you need to be in; you also know the general part of the state as well. Counties and cities help keep the problem of finding geographic locations from getting out of control.

However, if you took away the cites and counties, finding your way around the state would become next to impossible. Try to find 123 Main Street with no designation as to the city or county. It becomes almost impossible. Not only would every city road and county highway need to be uniquely named; you might never find them once you were done. For example, if you were looking for a particular road, and there were no cities or counties to reference, you would have to comb the entire state looking for that one road. Even if you had a road map, not knowing the general area to start in would make the task very daunting.

IS-IS domains are the equivalent to the counties in a state, and IS-IS areas are the cities. These areas and domains aid the routers in finding ESs quickly, especially in large environments.

IS-IS Areas

An IS-IS area is a single set of ESs and ISs. That is, a network of ESs (end systems) and ISs (intermediate systems) that all share the same area number or ID is considered one area. Figure 19.13 illustrates an IS-IS area.

FIGURE 19.13
An IS-IS area.

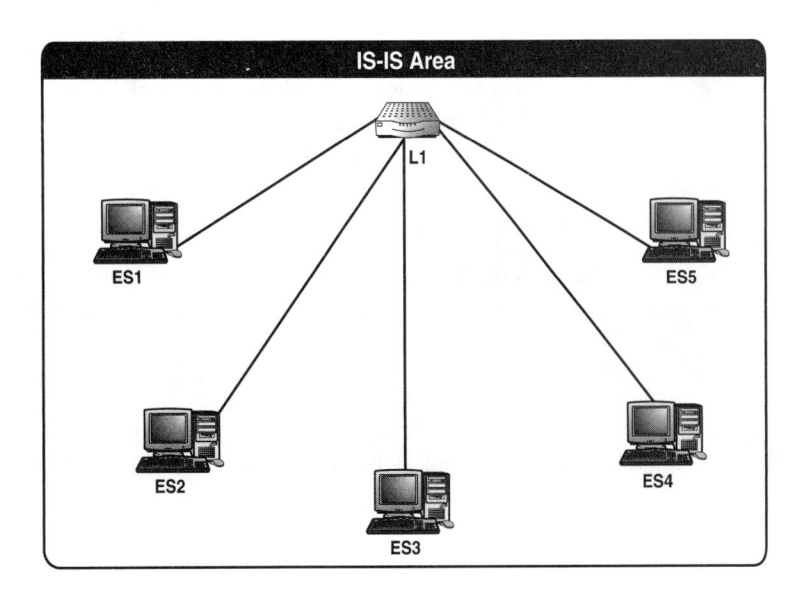

> **Note**
>
> The concept of IS-IS areas and domains is a direct reference back to the DECnet Phase IV architecture. All DECnet networks are divided into areas.
>
> If you are familiar with IP networks and IP subnetting, the concept of IS-IS areas and domains will not be that hard to follow. However, areas and domains do not correlate directly to their IP cousins. Rather, it is more accurate to say that IS-IS areas and domains together are equivalent to an IP subnet. IS-IS areas can be thought of as sub-subnets.

Areas tend to be fairly small and self-contained. A network architect would not necessarily design an area in the same fashion as he or she would design an IP subnet. IS-IS areas are not as general as IP subnets. An area is very localized.

Routing within areas, covered in detail in the "IS-IS Routing" section in this chapter, is accomplished by L1s (level 1 routers). Just as in DECnet Phase IV, L1s are used for intra-area data routing. L1s are the major interior routing devices of IS-IS areas. Keeping true to their DECnet counterparts, level 1 routers cannot route outside of their own local area. For that reason, a group of areas has routing requirements greater than the sum of its parts. (In other words, just by putting a bunch of areas in a room, you are not guaranteeing that they will communicate with each other. In fact, they won't.) It is because of this communication barrier that groups of related areas are considered domains and have different requirements from the smaller, more localized areas.

In IS-IS terms, a domain is a group of areas bridged by a pair of level 2 routers. Only level 2 routers can form a domain. One area with a level 1 router connected to a level 2 router (that also bridges another area) is not considered a domain. Figure 19.14 illustrates a valid IS-IS domain. Notice the two L2s with a backbone running between them. The presence of this L2 pair (with areas on either side) forms the IS-IS domain. Figure 19.15 shows an invalid IS-IS domain.

Having the correct area/domain layout on paper before you begin planning your IS-IS network can make all of the difference in the world. If you inadvertently end up with an area/domain configuration like the one in Figure 19.15, your environment will not route correctly.

As with every protocol, just having the correct physical layout is not enough. The protocol address must correspond to the physical topology. IS-IS's address scheme is a mixture of pure OSI routing address conventions and the DECnet Phase IV area/node MAC addresses.

FIGURE 19.14

A correctly formed IS-IS domain.

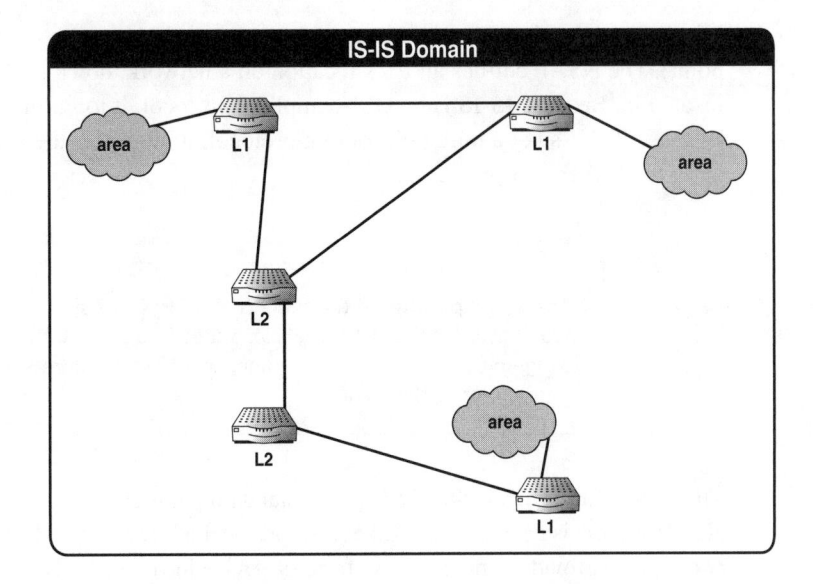

FIGURE 19.15

An incorrectly formed IS-IS domain.

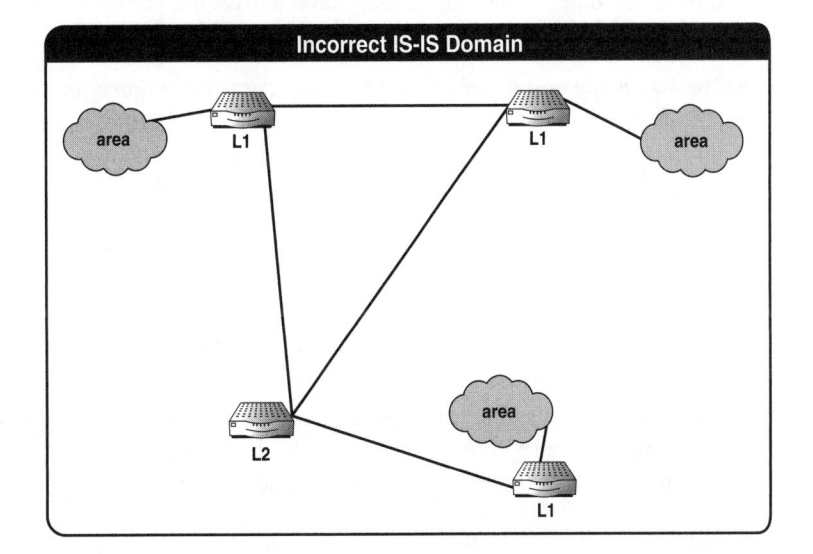

IS-IS Addresses

IS-IS's address scheme is derived from that of OSI and DECnet Phase IV. This was not done by accident. Combining the two architectures was a necessary task to ensure the interoperability of IS-IS and the DNA-based DECnet. This allows the protocol to easily route data on multiple platforms, for multiple routed protocols. IS-IS addresses are also key to defining IS-IS areas and routing domains.

Pure OSI protocols utilize an address known as an NSAP (network service access point). The NSAP defines an ES's location on a network, down to the area that it is located in. Because IS-IS is an OSI-compliant protocol, it too utilizes NSAP addresses. Because IS-IS is not a pure OSI routing protocol, it interprets the address a little differently than other OSI protocols.

> **Note** The actual purpose of the NSAP is to address the specific point in the network layer (of the OSI model) on a specific device. Rather than arbitrarily assigning an address to a machine, OSI chose to address the information entry point to the device.

The format for device addresses is pretty standard among network protocols, and the NSAP address is no exception. Like most protocol addresses, an NSAP is divided into two parts to provide a more precise form of device location. An NSAP is divided into an IDP (initial domain part) and a DSP (domain-specific part). The combination of these two parts determines the location of the point of entry for the device's network layer.

The IDP is the portion of the address that refers to the domain a device belongs to. The IDP itself also contains two parts, the AFI (authority and format identifier) and the IDI (initial domain identifier). The AFI specifies the authority assigning the address to the domain. The IDI specifies general information about the domain.

The second part of the NSAP, the DSP (domain-specific part) contains the literal address information. The DSP holds the address of the domain that a particular device belongs to. This is true for all pure OSI protocols; however, IS-IS is not a pure OSI protocol. IS-IS divides the NSAP address into two main portions: the area address and the system ID (a third part attached to the end of the NSAP is the address selector and is almost always set to 0). The area address, which incorporates the IDP of the NSAP, specifies the area (within a domain) to which the device belongs, whereas the system ID (much like a MAC address) addresses the actual device.

NSAP Area Address

The area address, composed of the NSAP IDP, indicates the area a device belongs to. All devices in a specific area have the same area address. The administrator assigns this address, consisting of at least one hexadecimal octet of data, at design time.

In an environment with multiple areas, the area address is very important to the routing of the network. All ESs and L1s in one area have the same area address, allowing for the correct identification of all systems in the area by extra-area devices.

NSAP System ID

The system ID identifies a system with an area. Just as the DECnet Phase IV systems use the area/node ID to modify the MAC address, IS-IS systems use a modified MAC address to create the system ID of the NSAP. The device-specific system ID is never shared or duplicated on an IS-IS network. For this reason, the system ID stands as a reliable marker for locating a system in an area.

IS-IS Packets

IS-IS routes data through the networking environment through the use of IS-IS packets. These packets encapsulate the data that IS-IS is routing around the network. Keep in mind, though, that not all packets are meant for shuttling data. Some packets are for the internal use of IS-IS devices. These packets help IS-IS determine the configuration and topology of devices connected to an IS-IS environment.

There are three types of packets used in the IS-IS environment: hello messages (HMs), link state packets (LSPs), and sequence number packets (SNPs). This section discusses how IS-IS uses each of these packet types to help devices route data from system to system.

If you were to dissect any packet, you could divide it into three major sections: the header, the data, and the checksum. Figure 19.16 illustrates a typical packet.

FIGURE 19.16

A typical packet.

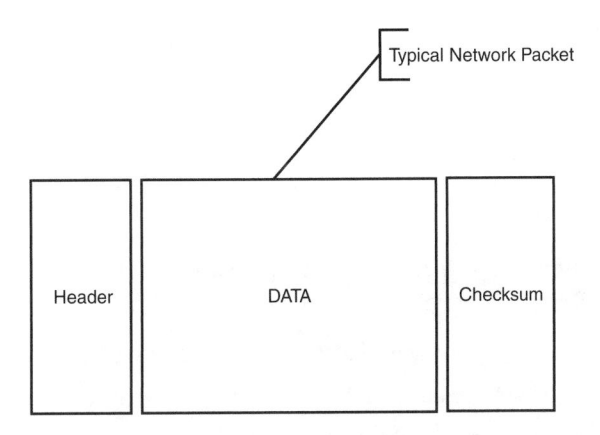

Most packet headers are fixed in length, depending on packet type. Most packet headers (in Ethernet or IS-IS packets, for example) are 8 bytes long, whereas others vary. In some cases, there may be a header length indicator after the header. The header length indicator tells the recipient device how long the header is. This lets the device easily determine when the header ends and the data begins.

The data portion of a packet is just that—the data that one system needs to send to another. This portion of the packet can vary in length depending on the amount of information being sent.

The checksum is usually the last part of a packet. The checksum represents the contents of the packet in a compact manner that the device can duplicate. A device can determine whether a packet is corrupt or incomplete by recalculating the checksum from the received data and comparing the result with the received checksum value.

All IS-IS packets follow the same basic format. An IS-IS packet consists of a header portion, a data portion, and an extended data portion. Figure 19.17 illustrates an IS-IS packet.

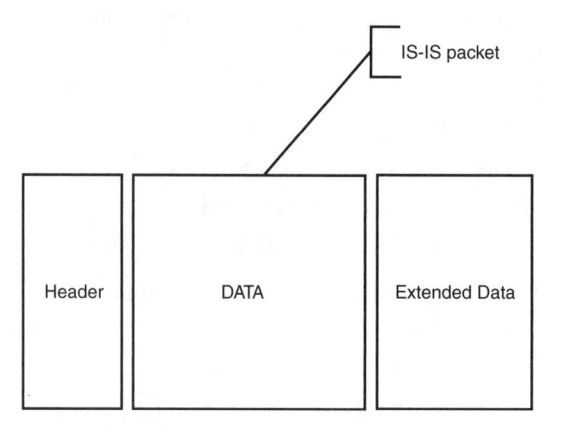

FIGURE 19.17

An IS-IS packet.

The 8-byte header is the part of the packet that we want to look at here. The header, regardless of the IS-IS packet type (HM, LSP, or SNP), is divided into eight 1-byte fields. These fields supply the recipient device with all of the information it needs to process the packet correctly.

Figure 19.18 illustrates an IS-IS packet with header information. The eight fields of an IS-IS header are:

- Protocol identifier—Identifies the packet as an IS-IS packet
- Length—Holds a value equal to the length of the header
- Version (1)—Specifies the version of IS-IS
- ID length—Specifies the length of the ID portion of the recipient's address
- Packet type—Designates the packet as being either LSP, HM, or SNP
- Version (2)—Restates the version of IS-IS being used

- Reserved—Reserved for future use
- MAA (maximum address area)—Specifies the maximum number of addresses in the current area

FIGURE 19.18

An IS-IS packet with header information.

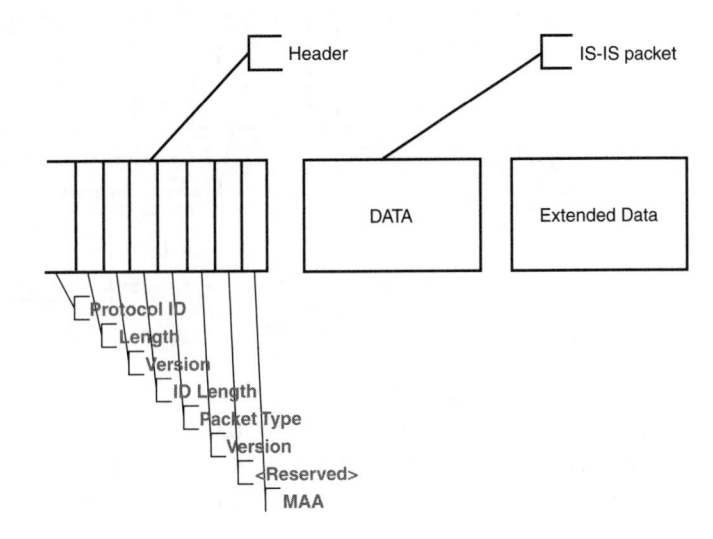

This packet format is the same for every IS-IS packet. The fields following the header, however, vary depending on the packet type. The fields after the header are the actual data being sent from system to system.

Each of the three IS-IS packet types also contains its unique fields. In the following sections we will examine them.

Hello Messages

Hello messages are used by IS-IS devices to alert others as to their functional presence on the network. Figure 19.19 illustrates a full hello message packet with header information. An IS-IS hello message has the following fields:

- Source ID—System ID of the device sending the message
- Manual address—The address of any manually entered area
- IS type—Indicates whether the IS sending the update is an L1 or L2
- Priority—Indicates the administrator-assigned priority of the router
- LAN ID—Specifies the LAN ID
- Designated IS system ID—Indicates the system ID of the designated IS

FIGURE 19.19

IS-IS hello message.

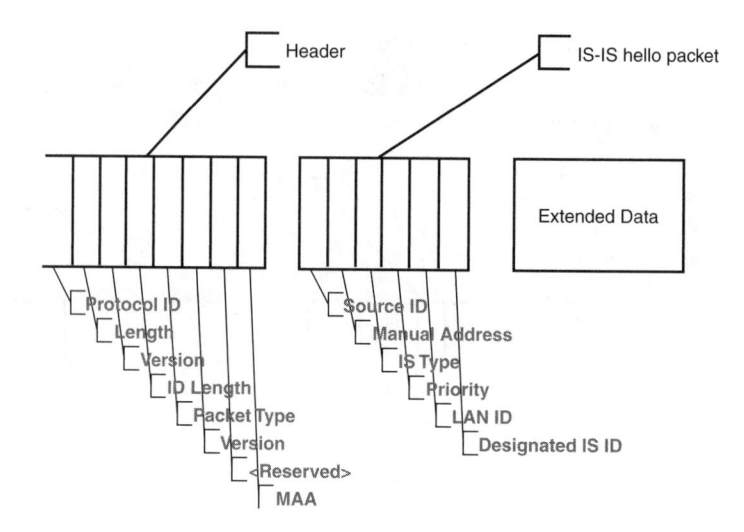

Header fields: Protocol ID, Length, Version, ID Length, Packet Type, Version, <Reserved>, MAA

IS-IS hello packet fields: Source ID, Manual Address, IS Type, Priority, LAN ID, Designated IS ID, Extended Data

An IS sends out a hello message periodically to inform the other ISs on the network that they are in a state to receive information. The packet also lets the recipient IS know the administrator-assigned priority, the IS type, and the address of the IS sending the hello message.

When an IS receives a hello message, it replies with a hello message of its own. This confirms that both links are functioning and no changes have occurred in the networking environment. After the functionality of the link between the two devices has been confirmed, the two ISs add each other's information to their lists of neighboring ISs.

Link State Packets

LSPs (link state packets) are the core of all link state protocols. The LSP is the delivery device for all routing updates. During a link state flood, all of the ISs on a network release LSPs to update the routing tables of the other routers in the environment.

An LSP must contain all of the pertinent information a router would need to move data correctly from one IS to another. Without correct and timely information, data released onto the network may never reach its intended recipient. The fields within an IS-IS LSP are:

- Source ID—System ID of the device sending the message
- Manual address—The address of any manually entered area
- IS type—Indicates whether the IS sending the update is an L1 or L2
- System ID (with cost)—Contains all of the sending IS's neighbors and their configured costs

- Designated IS system ID—Indicates the system ID of the designated IS
- Static adjacencies—Contains all of the statically configured ISs and their costs

There are only two field differences between the IS-IS hello message and the IS-IS LSP. However, those two differences are the difference between a routing network and a stagnant one. The LSP contains fields for routing table updates. When an IS receives an LSP, it inserts the sending device's system ID into its own routing table. Then it appends to that entry a list of that IS's direct neighbors and their costs.

> **Note:** Keep in mind that because L1s can have knowledge only of their local area, any foreign information that may be received is discarded.

After the LSPs are received and digested, the IS runs Dijkstra's algorithm against the new data to calculate the new optimal paths. Figure 19.20 illustrates a link state packet.

FIGURE 19.20
A link state packet.

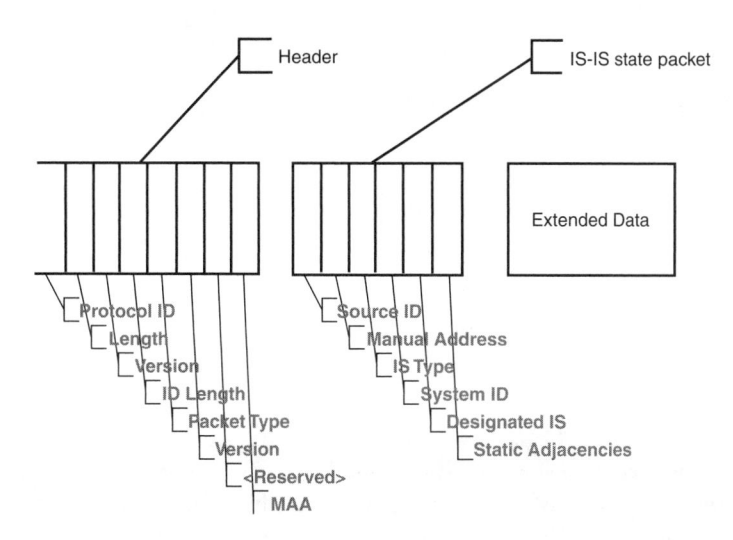

Header fields: Protocol ID, Length, Version, ID Length, Packet Type, Version, <Reserved>, MAA

IS-IS state packet fields: Source ID, Manual Address, IS Type, System ID, Designated IS, Static Adjacencies

Extended Data

Sequence Number Packets

The purpose of the sequence number packet (SNP) is to ensure that every IS being updated by LSPs is getting the correct LSP. If an IS receives an SNP that is out of sequence, the accompanying link state update is disregarded. An SNP has the following fields:

- Remaining life—Remaining life of the LSP (during this time the IS cannot accept any other updates)

- LSP ID—The ID number identifying the LSP
- LSP sequence number—Sequence number of the update
- Checksum—Used to ascertain the integrity of the packet

These fields tell the receiving IS whether it has the correct update and how long that update is valid. Figure 19.21 illustrates a sequence number packet with its header information.

FIGURE 19.21

A sequence number packet.

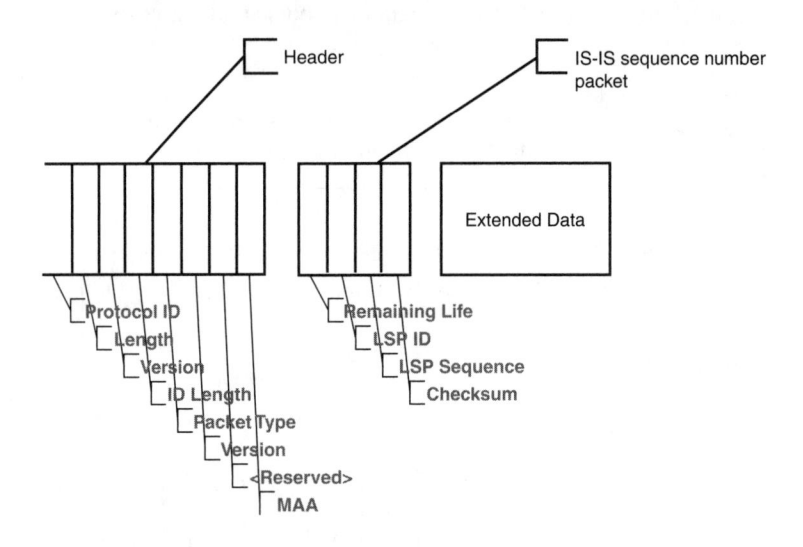

Header fields:
- Protocol ID
- Length
- Version
- ID Length
- Packet Type
- Version
- <Reserved>
- MAA

IS-IS sequence number packet fields:
- Remaining Life
- LSP ID
- LSP Sequence
- Checksum
- Extended Data

All of the packets discussed thus far are crucial to the successful operation of an IS-IS environment. In the following section we will discuss how all of these elements are combined to route data through an IS-IS network.

IS-IS Routing

Now that you know the history and the technology behind IS-IS, it's time to look into how it accomplishes its routing tasks. Routing in IS-IS is achieved through the successful and timely updating of the topological information pertaining to the local IS-IS areas.

IS-IS requires some "cohesiveness" to route efficiently. That is, all of the ISs on an IS-IS network cannot just run around doing what they please. They need to take direction from someone (or more realistically, something).

IS-IS, within its own areas and domains, elects one IS to be the master or designated IS. This IS is responsible for the actions of the environment.

> **Note:** This concept of a "master node" to watch over the operations of a network is not new. If you are familiar with the "master browser" in Microsoft networking or the "active monitor" in Token Ring, you've got the idea.

The first concept we need to cover is that of the designated IS. IS-IS nodes elect a designated IS to be the initiator during network events.

Designated IS

The major job of the designated IS is to send out LSPs that include LAN-wide information. The designated IS (after collecting the link state updates for the network) generates an overall picture of the networking environment and sends it to all other ISs on the LAN. This is done to control the number of redundant LSPs an IS may receive.

When an IS receives an LSP from the designated IS, all other LSPs are compared to it for accuracy. This also ensures that convergence occurs quickly.

During an IS election (to determine the designated IS), the ISs involved compare their priorities. After all of the ISs have compared their priorities, the IS with the highest priority is determined to be the designated IS. In the event that multiple ISs are found to have equal "highest priorities," they have an ID election.

> **Note:** IS priority is one of the administrator-assigned values. A network administrator will assign each IS a priority (an arbitrary numeric value, 1 being the highest). This value can be changed and, like the cost metric, is determined solely by the administrator.
>
> The priority field is also used in IS-IS hello messages to indicate the status of an IS. (In the event that an IS's priority changes, an LSP flood and an election would take place.)

The ISs with the highest priority then compare their MAC addresses. The IS holding the MAC address with the highest numerical value is elected the designated IS. The designated IS then resumes the job of collecting and distributing LSPs on behalf of the LAN as a whole (known as a pseudonode).

If one IS has interfaces that span multiple LANs, it is involved in the elections on all of them. In other words, elections occur based on the LAN an IS is present on. If an IS is present on more than one LAN, it participates in more than one election. Therefore, there is a chance that an IS can be a designated IS for more than one IS-IS networking environment. In any case, the designated IS treats the remaining ISs on its LAN as one entity, known as a pseudonode.

Pseudonodes

After a designated IS is chosen, the remaining ISs are grouped together into a pseudonode. The pseudonode is treated as one entity, when in reality it is a collection of the remaining ISs. IS-IS networks use these pseudonodes to receive information concerning the LAN as a whole.

The ISs in the pseudonode accept LSPs from the designated IS. During an LSP flood each IS sends an LSP to each IS it is connected to. (Obviously, an IS can send an update only to a device that it is directly connected to.) This LSP (known as a non-pseudonode LSP) contains all of the information about an IS's directly connected links.

Figure 19.22 illustrates an LSP flood with four ISs. During this flood, router A receives an LSP from router B stating that all of its links (router C) are functioning properly.

FIGURE 19.22

A link state flood with four nodes.

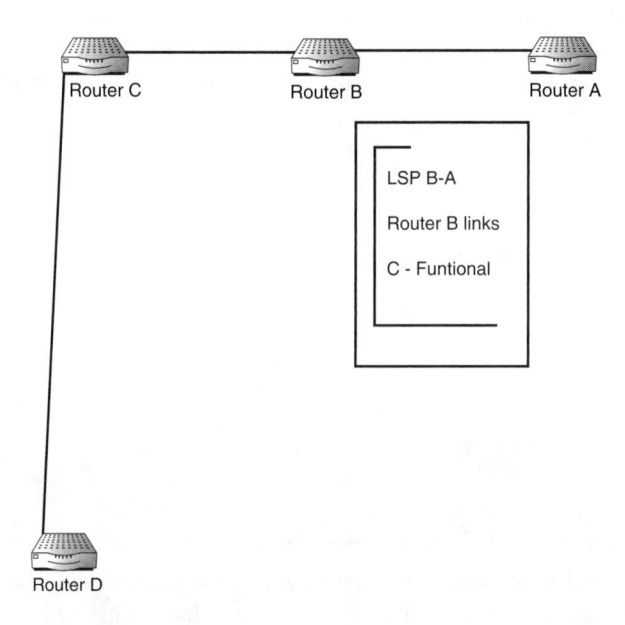

In its routing table, router A would know that routers B and C were functioning properly. Router A would have no way of knowing the state of router D.

If every router were to send every other router the updates for the entire network, a never-ending loop of updates would occur. Router A would be receiving updates about router D from routers B, C, and D. However, the concept of pseudonodes fixes this problem.

The job of the designated IS is to collect all of the update information and create a "master table" or picture of the network topology. The designated IS then sends one update to the pseudonode. All of the ISs in the pseudonode process this information against the updates from their neighbors. This keeps all of the ISs updated and keeps the network free of update loops.

Every IS is addressed differently to make it unique. IS-IS has to make arrangements for addressing a group of nodes as a pseudonode. IS-IS accomplishes this through the use of multicast addressing.

There are four Ethernet addresses that can be used for multicasting by IS-IS. The addresses are distinguished by destination. In other words, the address used depends on the group of devices being contacted. Table 19.1 shows the multicast addresses used by IS-IS and their intended destinations.

TABLE 19.1 Ethernet Multicast Addresses for IS-IS

0180C2000014	Used to contact all L1s only
0180C2000015	Used to contact all L2s only
09002B000005	Used to contact all ISs; this is the address used to contact the pseudonode
09002B000004	Used to contact all ESs only

All of the nodes on an IS-IS network know to process packets sent to the multicast addresses. The designated IS only needs to send one update to the pseudonode multicast address to have it processed by every device.

IS-IS Routing

Level 1 routers and level 2 routers move data differently within an IS-IS environment. The reason for this is simple: Level 2 routers have greater routing responsibilities than level 1 routers. Level 2 routers are responsible for moving data in an area, domain, and LAN-wide environment, whereas level 1 routers are responsible only for local areas.

With an L1 router, the source ES sends the packet to be routed to the nearest (directly connected) L1. Because the ES cannot move the data itself, it needs to go to either an L1 or an L2. The L1 now has some decisions to make based on the information in the header of that packet.

The L1 scans the header looking for the destination address of the packet (the destination address holds two important pieces of information, the destination area and the destination system). When the L1 finds the destination address, it decodes the destination area.

The L1 then compares the destination area of the packet with its own. (Remember that the L1 has topographical knowledge only of its own area; if the destination area does not match its own, the L1 forwards the packet on to the next router.) After comparing the destination area with its own, the L1 can come to one of two conclusions: Either the packet should be routed within the local area or it should be forwarded to a neighboring router.

> **Note** By this time the L1 has already received an LSP and Dijkstra's algorithm has been run against the updated information. Therefore, it can be assumed that the L1 is working from a complete and up-to-date picture of the network.

If the destination area is the local area, the router then rescans the header for the destination system. Also part of the destination address, the destination system tells the L1 exactly which ES to forward the packet to. If the destination area matches the local area but the destination system is unknown to the router, the packet is dropped.

If the destination area is not the L1's local area, the L1 examines its routing table to find the neighboring router that can reach the intended area. The packet is then routed to the L1 that governs the destination area. If the destination area cannot be found, the packet is dropped. Figure 19.23 illustrates this process.

The process is a little easier to understand when you can see it diagrammed as in Figure 19.23. Even without a visual sketch, the routing procedure for L1s is very straightforward. IS-IS is an efficient routing protocol that can move data pretty rapidly from one hop to another. There are relatively few routing decisions that need to be made, and the separation of duties between level 1 and level 2 routers makes the process even easier by allowing the router to focus on a specific area and not worry about the network as a whole.

The routing process for L2s is slightly different from that for L1s. When an L2 receives a packet, the first couple of steps in the routing process are the same: The router will scan the header for the destination address, then compare that address to its own. Because an L2 can have directly connected areas, the L2 determines the destination area and compares this against its own group of area L1s. If the destination area is one of the L2's level 1 neighbors, the packet is passed to the L1 on the destination area.

However, if the destination address does not match one on any of the L2's known areas, the L2 then looks at the prefix information.

FIGURE 19.23

IS-IS L1 routing.

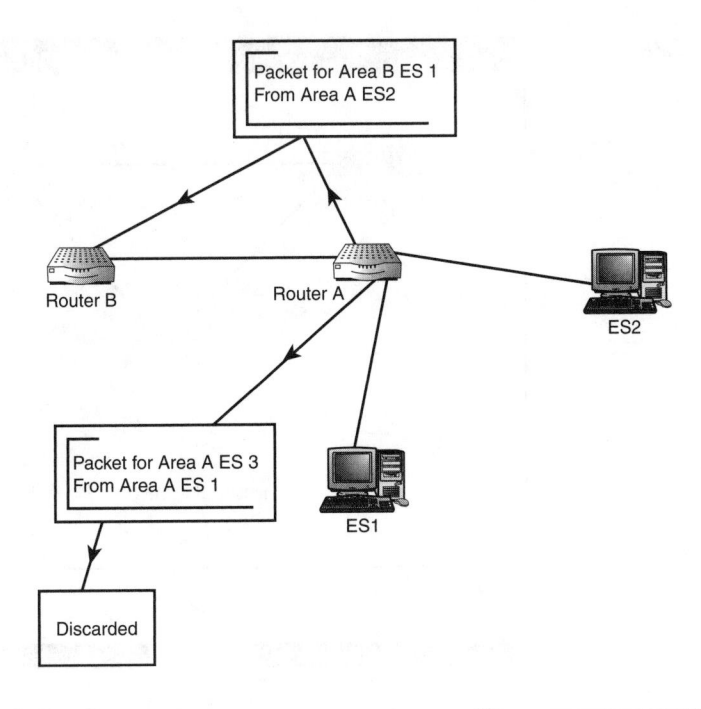

> **Note**
>
> Areas that are not local to the L2 are appended to a prefix in the L2's routing table. This not only allows the L2 to differentiate between local and nonlocal areas, but it helps the L2 determine where to send packets that are not local.
>
> These local and nonlocal areas are known as internal and external routes. Typically, internal routes are intradomain. This means that only two L2s will be involved. External routes can span multiple domains and any number of L2s.

If the packet is destined for an internal route, the packet is forwarded to the appropriate L1. Figure 19.24 illustrates internal route routing.

If the packet is destined for an external route, the L2 forwards the packet to its L2 neighbor. Figure 19.25 illustrates external route routing.

If the packet's destination area cannot be calculated, the packet is dropped.

IS-IS routing can be a complicated, advanced topic. However, this chapter was intended to provide a concise overview of how IS-IS differs from other routing protocols. The final section of this lesson focuses on the commands necessary to configure IS-IS on a Cisco router.

FIGURE 19.24

Internal route L2 routing.

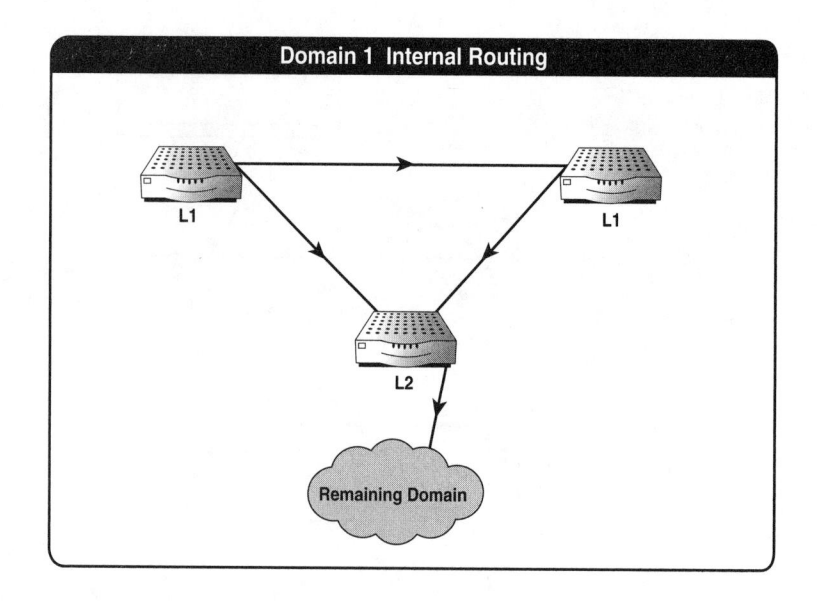

FIGURE 19.25

External route L2 routing.

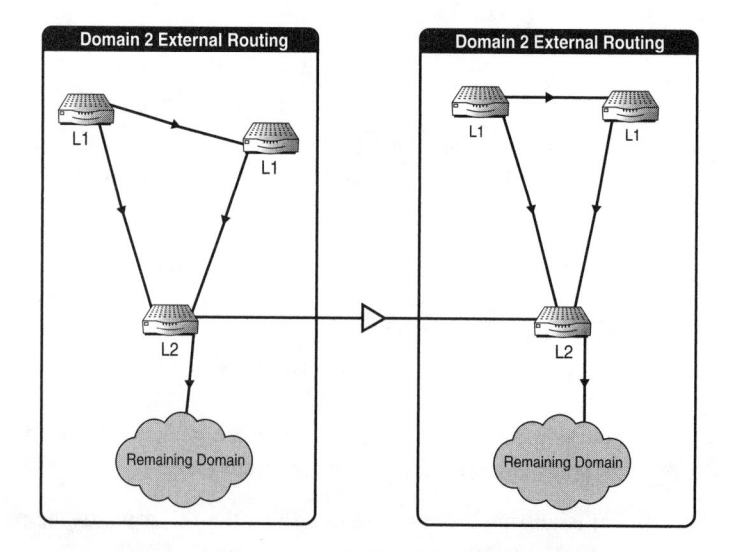

Configuring IS-IS

The first step in configuring a Cisco router to use IS-IS is to enable IS-IS routing and assign the area number. IS-IS configuration is performed from within router configuration mode. Use the router isis command to enable IS-IS routing.

```
Router#configure terminal
Router(config)#router isis 45
```

The parameter 45 in this code sample represents the area number to route. After the `isis` command is executed, the "net" (network address) needs to be established. The `net` command assigns the network address to the router. You can enter the net command as follows:

```
Router(config-router)# net 24.0001.001a.0000.0017.00
```

These two commands enable a Cisco router to participate in an IS-IS network on area 45. These are the only required commands for establishing an IS-IS-enabled router. However, there are some optional commands, such as `is-type` and `access-list`, that may prove useful.

The first is the `is-type` command. This command is used to indicate if the current router is an area router or a backbone router. In using the `is-type` command, a level 1 router is an area router, and a level 2 router is a backbone router. You can use the following example when executing the `is-type` command.

```
Router(config-router)# is-type level-1
```

Finally, you may want to establish some default routes into your AS. Establishing a default route requires a couple of steps. First, an access list must be created. The access list provides the rules that the default route works on. Second, a route map needs to be established referring back to the access list. The final step is to associate the default with the new route map. Using the following commands you can easily execute the establishment of a default route.

```
Router(config)#access-list 1 permit 10.0.0.0 0.255.255.255
Router(config)#route-map new
Router(config-route-map)#match ip route-source 1
Router(config-route-map)#^Z
Router(config)#router isis 399
Router(config-router)#default-information originate route-map new
Router(config-router)#^Z
```

> **Note** The use and syntax of access lists will be covered in depth in the next lesson.

At this point the router will have an established IS-IS area of 399 and a default route permitting incoming data from network 10.0.0.0.

Although there are many other commands associated with the operation of IS-IS, the ones we have covered today provide a good introduction to the functionality of Cisco routers.

Summary

- IS-IS is a routing protocol that was developed for use on the DECnet system.
- The IS-IS protocol was later adapted for use with IP and has become a high-end, robust routing protocol.
- Being a link state protocol, IS-IS uses the following default metrics to calculate the best path: delay, expense (cost), and reliability.

Q&A

Q With the number of routing protocols that already exist for IP, why was IS-IS adapted from DECnet?

A IS-IS is one of the most robust link state protocols in use. IP networks were growing to a size and structure that the IP native routing protocols were having trouble keeping up with. Therefore, because the next version of DECnet was already leaning toward IP support, converting IS-IS seem like the next logical step.

Quiz

Questions

1. How many default metrics are used by IS-IS?
2. Where are L2 routers found within the IS-IS domains?
3. What are the three steps for configuring a default router on an IS-IS router?

Answers

1. Three: delay, expense, and reliability.
2. The IS-IS backbone.
3. Define an access list, assign the access list to a route map, and reference the route map in the default route.

Exercise

1. Configure a default route on a router in IS-IS area 4. The router should allow all traffic from 198.118.26.0.

Week 3

Day 20

Introduction to Basic Cisco Security

Today's lesson focuses on two basic security techniques implemented on Cisco routers. Ask anyone familiar with Cisco routers what the number-one concern is in today's electronic business environments, and the answer will be security. Whether this means protecting your internal information from the threat of external exposure or holding company liability to a minimum by restricting access to internal devices, security is important.

Security itself, even Cisco security, is an immense, advanced subject. This lesson will serve to introduce you to two basic techniques that even novice Cisco users should be familiar with: IP access lists and NAT (network address translation). Combining NAT and access lists can produce a simple yet fairly secure environment. Both technologies are available on most Cisco routing platforms and under most IOS versions.

NAT is usually implemented on gateway routers—that is, routers with a direct external connection to the Internet. The concept behind NAT is that one routable IP address (or a pool of addresses) is assigned to one interface of the gateway router. Another interface of the router is configured with a nonroutable IP address that corresponds to the addresses of the local network. NAT then translates nonroutable IP traffic to routable IP traffic. NAT is good for basic security because the router performs address translation, making it exceedingly difficult for crackers to "piggyback" on IP traffic into and out of networks.

NAT works hand in hand with another basic security tool: IP access lists. Access lists provide a mechanism for the administrator to allow or deny routed protocol traffic based on certain criteria. These criteria can range from the port that the incoming traffic is using to the originating address.

Access lists should be an everyday part of routing maintenance. Looking back through the lessons in this book, a majority of the protocols used by routers operate through the use of access lists. There are two types: IP access lists and IPX access lists. In this lesson we will be examining the structures and concepts behind IP access lists.

IP Access Lists

An access list is an instruction sheet that tells a router how to deal with certain packets. Cisco routers use access lists to control the flow of information both into and out of the router. Although this lesson will focus on only two types of access lists (Standard IP and Extended IP), there are 11 different kinds that can be configured within Cisco routers:

- Standard IP
- Extended IP
- Protocol type-code
- DECnet
- Appletalk
- MAC (Media Access Control layer)
- Standard IPX
- Extended IPX
- IPX SAP
- Extended MAC
- IPX summary address

Note: Cisco routers can be configured for access control over almost any routed protocol. However, the most popular is IP.

Configuring a Cisco router to utilize access lists is a two-step process. The first step is to configure the actual access list. In other words, create a general rule that dictates how the router will deal with particular packets. The second step is to apply, or *bind,* that access list to an interface. The process of binding access lists to particular interfaces allows different lists to be bound to different interfaces.

Each access list is identified by a number. The number assigned to an access list is partially dictated by the type of access list being configured. Each type of access list is assigned a range of 100 addresses (meaning that there are 100 for each kind of access list that can be configured). Table 20.1 features the address ranges available to each kind of access list.

TABLE 20.1 Access List Numbers

Access List Type	Number Range
Standard IP	1–99
Extended IP	100–199
Protocol type-code	200–299
DECnet	300–399
Appletalk	600–699
MAC (media access control sublayer)	700–799
Standard IPX	800–899
Extended IPX	900–999
IPX SAP	1000–1099
Extended MAC	1100–1199
IPX summary address	1200–1299

Standard IP access lists always have a number between 1 and 99, and extended IP access lists will range from 100 to 199. These are the two types of access lists we will be focusing on for this lesson.

To configure an access list on a Cisco router, use the `access-list` command from global configuration mode. You use global configuration mode because you are only defining the rules of your access list. When you bind the access list to an interface, on the other hand, you do so from interface configuration mode. The following code sample shows the creation of a standard IP access list:

```
Router#configure terminal
Router(config)#access-list 1 permit 198.42.16.1
Router(config)#^Z
```

> **Note:** Cisco routers (when dealing with access lists) employ a rule known as implicit denial. Under implicit denial, anything that does not match the access list is denied. Following this rule (referring to the access list we just created), everything other than 186.42.16.1 would be denied access to the resources beyond this router.

The syntax for using the `access-list` command to configure a standard IP access-list is as follows:

`#access-list <access-list number> <action> <source address>`

The access-list configuration in the previous example simply states, "Permit traffic from IP address 198.42.16.1." The other option Cisco provides for the *<action>* parameter is deny. To create a standard IP access list that denies traffic from 10.36.149.8, use the following code:

```
Router#configure terminal
Router(config)#access-list 1 deny 10.36.149.8
Router(config)#^Z
```

Standard access lists are ideal for smaller environments, where implicit permission or denial of one or two addresses can secure a network. Standard access lists allow a user to create "blanket" rules in which all traffic from an address is either permitted or denied. Standard access lists offer little in the way of flexibility and customization.

Extended access lists give a Cisco user more control over the rules behind the type of packets that are allowed or denied. The syntax for creating extended IP access lists is as follows:

`#access-list <access-list number> <action> <protocol> <source address> <destination address> <port>`

There are more options for configuring extended access lists than there are for standard access lists. These extra options allow Cisco routers to filter traffic based on source, destination, protocol, or port. For example, to deny IP Telnet traffic (port 23) from 10.98.12.1 to 10.99.36.5, use the following code:

```
Router#configure terminal
Router(config)#access-list 100 deny IP host 10.98.12.1 host 10.99.36.5 23
Router(config)#^Z
```

> **Note**: Telnet traffic runs over IP port 23. Table 20.2 lists the more common IP services and their corresponding port assignments.

TABLE 20.2 Common IP Ports

Service	Port
SSH	22
Telnet	23
SMTP	25
HTTP	80
LDAP	389
MS NetMeeting	1024, 1503
HTTPs	443
SOCKS	1080
MS NetShow	1755
MSN Messenger	1863
Mirabilis ICQ	1024
AOL Instant Messenger	5190
AOL ICQ	5190
AOL	5190–5193
Dialpad.com	5354, 7175, 8680–8890, 9000, 9450–9460
pcAnywhere	5631
VNC	5800+, 5900+
Netscape Conference	6498, 6502
Common IRC	6665–6669
RealAudio and Video	7070
VocalTec Internet Conference	22555
MSN Gaming Zone	28800–29000
DirectX Gaming	47624, 2300–2400

The preceding access list example uses the keyword host before the source and destination addresses. If a user wants to make a much broader statement—for example, disabling HTTP traffic for the entire network—the any keyword is used:

```
Router#configure terminal
Router(config)#access-list 147 deny IP any 10.0.0.0 0.255.255.255 any 0.0.0.0
255.255.255.255 80
Router(config)#^Z
```

This statement blocks all local users (network 10.0.0.0) from accessing any Web sites (the broadcast range 0.0.0.0–255.255.255.255 on port 80). Using the any keyword can be dangerous, though. Services and users that legitimately need access to particular destinations may be blocked. Design your access lists carefully.

These two types of access lists, standard and extended, can be combined in any configuration to filter traffic in almost any way administrators see fit. Creating the access list is only half the equation, though; you still have to bind the access list to one or more interfaces.

When you bind an access list to an interface, the access-group keyword of the ip command is used from interface configuration mode. The command only allows one parameter: in or out. This parameter indicates whether the rule is to be applied to incoming or outgoing packets. You should use the following code to establish one standard and one extended access list. These access lists are then bound to the router's interface, ethernet 0.

```
Router#configure terminal
Router(config)#access-list 13 permit 128.53.12.1
Router(config)#access-list 108 deny IP host 198.20.13.118 host 128.53.12.1 80
Router(config)#^Z
Router#configure terminal
Router(config)#interface ethernet 0
Router(config-if)# ip address 198.20.13.115
Router(config-if)# ip access-group 108 out
Router(config-if)# ip access group 13 in
```

In this code sample, you created two access lists. The first permits incoming traffic from the source address 128.53.12.1, and the second rule states that all IP HTTP traffic from 198.20.13.118 to host 128.53.12.1 should be denied. This is an effective way to keep the user at address 198.20.13.118 from viewing the Web pages at address 128.53.12.1 80 while still allowing services from that site to access the local network.

One very important thing to keep in mind about access lists is the rule of implicit denial. If an access list is created and a packet does not meet the rules established in the access list, the packet is denied.

Access lists are a basic yet effective way to control the flow of traffic into and out of environments. Another tool that is equally effective, and works with access lists, is NAT.

NAT

NAT (network address translation) is a tool that allows gateway routers to map external IP addresses to internal IP addresses. This tool is most often used on gateway routers that control access to the Internet. Because of the growing shortage of IP addresses, many network administrators choose to implement local IP schemes that consist of public IP addresses. The problem with public IP addresses is that they cannot be routed over the Internet.

Using NAT, one private IP address is assigned to the gateway router. This router then performs address translation on all incoming and outgoing traffic, ensuring that the outgoing traffic is tagged with the private address and that the incoming traffic is correctly referred to the proper public address.

NAT is an effective security tool because the translation process changes the source and destination addresses of each packet, making it harder for crackers to access networks through IP services. NAT also relies on IP access lists to secure the translation process. NAT, like access lists, works on the concept of "inside" versus "outside" traffic. To fully configure NAT on a Cisco router, you need to define the inside and outside characteristics of the affected interfaces. On a gateway router it is assumed that at least one interface is addressed to the internal network and one interface is addressed to the Internet (or other external network). The internal interface is configured with an "inside" NAT rule, while the external interface uses an "outside" rule. There are four basic steps you should follow to configure NAT:

- Define the NAT interfaces.
- Configure the interface addresses.
- Configure the NAT address pool.
- Associate an access list with the NAT pool.

The first step in configuring NAT is to define the interfaces as either inside or outside. You can accomplish this from the interface configuration mode. In the following code sample, interface `ethernet 0` is configured as an inside interface, and the ISDN port is configured as the outside interface.

```
Router#configure terminal
Router(config)#interface ethernet 0
Router(config-if)#ip nat inside
Router(config-if)#interface bri 0
Router(config-if)#ip nat outside
Router(config-if)#^Z
```

The second step in configuring NAT is to ensure that each interface has a proper IP address. In other words, the inside interface must have a public address, and the outside interface must have a private address.

> **Note:** In such a scenario your ISP generally provides you with an address to define for the outside interface.

You can use commands like the following to establish the internal and external addresses:

```
Router#configure terminal
Router(config)#interface ethernet 0
Router(config-if)#ip address 198.65.1.1 255.255.0.0
Router(config-if)#interface bri 0
Router(config-if)#ip address 186.91.108.1 255.255.0.0
Router(config-if)#^Z
```

The interfaces of this router (Router) are configured for NAT. However, the router still does not know what to do with this information. A pool of translatable addresses needs to be established for the router to map to. That is, the router needs to be told what addresses are available to translate the inbound data into.

Forming NAT address pools is done from the global configuration mode of the router. The syntax you should use for forming a NAT pool is:

```
#ip nat pool <name> <address range> netmask <subnet mask>
```

The following code illustrates the creation of a NAT address pool:

```
Router#configure terminal
Router(config)#ip nat pool my_pool 198.65.1.1 198.65.254.254 netmask 255.255.0.0
Router(config)#^Z
```

In the foregoing example, you used the nat_pool command to create an address pool named my_pool for NAT to use in translating addresses. This particular pool uses the addresses from 198.65.1.1 to 198.65.254.254. Because the pools are named, different interfaces can use different address pools.

To configure NAT to use the pool named my_pool, we need first to create an access list detailing how to deal with the addresses in the pool. NAT can then be configured to use the pool addresses in accordance with the rules established in the access list. The access list you create must simply "permit" traffic to the addresses in our pool. You should enter the following commands to create your access list.

```
Router#configure terminal
Router(config)#access-list 1 permit 198.65.0.0 0.0.255.255
Router(config)#^Z
```

The final step you need to perform is to associate this access list with the NAT pool. The following commands illustrate how you would accomplish this.

```
Router#configure terminal
Router(config)#ip nat inside source list 1 pool my_pool
Router(config)#^Z
```

The `nat inside source` command states that all inbound NAT traffic that meets the rules of access list 1 can be translated to pool my_pool. After the rules are established, the router is ready to run. Any inbound packets not permitted by the access list are not translated by NAT and dropped.

Summary

The combination of NAT and IP access lists is a basic yet powerful security tool that all Cisco users should master. The traffic logic and flow can be sculpted to the needs of most businesses by using these two tools. You should remember the following information about Cisco security.

- Access lists are rule-based command structures detailing how a router should deal with packets.
- Access lists utilize a feature known as implicit denial.
- Any packets that do not meet the criteria of the access list are denied.
- NAT (network address translation) is used to translate the source and destination addresses of packets.
- NAT uses access lists to provide the rules by which it should perform translations.

The final lesson of this book is going to deal with understanding Cisco Catalyst Switch routing and PNNI.

Q&A

Q Does NAT need to be installed on a gateway?

A No, there is no rule that says NAT cannot be installed on a border router or other internal router that spans more than one network. However, its most popular use is to protect and monitor Internet traffic.

Quiz

Questions

1. What is the acceptable number range for extended IP access lists?
2. Which type of access list allows the user to block particular ports?
3. Is NAT configured globally or per interface?

Answers

1. 100–199.
2. Extended IP.
3. Both. The pool is configured in global mode, while the inside and outside interfaces are defined in the interface configuration mode of the IOS.

Exercises

1. Configure an extended access list to block inbound SMTP traffic.

Note
```
Router#configure terminal
Router(config)#access-list 100 deny IP any 0.0.0.0
255.255.255.255 any 0.0.0.0 255.255.255.255 25
Router(config)#^Z
```

2. Configure a router to NAT between the internal network 10.0.0.0 and the external Internet on IP address 115.68.43.1. The internal interface is ethernet 0 and the external interface is serial 0. The address of ethernet 0 is 10.101.23.1.

Note
```
Router#configure terminal
Router(config)#interface ethernet 0
Router(config-if)#ip address 10.101.23.1 255.0.0.0
Router(config-if)#ip nat inside
Router(config-if)#interface serial 0
Router(config-if)#ip nat outside
Router(config-if)#ip address 115.68.43.1 255.0.0.0
Router(config-if)#^Z
Router#configure terminal
Router(config)#ip nat pool exercise 10.0.0.0 10.254.254.254
netmask 255.0.0.0
Router(config)#access-list 1 permit 10.0.0.0 0.255.255.255
Router(config)#ip nat inside source list 1 pool exercise
Router(config)#^Z
```

WEEK 3

DAY 21

Understanding Cisco Catalyst Switch Routing and PNNI

The final lesson of this book presents a form of Cisco routing that we have yet to cover in this text. High-end Cisco devices known as Catalyst switches, are also capable of performing routing tasks even though they are switches. In particular, they have the ability to run a very useful routing protocol known as PNNI (Private Network to Network Interface). Because you may not have a Cisco Catalyst switch on hand (most people would not anticipate needing a switch for a lesson in routing), this lesson will be kept as brief as possible. Its main purpose is to introduce you to the routing protocols that exist on devices other than Cisco routers—specifically, on Cisco switches).

This lesson will introduce you to PNNI and the commands required to configure PNNI routing on a Cisco switch. The topics covered in this lesson include

- ATM (Asynchronous Transfer Mode) architecture
- The UNI signaling protocol
- PNNI hierarchy
- PNNI routing protocol
- PNNI and QOS
- PNNI signaling protocol
- PNNI crankback
- Configuring PNNI

PNNI, or Private Network-to-Network Interface, is a protocol used to pass data between ATM (Asynchronous Transfer Mode) switched networks. PNNI handles the routing of information to and from multiple ATM groups on a local or worldwide scale.

The term PNNI itself actually represents a logical interface through which multiple ATM networks can connect and communicate. PNNI as a specification includes suggestions and regulations for the routing of data between large networks of ATM systems.

The ATM Forum created PNNI in 1996 as an efficient way to route information between ATM environments. When the ATM Forum set out to create the standards that would later become PNNI, they looked to "pre-established" technologies to base the specifications on. This course of action enabled the members of the ATM Forum to save themselves years of work trying to create something (that might not work) or developing a technology that may already have been developed.

Note The ATM Forum (formed in 1991) is an alliance of corporations that work together toward greater acceptance of ATM technology in business. The member corporations of the ATM Forum set and accept standards and advances in ATM switching technology.

PNNI is actually divided into two main functions: the routing protocol and the signaling protocol. The PNNI routing protocol moves data from one ATM cluster or group to another. To route the very fast-moving ATM cells efficiently, the ATM Forum based the designs for the PNNI routing protocol on other link state routing protocols.

> **Note:** The PNNI routing protocol is based on link state protocols. That is, through the use of update packets, a node on the network can update other nodes as to the state of its links. In general, link state protocols tend to route data in a quick and efficient way.

The second function of PNNI is a signaling protocol. The signaling protocol is used to build and tear down connections between switches. This function is critical in ATM networks. Before PNNI could work in an ATM environment, it needed to handle requests for connections between two (or more) switches.

The PNNI signaling protocol was based on another ATM Forum specification, UNI (user-to-network interface). The UNI signaling protocol had been developed by the ATM Forum to be a quick, adaptable signaling protocol between public and private networks. With a few minor revisions, UNI was modified to become the PNNI signaling protocol.

This chapter will introduce you to the technology behind PNNI and the two PNNI protocols. However, before we can discuss how PNNI works, we need to understand basic ATM networking.

ATM Architecture

ATM (Asynchronous Transfer Mode) was developed to enable the high-speed transfer of data, voice, and video over public data lines. ATM, unlike many networks that people are familiar with, is a switch environment. That is, a connection-oriented protocol is used to create circuits between switches for the reliable transfer of data. Figure 21.1 illustrates a typical ATM architecture.

> **Note:** ATM does support connectionless transfer of data; however, this is seldom evoked. ATM efficiently transfers data over public line at rates up to 1 Gbps.

Most of the technologies that are common on networks today are connectionless (IP being the most popular). The overall, inescapable problem with connectionless transfer of data is that there is no guarantee the data reaches its intended destination. However, ATM, being connection oriented, builds "session length" circuits between switches. After the session is completed (all of the data has been transferred between the two switches), ATM then tears down the circuit. This allows another session to use one or both of the ports for another connection. Figure 21.2 illustrates the process of building and tearing down ATM connections.

FIGURE 21.1

An ATM network.

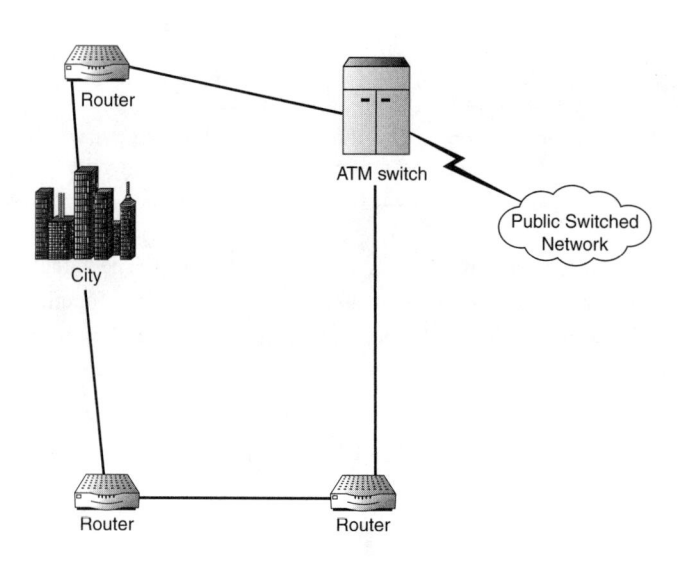

FIGURE 21.2

An ATM connection.

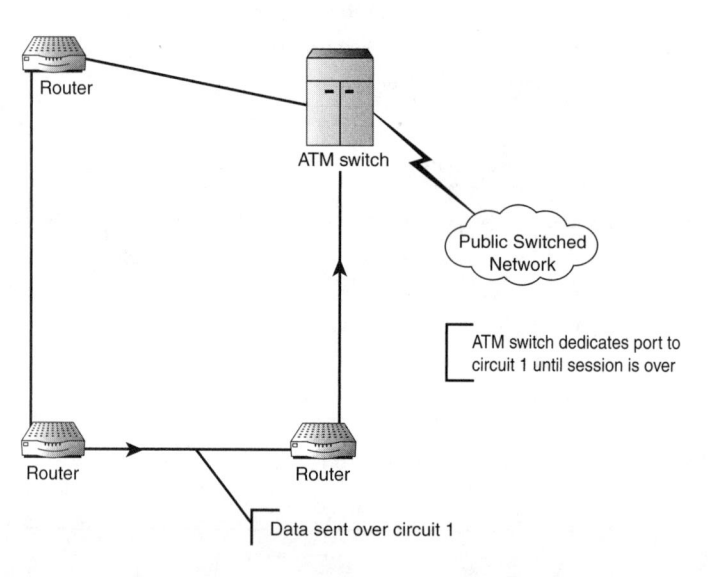

ATM is by no means the only architecture to use connection-oriented transfers of data. In fact IP's relative, TCP, is a connection-oriented protocol. Without a doubt, ATM is the best example of functional connection-oriented data transfer.

The key to ATM's quick transfer rates is the underlying format of its data. ATM does not transfer variable-length packets as most protocols do. Protocols such as IS-IS (Day 19) transfer packets that may vary in size depending on the data being transferred. Therefore, the receiving device must scan the header of the packet, determine the size of the data, and process the packet. With a variable-length packet the amount of time needed to process each packet changes from packet to packet. The larger the packet is, the longer it takes to process.

In contrast, ATM transfers data in a fixed-length format known as a cell. ATM cells, regardless of the amount of data being moved, are 53 bytes long. As shown in Figure 21.3, ATM cells consist of a 5-byte header and a 48-byte "payload" or data segment.

FIGURE 21.3
An ATM cell.

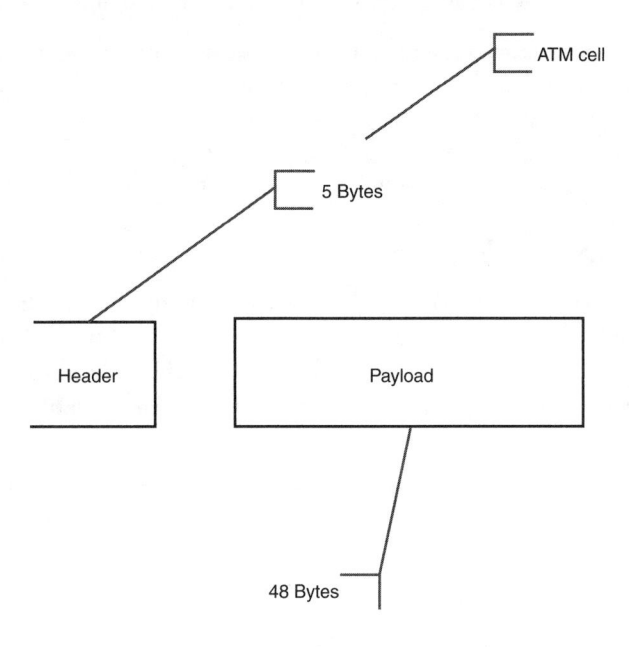

> **Note**
> Even though ATM cells are of fixed length (eliminating the need for a header length field), they still need a header. The header of an ATM cell specifies the source and destination of the payload.

The fixed length of ATM cells makes them perfect for carrying digital audio and video. Because receiving ATM devices do not have random bursts of slow and fast processing (dependent on packet size), the signals are received evenly and quickly. Any slowdown in the digitizing of the signal most likely is directly related to the sample rate of the video (or audio) and will not be noticed.

Another factor in ATM's success is the fact that it is asynchronous. *Asynchronous* means that ATM switches can send and receive signals at the same time. Therefore, a pair of switches can send each other data at the same time, cutting the transfer (circuit up) time in half.

ATM's asynchronous nature is due to its fixed cell format. Because ATM cells are a fixed 53 bytes in length, each switch knows how long it will take to receive a packet. Therefore, in between the sending of cells, the switch can open itself up to receive any cells arriving from the switch on the other end on the circuit.

Before we can further explore how ATM switching and signaling (and ultimately PNNI) work, we need to look at the layout of a typical ATM network. Since PNNI not only was created to work on ATM networks but was based on an existing protocol (UNI v3), you need to understand better the architecture of ATM switched sites. Understanding the architecture of an ATM site will help you learn the concepts behind PNNI.

ATM Network Layout

There are two types of ATM networks: public and private. A public ATM network exists in the public cloud. That is, somewhat like the Internet, a public ATM network is a group of public-access networks usually managed by a public telecom firm. A private ATM network, on the other hand, exists completely within the domain of one enterprise.

> **Note** Keep in mind that public ATM networks are composed almost entirely of ATM switches (known as public switches). Very few ATM end systems (ESs) exist in a public ATM network.

Of course, as with most rules in networking, the lines of definition are not always crystal clear. In fact, you can have two private ATM networks connected by a public one. In this case each network is its own group and not viewed as one entity (the private networks are private and the public ones are public). ATM networks are relatively simple in design but not in technology. ATM networks are based on an extremely advanced, complicated packet-switching technology.

Each device in an ATM network is either an ATM switch or an ATM end system. The ATM switch is the device that connects to the "mesh" of the network. That is, the ATM switch is the device that moves data to and from the network. In the early days of ATM, the ATM switch would have been the final point of presence on a company's network.

An ATM end system is any device on an ATM network that is not an ATM switch. Therefore, all PCs, routers, and printers are considered ESs. Because ESs have no switching capability, they forward all data to the ATM switch for transmission over the network.

When ATM was first developed, these two device classifications made designing ATM environments fairly easy. The first uses for ATM were in public switched networks. In other words, the company's local network connected to an ATM switch. The information from this ATM switch was then carried over the public switched network (usually a public telephone company). The public switched network carried the data to the ATM switch at the destination network. Figure 21.4 illustrates an ATM public switched network.

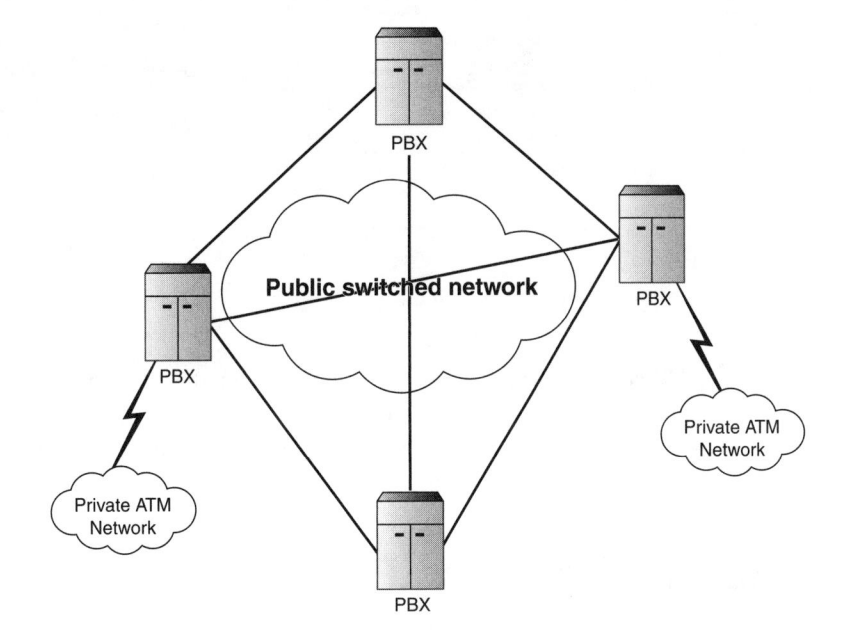

FIGURE 21.4

An ATM public switched network.

For the first ATM public networks, a set of protocols was developed: UNI (User-to-Network Interface) and NNI (Network-to-Network Interface). These protocols were created solely for the purpose of signaling to the public switches that another ATM switch had data to transmit. As Figure 21.5 illustrates, because there are two types of ATM networks (public and private), there are two types of UNI and NNI protocols.

UNI was developed to allow the ATM switch (or end system) on a private network to signal to an unknown public switch that it had data to send. UNI would then create a circuit between the two switches. After the session between the two switches was done, UNI would tear down the circuit. The private version of the protocol (P-UNI) could be used to connect ESs with private ATM switches.

FIGURE 21.5

The uses of UNI and NNI.

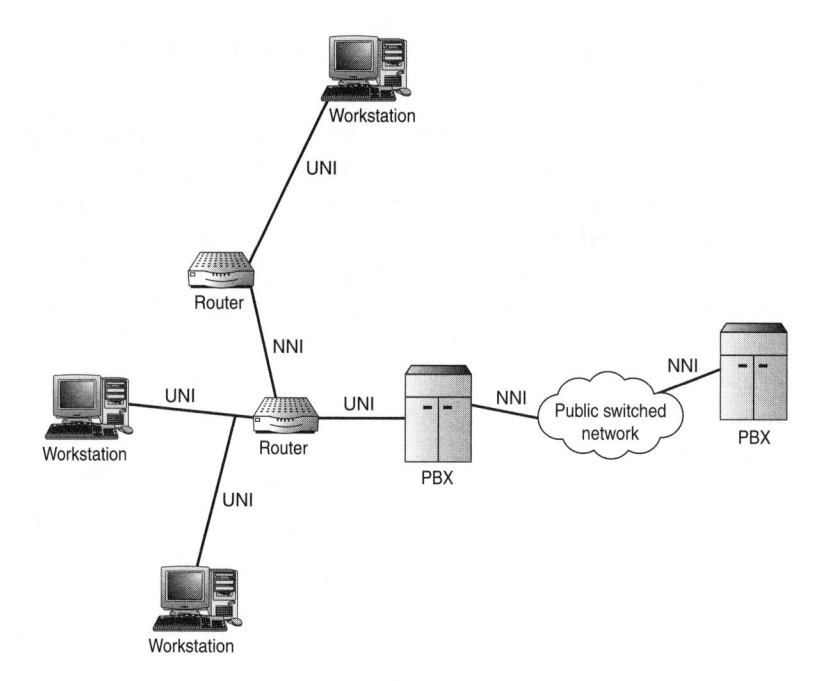

As ATM networks began to grow, a protocol had to be developed to handle the intense communicational load of switch-to-switch signaling. NNI (and its private counterpart, PNNI) were developed just for this purpose. NNI was modeled after UNI to ensure that proper communication standards were adhered to.

The UNI Signaling Protocol

UNI (user node interface) is a signaling protocol that enables the establishment of communication between ESs and private switches or between private switches and public switches. Signaling protocols send specially formatted messages to switches. The receiving switch then allows for an open line (or circuit) of communication between the devices.

UNI can signal for two types of circuits to be open in an ATM environment: point-to-point or point-to-multipoint. Figures 21.6 and 21.7 illustrate point-to-point and point-to-multipoint communications, respectively.

When UNI opens a point-to-point circuit, one system contacts another and requests a session. Once the receiving system accepts the signal, a circuit is opened between the two. Acting much like a direct cable connection, a point-to-point circuit allows communication between two systems or points.

FIGURE 21.6

A *point-to-point* circuit.

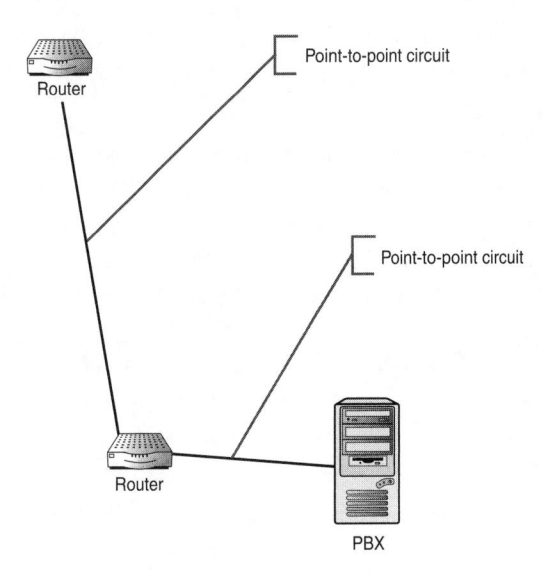

FIGURE 21.7

A *point-to-multipoint* circuit.

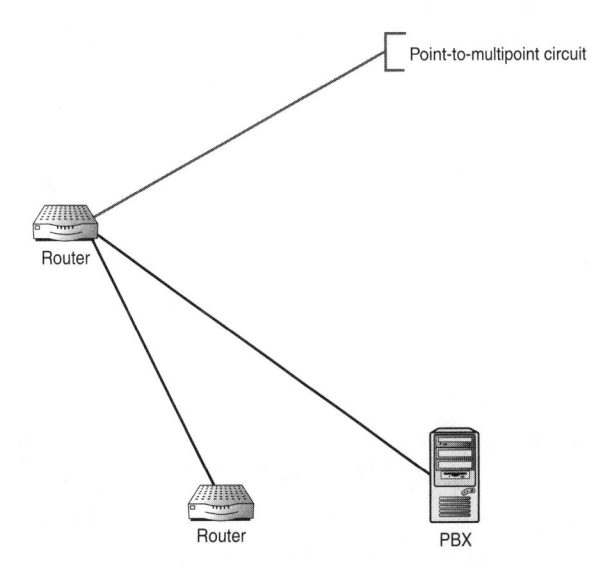

The major advantage to a point-to-point circuit is the use of asynchronous ports. A point-to-point ATM connection can establish bidirectional communication between systems. This is very desirable in a networking environment, because it enables two systems to hold interruptible sessions.

A point-to-multipoint connection is established when one system needs to open a circuit with multiple systems. One possible reason for opening a point-to-multipoint circuit is for multicasting.

The major disadvantage to ATM point-to-multipoint connections is they are not asynchronous. A point-to-multipoint circuit allows communication in only one direction (from the point to the multipoints). This is not a problem related to the UNI protocol; rather, the fields in the ATM cell do not allow for the entries necessary to open a point-to-multipoint asynchronous (known as multipoint-to-multipoint) circuit.

The ATM Cell Structure and Signaling Protocol

A standard ATM cell has a 5-byte header. This header contains the information required for any system to determine what kind of cell it is, whom it is intended for, and who sent it. The header itself contains different fields depending on the cell type; for example, a UNI cell header contains different fields than an NNI cell header does. Figure 21.8 illustrates the fields in a UNI cell header. The UNI cell header has the following fields:

- Generic flow control (4 bits)—Generally unused.
- Virtual path identifier (8 bits)—Identifies the next hop toward the cell's intended destination. (A cell may need to travel through multiple switches before reaching its destination.)
- Virtual channel identifier (16 bits)—Helps the current switch identify the next switch to receive the cell.
- Payload type (3 bits)—Identifies the contents of the cell.
    - Bit A—If this bit is on, the payload contains data.
    - Bit B—Indicates congestion.
    - Bit C—Marker used to signal the last in a series of cells.
- Congestion loss priority (1 bit)—Used by the switch to discard any cell that has taken too long to reach its destination.
- Header checksum—Used to check the integrity of the header.

As the cell is passed through the network, each switch modifies the virtual path identifier and the virtual channel identifier to aid in the successful routing of the cell. As each switch passes the cell along, the path taken by the cell is marked as shown in Figure 21.9.

When the cell reaches its final destination, the last switch makes a decision to either accept or reject the circuit. If the switch accepts the cell, the path the cell took to reach its destination is turned into a circuit. Figure 21.10 illustrates a UNI circuit.

FIGURE 21.8

The fields in a UNI cell header.

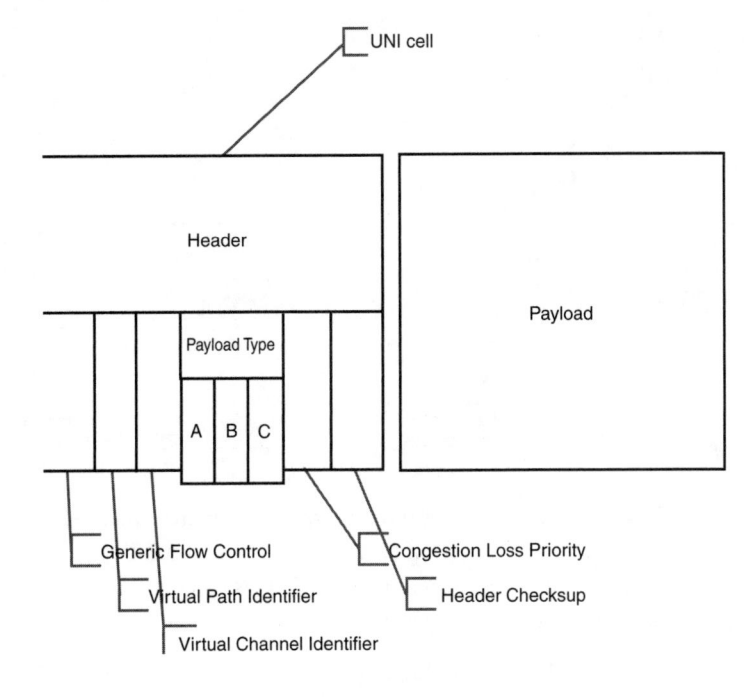

FIGURE 21.9

A UNI cell being routed.

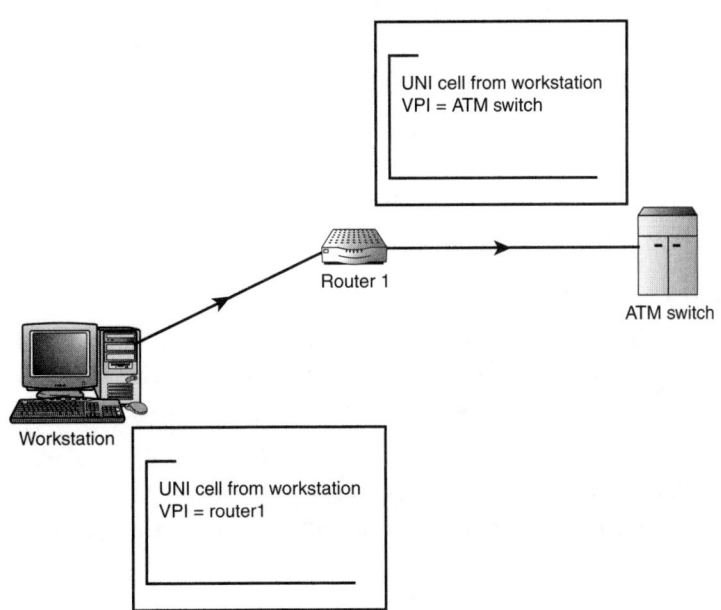

FIGURE 21.10

A UNI circuit.

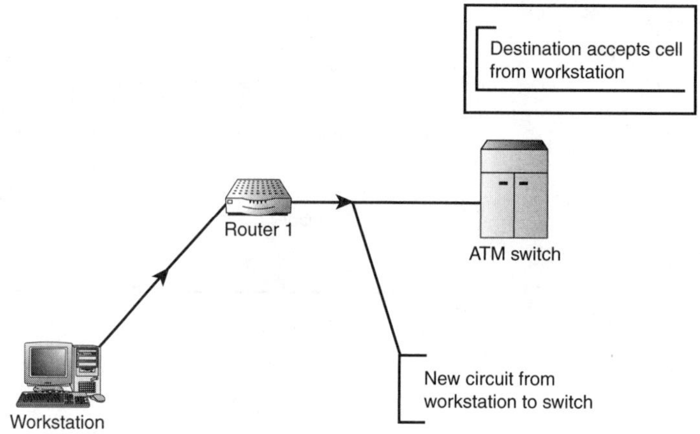

UNI is a good protocol for moving information around an ATM network. However, when the communication requirements dictate that a circuit be open between two private switches, a different protocol is needed. This protocol is known as PNNI, the Private Network-to-Network Interface.

UNI does not have the routing or signaling capacity needed to handle the complete task of establishing and tearing down circuits, as well as to advertise routing paths. When the members of the ATM Forum set out to create a protocol to supply the routing and signaling capacity that UNI lacked, they started with UNI.

By modeling the new Private Network-to-Network Interface after UNI, they were assured of a good base to build the protocol on. The following sections describe the PNNI protocol, how it works, and why it was modeled as it was.

PNNI Hierarchy

PNNI networks follow a hierarchy: Certain systems or groups of systems are granted precedence over others to establish optimal paths. This section describes how the PNNI hierarchy works and how it fits the ATM architecture.

If PNNI did not accommodate a routing hierarchy, the networks would be formed in a flat manner: Every group or cluster of systems would be equal to every other. Being flat (from a routing perspective) can hurt a network in a couple of ways.

The first way a flat routing environment can hurt a network is by increasing the amount of memory and processing power needed to make routing decisions. If every system of the network is on the same level, there is no way for a routing scheme to separate them into smaller groups. A router using an algorithm to calculate a routing path needs to compute that path using every system on the network as a variable. Keeping track of such variables would take a very large amount of memory. Crunching the numbers required for calculating the paths of that many systems would take even more processing power.

The second problem with having a flat routing environment is that you give up some speed. The more variables a router must consider when making a decision, the longer that decision takes. On a flat network, every system must be considered by the router as a possible variable. On a larger network, the processes of routing data could require the use of so many variables that network speed would be unbearably slow.

PNNI guards against problems associated with flat networks by implementing a hierarchical network scheme. PNNI places every system into a group; those groups are then placed into larger groups, creating endless possibilities for the size of the hierarchy that can encompass a network. The smallest group, considered the base for everything else in the hierarchy, is known as a peer group.

PNNI Peer Groups

PNNI networks are divided into peer groups (PGs). Every peer group has its own address on the network. This address (known as a PG number or group address) is unique to a group and shared by all of the members of the PG.

How the end systems are separated into peer groups depends on the address of the switch. Because a PG is designated by the common address of its members, and a member's address is derived from the switch it is attached to, the separation of the PGs depends on the addressing of the switches.

The purpose of a PNNI peer group is purely for routing. Within a peer group, the ESs and their switches pass data among themselves and the other members of the group. This limits the amount of traffic that is passed from switch to switch. Being the lowest member of a hierarchy thus has its advantages.

For PNNI routing purposes, the members of a peer group can have topographical knowledge only of the systems in that group. Systems of a given PG never know the specific composition of any other peer group. Therefore, by creating a lowest-level group like this, PNNI can control the amount of data that border nodes need to process.

> **Note:** A border node is an ATM switch that connects peer groups. Through a border node, information can be sent from one peer group to another.

PNNI NSAP Addressing

Most private ATM networks use the NSAP (network service access point; see Day 19) addressing format.

> **Note:** Other protocols, such as IS-IS, also utilize the NSAP address format, or a modified version of it.

The 20-byte NSAP address for ATM is composed of some network-specific fields and the device's MAC address. Figure 21.11 illustrates the fields that make up an NSAP address. The fields of the NSAP address in PNNI are:

- AFI: Authority format identifier—Specifies the authority assigning the address.
- ICD: International code designator—Specifies the addressing authority (used for international uniqueness).
- Address type—Signifies whether the address is ICD, NSAP, or DCC (Data Country Code).
- Switch ID—The MAC address of the switch.
- End system identifier—The MAC address of the end system.
- Selector—Unused.

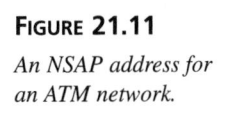

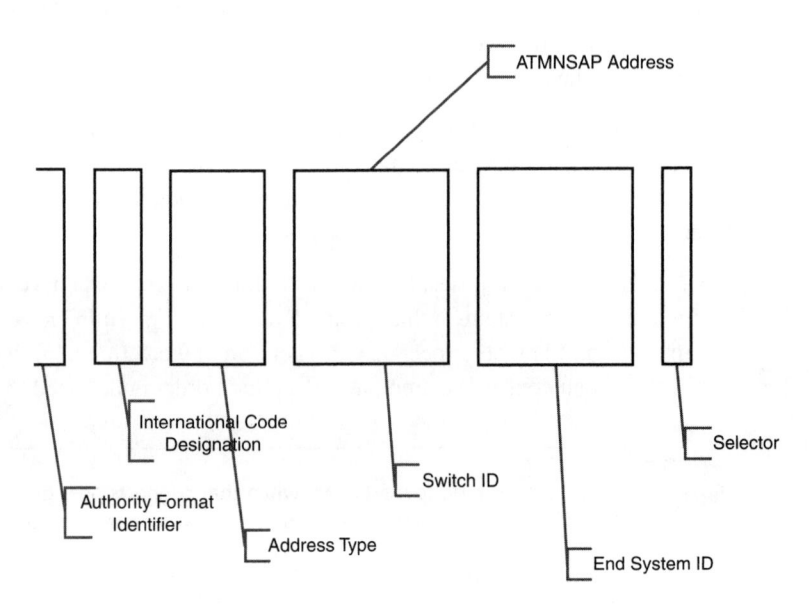

FIGURE 21.11

An NSAP address for an ATM network.

Figure 21.12 illustrates a populated ATM switch address (the example used supplies the AFI and ICD of Cisco Systems).

FIGURE 21.12

An ATM switch address.

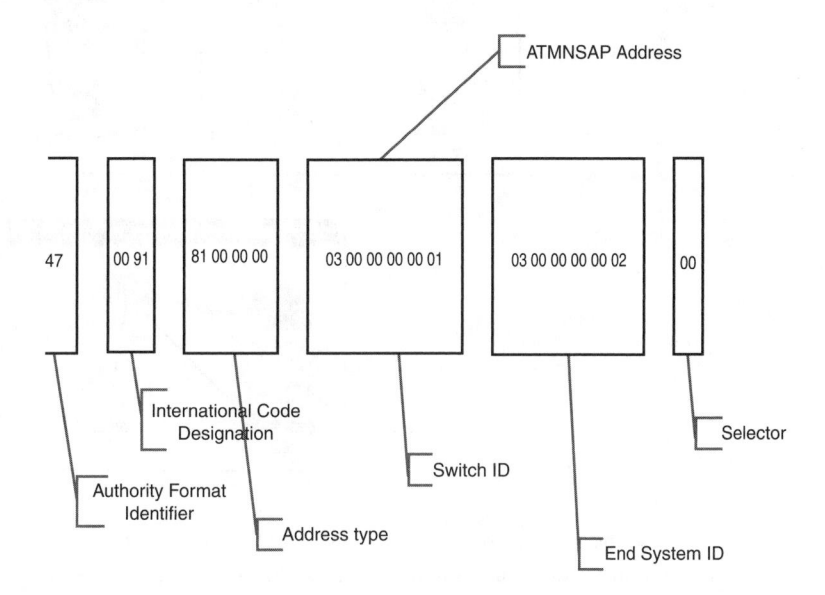

```
         ATMNSAP Address
47 | 00 91 | 81 00 00 00 | 03 00 00 00 00 01 | 03 00 00 00 00 02 | 00
```

- International Code Designation
- Authority Format Identifier
- Address type
- Switch ID
- End System ID
- Selector

In a peer group all systems share a 12-byte identifier. This identifier is actually the first 12 bytes of the switch's 13-byte ATM address; the 13th byte is the switch identifier. Because the first 12 bytes of the ATM address are constant for every ES in the PG, these bytes are the peer group number.

One unique aspect of the ATM switch address format applies to the ATM switch itself. According to the logic used to form the PG number (the MAC address of an ATM switch is the end system ID of all other devices in the same peer group), the address field's end system ID and switch ID are identical on an ATM switch within a peer group.

When a new ES is attached to the switch, it adopts the switch's end system identifier as its switch ID. The ES's MAC address is then used to populate its own end system identifier field.

Using the preceding logic to form ATM addresses, PNNI can dynamically create peer groups. Whenever an end system is connected to an ATM switch, it is dynamically assigned the NSAP address and is adopted into the peer group. Peer groups are at the heart of the PNNI hierarchy model. Figure 21.13 shows three ATM peer groups.

As illustrated in Figure 21.13, the new peer groups are identified by the peer group numbers.

FIGURE 21.13

Three ATM peer groups.

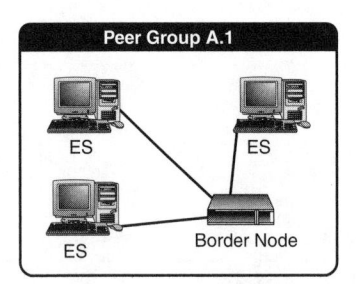

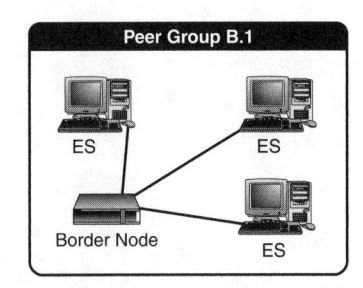

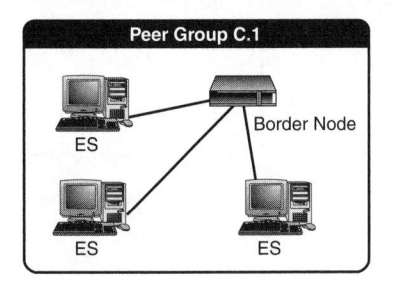

Because the first 12 bytes of the ATM address (see Figure 21.13) are the same for every node in the peer group, a letter can be used to represent them (in our example we use the letter A). The number after the dot is the 13th bit of the ATM address (of the ATM switch). This number is unique to the switch and completes the representation of the peer group number. The MAC address of each node is then attached to this peer group number to represent each individual end system.

Before routing can begin between the new peer groups, one more step needs to be taken. Each peer group switch needs to be assigned a PNNI level. This level determines the peer group's standing in the PNNI hierarchy. The group with the lowest PNNI level number is considered the dominant group. The dominant peer group is given routing priority over other PGs. A PNNI level can be any numeric value from 0 to 104.

A peer group with level that you configure as 104 has a very low routing priority compared to a PG with a level of 0. By employing levels, the peer groups can be continuously combined into larger and larger entities. For example, in Figure 21.13 the peer groups A.1 and A.2 can be considered one larger group. The peer group with the lowest level ID handles the routing decisions in this larger group.

By continually combining peer groups into larger entities, PNNI eliminates the problems of a flat routing network. Even though the members of a peer group have knowledge only of the topography of their peer group, the lower-level switches have topographical knowledge of each peer group above them.

> **Note:** The topology of a peer group refers to the location of the end systems in relation to the switch.

To keep the routing traffic between switches to a minimum, each peer group acts as a self-contained network. In Figure 21.13, if an end system in peer group A.1 needs to send data to an end system in peer group A.2, it must follow a few steps to get there. The switch in A.1, not having direct knowledge of the end systems in A.2, determines that the cell is not meant for the local peer group. The switch then forwards the packet to the switch for peer group A.2 (routing protocols take over from here).

As these groups grow in size, the amount of memory needed to keep track of the topology and handle the routing requests grows as well. Therefore, a concept of PNNI hierarchy is needed to allow the potential limit of the PNNI architecture to be circumvented.

> **Note:** One of the keys to the success of the PNNI network structure is its ability to scale to networks of almost any size. The PNNI hierarchy model, with its use of peer group numbers and peer group levels, can be adapted to almost any network.

Through the use of PNNI levels, groups A.1 and A.2 can be considered one higher-level peer group. The switch with the lowest level handles the routing for the higher-level group. Figure 21.14 illustrates a PNNI network with peer groups that have been divided into levels.

> **Note:** The structure of the graphic in Figure 21.14 has been modified to a pyramid to illustrate better the concept of PNNI leveling.

By taking the logic of PNNI levels and extending it to hundreds of switches, PNNI networks can be scaled to almost any size. Once the PNNI levels have been determined, the environment is ready for routing. PNNI handles the passing of data from switch to switch.

As we briefly discussed earlier in the chapter, PNNI is actually split (by function) into two different protocols. The process of routing data on an ATM network requires special considerations on the part of the protocols being used. Therefore, in addition to the routing protocol of PNNI, a separate signaling protocol had to be added.

FIGURE 21.14

PNNI levels.

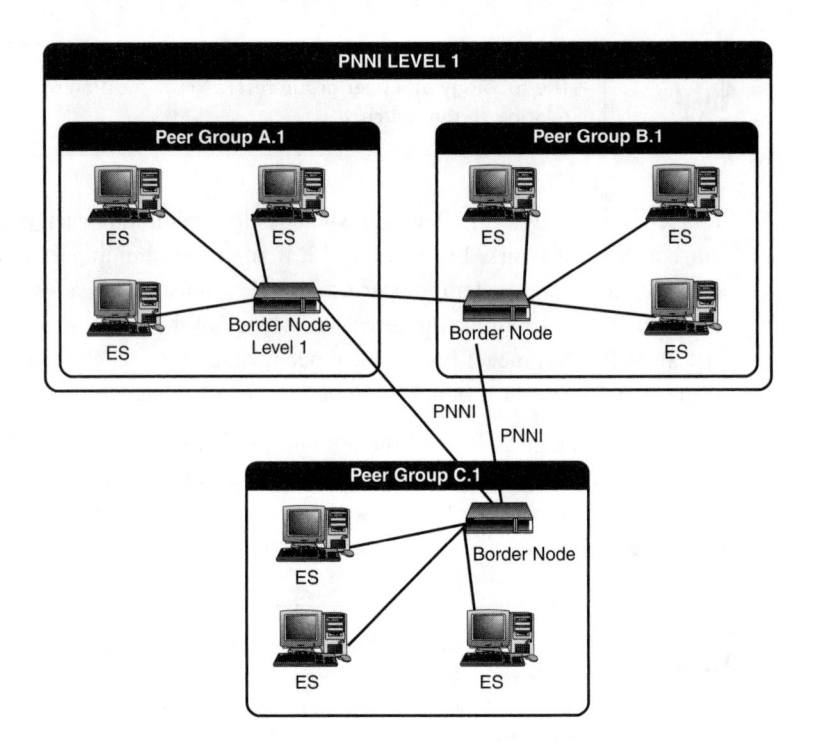

After the data is sent from an end system to a switch, the PNNI signaling protocol notifies the destination switch that a session is being requested. This is the first job duty of PNNI. The signaling protocol then builds a circuit between the two points. (This process is described in detail in the later section on "PNNI Signaling Protocol.")

After the circuit is open, the second function of PNNI kicks in. As described in the next section ("PNNI Routing Protocol"), the PNNI routing protocol handles the actual moving of the data from switch to switch. Figure 21.15 illustrates a PNNI network. The notation in the figure shows what protocols work in certain areas of the ATM environment.

Following the flow of data (via protocols) on an ATM network can be rather confusing if you have never seen it before. Even though the signaling portion of PNNI may seem a bit foreign, the routing part is pretty straightforward.

PNNI Routing Protocol

The PNNI routing protocol is based on the very successful link state category of protocols. Let's quickly review link state protocols before discussing the technology behind the PNNI routing protocol.

FIGURE 21.15

An ATM environment map with protocols.

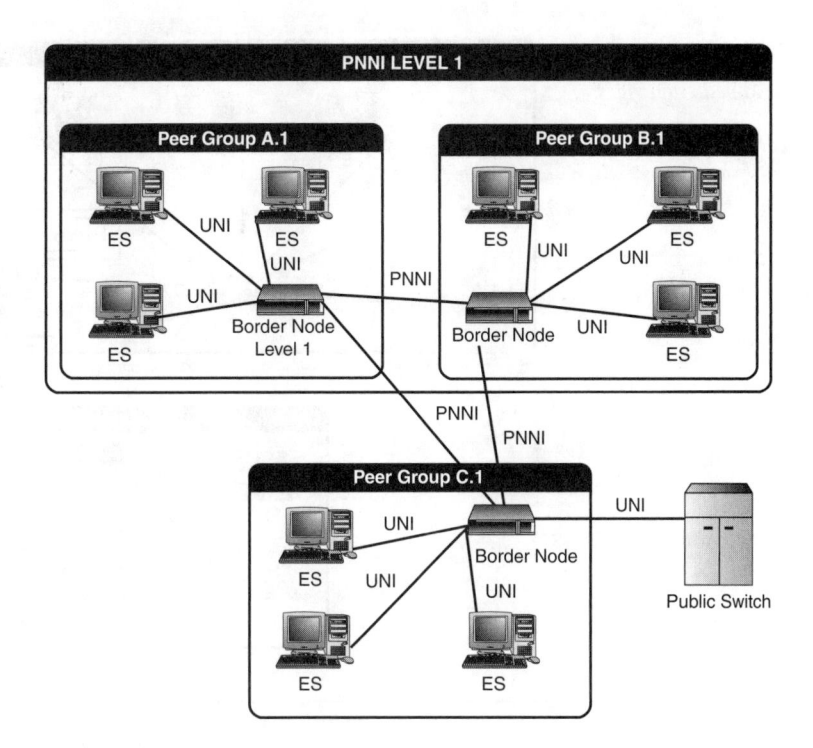

Every switch on an ATM network advertises the state of its links through hello messages. These messages are distributed to every other switch in the ATM environment regardless of peer group. The receiving systems digest the information in the hello message and formulate an overall picture of the network. Figure 21.16 illustrates the passing of a hello message on an ATM network.

In Figure 21.16, switch A.1 advertises to switches B.1 and A.2 the states of all end systems directly attached to it. In other words, switch A.1 tells A.2 and B.1 that the five end systems connected to it are up and functional. Included with this hello message are all of the metrics needed to associate the particular systems with a path.

When switch A.2 receives the hello message from A.1, it realizes (from the peer group ID) that A.1 is in its peer group. The two routers then form a link establishing that they are in the same peer group.

The process of sending hello messages is known as a link state flood. During this process every system involved floods the network with hello messages, advertising the state of its links. These messages are digested by all of the switches on the network. Link state floods have a tendency to be very bandwidth and processor intensive.

FIGURE 21.16

ATM hello messages.

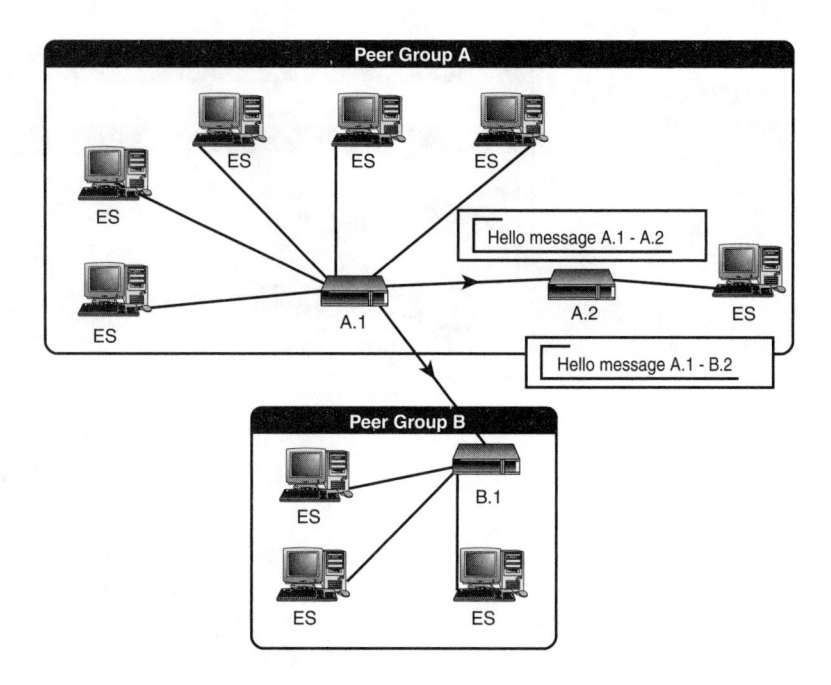

> **Note**
>
> Hello messages or link state floods are initiated by a change in the ATM environment. These changes can be the destruction or restoration of a link, the change of a routing metric, or other administrative environmental change. Some changes however, like those to certain QOS (quality of service) metrics, may not be great enough to kick off a link state flood.

Because every switch sends out the advertisements, the hello message floods are worse on larger networks than they are on smaller ones. Regardless of how many switches are on the network, one precaution makes a lot of difference in how the switches handle the floods: An ATM switch always processes a hello message before processing a cell for routing. By that, more memory (and a larger processor, if possible) will aid the switch in processing the messages quickly. By processing the hello messages as quickly as possible, the switches can return to normal operation sooner. This process (obtaining the latest network routing information quickly) is known as convergence.

Convergence occurs when every switch is operating with the same picture of the network—that is, every switch has processed the hello messages and agreed that the contents of those messages describe the current network topology. (In general, link state protocols, like PNNI, have a faster convergence time than others.)

Routers, no matter what protocols they are using, need to have the most up-to-date topology information to make the best decisions. Link state protocols use the information in the hello messages (which creates the switch's routing table) to calculate the shortest path between systems. Like other link state protocols, PNNI works on a "shortest path" basis. A PNNI device always tries to choose the shortest possible path between two systems.

Deciding which path is the shortest is the job of the routing algorithm. The routing algorithm is a formula used by the PNNI device to use the metrics found in its routing table in order to calculate the best path to a destination. PNNI devices are configured with different metrics to indicate a device's likelihood of being chosen as the shortest path. PNNI uses the following metrics to describe a device:

- Administrative weight (AW)—An administrator-assigned cost; the metric is purely arbitrary.
- Available cell rate (AvCR)—The bandwidth of a line
- Maximum cell transfer delay (MaxCTD)—The delay experienced in transmitting cells over a particular link
- Cell loss ratio (CLR)—The number of cells typically lost over a particular link
- Cell delay variation (CDV)—A combined metric representing the link's CLR minus the average CLR for the environment (CLR – Avg. CLR)
- Maximum cell rate (MaxCR)—The maximum cell capacity of the line

Each of these metrics has an assigned value, either dynamically or statically. The values are used by PNNI's routing algorithm to calculate the overall value or usefulness of a particular link in reaching the cell's ultimate destination. If the combination of the metrics proves that the current link is the ideal link for routing, the cells are forwarded across the line.

All of the metrics listed, with the exception of administrative weight, are considered QOS metrics. QOS (quality of service) routing is a standard set forth in RFC 2386.

PNNI and QOS

PNNI adheres to the QOS specifications for ATM. That means that ATM supports the same metrics for providing a consistent level of routing service to the end systems as every other QOS-compliant architecture. Although many protocols have been adapted or enhanced to meet QOS standards, PNNI was designed to handle QOS natively. In other words, no extra hardware or software to implement the metrics is required for QOS ATM routing.

Metrics such as maxCR and CLR are used to ensure that a cell will be forwarded over a link that can handle it. The QOS metrics (maximum cell transfer delay, cell loss ratio, cell delay variation, and maximum cell rate) and the administrative metric of administrative weight are all statically defined. That is, they rarely change without the administrator's intervention.

The QOS metric of available cell rate is a dynamic metric that can fluctuate depending on the current link traffic. Because this metric is dynamic, a change in this cost generally does not cause a link state update. A change in the available cell rate must surpass a preset threshold to trigger a network-wide update.

When a cell needs to be routed on a PNNI network, the signaling protocol requests a minimum (QOS) value that the circuit needs to route the cell successfully.

> **Note**
> Depending on the switch being used in the ATM environment, a different QOS algorithm may be used to help determine the available paths. PNNI allows for two different QOS algorithms, simple GCAC (Generic Call Admission Control) and complex GCAC.
>
> Simple GCAC weighs only the available cell rate metric in making a decision, whereas complex GCAC uses available cell rate and two new metrics: cell rate margin and variance factor.

For example, the PNNI signaling protocol might request that the circuit have a certain bandwidth; then only links that fall within that QOS bandwidth metric can be considered by the algorithm as a possible path. Figure 21.17 illustrates a QOS circuit request.

In Figure 21.17, data is attempting to be routed from A.1 to C.4. The signaling protocol (covered in the section "PNNI Signaling Protocol") requests that a link with at least 56 Kbps of constant bandwidth be opened to route the cells. This request automatically excludes the link between B.1 and C.1 from consideration for carrying the cells.

PNNI determines what paths are used for routing data by weighing each link's metrics against a routing algorithm. This algorithm examines the cost associated with every link and determines which is the best to use.

The algorithm of choice for many link state protocols is Dijkstra's algorithm. PNNI is no exception. PNNI can utilize this algorithm very well (see Day 17, "Configuring OSPF," for a complete description of Dijkstra's algorithm; we will discuss it only briefly here). Once the considerations for QOS have been made, the algorithm can then choose the shortest path for the data.

FIGURE 21.17

QOS routing.

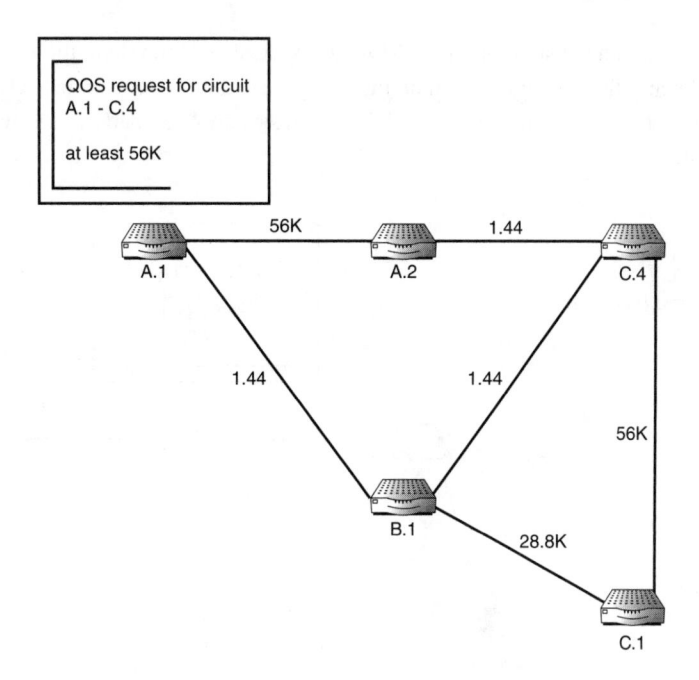

Dijkstra's algorithm uses the metrics assigned to each link to determine the shortest path between all possible points on a network simultaneously. That is, Dijkstra's algorithm dynamically calculates the costs of every link on the network at the same time. This makes the algorithm a very quick and reliable way to determine paths.

Combining native QOS and shortest-path routing is one of the attributes that make PNNI an attractive protocol, especially for the ATM environment. The PNNI routing protocol is only half of the picture. ATM as an architecture is circuit based. Therefore, circuits need to be established before data can be routed over them. The job of establishing these circuits falls to the PNNI signaling protocol.

PNNI Signaling Protocol

The PNNI signaling protocol is the portion of PNNI that is required to establish and tear down connections between devices. The signaling protocol takes into account any metrics, including QOS, to request that circuits be opened for routing purposes. Once the signaling protocol has successfully built a circuit between two points, the PNNI routing protocol can take over.

When an end system on an ATM network needs to send data, the PNNI signaling protocol starts the process by contacting the closest directly connected ATM switch and notifying it of the request. Figure 21.18 illustrates an ATM end system with a routing request.

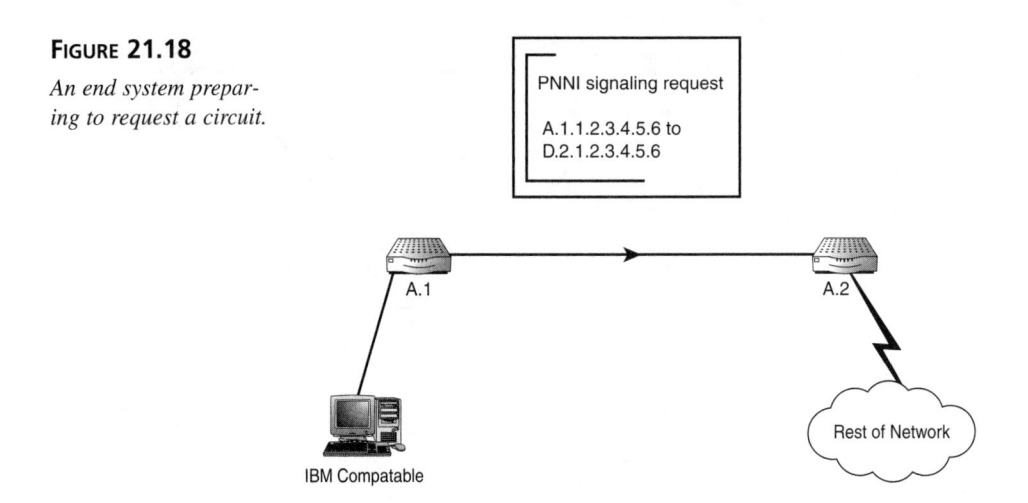

FIGURE 21.18

An end system preparing to request a circuit.

```
PNNI signaling request
A.1.1.2.3.4.5.6 to
D.2.1.2.3.4.5.6
```

A.1 → A.2

IBM Compatable

Rest of Network

In Figure 21.18, the PNNI signaling protocol contacts switch A.1 on behalf of the end system. The signaling protocol notifies the switch that the end system is requesting that the switch open a circuit to an end system in the D peer group.

> **Note** Even though the end system knows which specific end systems it needs to contact in peer group D, it has no topographical knowledge of that group. It would simply request the circuit to the border node of the peer group. Peer group D's border node would then route the cells to the correct end system.

The signaling protocol also sends along a set of QOS requests. These requests (or minimum requirements) are passed from switch to switch. When a switch receives the QOS requirements, it first finds the links that can meet those metrics. The remaining links are exempt from consideration. The request is then passed down the optimal link to the next switch.

> **Note** If no links are found that meet the QOS requirements of the signaling request, the request is denied. The information from the source end system is then discarded.

Eventually the signaling request reaches the destination border node. Here, the switch can either accept or deny the circuit. If the circuit is accepted, the border node passes the cells to the destination end system, and a circuit is established between the two systems. If the destination border node refuses the request, the data from the end system is discarded.

Figure 21.19 illustrates an ATM network with all of the metrics populated. Let's look at the path the signaling protocol would take from end system A.1.X.X.X.X.X.X to end system D.1.X.X.X.X.X.X.

FIGURE 21.19

An ATM network signaling example.

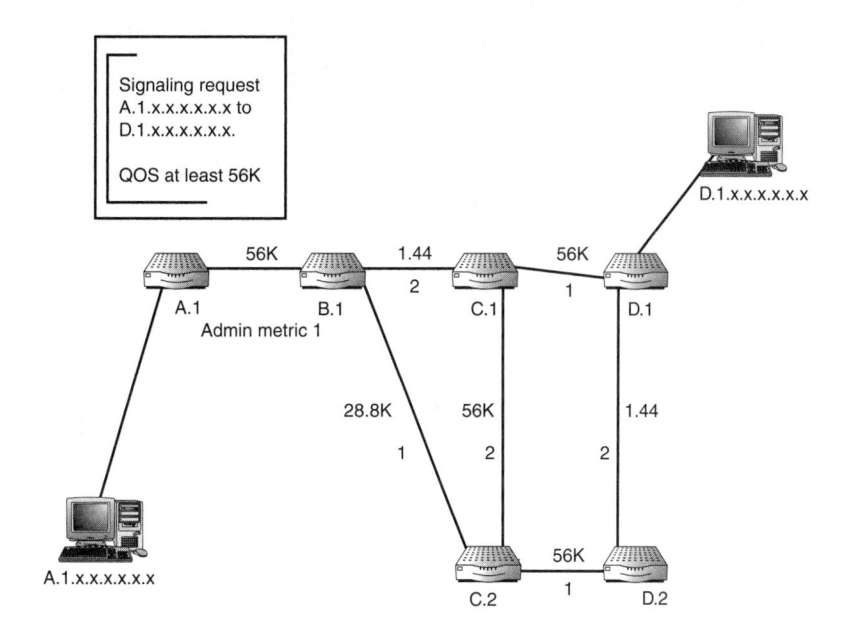

In Figure 21.19, the signaling protocol would send the request to switch A.1. The QOS requirements call for a line with at least 56 Kbps of bandwidth. Therefore, when A.1 receives the signaling request, it evaluates all of its links to determine which have 56 Kbps of bandwidth. In this case there is only one link (B.1), and it does have 56 Kbps. The signaling request is then forwarded to B.1.

At B.1 the switch has two choices: The cells can be sent over the B.1–C.1 link or the B.1–C.2 link. Because the B.1–C.2 link does not meet the QOS requirements, the link is not considered for the path. The request is then forwarded to C.1.

When C.1 gets the request, it has two choices. The links C.1 to C.2 and C.1 to D.1 both meet the QOS requirements for the circuit. The switch then turns to its routing algorithm, which determines that the shortest path is the link C.1 to D.1. The signaling request is then forwarded to D.1.

D.1 recognizes that the end system D.1.X.X.X.X.X.X is in its peer group. ATM switch D.1 can then accept the circuit request by forwarding it to end system D.1.X.X.X.X.X.X, or it can reject the request. If D.1 accepts the request, a circuit is established between the two end systems. Figure 21.20 illustrates the completed circuit.

FIGURE 21.20

A completed ATM circuit.

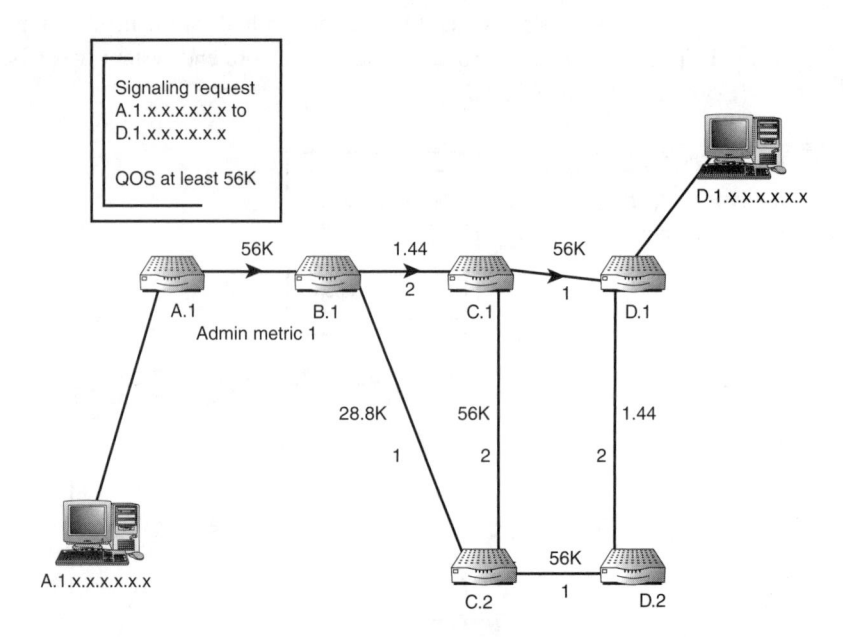

If the signaling request is rejected by D.1, the switches C.1, B.1, and A.1 are so notified with a return message. This message cancels the circuit's requests on the switches and discards any cells (pertaining to the circuit) that the switch may have processed.

When the end system A.1.X.X.X.X.X.X completes its session with D.1.X.X.X.X.X.X, regardless of whether the signal was accepted or rejected, the PNNI signaling protocol tears down the circuit, leaving the links clear for routing.

Because some of the QOS metrics are dynamically assigned, there is a chance that they might change during a transmission. PNNI has a built-in mechanism to deal with such an event, called *crankback*. PNNI can implement its crankback mechanism if QOS metrics change unfavorably during a transmission.

PNNI Crankback

During the lifespan of a circuit a QOS metric, such as available cell rate, may change. If a QOS metric changes detrimentally with respect to the circuit (for example, the circuit requires a delay of 10 ms and the delay jumps to 200 ms), the PNNI protocol performs an action known as a crankback. Look at the circuit in Figure 21.21. During a crankback the protocol rolls back the circuit to the last ATM switch that still meets the QOS requirements. Figure 21.22 shows a circuit being rolled back during a crankback operation.

FIGURE 21.21

A completed ATM circuit with QOS metrics.

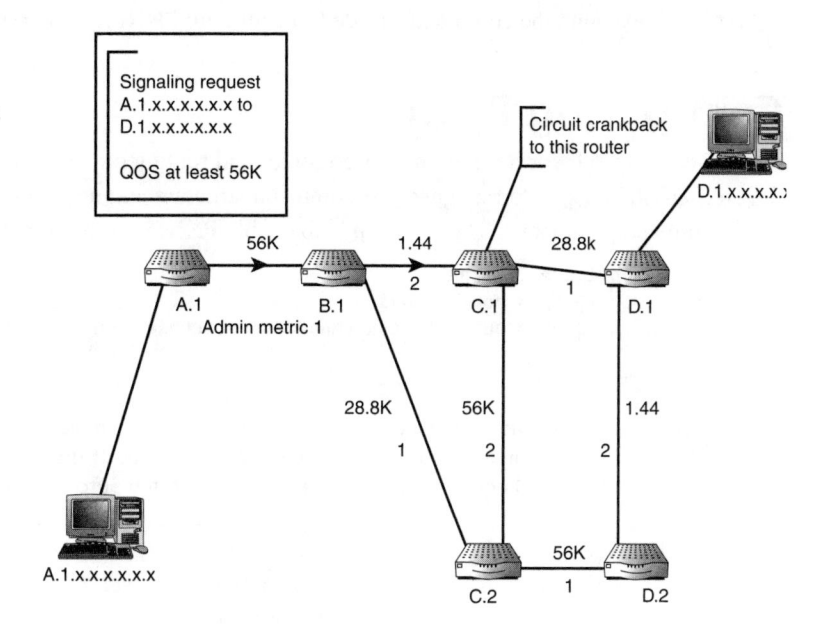

FIGURE 21.22

A circuit crankback.

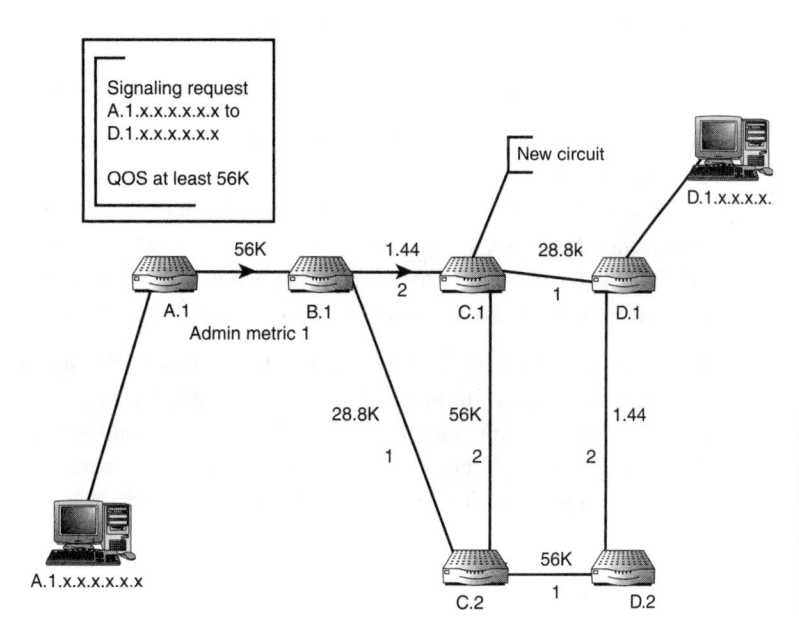

The circuit is then rebuilt from the last good switch. While the circuit is rebuilt, the QOS requirements are re-evaluated.

Now that we have discussed the concepts behind ATM switching and PNNI routing, it's time to examine the commands needed to configure PNNI routing on a Cisco switch.

Configuring PNNI

The commands for routing on a Cisco router and routing on a Cisco switch are not that different. You should recognize the command structure and understand the purpose of the command parameters. The first step is to enable PNNI routing on the switch:

```
Switch#configure terminal
Switch(config)#atm router pnni
Switch(config-atm-router)# aesa embedded-number left-justified
```

> **Note:** The last command executed in the previous example is used to enable PNNI version 2 encoding. The E.164 address prefixes of the end systems (aesa, for "ATM end system address") will be converted automatically.

The `atm router` command enables PNNI routing. However, there are some peripheral commands that you should be aware of. For example, to specify the ATM address of the switch, use the `atm address` command:

```
Switch#configure terminal
Switch(config)#atm address 52.000a.c001.034b.000.06a7.0001. ..
```

The three periods at the end of the command execution string indicate to the switch that the address entered is the prefix and the default MAC address should be appended to it to form the ATM address. As is apparent from their name, the main function of switches is not routing. However, switches do offer the ability to utilize a very effective routing protocol. Unfortunately, there are many more commands associated with ATM and PNNI than can be covered in one lesson of a book focused on routing.

The purpose of covering the topics in this lesson was to familiarize you with the protocol as many environments utilize both Cisco routers and Cisco switches. There are many resources both in print and online that elaborate on the subjects and topics covered here. Having reached the end of this book, I hope you have acquired the basic knowledge needed to understand introductory Cisco routing.

Congratulations! You have finished the core elements needed to understand basic Cisco router functionality and techniques. With this chapter, you have also learned some move advanced Cisco switch routing techniques. For more information about any of the topics we have covered, try the Cisco online knowledge base, at www.cisco.com, or any of the other routing books from SAMS Publishing.

APPENDIX

Cisco Command Reference

The following is a fairly comprehensive list of Cisco IOS commands, their parameters, and their related meanings. The commands for user and privilege modes have been included within this reference. Although many of the definitions and usage characteristics of these commands can be found in the Cisco IOS, beginners will find a simple reference like this most useful. Sample statements have been given to illustrate command syntax and execution.

> **Note** The brief explanations for each command are adapted from the Cisco help system.

User Mode Commands

access-enable

Cisco Explanation

Create a temporary access list entry. (This command is allowed for virtual lines only.)

Parameters

Parameter	Explanation
host	Enable a specific host only
timeout	Maximum idle time to expire this entry
<1-9999>	Access list idle timeout
timeout	Maximum idle time to expire this entry
<1-9999>	Access list idle timeout

Syntax Example

```
>access-enable host timeout 1
```

access-profile

Cisco Explanation

Apply user-profile to interface. (This command is allowed for virtual lines only.)

Parameters

Parameter	Explanation
ignore-sanity-checks	Ignore all sanity check errors (used to ignore errors resulting from incorrect formatting of AV pair authentication information)
merge	Merge old and new per-user profiles, removing only access lists
ignore-sanity-checks	Ignore all sanity check errors (used to ignore errors resulting from incorrect formatting of AV pair authentication information)
replace	Remove old per-user config, replace with new config
ignore-sanity-checks	Ignore all sanity check errors (used to ignore errors resulting from incorrect formatting of AV pair authentication information)

Syntax Example

```
>access-profile merge
```

connect
Cisco Explanation
Open a terminal connection to another device. The only parameter is the external device's name or address.

Parameters

Parameter	Explanation
WORD	IP address or hostname of a remote system

Syntax Example
>connect RouterA

disable
Cisco Explanation
Turn off privileged commands. This command takes the specific privilege mode number as an optional parameter.

Parameter

Parameter	Explanation
(0-15)	Level number

Syntax Example
>disable 14

disconnect
Cisco Explanation
Disconnects an existing network connection (that is, a remote session). This command takes either the connection name or the connection number as a parameter.

Parameters

Parameter	Explanation
<1-20>	The number of an active network connection
WORD	The name of an active network connection

Syntax Examples

```
>disconnect 1
>disconnect RouterA
```

enable

Cisco explanation: Turn on privileged commands. If the administrator has established different access levels, the level number can be an optional parameter.

Parameter	Explanation
(0-15)	Level number

Syntax Example

```
>enable 14
```

exit

Cisco explanation: Exit from the EXEC. Used to quit an IOS session; takes no parameters.

Syntax Example

```
>exit
```

help

Cisco Explanation

Description of the interactive help system; takes no parameters.

Syntax Example

```
>help
```

lock

Cisco Explanation

Locks the terminal. The lock command locks the screen of a remote terminal. This command takes no parameters.

Syntax Example

```
>lock
```

login

Cisco Explanation

Log in as a particular user.

This command authenticates the router user to a specific login server. It takes no parameters if a login server is not available.

Syntax Example

>login

logout

Cisco Explanation

Exit from the EXEC. This command takes no parameters.

Syntax Example

>logout

name-connection

Cisco Explanation

Name an existing network connection. This command is used to name a remote session connection for simplifying the process of referring to multiple locations. This command takes no parameters, but it will initiate a menu-driven dialog.

Syntax Example

>name-connection 1 RouterA

pad

Cisco Explanation

Open an X.29 PAD (packet assembler/disassembler) connection. This command is used to connect to an external X.25 PAD device.

Parameters

Parameter	Explanation
WORD	X.121 address or name of a remote system

Syntax Example

>pad Remote

ping

Cisco Explanation

Send echo messages.

Parameters

Parameter	Explanation
WORD	Ping destination address or hostname
ip	IP echo
WORD	Ping destination address or hostname
ipx	Novell/IPX echo
WORD	Ping destination address or hostname
tag	Tag encapsulated IP echo
WORD	Ping destination address or hostname

Syntax Examples

`>ping 10.25.123.3`

`>ping ip 10.25.123.3`

ppp

Cisco Explanation

Start IETF Point-to-Point Protocol (PPP).

Parameter

Parameter	Explanation
negotiate	Use PPP negotiated IP address

Syntax Example

`>ppp negotiate`

resume

Cisco Explanation

Resume an active network connection. This command accepts several options introduced by a slash /, any of which can be used.

Options

Option	Explanation
/debug	Print parameter changes and messages
/echo	Perform local echo
/line	Enable Telnet line mode
/next	Step to next network connection
/nodebug	Do not print parameter changes and messages
/noecho	Disable local echo
/noline	Disable Telnet line mode
/nostream	Disable stream processing
/set	Set X3 connection options
/stream	Enable stream processing

Parameters

Parameter	Explanation
<1-20>	The number of an active network connection
WORD	The name of an active network connection or connection options

Syntax Example

```
>resume /noecho RouterA
```

rlogin

Cisco Explanation

Open an rlogin connection.

Parameter

Parameter	Explanation
WORD	IP address or hostname of a remote system

Syntax Example

```
>rlogin 10.25.123.3

>rlogin RouterA
```

show

Cisco Explanation

Show running system information. The show command is a very comprehensive command used to view and monitor many of the statistics of the router.

Parameters

Parameter	Explanation
clock	Display the system clock
detail	Display detailed information
dialer	Dialer parameters and statistics
maps	Show dialer maps
flash:	Display information about flash: filesystem
all	Show all possible flash info
chips	Show flash chip information
detailed	Show flash detailed directory
err	Show flash chip erase and write retries
summary	Show flash partition summary
history	Display the session command history
hosts	Show IP domain name, lookup style, name servers, and host table
WORD	Hostname for specific information
location	Display the system location
Modemcap	Show Modem Capabilities database
WORD	Modem entry to use
ppp	Show PPP parameters and statistics
bap	Show PPP Bandwidth Allocation Protocol (BAP) parameters and statistics
group	BAP group information
WORD	Group name
queues	BAP queue information
multilink	Show Multilink PPP bundle information
queues	Show PPP request queues
rmon	Show RAM Monitor (RMON) statistics
alarms	Display the RMON alarm table
events	Display the RMON event table

continues

Parameter	Explanation
events	Display the RMON event table
alarms	Display the RMON alarm table
rtr	Display Response Time Reporter (RTR) results
application	RTR Application
full	Listed output
tabular	Compact output
collection-statistics	RTR statistic collections
<1-2147483647>	Entry number
full	Listed output (selected entry)
tabular	Compact output (selected entry)
full	Listed output (all collections)
tabular	Compact output (all collections)
configuration	RTR Configuration
<1-2147483647>	Entry number
full	Listed output (selected entry)
tabular	Compact output (selected entry)
full	Listed output (all configurations)
tabular	Compact output (all configurations)
distributions-statistics	Display RTR statistic distributions
<1-2147483647>	Entry number
full	Listed output (selected entry)
tabular	Compact output (selected entry)
full	Listed output (all distributions)
tabular	Compact output (all distributions)
history	RTR history
<1-2147483647>	Entry number
full	Listed output (selected entry)
tabular	Compact output (selected entry)
full	Listed output (all history)
tabular	Compact output (all history)
operational-state	RTR operational state
<1-2147483647>	Entry number
full	Listed output (selected entry)

continues

Parameter	Explanation
tabular	Compact output (selected entry)
full	Listed output (all state)
tabular	Compact output (all state)
reaction-trigger	RTR reaction trigger
<1-2147483647>	Entry number
full	Listed output (selected entry)
tabular	Compact output (selected entry)
full	Listed output (all reactions)
tabular	Compact output (all reactions)
totals-statistics	RTR statistics totals
<1-2147483647>	Entry number
full	Listed output (selected entry)
tabular	Compact output (selected entry)
full	Listed output (all totals)
tabular	Compact output (all totals)
sessions	Show information about Telnet connections
snmp	Show SNMP (Simple Network Management Protocol) statistics
tacacs	Show TACACS+ (Terminal Access Controller Access Control System) server statistics
terminal	Display terminal configuration parameters
traffic-shape	Display traffic rate shaping configuration
Ethernet	IEEE 802.3
<0-1>	Ethernet interface number
Null	Null interface
<0-0>	Null interface number
queue	Show shaping queue contents
Ethernet	IEEE 802.3
<0-1>	Ethernet interface number
Null	Null interface
<0-0>	Null interface number
statistics	Traffic rate shaping statistics
Ethernet	IEEE 802.3
<0-1>	Ethernet interface number

continues

Parameter	Explanation
Null	Null interface
<0-0>	Null interface number
users	Display information about terminal lines
all	Include information about inactive ports
wide	Use wide format (including inactive ports)
wide	Use wide format
version	System hardware and software status

Syntax Example
>show system detailed

slip
Cisco Explanation
Start Serial-Line IP (SLIP).

Syntax Example
>slip

systat
Cisco Explanation
Display information about terminal lines.

Parameter

Parameter	Explanation
all	Include information about inactive ports

Syntax Example
>systat all

telnet
Cisco Explanation
Open a Telnet connection with a remote router or other Telnet device.

Parameter

Parameter	Explanation
WORD	IP address or hostname of a remote system

Syntax Examples

```
>telnet 10.25.123.3

>telnet RouterA
```

`terminal`

Cisco Explanation

Set terminal line parameters.

Parameters

Parameter	Explanation
autohangup	Automatically hang up when last connection closes
session-timeout	Automatically hang up when current session Times-out
data-character-bits	Size of characters being handled
<7-8>	Bits per character
databits	Set number of data bits per character
<5-8>	Number of databits
default	Set a command to its defaults
Accepts any valid parameter	
dispatch-character	Define the dispatch character
CHAR or <0-127>	Dispatch character or its decimal equivalent
dispatch-timeout	Set the dispatch timer
<0-4294967294>	Dispatch timer in milliseconds
domain-lookup	Enable domain lookups in show commands
download	Put line into 'download' mode
editing	Enable command line editing
escape-character	Change the current line's escape character
BREAK	Cause escape on BREAK
CHAR or <0-255>	Escape character or its ASCII decimal equivalent
DEFAULT	Use default escape character
NONE	Disable escape entirely

continues

Parameter	Explanation
soft	Set the soft escape character for this line
BREAK	Cause escape on BREAK
CHAR or <0-255>	Escape character or its ASCII decimal equivalent
DEFAULT	Use default escape character
NONE	Disable escape entirely
exec-character-bits	Size of characters to the command exec
<7-8>	Bits per character
flowcontrol	Set the flow control
NONE	Set no flow control
hardware	Set hardware flow control
in	Listen to flow control from the attached device
out	Send flow control information to the attached device
software	Set software flow control
in	Listen to flow control from the attached device
lock	Ignore network host requests to change flow control
out	Send flow control information to the attached device
full-help	Provide help to unprivileged user
help	Description of the interactive help system
history	Enable and control the command history function
size	Set history buffer size
<0-256>	Size of history buffer
hold-character	Define the hold character
CHAR or <0-255>	Hold character or its decimal equivalent
international	Enable international 8-bit character support
ip	IP options
netmask-format	Change display of netmasks
bit-count	Display netmask as number of significant bits
decimal	Display netmask in dotted decimal
hexadecimal	Display netmask in hexadecimal
tcp	TCP options
input-coalesce-threshold	Set the threshold that triggers packet coalescing (20 default)
length	Set number of lines on a screen
<0-512>	Number of lines on screen (0 for no pausing)

continues

Parameter	Explanation
no	Negate a command or set its defaults
notify	Inform users of output from concurrent sessions
padding	Set padding for a specified output character
CHAR or <0-127>	Character to be padded
parity	Set terminal parity
even	Even parity
mark	Mark parity
none	No parity
odd	Odd parity
space	Space parity
rxspeed	Set the receive speed
<0-4294967295>	Receive speed
special-character-bits	Size of the escape (and other special) characters
<7-8>	Bits per character
speed	Set the transmit and receive speeds
<0-4294967295>	Transmit and receive speeds
start-character	Define the start character
CHAR or <0-255>	Start character or its decimal equivalent
stop-character	Define the stop character
CHAR or <0-255>	Stop character or its decimal equivalent
stopbits	Set async line stop bits
1	One stop bit
1.5	One and one-half stop bits
2	Two stop bits
telnet	Telnet protocol-specific configuration
break-on-ip	Send break signal when interrupt is received
ip-on-break	Send interrupt signal when break is received
refuse-negotiations	Suppress negotiations of Telnet Remote Echo and Suppress Go Ahead options
speed	Specify line speeds
<1-4294967295>	Default speed
sync-on-break	Send a Telnet Synchronize signal after receiving a Telnet Break signal

continues

Parameter	Explanation
transparent	Send a CR as a CR followed by a NULL instead of a CR followed by a LF
terminal-type	Set the terminal type
WORD	Terminal type
transport	Define transport protocols for line
all	All protocols
none	No protocols
pad	X.3 PAD (packet assembler/disassembler)
rlogin	Unix rlogin protocol
telnet	TCP/IP Telnet protocol
txspeed	Set the transmit speeds
<0-4294967295>	Transmit speed
width	Set width of the display terminal
<0-512>	Number of characters on a screen line

Syntax Example

```
>terminal autohangup session-timeout
```

traceroute

Cisco Explanation

Trace route to destination

Parameters

Parameter	Explanation
WORD	Trace route to destination address or hostname
appletalk	AppleTalk trace
WORD	Trace route to destination address or hostname
clns	ISO Connectionless Network Service (CLNS) trace
WORD	Trace route to destination address or hostname
ip	IP trace
WORD	Trace route to destination address or hostname
ipx	IPX trace
WORD	Trace route to destination address or hostname

continues

Parameter	Explanation
oldvines	VINES (Virtual Integrated Network Service) trace (Cisco)
WORD	Trace route to destination address or hostname
vines	VINES trace (Banyan)
WORD	Trace route to destination address or hostname

Syntax Examples

```
>traceroute RouterA

>traceroute 10.25.123.3

>tracerouter ip 10.25.123.3
```

tunnel

Cisco Explanation

Open a tunnel connection.

Parameter

Parameter	Explanation
WORD	Address or hostname of a remote system

Syntax Example

```
>tunnel RouterA
```

where

Cisco Explanation

List active connections.

Syntax Example

```
>where
```

x28

Cisco Explanation

Become an X.28 PAD (packet assembler/disassembler). Any combination of the x.28 parameters can be used together.

Parameters

Parameter	Explanation
debug	Turn on debug messages for X.28 mode
escape	Set the string to escape from X.28 PAD mode
noescape	Never exit X.28 mode (use with caution)
nuicud	All calls with NUI (Network User ID) are normal charge with the NUI placed in call user data
profile	Use a defined X.3 profile
reverse	All calls default to reverse charge
verbose	Turn on verbose messages for X.28 mode

Syntax Examples

>x.28 debug nuicud

>x.28 escape nuicud debug

x3

Cisco Explanation

Set X.3 parameters on PAD.

Parameter

Parameter	Explanation
<0-22>:<0-255>	X.3 PAD parameters and values

Syntax Example

>X3 5:225

Privilege Mode Commands

The following is a selection of privilege mode commands and their uses. There are many more commands that can be run in privilege mode, but only those commands that do not also appear in user mode have been included.

> **Note:** Keep in mind that any or all of these commands can be blocked from certain users through privilege mode access levels.

access-template
Cisco Explanation
Create a temporary access list entry. This command creates a temporary access list, which users can invoke for a limited period of time.

Parameters

Parameter	Explanation
<100-199>	IP extended access list
WORD	Name of temporary list within the access-list
A.B.C.D	Source address
A.B.C.D	Source wildcard bits
A.B.C.D	Destination address
A.B.C.D	Destination wildcard bits
timeout	Maximum idle time to expire this entry
<1-9999>	Access list idle timeout
any	Any destination host
host	A single destination host
Hostname or A.B.C.D	Source address
A.B.C.D	Destination address
A.B.C.D	Destination wildcard bits
timeout	Maximum idle time to expire this entry
<1-9999>	Access list Idle timeout
any	Any source host
A.B.C.D	Destination address
A.B.C.D	Destination wildcard bits
timeout	Maximum idle time to expire this entry
<1-9999>	Access list idle timeout
host	A single source host
Hostname or A.B.C.D	Source address
A.B.C.D	Destination address
A.B.C.D	Destination wildcard bits
timeout	Maximum idle time to expire this entry
<1-9999>	Access list idle timeout

continues

Parameter	Explanation
<2000-2699>	IP extended access list (expanded range)
accepts the same parameters as IP extended access list	
WORD	Access list name

Syntax Example

```
#access-template 100 test 10.25.123.3 0.255.255.255 10.35.124.4 0.255.255.255
timeout 1
```

cd

Cisco Explanation

Change current directory.

Parameters

Parameter	Explanation
flash:	Directory name
flh:	Directory name
null:	Directory name
nvram:	Directory name
system:	Directory name

Syntax Example

```
#cd flash: files
```

clear

Cisco Explanation

Reset functions.

Parameters

Parameter	Explanation
access-list	Clear access list statistical information
counters	Clear access list counters
<0-199>	Access list number
WORD	Access list name
access-template	Clear access template

continues

Parameter	Explanation
<100-199>	IP extended access list
See `access-template` *for a list of access-list parameters*	
<2000-2699>	IP extended access list (expanded range)
See `access-template` *for a list of access-list parameters*	
`arp-cache`	Clear the entire ARP (Address Resolution Protocol) cache
`bridge`	Reset bridge forwarding cache
<1-255>	A bridge group number
`cdp`	Reset CDP (Cisco Discovery Protocol) information
`counters`	Clear CDP counters
`table`	Clear CDP table
`counters`	Clear counters on one or all interfaces
`Ethernet`	IEEE 802.3
<0-1>	Ethernet interface number
`line`	Terminal line
<0-5>	First Line number
<1-5>	Last Line number
`console`	Primary terminal line
<0-0>	First Line number
`vty`	Virtual terminal
<0-4>	First Line number
<1-4>	Last Line number
`Null`	Null interface
<0-0>	Null interface number
`dialer`	Clear dialer statistics
`frame-relay-inarp`	Clear inverse ARP entries from the map table
`host`	Delete host table entries
`WORD`	Hostname to delete (* for all entries)
`interface`	Clear the hardware logic on an interface
`Ethernet`	IEEE 802.3
<0-1>	Ethernet interface number
`Null`	Null interface
<0-0>	Null interface number
`ip`	IP

continues

Parameter	Explanation
access-list	Clear access list statistical information
See access-template for a list of access list parameters	
access-template	Access template
See access-template for a list of access list parameters	
accounting	Clear IP accounting database
checkpoint	Clear IP accounting checkpoint database
cache	Delete cache table entries
A.B.C.D	Address prefix
A.B.C.D	prefix mask
eigrp	Clear IP-EIGRP
<1-65535>	Autonomous system number
neighbors	Clear IP-EIGRP neighbors
A.B.C.D	IP-EIGRP neighbor address
Ethernet	IEEE 802.3
<0-1>	Ethernet interface number
Null	Null interface
<0-0>	Null interface number
neighbors	Clear IP-EIGRP neighbors
A.B.C.D	IP-EIGRP neighbor address
Ethernet	IEEE 802.3
<0-1>	Ethernet interface number
Null	Null interface
<0-0>	Null interface number
nat	Clear NAT (Network Address Translation)
statistics	Clear translation statistics
translation	Clear dynamic translation
nhrp	Clear Next Hop Resolution Protocol (NHRP) cache
A.B.C.D	Destination network to delete
A.B.C.D	Destination network mask
ospf	Clear OSPF commands
counters	OSPF counters
neighbor	Neighbor statistics per interface or neighbor id
Ethernet	IEEE 802.3

continues

Parameter	Explanation
<0-1>	Ethernet interface number
Hostname or *A.B.C.D*	Neighbor ID
Null	Null interface
<0-0>	Null interface number
redistribution	Route redistribution
prefix-list	Clear prefix list
WORD	Name of a prefix list
redirect	Clear redirect cache
route	Delete route table entries
*	Delete all routes
A.B.C.D	Destination network route to delete
rtp	Clear RTP/UDP/IP header-compression statistics
header-compression	RTP/UDP/IP header-compression statistics
Ethernet	IEEE 802.3
<0-1>	Ethernet interface number
Null	Null interface
<0-0>	Null interface number
ipx	Reset Novell/IPX information
accounting	Clear IPX accounting database
checkpoint	Clear IPX accounting checkpoint database
cache	Clear IPX fast switching cache
eigrp	Clear Novell-EIGRP
route	Remove IPX routing table entry
neighbors	Clear Novell-EIGRP neighbors
Ethernet	IEEE 802.3
<0-1>	Ethernet interface number
N.H.H.H	Novell-EIGRP neighbor address
Null	Null interface
<0-0>	Null interface number
spx-spoof	Clear IPX SPX spoof table
line	Reset a terminal line
<0-5>	Line number
console	Primary terminal line

continues

Parameter	Explanation
<0-0>	Line number
vty	Virtual terminal
<0-4>	Line number
logging	Clear logging buffer
snapshot	Clear Snapshot timers
quiet-time	Clear quiet time, enter active time if client side
Ethernet	IEEE 802.3
<0-1>	Ethernet interface number
Null	Null interface
<0-0>	Null interface number
tcp	Clear a TCP connection or statistics
line	TTY line
<0-0>	Line number
local	Local host address/port
Hostname or *A.B.C.D*	Local host name or IP address
<1-65535>	Local TCP port
remote	Remote host address/port
Hostname or *A.B.C.D*	Remote host name or IP address
<1-65535>	Remote TCP port
statistics	TCP protocol statistics
tcb	TCB address
<0x0-0xFFFFFFFF>	TCB address
x25	Clear X.25 circuits
Ethernet	IEEE 802.3
<0-1>	Ethernet interface number
H.H.H	CMNS host MAC address
xot	Clear an XOT (X.25-Over-TCP) VC
remote	Show XOT VCs to one remote host
A.B.C.D	host IP address
<1-65535>	port number
local	Show XOT VCs from one local host
A.B.C.D	host IP address
<1-65535>	port number

Syntax Example

`#clear counters`

clock

Cisco Explanation

Manage the system clock.

Parameters

Parameter	Explanation
set	Set the time and date
hh:mm:ss	Current Time
<1-31>	Day of the month
MONTH	Month of the year
<1993-2035>	Year
MONTH	Month of the year
<1993-2035>	Year

Syntax Example

`#clock set 12:00:00 1 January 2000`

copy

Cisco Explanation

Copy from one file to another.

Option

Option	Explanation
/erase	Erase destination file system

"From" Parameters

Parameter	Explanation
flash:	Copy from flash: file system
flh:	Copy from flh: file system
ftp:	Copy from ftp: file system
null:	Copy from null: file system

continues

Parameter	Explanation
nvram:	Copy from nvram: file system
rcp:	Copy from rcp: file system
running-config	Copy from current system configuration
startup-config	Copy from startup configuration
system:	Copy from system: file system
tftp:	Copy from tftp: file system

"To" Parameters

Parameter	Explanation
flash:	Copy to flash: file system
flh:	Copy to flh: file system
ftp:	Copy to ftp: file system
null:	Copy to null: file system
nvram:	Copy to nvram: file system
rcp:	Copy to rcp: file system
running-config	Copy to current system configuration
startup-config	Copy to startup configuration
system:	Copy to system: file system
tftp:	Copy to tftp: file system

Syntax Example

`#copy running-config startup-config`

debug

Cisco Explanation

Debugging functions (see also undebug).

Parameters

Parameter	Explanation
aaa	AAA (Authentication, Authorization, and Accounting)
access-expression	Boolean access expression
all	Enable all debugging
arp	IP ARP (Address Resolution Protocol) and HP Probe transactions

continues

Parameter	Explanation
async	Aync interface information
callback	Callback activity
cdp	CDP (Certificate Discovery Protocol) information
chat	Chat scripts activity
compress	COMPRESS traffic
condition	Condition
confmodem	Modem configuration database
custom-queue	Custom output queueing
dhcp	DHCP (Dynamic Host Configuration Protocol) client activity
dialer	Dial on Demand
dnsix	DNSIX (Department of Defense Intelligence Information System Network Security for Information Exchange) information
domain	Domain Name System
dxi	ATM-DXI (Asynchronous Transfer Mode—Data Exchange Interface) information
eigrp	EIGRP (Enhanced Interior Gateway Routing Protocol) information
entry	Incoming queue entries
ethernet-interface	Ethernet network interface events
frame-relay	Frame Relay
interface	interface
ip	IP information
ipx	Novell/IPX information
lapb	LAPB (Link Access Protocol Balanced) transactions
list	Set interface, access list, or both for the next debug command
llc2	LLC2 Type II Information
modem	Modem control/process activation
nhrp	NHRP (Next Hop Resolution Protocol)
packet	Log unknown packets
pad	X.25 PAD (packet assembler/disassembler) protocol
ppp	PPP (Point to Point Protocol) information
priority	Priority output queueing

continues

Parameter	Explanation
radius	RADIUS (Remote Authentication Dial-In User Service) protocol
rtr	Response Time Reporter (RTR) monitor information
serial	Serial interface information
smf	Software MAC filter
snapshot	Snapshot activity
snmp	SNMP (Simple Network Messaging Protocol) information
sntp	SNTP (Simple Network Time Protocol) information
spantree	Spanning tree information
standby	Hot standby protocol
tacacs	TACACS (Terminal Access Controller Access Control System) authentication and authorization
tbridge	Transparent bridging
telnet	Incoming Telnet connections
tftp	TFTP (Trivial File Transfer Protocol) debugging
tunnel	Generic Tunnel Interface
vprofile	Virtual Profile information
vtemplate	Virtual Template information
x25	X.25, CMNS (Connection Mode Network Service), and XOT (X.25 over TCP) information
x28	X.28 mode

delete

Cisco Explanation

Delete a file.

Parameter

Parameter	Explanation
flash:	File to be deleted

Syntax Example

```
#delete flash: aa3424.bin
```

dir
Cisco Explanation
List files on a file system.

Parameters

Parameter	Explanation
/all	List all files
flash:	Directory or file name
flh:	Directory or file name
null:	Directory or file name
nvram:	Directory or file name
system:	Directory or file name

Syntax Example
`#dir /all`

erase
Cisco Explanation
Erase a file system.

Parameters

Parameter	Explanation
flash:	File system to be erased
nvram:	File system to be erased
startup-config	Erase contents of configuration memory

Syntax Example
`#erase startup-config`

more
Cisco Explanation
Display the contents of a file.

Options

Option	Explanation
/ascii	Display binary files in ASCII encoding
/binary	Force display to hex/text format
/ebcdic	Display binary files in EBCDIC encoding

Parameters

Parameter	Explanation
flash:	File to display
flh:	File to display
ftp:	File to display
null:	File to display
nvram:	File to display
rcp:	File to display
system:	File to display
tftp:	File to display

Syntax Example
#more /ascii system:

pwd
Cisco Explanation
Display current working directory.

Syntax Example
#pwd

reload
Cisco Explanation
Halt and perform a cold restart.

Parameters

Parameter	Explanation
LINE	Reason for reload
at	Reload at a specific time/date
hh:mm	Time to reload (hh:mm)
<1-31>	Day of the month
LINE	Reason for reload
MONTH	Month of the year
cancel	Cancel pending reload
in	Reload after a time interval
mmm or hhh:mm	Delay before reload
LINE	Reason for reload

Syntax Example

`#reload in 30 for maintenance`

rsh

Cisco Explanation

Execute a remote command.

Parameters

Parameter	Explanation
WORD	IP address or hostname of `rsh` server
/user	Specify remote username
LINE	Command to be executed remotely

Syntax Example

`#rsh RouterA reload`

setup

Cisco Explanation

Run the setup command facility.

Syntax Example

`#setup`

test

Cisco Explanation
Test subsystems, memory, and interfaces.

Parameters

Parameter	Explanation
eigrp	IPX EIGRP test commands
<1-65535>	AS number
1local	Neighbor states 1
<1-FFFFFFFE>	IPX address
1successor	Neighbor states 3
<1-FFFFFFFE>	IPX address
2local	Neighbor states 1–2
<1-FFFFFFFE>	IPX address
2successor	Neighbor states 3–2
<1-FFFFFFFE>	IPX address
3local	Neighbor states 1–0
<1-FFFFFFFE>	IPX address
4local	Neighbor states 1–0–2
<1-FFFFFFFE>	IPX address
5local	Neighbor states 1–0–FC fail–1
<1-FFFFFFFE>	IPX address
6local	Neighbor states 1–2–FC fail–3
<1-FFFFFFFE>	IPX address
ack	Toggle EIGRP fast acking
delete	Delete a phony entry in the topology table
ifs	IFS TEST code
appn	APPN commands
read	Read APPN file
Hostname or *A.B.C.D*	Destination address
LINE	Filename only
write	Write APPN file
Hostname or *A.B.C.D*	Destination address
LINE	Filename only

continues

Parameter	Explanation
boot	Parse the bootstrap boot command line
LINE	Remainder of the bootstrap boot command
defaults	Show default boot files
show	Show related commands
hidden	Toggle display of hidden file systems and files
slot	Produce core dump of slots on crashes
<0-32>	Slot number
WORD	URL for slot core destination
WORD	URL for slot core destination

Syntax Example

`#test ifs appn read RouterA test_file`

verify

Cisco Explanation

Verify a file.

Parameter

Parameter	Explanation
flash:	File to be verified

Syntax Example

`#verify flash: aaa8764.bin`

write

Cisco Explanation

Write running configuration to memory, network, or terminal.

Parameters

Parameter	Explanation
erase	Erase nonvolatile (flash) memory
memory	Write to nonvolatile memory
network	Write to network TFTP server
flash:	URL of destination file

continues

Parameter	Explanation
ftp:	URL of destination file
null:	URL of destination file
nvram:	URL of destination file
rcp:	URL of destination file
system:	URL of destination file
tftp:	URL of destination file
terminal	Write to terminal

Syntax Example
`#write memory`

INDEX

? (help system wildcard character), 78
[ ] (input request delineators), 72
/ (input request separator), 72
 # (privilege mode command prompt), 70
 # (startup messages, decompression symbol), 74
% (status message alert character), 72
> (user mode command prompt), 69, 70

A

ABRs (area border routers), in OSPF, 331
access-enable command, 458
access levels, 63
access list
 implicit denial, 420
 IP, 422
access-list command, 415, 419
access-profile command, 458
access-template command, 474
alert messages, 71–72
algorithm. *See* **routing algorithms**
algorithms
 Bellman-Ford distance vector, 313
 Dijkstra's, 332–335, 412, 448–449
 distance vector, 276, 313
 DUAL (Diffusing Update Algorithm), 321–322
 GCAC (Generic Call Admission Control), 448
 link state, 332
 routing, 447
application layer (of OSI model), 160
area command, 343
 no-redistribution parameter, 344
 no-summary parameter, 344
ARIN (American Registry for Internet Numbers), 352
ARPAnet, 11
AS (autonomous system), 311, 328–329, 348, 349–360
 areas, 330
  ABRs (area border routers), 331
  NSSAs (not-so-stubby areas), 330–331
  stub, 330
 AS-Set, 370
 BGP, 348

492 AS (autonomous system)

DR (designated router), 331
multihomed, 353–354
next hop, 371
requirements, 351
stubs, 352
system numbers, 351–354
    IP address linking, 355–360
    private range, 352
transit, 354
ASN (Autonomous System Number), 317, 351–360
asynchronous, defined, 432
ATM (Asynchronous Transfer Model), 428, 429–432
  cell structure, 436–438
  cells, 431–432
    header, 431
  networks
    ATM switches, 432
    ES (end systems), 432–433
    private, 432
    public, 432
    public switched, 433
  switch address, 441
atm address command, 455
atm router command, 455
ATM switches, 432
auto-cost command, 344–345
auxiliary passwords, 127

B

backbone, in OSPF, 338
backup strategies, 142
bandwidth-percentage command, 323
banners, creating, 134
Basic Management Setup, 106, 111–116
BBS (bulletin board servers), 16–17
Bellman-Ford distance vector algorithm, 313
BGP (Border Gateway Protocol), 276
  autonomous systems (ASs), 348, 349–360
  AS-Path, 370
  AS-Set, 370
  border gateways, 357–358
  comment routing errors, 361
  confederation configuration, 375
  confederation number, 374
  confederations, 372–375
  dynamic route redistribution, 362
  EBGP (Exterior Border Gateway Protocol). *See* EBGP
  EBGP multihop peering, 358, 359
  flap dampening, 366
  headers, 367–370
    common, 367–368
    keep-alive message, 370
    notification message, 370
    open message, 368–369
    update message, 369
  IBGP (Interior Border Gateway Protocol). *See* IBGP
  local preference, 372
  next hop, 371
  peering sessions, 358–360
  route flapping, 366
  route maps, 363–365
  route reflection, 377
  router restarts, 359
  routing mesh, 358
  speakers, 356
  stubs, 353
  synchronization, 375–376
  TCP port, 179, 358
  version 4, 348
bgp confederation command, 375
binary backup, 140
Boot Loader messages, 73–74
border gateway router, in OSPF, 329
border node, 451
break key sequence, 56
B2B (business-to-business) communications, 253
bus network, 287

C

cabling, 107
  Ethernet, 107
  Ethernet pinouts, 108–109
  RJ-45 to DB9 adapters, 108
Catalyst switches, 427
CCO (Cisco Connection Online) site, 43, 238
cd command, 475
channels (ISDN)
  B (bearer), 256
  D (data), 256
CIDR (Classless Inter-

DECnet 493

Domain Routing), 182
Cisco Career
   Certifications, 8
   exams, 9
Cisco Certified
   Internetwork Engineer
   (CCIP), 9
Cisco Certified Network
   Associate (CCNA), 8
Cisco Certified Network
   Professional (CCNP), 9
Cisco hardware
   7500 series router, 21
   1600 series, 254
   1600 series router, 22
   catalyst switch, 427
   SOHO line, 20
Cisco IOS (Internet
   Operating Systems). *See
   also* IOS
   basic package, 42
   basics, 40–41
   feature pack, 42
   service agreements, 43
   setup mode, 40
   updating, 41–43
Cisco IOS command interpreter
   privilege mode, 57–58
   user mode, 57
Cisco CCO Web site, 150
Cisco website, 43
clean router, defined, 106
clear command, 475–480
CLNP (Connectionless
   Network Protocol),
   389–390
clock command, 480
command prompt, 69
CompuServe, 17
confederation number

(BGP), 374
configuration files, 119–123
   editing, 122–123
   private-config, 121
   running-config, 120,
      122–123
   startup-config, 119–120,
      122–123
   viewing, 120–122
configuration file backups,
   147–151
   reasons to back up, 147
   TFTP servers, 148–151
      Cisco Remote
         Software Loader,
         150
      copy command, 149
      copying files to an
         offline spare, 151
      copying files to a TFTP
         server, 151
      keeping backups without a TFTP server,
         149
      obtaining the IOS
         image, 149–150
   what to back up, 148
configure command, 125,
   126, 132
configure terminal command, 188
confreg command, 130
connect command, 207, 459
connectionless service, 165
connection-oriented service,
   LLC (Logical Link
      Control), 165
console passwords, 127–128
console ports, 107
convergence, 101, 281, 392
   achieving, 102–103

defined, 101
copy command, 480–481
crossover cable, Ethernet,
   108–109
Ctrl+A as function key, 67
Ctrl+B as function key, 67
Ctrl+E as function key, 67
Ctrl+F as function key, 67
Ctrl+N as function key,
   67–68
Ctrl+P as function key, 67–68
Ctrl+Z, use of, 227

D

DARPA. *See* ARPAnet
data, 161–162
   formats, 162, 171
   frames, 164
   packets. *See* packets
   segments, 161
   user, 161
data encapsulation, 91, 95
   versus data encryption, 92
data encryption, 92
   versus data encapsulation,
      92
data frame, 261
data link layer, 90
data link layer (of OSI
   model), 164
data packets. *See* packets
debug command, 481–483
DECnet, 380–381
   areas, 382
   DRP (DECnet Routing
      Protocol)
      HM (hello message),
         386–388
      MAC (Media Access

Control), addresses, 382–384
nodes, 382
   ES (end system), 384
   L1 (level 1 router), 384–385
   L2 (level 2 router), 385–386
   Phase V, 389
delete command, 483
dialer command, 264
Dijkstra's algorithm, 332
dir command, 120, 484
disable command, 79, 459
disconnect command, 459–460
distance vector algorithms, 276
   Bellman-Ford, 313
distribute-list command, 363
DNA (Digital Network Architecture), 380
DR (designated router) in OSPF, 331
DRAM, IOS image requirements, 55
DUAL (Diffusing Update Algorithm), 321–322
dynamic updating, 277–280

E

EBGP (Exterior Border Gateway Protocol). *See also* **BGP**
   configuration, 360–372
   EGP, 371

EIGRP (Enhanced Interior Gateway Routing Protocol), 310–311, 362
   autonomous system number (ASN), 323
   configuring, 322–323
   DUAL (Diffusing Update Algorithm), 321–322
   hello packets, 322
   versus IGRP, 321–322
   versus RIP, 310–313
enable command, 79, 113, 126, 188, 460
enable password, 126
encapsulation methods, 240–244
   Ethernet_SNAP, 243
   Ethernet_II, 242
      header fields, 242
Enter key as function key, 65–66
erase command, 484
Esc+B as function key, 67
Esc+F as function key, 67
Ethernet
   configuration, 115–116
   crossover cable, 108
   interface, 131–135
   pinouts, 108–109
   rollover cable, 108–109
   standard cables, 107
exit command, 460
extended setup, 112, 117–119

F

FDDI (Fiber Distributed Data Interface), 37

flap dampening, 366
flapping, 366
   BGP route, 366
Flash Load Helper, 51
flash memory, 44
   dual banks, 48
   Flash Loader Helper, 51
   flash SIMM, 48
   memory chips, 48
   partitioning, 49–50
   TFTP (Trivial File Transfer Protocol), 50
flat routing environment, 438–439
flooding, 330, 391–396
Frame Relay, 22, 267–269
   configuring, 269–271
   DCE (Data Circuit terminating Equipment), 267–268
   DLCI (Data Link Connection Identifier), 268
   DTE (Data Terminal Equipment), 268
   IETF (Internet Engineering Task Force) encapsulation method, 269
   LMI (Local Management Interface) updates, 268–269
   multiplexer, 268
frame-relay map command, 270–271
function keys
   Ctrl+A, 67
   Ctrl+B, 67
   Ctrl+E, 67
   Ctrl+F, 67
   Ctrl+N, 67–68

Ctrl+P, 67–68
Esc+B, 67
Esc+F, 67

G

gateway, 311–312
  border, 357
  default, 97, 190
  defined, 311
  exterior environments, 312
  interior environments, 312
GCAC (Generic Call Admission Control)
  complex, 448
  simple, 448
GEnie, 17
Gopher, 17
GUI (graphical user interface), 61–62

H

hardware. *See also* Cisco hardware
  backups
    offline, 139–140, 142–145
    online, 139–140, 145–147
help command, 460
help system, 75–78
  context-sensitive, 78
  full, 75–78
  partial, 75
  using wildcards, 78
hexadecimal digits, 236
  0x notation, 237

hold-down timers, 320
  RIP, 293–294
hop count limit
  hops versus nodes, 315
  IGRP, 314–315
hops, 197
hostname, 112
  setting, 125
hostname command, 125
HyperTerminal, 56
hubs, 98

I

IBGP. *See also* BGP
  confederations, 375
  routing configuration, 372–377
ICMP (Internet Control Message Protocol), 188, 193
  echo packets, 195
  tools, 193–204
    ping, 194–195
    ping (privilege mode), 198–201
    ping (user mode), 195–198
    traceroute, 201–204
IGP (Interior Gateway Protocol), 310, 311, 371
IGRP (Interior Gateway Routing Protocol), 309–311, 313
  as an autonomous system (AS), 311
  ASN (Autonomous System Number), 317
  Bellman-Ford distance vector algorithm, 313

configuring, 317–318
versus EIGRP, 321–322
hold-down timers, 320
as IGP protocol, 311
load balancing, 315–316
metrics, 313
  bandwidth, 314
  hop count, 314–315
  internetwork delay, 314
  load, 314
  reliability, 314
modifying timers, 319–320
  hold-down, 319
  route removal, 319
  route timeout, 319
  route update, 319
versus RIP, 310–313
split horizon, 321
unequal cost, 318
updates, flash, 317
updating routing tables, 316–317
input request, 71–72
interface command, 189, 227
interface configuration, 131–134
  administratively down, 132
  administratively up, 132
  IP address, 133
  line protocol down, 133
Internet, 311
  routing, 16–19
interoperability, 88
IOS (Internet Operating System), 61–62, 159, 457
  access enable, 458
  access levels, 63
  access-list command, 419
  access profile command, 458

IOS (Internet Operating System)

access template, 474–475
banner message, 69
bgp confederation command, 375
cd, 475
clear, 475–480
clock, 480
command prompt, 69
command processing
   partial command recognition, 79
   privilege mode, 62–63
   user mode, 62–63
connect command, 459
copy command, 480–481
debug command, 481–483
delete command, 483
dir command, 484
disable command, 459
disconnect command, 459–460
distribute-list command, 363
   hostname, 69
   mode indicator, 70
   submode indicators, 70
enable command, 460
erase command, 484
exit command, 460
function keys (advanced command editing system), 64–68
   Ctrl+A, 67
   Ctrl+B, 67
   Ctrl+E, 67
   Ctrl+F, 67
   Ctrl+N, 67–68
   Ctrl+P, 67–68
   enter, 65–66
   Esc+B, 67
   Esc+F, 67
   spacebar, 66
help command, 460
help system, 75–78
   context-sensitive, 78
   full, 75–78
   partial, 75
input request, 71–72
ip command, 189–192
ip as-path command, 365
IP feature pack, 117, 184, 188
IP/IPX feature pack, 117
IPX service pack, 234
lock command, 460
login command, 461
logout command, 461
main components, 69
more command, 484–485
name-connection command, 461
nat inside source command, 425
neighbor command, 359
network command, 317
no metric holddown command, 320
no statement, 128–129
no synchronization command, 376
pad command, 461
ping command, 79–80, 194–195, 462
ppp command, 462
privilege mode commands, 473–489
processor speed, 64
pwd command, 485
redistribute static command, 363
reload command, 485–486
resume command, 462–463
rlogin command, 463
router bgp command, 356–357
router configuration mode, 317
rsh command, 486
setup command, 486
show command, 80–83, 121, 305, 464–467
size, 64
slip command, 467
status messages
   alert, 72
   startup, 70
systat command, 467
telnet command, 467–468
terminal command, 76–77, 468–471
test command, 487–488
timer basic command, 319
traceroute command, 201–204, 471–472
tunnel command, 472
user mode commands, 458–473
variance command, 318–319
verify command, 488
write command, 488–489
x3 command, 473
x28 command, 472–473

IOS images
compressed, 46
flash memory, 46
uncompressed, 46

IOS startup messages
Boot Loader messages, 73–74
restricted rights legend, 74

IP (Internet Protocol), 158, 176–184
access list, 419–422
binding, 419

extended, 420
   list numbers, 419
   standard, 419–420
   types, 418
address, 215
address classes, 177–179
   class A, 177–178
   class B, 178
   class C, 178–179
   class D, 179
   class E, 179
classful
   class A, 170
   class C, 170
   defined, 170
   mask addresses, 170
classless, 170–171
   CIDR (Classless Inter-
      Domain Routing),
      171
   supernet address, 171
header fields
   checksum, 94
   destination address, 94
   flag, 93
   fragment offset, 93
   identifier, 93
   length, 93
   next, 94
   options, 94
   protocol, 94
   source address, 94
   Time To Live (TTL),
      93–94
   total length, 93
   type of service (TOS),
      93
   version, 93
interfaces, 188–193
license, 215–216
node addresses. *See* host
   addresses

ports, 421
reserved IP addresses, 176
reserved router addresses,
   98
and router functionality,
   184
scheme, 215
subnet mask, 180
subnetting, 180–182,
   215–223
   computation of,
      181–182
supernetting
   computation of, 183
version IP-6, 215
IP access lists, 418–422
IP addresses, and ASN, 355
**ip address command, 133,
   192**
ip as-path command, 365
ip classless command, 189
ip command, 189
**ip default-gateway com-
   mand, 190**
ip route command, 228
   parameters, 229
   perm option, 190
ip routing command, 189
IP-6, 93
**IPX (Internetwork Packet
   Exchange), 158, 233–235**
   addressing
      MAC (Media Access
         Control) address, 237
   addresses, 235–237
      compared to IP
         addresses, 235
      hexadecimal format,
         235–237
      network host, 235
   configuring, 237–244

encapsulation methods,
   240–244
encapsulation methods,
   240
history of, 234
routing, 244–249
ipx interface command, 248
**IPX/IP basic feature pack,
   237–238**
**ipx network command,
   239–240**
**ipx route command, para-
   meters, 246–247**
**ipx routing command,
   238–239**
**ISDN (Integrated Services
   Digital Network), 21, 22,
   255–261**
   BRI (Basic Rate
      Interface), 256
      B channel, 256
      D channel, 256
   configuring, 261–264
      encapsulation method,
         263
      protocol address, 263
      SPIDs, 263
      switch type specifying,
         262–263
   equipment types
      NT1 (Type-1 network),
         257
      NT2 (Type-2 network),
         257
      TA (terminal adapter),
         257
      TE1 (Type-1), 257, 261
      TE2 (Type-2), 257
   frames, 261
   LAPD (Link Access
      Protocol [for
      channel] D), 258

protocol categories
  E, 258
  I, 258
  Q, 258
reference points
  type R, 258
  type S, 258
  type T, 258
  type U, 258
SOHO (Small Office/Home Office) users, 255
IS-IS (Intermediate System to Intermediate System protocol), 379–381
  addresses, 398, 401–402
  algorithm, 397–398
  areas, 398–400
  CLNP (Connectionless Network Protocol), 389–390
  configuring, 414–415
  domains, 398–399, 400–401
  IS, designated, 409–410
    master table, 411
  IS priority, 409
  link state routing, 391–393
  metrics
    cost, 396–398
    delay, 396
    error, 396
    expense, 396
  packets
    checksum, 403, 404
    data, 403, 404
    extended data, 404
    header, 403, 404–405
  hello messages, 405–406
  LSP (Link State Packet), 406–407
  SNP (Sequence Number Packet), 407–408
  pseudonodes, 410–411
  multicast addressing, 411
  routing, 408–409, 411–414
    external route, 413
    internal route, 413
is-type command, 415

L

LAN (Local Area Network) interfaces, 18
LAN sniffers, connection-oriented, 168
line command, 127, 205
line properties, 127
line protocol, 133
link state algorithms
  OSPF, 332
load balancing, 319
  IGRP, 315–316
lock command, 460
login command, 461
logout command, 461
LSA (link state advertisement), 329–330
  flooding, 330, 391–396
    convergence and, 392
  LSP (LSA packets), 392–393
  remaining-life field, 394–395
  sequence field, 395
Lynx, 17

M

MAC (Media Access Control), 164, 237
MAC (Media Access Control) addresses, 90, 382–384
master mode, 409
Media Access Units (MAU), 12
memory architecture, 44–48
  model name indicators, 44
  RFF (Run-from-flash) routers, 44–46
Microsoft
  Hyperterminal, 56
mode indicators, 70
more command, 484
multicasting, 170
multihomed AS
  BGP, 353

N

name-connection command, 78, 461
NAT (Network Address Translation), 417–418, 423–425
  configuration, 423–425
  inside source lists, 425
  inside versus outside interfaces, 423

IP address pools, 424
public versus private IP addresses, 424
nat inside source command, 425
neighbor command, 359
net command, 415
NetBEUI, 166
network command, 300, 317, 342
network layer, of OSI model, 88–90, 163-164
Cisco routers and, 88–90
and routing, 163
network routing. *See* **routing**
networks
home office, 20
mainframe-based, 11
PC-based, 12
segmented, 14, 224–228
router configuration, 225–228
router placement, 225
Token Ring, 11, 12
VPN (virtual private networks), 22–23
networking
defined, 10
serial connections versus networking, 10
no metric holddown command, 320
no statement, 128–129
no synchronization command, 376
North American switch types, 263
notify command, 208
Novell NetWare, 233, 234
NSAP (Network Service Access Point), 440–444
area address, 402
DSP (Domain Specific Part), 402
IDP (Initial Domain Part)
AFI (Authority and Format Identifier), 402
IDI (Initial Domain Identifier), 402
system ID, 403
NSSA (not-so-stubby area), OSPF, 331, 338
NVRAM (nonvolatile RAM). *See* **flash memory**

O

OSI (Open Systems Interconnect) model, 159–160, 175, 380–381
application layer, 160
data link layer, 164–165
connectionless service, 165
connection-oriented services, 165
MAC (Media Access Control) sublayer, 164–165
system addresses, 90
described, 159–160
network layer, 88–90, 163–164
and routing, 163
protocol addresses, 89–90
NSAP (Network Service Access Point), 402
physical layer, 165–166
presentation layer, 161
session layer, 161, 167
transport layer, 161
OSPF (Open Shortest Path First), 276, 327–332
areas, 338–340
ABRs (Area Border Routers), 331, 339
backbone, 338
NSSAs (not-so-stubby areas), 330–331, 340–341
stub, 330–331, 340
AS (Autonomous System), 328–329
border gateway router, 329
configuring, 341–345
DR (Designated Router), 331
flooding, 330
link state algorithm, 332
LSA (Link State Advertisement), 329–330
metric determination, 335
packet, type field, 337
route redistribution, 341
updates, 336
database description, 338
hello message, 338
link state acknowledgment, 338
link state request, 338
link state update, 338
virtual link, 339

P

packets, 95, 163
analyzers, 168

broadcast, 322
echo, 195
headers, 95
hello, 322
IPX, 243
IPX encapsulated, 244
protocol size specifications, 95
session-open, 168
size range, 93
tear-down, 167
pad command, 461
passive interface command, 303
password recovery, 129–131
password removal, 128–129
passwords, 125–131
   auxiliary, 127
   console, 127–128
   enable, 126
   encrypted, 126
   plain text, 113
   recovery, 129–131
   removal, 128–129
   secret, 113, 126
   virtual terminal, 126
pay-per-use service, 255, 256
peering sessions
   BGP, 358–360
physical backups, 138–147
   backup routers, 141–147
      offline, 142–145
      online, 145–147
      load balancing, 145–147
         Spanning Tree Protocol (STP), 147
      switches versus hubs, 146
   power supply backups, 138–141

Cisco multiple power units, 141
offline, 139
online, 139
surge protection, 139
uninterruptible power supply (UPS), 138–140
reasons to back up, 138
routing environment, 138
physical layer (of OSI model), 165
ping command, 79–80, 194–195, 462
   hop limit, 197
   ip option, 196
   output message icons, 197
   privilege mode, 198–201
      DF bit, 200
      record, 201
   tag option, 196
   TTL (Time To Live), 196
   status icon, 80
   user mode, 195–198
PNNI (Private Network-to-Network Interface), 427
   ATM (Asynchronous Transfer Model) and, 428
   configuring, 454–455
   crankback, 452–454
   hierarchy, 438–444
   metrics, 447
   NSA (Network Service Access Point) addressing, 440–444
   peer group
      level, 442
      topology, 443
   PGs (peer groups), 439
   QOS (quality of service) and, 447–449

routing algorithm, 447
routing protocol, 428–429, 444, 447
signaling protocol, 429, 444, 449–452
QOS requirements, 450
power supply loss
   protection, 138–141
ppp command, 462
presentation layer (of OSI model), 161
privilege mode, 49, 54
Prodigy, 17
protocols, 157–159
   categorization, 158–159, 166–171
   classful IP
      class A, 170
      class C, 170
      defined, 170
      mask addresses, 170
   classful versus classless, 169–171
   classless IP, 170–171
      CIDR (Classless Inter-Domain Routing), 171
      supernet address, 171
   classless versus classful, 169–171
   connectionless, 168–169
      versus connection-oriented, 167–169
      disadvantages of, 169
   connection-oriented, 167–168
      advantages of, 168
      versus connectionless, 167–169
      defined, 167
      session-open packet, 168

session process,
    167–168
  tear-down packet, 167
encapsulation, 171–172
  checksum, 172
  data size, 172
  destination address,
    172
  origin address, 172
  sequence number, 172
link state, 327
  LSAs (Link State
    Advertisements),
    391–393
nonroutable, 166
routed, 390
  CLNP (Connectionless
    Network Protocol),
    389–390
  IP (Internet Protocol),
    92–94, 158, 188–193,
    215
  IPX (Internetwork
    Packet Exchange),
    158, 233–244
  WAN (Wide Area
    Network), 253–255,
    262
routing, 390
  BGP (Border Gateway
    Protocol), 348–377
  EIGRP (Enhanced
    Interior Gateway
    Routing Protocol),
    310–311, 321–323
  IGRP (Interior
    Gateway Routing
    Protocol), 309–311,
    313, 317–318
  IS-IS (Intermediate
    System to
    Intermediate System),
    379–415

OSPF (Open Shortest
    Path First), 327–332
PNNI (Private Network
    to Network
    Interface), 427–429,
    444, 447
RIP (Routing
    Information
    Protocol), 286–311
routing versus routed, 117,
    158
stacks. *See* protocols,
    suites
suites, 159
UNI (User Node
    Interface), 434–436
protocol headers, 91–94
PSN (public switched network), 261, 433
public switches. *See* **ATM switches**
PVC (permanent virtual circuit), 266
pwd command, 485

Q

QOS (quality of service), 447–449
  GCAC (Generic Call
    Admission Control)
    algorithm, 448
  metrics
    available cell rate, 448

R

RAM
  dynamic (DRAM), 32

nonvolatile (NVRAM).
    See flash memory
  static (SRAM), 32
**recovering passwords,
    129–131**
redistribute static command, 363
**refuse-message command,
    209**
**reload command, 124,
    485–486**
**removing passwords,
    128–129**
restricted rights legend, 74
**resume command, 208,
    462–463**
**RFF (Run-from-Flash)
    routers, 44–46**
  advantages, 45–46
  boot process, 45
  disadvantages, 46
  upgrading IOS images
    dual flash banks, 48
    Flash Load Helper, 51
    partitioning, 49–50
    TFTP, 50
**RFR (Run-from-RAM)
    routers, 46–48**
  advantages, 47
  boot process, 47
  disadvantages, 48
  upgrading IOS images,
    51–53
**RIP (Routing Information
    Protocol), 276, 309–311**
  configuration, 299–300
    network command, 300
    router command, 300
    router rip command,
    300
  and data encapsulation,
    295

hold-down timers, 288, 293–294
hop count limit, 288, 291–292
as IGP, 310
versus IGRP and EIGRP, 310
maintenance, 301–306
modifying timers, 301–302
　timer basic command, 301
　neighbor configuration
　auto detection, 302
　neighbor command, 302
　passive interface command, 303
　show running-config command, 303
operation of, 295–298
overview, 286
protocol headers, 295–296
reattached protocol headers, 297
route poisoning, 288, 292
routing algorithm, 294–295
and routing loops, 287–288
routing tables, 296
　cost field, 289
　flag field, 289, 290
　network field, 289
　next hop field, 289
　RAM storage, 289
　timer field, 289–290
routing table updating
　fields, 299
　triggers, 298
show commands, 305

single environment, 295
split horizon, 288, 293
technology, 287–288
version command, 303, 305
version of, 304
viewing stats, 305–306
and WAN connections, 286
RJ-45 connector, 107
rlogin command, 209, 463
rollover cables, 108–109
　pinouts, 109
ROM monitor (ROMMON mode), 130
route maps (BGP), 363–365
routed protocols, 390
　CLNP (Connectionless Network Protocol), 389–390
　IP (Internet Protocol), 92–94, 158, 188–193, 215
　IPX (Internetwork Packet Exchange), 158, 233–244
　versus routing protocols, 103
　WAN (wide area network), 253–255, 262
router bgp command, 356–357
router command, 300
router configuration, 105–106
　basic management setup, 111–116
　clean, 106
　　setup dialogs, 109
　configuration files, 119–123

Ethernet interface, 115–116, 118
extended setup, 112, 117–119
hostname, 112, 125
individual item configuration, 124–131
line properties, 127
passwords, 125–131
reconfiguration, 106, 123–124
secret passwords, 113
SNMP (Simple Network Management Protocol), 114
via telnet, 107
virtual terminal passwords, 114
router isis command, 414–415
router rip command, 300
routers
　best path, 168
　border, 19
　configuration backups, 147–152
　connecting to, 107–109
　DB9 ports, 107
　DSL, 18
　Ethernet, 18
　history, 10–16
　　Cisco, 15–16
　　mainframe-based networks, 11
　　PC-based networks, 12
　　subnetworks, 14
　hops, 290
　Internet, 16–19
　IP functionality of, 184
　ISDN, 18
　LAN (Local Area Network) interfaces, 18

of last resort, 190
neighbors, 290
network size limits, 290
physical backups,
  138–147
security
  IP access list, 419–422
  NAT. See NAT
in segmented networks,
  224–228
signal corruption, 290
T-lines, 18
TTL (Time To Live), 290
WAN (Wide Area
  Network) interfaces, 18
WIC (WAN Interface
  Card), 254
routes
dynamic, 228
static, 228–230
routing
complex, 99–100
mechanics of, 95–103
routing loops, 287–288
routing tables. See routing
  tables
simple, 96–99
updates, within RIP, 298
updating, 276
routing algorithms, 274–277
Bellman-Ford distance
  vector, 313
defined, 274
distance vectors, 276
DUAL (Diffusing Update
  Algorithm), 321–322
link state, 277
metrics, 275
RIP, 294–295
routing hardware, 25–26.
See also Cisco hardware
external, 27–32

console port, 29–30
flash memory, 31
status panel, 28
WAN expansion ports,
  30–31
general, 26
internal
  case, 27–28
  DRAM (Dynamic
    RAM), 32
  processor, 32
series-specific, 26
  800 Series, 33–34
  enterprise series, 36–37
  4000 Series, 36–37
  1600 Series, 34–35
  2500 Series, 36
routing protocols
algorithms, 274–277
  defined, 274
  distance vectors, 276
  link state, 277
  metrics, 275
BGP (Border Gateway
  Protocol), 276, 348–377
convergence, 281
dynamic updating,
  277–280
  routing tables, 278–280
EGP (Exterior Gateway
  Protocol), 286
EIGRP (Enhanced Interior
  Gateway Routing
  Protocol), 310–311,
  321–323
IGP (Interior Gateway
  Protocol), 286
IGRP (Interior Gateway
  Routing Protocol), 118,
  309–311, 313, 317–318

IS-IS (Intermediate
  System to Intermediate
  System), 379–415
OSPF (Open Shortest Path
  First), 276, 327–345
PNNI (Private Network-
  to-Network Interface),
  427–429, 444, 447
RIP (Routing Information
  Protocol), 118, 276,
  286–311
versus routed protocols,
  103
standard base units, 349
routing tables, 19, 100, 163
and algorithms, 275
and dynamic updating,
  278–280
convergence, 101,
  102–103
gateways, 101
RIP, 288
routing metrics, 102
update triggers, 298
updating the IGRP tables,
  316–317
rsh command, 486

S

secret passwords, 126
security, 417
  IP access list, 419–422
  NAT. See NAT, 417
segments, 162
session layer (of OSI
  model), 161, 167
setup command, 122, 124,
  486

show command, 80–83, 121, 305, 464–467
  arguments, 80–82
  interfaces, 83, 133
  running-config, 83
  startup-config, 83
show interface command, 132, 133
show running-config command, 303
show version command, 129, 237–238
shutdown command, 119, 133
slip command, 467
SNMP (Simple Network Management Protocol), 114
SOHO hardware, 20
spacebar, as function key, 66
speakers, BGP, 356
SPID (Service Profile ID), 256
split horizon
  IGRP, enabling/disabling, 320
  RIP, 293
startup-config file, 111
static route command, 264
status messages
  alert messages, 71–72
  startup, 70
stub
  area, in OSPF, 330–331, 340
  AS, in BGP, 352–353
subinterfaces, 270
subnet mask, 180
subnetting, 180–182, 214–223
  calculations, 218–224
  disadvantages, 217–218
  need for, 214–215

  number of potential hosts, 218
  number of potential networks, 218
  static route configuration, 228–230
  subnet mask, 219
supernetting, 183
SVC (Switched Virtual Circuit), 266–267
switches, 64, 98
switching protocols, 267
systat command, 467
systems addresses, 90

T

TCP (Transmission Control Protocol), 162, 167, 175, 187–188
  differences between TCP and IP, 175
TCP/IP protocol suite. *See* TCP and IP
Telnet, 126, 188
  remote administration, 204–209
  speed parameter, 205
telnet command, 207, 467–468
terminal command, 76–77, 468–471
test command, 487–488
TFTP (Trivial File Transfer Protocol), 50, 54, 55, 148–151
ticks, 247
Time To Live (TTL), 93–94, 196, 290
  RIP, 291

timer basic command, 301, 319
Token Ring, 11, 12
traceroute command, 201–204, 471–472
  privilege mode, 202–204
  part number parameter, 203
transport layer (of OSI model), 161
Trumpet, 17
tunnel command, 472

U

UI (User Interface)
  command line, 62
  GUI, 61–62, 64
  HTML-based interface, 64
UNI (User to Network Interface), 433, 434–438
  cell, 436–437
  header, 436
  circuit, point-to-multipoint, 435, 436
  circuit, point-to-point, 434–435
uninterruptible power supply (UPS), 138–140
update timers
  IGRP, 319
update triggers, 298

V

variance command, 318–319
verify command, 488
version command, 304, 305

virtual terminal passwords, 114, 126–127
VPN (Virtual Private Networks), 22–23

W

WAN (wide area network)
Frame Relay, 267–269
interfaces, 18, 20
ISDN (Integrated Services Digital Network), 21, 255–261
protocols, 253–255, 262
X.25, 265
where command, 472
WIC (WAN Interface Card), 254
write command, 488–489

X

Xerox, 287
Xerox PUP protocol, 286
Xmodem, 55, 56
x3 command, 473
x28 command, 472–473
X.25, 265
  PVC (Permanent Virtual Circuit), 266

Hey, you've got enough worries.

Don't let IT training be one of them.

Get on the fast track to IT training at InformIT,
your total Information Technology training network.

InformIT | www.informit.com | SAMS

- Hundreds of timely articles on dozens of topics ■ Discounts on IT books from all our publishing partners, including Sams Publishing ■ Free, unabridged books from the InformIT Free Library ■ "Expert Q&A"—our live, online chat with IT experts ■ Faster, easier certification and training from our Web- or classroom-based training programs ■ Current IT news ■ Software downloads
- Career-enhancing resources

InformIT is a registered trademark of Pearson. Copyright ©2001 by Pearson.
Copyright ©2001 by Sams Publishing.